LEARNING AND EXPANDING WITH ACTIVITY THEORY

This book is a collection of essays on cultural-historical activity theory as it has been developed and applied by Yrjö Engeström. The work of Engeström, rooted in the legacy of Vygotsky and Leont'ev, focuses on current research concerns that are related to learning and development in work practices. Engeström's publications encompass various disciplines and develop intermediate theoretical tools to deal with empirical questions. In this volume, Engeström's work is used as a springboard to reflect on the question of the use, appropriation, and further development of the classic heritage within activity theory. The book is structured as a discussion among senior scholars, including Engeström himself. The work of the authors applies classical activity theory to pressing issues and critical contradictions in local practices and larger social systems.

Annalisa Sannino is University Lecturer in the Department of Education at the University of Helsinki in Finland. She completed her Ph.D. in psychology at the University of Nancy in France and worked as a researcher in the Department of Education at the University of Salerno in Italy. Her research is focused on discourse, experiencing, and learning in interventions in educational institutions and work organizations. She has published research articles in refereed journals in English, French, and Italian.

Harry Daniels is Professor of Education, Culture, and Pedagogy and Director of the Centre for Sociocultural and Activity Theory Research at the University of Bath in the United Kingdom. From 2002 to 2005, he was editor of the international journal *Mind, Culture, and Activity*. His research interests include sociocultural and activity theory, innovative learning in the workplace, special needs and social exclusion, and patient and career information seeking. In 2001, he published the book *Vygotsky and Pedagogy*, which has subsequently been translated into several languages.

Kris D. Gutiérrez is Professor of Social Research Methodology at the University of California, Los Angeles. Her current research interests include the sociocultural contexts of literacy for language minority students. Her research also focuses on understanding the relationship between language, culture, development, and pedagogies of empowerment. In 2005, Gutiérrez received the Sylvia Scribner Award of the American Educational Research Association.

Learning and Expanding with Activity Theory

Edited by

Annalisa Sannino
University of Helsinki

Harry Daniels
University of Bath

Kris D. Gutiérrez
University of California, Los Angeles

 CAMBRIDGE
UNIVERSITY PRESS

CAMBRIDGE UNIVERSITY PRESS
Cambridge, New York, Melbourne, Madrid, Cape Town,
Singapore, São Paulo, Delhi, Tokyo, Mexico City

Cambridge University Press
32 Avenue of the Americas, New York, NY 10013-2473, USA

www.cambridge.org
Information on this title: www.cambridge.org/9780521758109

First published 2009
Reprinted 2011

A catalog record for this publication is available from the British Library.

Library of Congress Cataloging in Publication Data

Learning and expanding with activity theory / [edited by] Annalisa Sannino,
Harry Daniels, Kris D. Gutiérrez.
   p.   cm.
Includes bibliographical references and index.
ISBN 978-0-521-76075-1 (hardback) – ISBN 978-0-521-75810-9 (pbk.)
1. Action theory. 2. Intentionalism. 3. Act (Philosophy)
4. Engeström, Yrjö, 1948– 5. Learning. I. Sannino, Annalisa.
II. Daniels, Harry. III. Gutiérrez, Kris D. IV. Title.
B105.A35L43 2009
150.19′8–dc22   2008037807

ISBN 978-0-521-76075-1 Hardback
ISBN 978-0-521-75810-9 Paperback

CONTENTS

CONTRIBUTORS

FRANK BLACKLER
Lancaster University Management
School, United Kingdom

SUSANNE BØDKER
University of Aarhus, Denmark

YVES CLOT
Conservatoire National des Arts
et Métiers, Paris, France

MICHAEL COLE
University of California, San Diego,
United States

HARRY DANIELS
University of Bath, United Kingdom

TURI ØWRE DIGERNES
InterMedia, University of Oslo,
Norway

ANNE EDWARDS
University of Oxford, United
Kingdom

RITVA ENGESTRÖM
University of Helsinki, Finland

YRJÖ ENGESTRÖM
University of Helsinki, Finland

NATALIA GAJDAMASHKO
Simon Fraser University, Burnaby,
Canada

KRIS D. GUTIÉRREZ
University of California,
Los Angeles, United States

SHUTA KAGAWA
University of Tsukuba, Japan

VLADISLAV A. LEKTORSKY
Russian Academy of Sciences,
Moscow, Russia

STEN LUDVIGSEN
InterMedia, University of Oslo,
Norway

ÅSA MÄKITALO
Göteborg University, Sweden

REIJO MIETTINEN
University of Helsinki,
Finland

YUJI MORO
University of Tsukuba, Japan

WOLFF-MICHAEL ROTH
University of Victoria, Canada

GEORG RÜCKRIEM
University of the Arts, Berlin,
  Germany

DAVID R. RUSSELL
Iowa State University,
  United States

ROGER SÄLJÖ
Göteborg University, Sweden

ANNALISA SANNINO
University of Helsinki, Finland

JAMES R. TAYLOR
University of Montreal, Canada

JAAKKO VIRKKUNEN
University of Helsinki, Finland

KATSUHIRO YAMAZUMI
Kansai University, Osaka, Japan

EDITORS' INTRODUCTION

ANNALISA SANNINO, HARRY DANIELS, AND
KRIS D. GUTIÉRREZ

In 1884 the Finnish realist artist Albert Edelfelt completed a painting entitled *Boys on the Shore*. In the painting three boys are playing with small handmade sailing boats on the shore. There is an expansive view of the horizon in the background, with sailboats in the harbor. The painting provides a dynamic perspective on a world of possibilities experienced in the play of the three boys. At the same time, corresponding historically consolidated activities are carried out in the background. The three boys are involved in different ways in a joint action, oriented toward the movement of a boat in the water. The painting powerfully depicts the contrast between the strength and the fragility of the collective action. Two boys are positioned precariously on rocks, while the third is about to move toward them, stepping on an uneven and slippery surface. One of the boys is leaning toward the water with a wooden stick in his hand, trying to guide his boat through the current.

The scene in this painting metaphorically illustrates key features of the process of expansion as described in Yrjö Engeström's book *Learning by Expanding* (1987). Engeström's comment on children's play could well apply to Edelfelt's painting:

> Old and new, regressive and expansive forms of the same activity exist simultaneously in the society. Children may play in a reproductive and repetitive manner, but they do also invent and construct new forms and structures of play, new tools and models for play activity. Their playing seems to become increasingly consumptive and pre-fabricated, the exchange-value aspect seems to dominate it more and more as the toys and games have become big business. But is it so simple and uni-directional? What are the inner contradictions and historical perspectives of the play activity of our children? Once in a while parents are astonished as they find their children playing something which does not seem to fit any

Figure I.1. *Boys on the Shore* (Albert Edelfelt, 1884).

preconceived canons: something new has been produced "from below." Sometimes these inventions from below become breakthroughs that significantly change the structures of play activity. (1987, pp. 173–174)

Expansion is a form of learning that transcends linear and socio-spatial dimensions of individual and short-lived actions. Within the expansive approach, learning is understood in the broader and temporally much longer perspective of a third dimension, that is, the dimension of the development of the activity (Engeström, 1999c, p. 64). Expansion is the result of a transition process from actions currently performed by individuals to a new collective activity. A transition from action to activity is considered expansive when it involves the objective transformation of the actions themselves and when subjects become aware of the contradictions in their current activity in the perspective of a new form of activity. In this sense, learning by expanding can be defined as a "thoughtfully mastered learning activity" (Engeström, 1987, p. 210). The zone of proximal development characterizes this process: "In activity-theoretical terms, activity systems travel through zones of proximal development … , a terrain of constant ambivalence, struggle, and surprise" (Engeström, 1999c, p. 90).

By editing this book, we wanted to promote these kinds of exchanges – ambivalent, sometimes conflictual, and always unpredictable in their outcomes – between scholars who relate in different ways to activity theory. This book is a collection of essays about cultural-historical activity theory as it has been developed and applied by Yrjö Engeström. The work of Engeström, rooted in the legacy of Vygotsky and Leont'ev, focuses on current societal concerns that are related to learning and development in work practices. Engeström's publications are diverse, cross various disciplines, and develop intermediate theoretical tools to deal with empirical questions. In this volume, Engeström's work is used as a springboard to reflect on the question of the use, appropriation, and further development of the classic heritage within activity theory.

We see the exchanges in this volume as the beginning of an interesting process of learning and expanding with activity theory. "Expansion is qualitative transformation and reorganization of the object. On the other hand, expansion does not imply an abrupt break with the past or a once-and-for-all replacement of the existing object with a totally new one. Expansion both transcends and retains previous layers of the object" (Engeström, Puonti, & Seppänen, 2003, pp. 181–183). The book constructs Engeström's work as an object of academic discussion. Through the book, this object begins to expand as the authors redefine Engeström's work in the context of their respective analyses. "The creation, mastery, and maintenance of such expanded objects is a demanding and contradictory challenge to the parties involved. Expanded objects require and generate, and are constructed by means of novel mediating instrumentalities" (Engeström, Puonti, & Seppänen, 2003, p. 154). Like the wooden stick used by one of the boys in Edelfelt's painting, the contributions by the authors of this volume can be seen as mediating instrumentalities that allow one to reconceptualize activity theory in connection to related fields.

The authors in this volume address themes central to the classical roots of cultural-historical activity theory and to the theory and methodology Yrjö Engeström has developed. These themes include units of analysis, mediation and discourse, expansive learning and development, agency and community, and interventions. In this way, the structure of the book follows the conceptual genesis of activity theory. We begin with the foundational concepts of units of analysis and of mediation and discourse, and then move to further theoretical developments, namely expansive learning and development, and agency and community. The final theme of interventions represents the pragmatic side of the theory, as well as an open ending that reflects the fact that activity theory is far from complete.

Each author takes at least one of the five themes as a point of connection between Engeström's ideas and the author's own work. Engeström (1996b) proposed the notion of three generations of activity theory. He initiated the third generation of activity theory, which expands the unit of analysis to encompass relations between multiple activity systems. This volume covers different generations of activity theorists. Among them, ideas of the third generation are strongly represented, while the chapters are overall firmly rooted in the legacy of the first and second generations. The work of the authors applies classical activity theory to pressing issues and critical contradictions in local practices and larger social systems. The general aim is for each contribution to show how these theoretical and methodological resources can be used for practical applications and empirical challenges. The authors illustrate how these themes have been developed in their own inquiries and discuss the challenges that these developments evoke for future research and theorizing.

The first chapter, by Annalisa Sannino, Harry Daniels, and Kris D. Gutiérrez, is a review of the ways activity theory and the work of Yrjö Engeström promote dialogue between theory and practice, as well as between the past, the present, and the future. This chapter contributes to recent discussions concerning the legitimacy of activity theory as a unified theory. The authors point out two distinctive features of activity theory that can define the boundaries of the field. Activity theory is both a practice-based theory and a historical and future-oriented theory. The authors demonstrate how the theoretical contributions of the founders of cultural-historical activity theory are solidly grounded in practice. Also, activity theory has the peculiar and distinctive characteristic of developing as an integral part of the historical turmoil through which activity theorists have lived. The authors recollect two phases of turmoil in the development of activity theory: first, the Russian Revolution, which triggered the engagement of the founders, and second, the student movement through which activity theory was rediscovered and further developed in Europe. Finally, the chapter traces the steps taken by Yrjö Engeström in his work to promote dialogues between theory and practice, on the one hand, and between the past, the present, and the future, on the other; the authors discuss the texts that have most prominently influenced him and demonstrate how these readings are intertwined with historical circumstances in the development of his ideas. This historical review of activity theory and of Engeström's work sets the context for the other chapters in this volume.

The chapters in the first part address the units of analysis. The adoption of object-oriented and artifact-mediated activity as a new unit of analysis is one of the main contributions of cultural-historical activity theory. This methodological innovation represents a challenge to traditional thinking in human and social sciences, which rely on deep-seated individualism and on views of society as an anonymous structure. Object-oriented and artifact-mediated activity as a unit of analysis retains the importance of subjectivity, while integrating it with cultural means and constraints that inescapably characterize human practices. In doing so, this unit of analysis integrates society into activity. At the same time, there is a fruitful debate within activity theory on how to ensure that the subject, including emotions and the body, is fully taken into account in the formulation of the unit of analysis.

Frank Blackler expands the unit of analysis by putting it into use in the field of organization studies. He outlines recent contributions in this field that adopt concrete and situated activity systems, rather than the abstract systems of formal organizations, as the unit of analysis. The author emphasizes the relevance of the theory of expansive learning in analyzing how historically located organizations can influence their own work. Further necessary developments of the theory and of related interventions in organizations are highlighted. They correspond to the need to design interventions based on the recognition of complex organizational dynamics, such as hierarchy and disadvantage, and on a vision of work change. The development of intervention research requires further exploration of the nature of social and organizational re-mediation with regard to institutionalized power structures.

David R. Russell discusses how the theory of expansive learning has been adapted to writing, activity, and genre research in recent and ongoing studies of professional communication and writing. Research on written communication analyzes primarily texts. Contexts are examined through the history and ethnography of organizations to give a principled account of development over longer timescales. The author points out ways in which the theory of expansive learning has been modified in its uptake and ways in which those modifications challenge and potentially expand the theory and related methods for activity-theoretical researchers outside the field of written communication. Genre as social action is used as a unit of analysis to understand how organizations change. In particular, the concept of genre systems allows the analysis of written genres in and between organizations. The focus on genre systems is considered instrumental for studying coordination and interactions across boundaries and among activity systems. Both moment-to-moment coordination and historical development are seen to materialize through written genre systems that last over time and move in space.

Wolff-Michael Roth discusses the inclusion of sensuous aspects of work, such as emotion, identity, and ethico-moral dimensions, in the model of the activity system. He illustrates how one might collect salient data for this purpose. The author presents a case study of the work in a salmon hatchery, based on five years of ethnographic fieldwork, with the aim of demonstrating that sensuous aspects of work are woven into practical activities. He suggests that, by taking into account sensuous aspects of work together with the structural dimensions of the activity system, the link between emotions and participation in activity can be preserved. By acting as participant-observer and by observing participants in the work practice, the researcher has access to different perspectives and ways of experiencing work.

The second part of this volume addresses the concepts of mediation and discourse. It focuses on how culture is foundational to human activity in the form of mediating tools, language, signs, symbols, and categories. This theme is particularly relevant in an era in which technology and digital media are both empowering and controlling human practices. Since all activity is mediated, the study of technologies must be embedded in human activities where tools and media are generated, used, and modified. Technological and discursive mediation are unavoidably intertwined in every activity.

Vladislav A. Lektorsky addresses in his chapter the relations between collective activity and individual subject, between internalization and externalization, and between reflection and change. The chapter elucidates in particular the key activity-theoretical notions of subject and mediation. These notions are reconceptualized respectively in terms of collective subject and reflective mediation. The latter is seen as a means of promoting change in activities and creating new collective activities. Interventionist research is discussed as a particular kind of reflective mediation. Lektorsky argues that when the results of research are accepted by a community, the knowledge obtained may re-mediate activities and change human reality.

Georg Rückriem argues that digital technology is radically affecting the nature of human activity and that this transformation has not been sufficiently recognized in activity theory. The chapter openly takes activity theorists to task for being captive to the old culture dominated by the medium of print. The chapter highlights the shortcomings of the activity-theoretical concept of mediation and the related concepts of tool, symbol, and artifact. Rückriem claims that mediation is regularly regarded only in relation to specific activity systems within societies, rather than focusing on the "leading medium" of the contemporary society itself. The author argues that in order to come to grips with contemporary global challenges such as Web 2.0, activity theory needs to reinvent itself by learning from media history and media theory.

Åsa Mäkitalo and Roger Säljö analyze how a social dilemma involving burnout, stress, and long-term sick leaves is negotiated as an object of institutional activities by trade unions and employers in labor market organizations. The chapter focuses on the use of institutional categories in local discussions to define the dilemma and possibilities of the transformation of existing categories in response to local tensions and challenges. The analysis points out the need to reconsider institutionally well-established categories as potential discursive tools for designing new strategies and activities.

The third theme elaborated in this volume is expansive learning and development as collective transformations in activity systems. Activity theorists argue that this type of learning and development is increasingly relevant to our ability to understand how to deal with the discontinuities and disruptions of everyday life, which interestingly reflect major uncertainties on societal and global scales.

Michael Cole and Natalia Gajdamashko address the problem of teleology in human development. The authors take as starting points the question of teleology in development as treated by Engeström in *Learning by Expanding* and his characterization of development as a process of breaking away and opening up. Teleology is discussed in relation to phylogeny, cultural history, and ontogeny and their respective timescales. The authors examine three principles of development that were originally identified by Engeström as unappreciated by developmentalists: development as destruction and rejection of the old, development as collective transformation, and development as interwoven dialectics of vertical and horizontal movements. The chapter highlights the ways in which Engeström's approach fits with theories of human development and special contributions arising from his works.

Jaakko Virkkunen compares the conceptualizations of knowledge creation in the theories of Engeström and of Nonaka and Takeuchi. An empirical case from Nonaka and Takeuchi's work is reinterpreted through the lenses of both theories. As a result of the comparison, the author argues that a fundamental difference between the two theories lies in their approach to historical development. Consequently, concepts such as inner contradiction, object, and generalization have very different meanings in the two theories.

Reijo Miettinen focuses on the concept of contradiction as defined in the theory of expansive learning and on its uses in empirical studies of health care work, based on the methodology of developmental work research. Drawing on Marx's *Grundrisse* concerning the inner contradiction of capitalist production, the author argues that high-technology capitalism with its new forms of distributed production, exemplified by Linux, Wikipedia, and Synaptic Leap, directly challenges the logic of capitalist production. On this basis, the author solicits a broader analysis of contradictions that would also include further conceptualization of relations between contradictions.

Shuta Kagawa and Yuji Moro take up the legacy of Spinoza's philosophy as a resource for elucidating and expanding the concept of activity to include local interactions and affective aspects of learning. For this purpose, three key concepts in Spinoza's works are considered particularly important: multitude of activity, constrained forms of individual agency, and imaginative-discursive practice. The authors also apply Spinoza's concepts of imagination and discourse to the problem of transfer in learning. Spinoza's concept of discursive practice as a form of activity is used to illustrate the significance of discourse in student nurses' transitive learning.

The increasing emphasis in activity-theoretical research on the possibility of human beings' gaining influence and agency over their own lives and in collective institutions is reflected in the fourth theme of agency and community. Activity theory has been sometimes mistakenly read as a fixed theory of impersonal systems and structures. In fact, the object of activity theory is to analyze human lives involved in collective activity systems. The challenge here is to work out a new understanding of agency as collaborative, dialogic, and reflective subjectivity. We acknowledge that agency and community are emergent themes. Although they can be traced back to Vygotsky's works, they remain long-term research challenges in activity theory.

Anne Edwards draws on two tentative notions recently used by Engeström with regard to the issue of agency in interorganizational collaboration, namely collaborative intentionality capital and object-oriented interagency. While Engeström discusses these notions in terms of collective intentionality and distributed agency, this chapter proposes the concept of relational agency as a means to shift the focus from the systemic nature of work activity to joint actions within and across activity systems. Relational agency is offered as an enhanced form of personal agency and is defined as a capacity to recognize, examine, and work with the resources offered by other practitioners in collaborative action on an object of professional activity. The argument is backed up with empirical evidence from two studies on practitioners in various organizations aiming at the prevention of social exclusion of vulnerable children and youth.

Katsuhiro Yamazumi examines a particular type of agency, called expansive agency, emerging in a project of collaboration between a university, schools, and various community organizations. The project exposes students to food-related productive practices. Contradictions between the logics of the different activity systems involved are depicted as factors that at the same time obstruct and energize learning. These contradictions can bring about agency in efforts to master and cultivate shared objects between the different activity systems.

James R. Taylor argues that the concept of community needs to be explicitly problematized and further conceptualized within activity theory. Rather than merely a parameter or a context, community is discussed in this chapter in terms of a constructed outcome and object of an activity. Using a revised version of coorientation theory, the author suggests that the construction and existence of a community firmly tie subjects in coorientational relationships that inevitably involve authority.

Sten Ludvigsen and Turi Øwre Digernes focus on the activity-theoretical notion of object to understand the work of productive research communities. In particular the chapter addresses the impact of leadership on the research group's work in a community within humanities and a community within computer science. The analysis of common traits and differences between the two communities points out learning potentials and affordances for the integration of research Fellows in these communities. Microprocesses of negotiation are seen as an emerging object that redirects the work of researchers. The analysis suggests that the type of research focus, whether more or less open, adopted by a scientific community might affect these negotiations differently, influencing productivity and opportunities of integration by young researchers.

The final theme organizing this volume concerns interventions as conceptualized in the framework of the theory of expansive learning. Interventions are seen as a direct continuation of the lineage of the research of the founders of activity theory. The strong connection between the classic work of these Russian scholars and tangible transformations in human life is already described in the first chapter of this volume. However, interventions in the years of the founding scholars were typically focused on one subject at a time. Today interventions are also realized in collective settings, in order to promote the development of complex activity systems. The methodology of developmental work research and the Change Laboratory are well-known examples of attempts to move in this direction in Engeström's work. Intervention literature is still relatively limited, and constructive methodological debates are only beginning to be undertaken within activity theory.

Ritva Engeström discusses three interventionist studies in cleaning work and health care based on the methodology of developmental work research. She examines how subjectivity was constructed in these studies using the activity system as a unit of analysis. The author suggests that subjectivity may be examined in three interrelated activities: the central activity, the learning activity, and the activity of sense-making and experiencing. She argues that the collective nature of the subject is a result of collaboration between researchers and practitioners within interventions, in which the participants make conscious efforts at co-construction and joint learning.

Susanne Bødker discusses the relationship between participatory design research and developmental work research, in particular the Change Laboratory method. The author points out that today the participation of users in design can no longer be limited to workers in a given practice. Because technology and artifacts today cross the boundaries of work and personal life, it is necessary for participatory design to involve users considered within the perspective of their entire lives. Commonalities and differences between participatory design research and developmental work research are highlighted with regard to issues of work across organizational settings, design as a process going beyond work communities, exploration of the unknown, and consumerism.

Yves Clot explores connections and differences between the framework of expansive learning and the French intervention approach called the Clinic of Activity. Three main issues are discussed: transformative action in workplace interventions, the collective dimensions of human activity, and modeling as a tool for developing the action of the subjects. The author points out that the will to act in the real world allows activity theory to offer an alternative to positivism in science. This orientation is rooted in the indirect methods advocated by Vygotsky: One has to transform in order to understand. A psychological subject does not function in opposition to the social world. Not only does the subject exist in a collective; the collective also exists in the subject. The relationship between the theoretical model of activity and the transformative actions of practitioners is seen, from a Vygotskian point of view, as an example of the relation between everyday concepts and scientific concepts.

The last chapter of the volume is an epilogue written by Yrjö Engeström as a response to and reflection on the other chapters.

Before completing this introduction to the volume, we cannot fail to mention all those who contributed to its preparation. Our thanks go to the following colleagues for reviewing the chapters: Paul Adler, Susanne Bødker,

Mariane Cerf, Michael Cole, Jan Derry, Anne Edwards, Marilyn Fleer, Kai Hakkarainen, Martin Hildebrand-Nilshon, Hannele Kerosuo, Philippe Lorino, Sten Ludvigsen, Åsa Mäkitalo, Vesa Oittinen, Sami Paavola, Paul Prior, Wolff-Michael Roth, Roger Säljö, Peter Sawchuk, Falk Seeger, Berthel Sutter, James R. Taylor, Terttu Tuomi-Gröhn, Jaakko Virkkunen, and Gordon Wells. Most of all, we express our gratitude to Yrjö Engeström for his work, which keeps inspiring us. In recognition of his 60th birthday, this book is dedicated to his life engagement and timeless contribution to the field of activity theory.

1

Activity Theory Between Historical Engagement and Future-Making Practice

ANNALISA SANNINO, HARRY DANIELS, AND
KRIS D. GUTIÉRREZ

Activity theory seeks to analyze development within practical social activities. Activities organize our lives. In activities, humans develop their skills, personalities, and consciousness. Through activities, we also transform our social conditions, resolve contradictions, generate new cultural artifacts, and create new forms of life and the self.

The legitimacy of activity theory as a unified theory has been the subject of various discussions. Holzman (2006), for example, argues that there is no unified perspective on activity theory. Holzman uses the term "activity theory" to cover a wide variety of approaches inspired by Vygotsky: among others, cultural-historical activity theory and sociocultural psychology. Such a broad view of activity theory contributes to a misrepresentation of the theory as fragmented and scattered across multiple perspectives. Further, this view brings with it the risk of losing focus on the actual nature of activity, which is the core of activity theory. An emphasis on psychological approaches without consideration of anthropological, sociological, historical, and linguistic characteristics of activity is risky and narrows the focus to the study of specific and limited aspects of activity. As a unified theory, activity theory has shown consistent viability throughout its history, beginning in the 1930s when Leont'ev formulated its basic principles and proposed the structure of activity. In addition, activity theory today attracts more interest globally than ever before. The term "unified" does not refer to a closed and fixed theory. However, it rules out an interpretation of activity theory as an eclectic grouping of multiple theories.

Conceiving of activity theory as a psychological theory ignores its multidisciplinary nature. As Davydov (1999a) writes, "The problem of activity and the concept of activity are interdisciplinary by nature. ... The issue of activity is not necessarily connected with psychology as a profession. It is connected at present because in the course of our history activity turned out to be the thing on which our prominent psychologists focused their attention as early as in the Soviet Union days. Things just turned out to be this way" (p. 50). This historical circumstance has given rise to the prominence of activity theory in psychology. Today, however, activity theory is redefining itself and proving its generative potential across a wide range of disciplines and fields of social practice.

Davydov (1999a, 1999b) argues that the generative potential of activity theory is based on its nature as a monistic theory. Activity theory is a theory of the activity structure and of the content of the activity germ cell. The content of the activity germ cell stems from the interaction between individual and collective activities within an ontogenetic and historical perspective. As Scribner (1997), Engeström, and others (Engeström, 1987; Engeström, Miettinen, & Punamäki, 1999) have pointed out, activity theory addresses the foundational theoretical issue of activity as the primary unit of analysis and, thus, provides both a theory of human activity and a productive method for its study.

In *Perspectives on Activity Theory*, Engeström (1999a) acknowledges the risk of activity theory's becoming "an eclectic combination of ideas before it has a chance to redefine its own core" (p. 20). However, Engeström envisions a different future for the field, proposing that "the current expansive reconstruction of activity theory will actually lead to a new type of theory. Essential to this emerging theory is multivoicedness coexisting with monism" (Engeström, 1999a, p. 20). One distinctive theoretical feature of activity theory, for example, concerns the issue of change. As Minnis and John-Steiner (2001) argue, "The delineating factor [between activity theory and the theories dominant in Western psychology and sociology] is that activity theory requires a systematic examination of change. This can be done by provoking, facilitating, and documenting change" (p. 308).

This chapter contributes to these discussions on activity theory as a legitimate theory, unified by scientific contributions to its object of study, that is, activity. Activity theory is grounded in the lineage of Leont'ev's works and recognizes a unifying thread between the works of Leont'ev and other Russian scholars, such as Vygotsky, Luria, Meshcheryakov, and Davydov. This thread may be articulated as follows: Not only is activity an abstract principle of explanation or a general theoretical notion; it is a concept that denotes the basic unit of concrete human life.

THE CONCEPT OF ACTIVITY AS THE CORE

From an activity-theoretical perspective, human life is fundamentally rooted in participation in human activities that are oriented toward objects. Thus, human beings are seen as situated in a collective life perspective, in which they are driven by purposes that lie beyond a particular goal. Object-oriented activities, then, are the core of activity theory and distinguish it from other approaches. Sociocultural theories, for instance, focus on action rather than on activity (Wertsch, 1991). Here we wish to highlight an important difference between sociocultural approaches and activity theory. As a unit of analysis, a focus on action does not account for the historical continuity and longevity of human life. Activity theory conceptualizes actions in the broader perspective of their systemic and motivational context and, thus, aims at going beyond a given situation. The emphasis on action alone does not fulfill the research agenda in activity theory, according to which actions are studied in historically evolving collective activities.

Further, the boundaries of the field of activity theory are defined by two distinctive features. First, activity theory is a practice-based theory. Second, it is a historical and future-oriented theory. We argue that there are methodological issues that distinguish an activity-theoretical approach from traditional approaches to research. Activity theory involves the researcher throughout the course of the development, stagnation, or regression of the activities under scrutiny, as well as in the activities of the research subjects. This deep involvement in everyday human life is a crucial resource of activity theory.

We elaborate these issues in the following sections of the chapter. We first take up the issue of dialogue between theory and practice. Then we focus on dialogue between the past, the present, and the future. Finally, we trace the work of Yrjö Engeström, one of the most representative contemporary activity theorists, whose work has promoted dialogues between theory and practice, on the one hand, and between the past, the present, and the future, on the other.

ON THE DIALOGUE BETWEEN THEORY AND PRACTICE

In recent years, scholars have declared a practice turn in social sciences (Schatzki, Knorr Cetina, & von Savigny, 2000). This proclaimed practice turn can be traced back to Marx's idea of revolutionary practice, in which theory is not only meant to analyze and explain the world, but also to facilitate practices and promote changes. However, the social turn in activity theory is already found in the early work of Vygotsky, who drew on Marx's ideas 80 years ago. Since Vygotsky's work with children who were affected by the Russian Civil War, this practice-based approach has persisted. We see this approach in the work of many of the founders of cultural-historical activity theory, including Luria, Leont'ev, Galperin, Zaporozhets, Meshcheryakov, and Davydov, who engaged in various kinds of interventions in multiple settings. This dialogue between theory and practice is an essential component of activity theory and warrants discussion and exemplification. We begin with a discussion of how the dialogue between theory and practice was originally conducted. We will provide examples of concrete research inquiries by these and other scholars – research that met specific practical needs of people and that led to material changes in the lives of the subjects.

According to Yaroshevsky (1989), there is a clear connection between the works of Vygotsky during the Gomel period in the early 1920s and his practice as a teacher of literature. In the same period, Vygotsky established a psychological laboratory at the Gomel Teacher Training School. During these years, the country was actively concerned with the challenge of providing infrastructures for homeless children and for children with special needs. Vygotsky's laboratory aimed at carrying out experiments with schoolchildren and children with multisensory impairment living in state-run children's homes. Luria (2005), reflecting on Vygotsky's work in this period, wrote, "Vygotsky's work at the teachers college brought him in contact with the problems of children who suffered from congenital defects – blindness, deafness, mental retardation – and with the need to discover ways to help such children fulfill their individual potentials" (p. 39). Vygotsky's intellectual work was driven by these practical concerns of his time.

The connection to practice was later explicitly presented as a central component within Vygotsky's (1997a) discussion of overcoming the crisis in psychology:

> Confrontation [with a highly developed – industrial, educational, political, or military – practice] compels psychology to reform its principles so that they may withstand the highest test of practice. It forces us to accommodate and introduce into our science the supply of practical psychological experiences and skills which has been gathered over thousands of years. ... The importance of the new practical psychology for the *whole* science cannot be exaggerated. The psychologist might dedicate a hymn to it.
>
> ... Practice pervades the deepest foundations of the scientific operation and reforms it from beginning to end. Practice sets the tasks and serves as the supreme judge, as its truth criterion. It dictates how to construct the concepts and how to formulate the laws. (pp. 305–306, emphasis in original)

Even before meeting Vygotsky, Luria and Leont'ev shared an intensive period of research on emotions during which they "decided that one way to overcome ... inadequacy in our own and others' previous research was to work directly with people who were experiencing strong emotions in real life situations. The people we chose were actual or suspected criminals. ... This work turned out to be of practical value to criminologists, providing them with an early model of a lie detector" (Luria, 2005, pp. 34–36). Luria's subsequent academic work from the late 1920s on is indivisible from his practice as a medical doctor. He developed new methods of neuropsychological examination of patients with brain damage through his medical practice at the Burdenko Institute of Neurosurgery. In addition to diagnoses, Luria's work resulted in the development of a number of treatments for restoring speech in patients who had experienced trauma or suffered from aphasia.

Leont'ev also worked actively with injured solders to rehabilitate their movement functions. Gal'perin, Zaporozhets, and Rubinshtein were among a group of prominent scientists who collaborated with him in this endeavor. As underscored by Levitin (1982), this work led to theoretical results and concrete innovations that were strongly practice based: "It was shown that the rehabilitation of lost movement essentially depends on the general character of the patient's activity and the motives, goals, and means of this activity. The research data thus obtained was used to develop new effective methods of labor therapy and therapeutic exercises which were widely used at military hospitals" (p. 106). In a volume that reports the numerous results of this work, Leont'ev and Zaporozhets (1960) explicitly refer to the role of rehabilitation practice in understanding the symptoms connected to injured limbs: "It is difficult to over-estimate the importance of a correct understanding of these symptoms in the practice of rehabilitation. The most direct way to understand them is by careful observation of motor manifestations" (p. 194).

Similarly, Meshcheryakov devoted his life to the education of children with multisensory impairment. His book *Awakening to Life* (1979) is a thorough report of the development and implementation of Meshcheryakov's method in the Zagorsk boarding school. This method consisted of progressively guiding the child with multisensory impairment to perform independent actions. First, the child carries out the action with the help of the teacher, who directs the child's hand. Progressively the child recognizes a particular touch by the teacher as a sign to perform the learned action. Finally, the child learns to autonomously contribute to collective productive activities. At a time when children with multisensory impairment were relegated to the category of retarded subjects, Meshcheryakov's work led to generations of children with multisensory impairment who not only learned to move independently in their environment, but also became fully integrated in the society and obtained the highest academic degrees.

Within activity theory, even the most theoretically oriented representative – the philosopher Il'enkov – grounded his philosophy in the educational practices in the boarding school directed by Meshcheryakov in Zagorsk for children with multisensory impairment. Il'enkov (quoted by Levitin, 1982) publicly affirmed the following: "The enormous work being carried out by Meshcheryakov, while it is important for the study of the handicapped and for education, is above all important and necessary for those of us who study philosophy. The problems posed by the education of children with multisensory impairment are epistemological problems. The neurophysiologist deciphering mechanisms of the brain inaccessible to direct analysis, the astronomer describing remote galaxies, and the physicist studying invisible particles – all of them, in the final analysis, are exploring the world hidden from the sense organs at our disposal" (Levitin, 1982, p. 298).

Davydov's (1990) book, *Types of Generalization in Instruction,* is a careful analysis and a harsh critique of contemporary school instructional practices in the Soviet Union. According to the author, teaching in Soviet schools was based on anachronistic concepts and methods that facilitated mainly empirical thinking and neglected more effective forms of rational cognition, that is, scientific and theoretical thinking. Davydov's work comprises an impressive set of large-scale, long-term interventions of developmental teaching in schools. These inquiries were aimed at promoting scientific and theoretical forms of thinking through new methods of designing school subjects in line with the dialectical method of ascending from the abstract to the concrete.

For Davydov (1990), "study of the principles governing mental activity occurs *on the basis of and in the form of experimental instruction* (p. 373, emphasis in original). Moreover, Davydov (1988) connects the practice of experimental teaching with the nature itself of the method of formative experiments initiated by Vygotsky and developed further within his tradition:

> The essence of that method consists in having psychologists draw up a project of a new type of activity for children that is in line with a meaningful social mandate to be analyzed in the more or less distant future. Then they join forces with educators to shape that type of activity in schoolchildren. ... The original elaboration and testing of this project (model) is done under experimental conditions. But when

the appropriate effect has been achieved in the sphere of children's consciousness, the shaping in them of a new type of activity can be transferred to a broader range of practice. (p. 73)

Transformation is a key theoretical notion for Davydov (1999b), who distinguishes the concept from the notion of change as used in everyday language. "Many changes of natural and social reality carried out by people affect the object externally without changing it internally. Such changes can hardly be called transformations. Transformation means changing an object internally, making evident its essence and altering it" (Davydov, 1999b, p. 42). For Davydov, the philosophical roots of activity theory found in the works of Hegel and Marx imply a particular type of activism. This activism does not coincide with technicist activism. Quoting Davydov (1999b): "Technicist activism ... has no humanistic origins. Instead of developing the essence of reality according to its own laws it disfigures it, mutilates it, and changes it without taking into account the historical interests of humans and realistic possibilities of the reality itself. Such activism does not coincide with the activity theory of Marx and Hegel, according to which people dealing with an object may only use the measure that belongs to that object" (p. 43). Thus, a humanist activism is grounded in historical realities.

Activity theory, as a practice-based theory, is grounded in practice both theoretically and concretely. On this basis, we argue that the very nature of activity theory relies on establishing a bridge between theory and practice. On the one hand, as previously addressed in the works by the founders, the study of higher mental functions was made possible by turning to the observation of concrete life situations. On the other hand, transformations of real practices are promoted while research within activity theory is performed. In this sense, we identify a dual role of practice in the works of the founders. From a theoretical point of view, practice is the epistemological source of knowledge, and it is their very concrete involvement in practice and activism that characterizes the lives and contributions of the founders.

ON THE DIALOGUE BETWEEN THE PAST, THE PRESENT, AND THE FUTURE

Activity theory is based on the collective heritage of the founders, in particular Vygotsky, Luria, and Leont'ev. With the collective foundational work of the troika, activity theory is unique in human and social sciences. This collective contribution stands in contrast to other approaches typically based on a single individual's endeavors – for example, psychoanalysis on Freud's works and genetic epistemology on Piaget's works. Also, activity theory has the distinctive characteristic of developing as an integral part of the periods of historical turmoil in which activity theorists have lived. We recollect two such periods in the development of activity theory: first, the Russian Revolution, which triggered the engagement of the founders, and the European student movement of the 1960s, through which activity theory was rediscovered and further developed in Europe 50 years later.

The Russian Revolution was the consequence of extenuating and continuous conflicts during which the country experienced unsustainable conditions of inequality. The Bolsheviks, under the leadership of Lenin, were able to read the population's need for a radical political and social change. In November 1917, organized masses of workers and soldiers marched in the streets and took over Petrograd, where power had been in the hands of the Russian Provisional Government since the czar's abdication. John Reed's (1935) book, *Ten Days That Shook the World,* is a condensed diary that vividly captures the spreading fervor in the ten days when the actual insurrection happened. Far from bringing peace to the country, these events led to a civil war that lasted until 1922. Officers with monarchist ideals organized a loose army of counterrevolutionary forces aimed at opposing Lenin's power. The fact that Lenin was running a state during a civil war did not prevent new positive energy from spreading throughout the country.

Although Russia was taking only the first steps as a new type of society, the period immediately after the revolution was simultaneously a period of creative turmoil and one of great enthusiasm for the arts and sciences. And there was a lot of experimentation in cultural and political life. These years established the conditions for the growth of extraordinary creative efforts in all domains of cultural and social life. During the years when Vygotsky lived in Gomel after completing his legal studies, the whole society was displaced and considerable political attention was focused on homeless and pedagogically neglected children. A few years later, Luria and Leont'ev met Vygotsky, who represented a new psychology that they could collectively pursue.

What triggered this lifetime engagement under extremely difficult post-revolution conditions? Russia had been ruled for centuries by despots, and thus the revolution was a unique historical turn for the country. For a large number of artists, intellectuals, and academics, it meant a unique opportunity to build a new society. They became completely involved in this cause, exhilarated that they were sharing the vision of a better world for all. A. A. Leont'ev (2005) writes that his father, A. N. Leont'ev, decided to study psychology because "as a witness of the events of the Revolution and the Civil War ... Leont'ev developed a desire – as he recalled in old age – *to philosophically understand and make sense of* what was happening" (p. 13, emphasis in original). A. A. Leont'ev, sketching his father's autobiography, cites Leont'ev's shift from a desire to become an engineer to a commitment to studying psychology: "Then technical interests somehow disappeared on their own, and philosophical problems emerged. It was these problems that led me one fine day to the Institute of Psychology, where I asked: where does one study to be a psychologist?" (A. A. Leont'ev, 2005, p. 13). A need to make sense of historical turmoil was the driving force behind the formation of what was to become activity theory.

The revolution served as a catalyst for these scientists to come together and work collectively in the development of activity theory. Luria cites the influence of the fervor of the post-revolution years on him and his colleagues that lingered throughout their lives, including the period of the Second World War.

"The unity of purpose of the Soviet people so clearly felt during the great revolution and the subsequent years reemerged in new forms. A sense of common responsibility and common purpose gripped the country. Each of us knew we had an obligation to work together with our countrymen to meet the challenge" (Luria, 2005, p. 138).

When Stalin succeeded Lenin in 1924, the Soviet Union gradually transformed into a dictatorship. This led to a 30-year period of stagnation during which intellectuals and academics who deviated from the Stalinist ideology were politically attacked for their work and eventually physically threatened, marginalized, or killed. Vygotsky and his colleagues had to flee to the Ukraine for safety. A. A. Leont'ev (2005) refers to these years when Vygotsky and his colleagues were all in Moscow as a dangerous time: "The position of Vygotsky and his team at the Institute of psychology became less and less secure with each year" (p. 27). From this time on, it became increasingly difficult for these scholars to pursue their work. The pedologist movement in which Vygotsky was involved was condemned, and even after Vygotsky's death, his books were removed from his archives.

However, Stalinism was not immediately seen as a reactionary and inhumane regime. The communist ideals in the Soviet Union were largely humanistic, and millions of people believed that in the name of these ideals they were all building a better future. In those years with Stalin in power, few in the West could understand the extent of the internal terror in the Soviet Union. Great intellectuals like Jean-Paul Sartre and prominent artists like Pablo Picasso were supporters of Soviet communism, which they considered to be a viable alternative to capitalism and U.S. imperialism. Only in the late 1950s did the horrors of Stalinism gradually begin to come to light. The realization of what actually happened in the Soviet Union during the regime of Stalin led numerous scholars from all over the world to turn their attention to banned or previously unknown works produced by Russian academics.

A few years after Stalin's death, Leont'ev received the Lenin Prize. This was an important sign that the new kind of psychology initiated by Vygotsky was finally acceptable. This event, however, was not a sign of a consistently positive atmosphere with regard to the work of these scholars. As late as the 1980s, scholars such as Davydov were prevented at times from traveling abroad. Until 1990, when the Soviet Union ceased to exist, the legacy of Stalinism continued and the state system Stalin built continued to be based on coercion and extreme control. Activity theory, then, must necessarily be understood in the context of this complex historical framework.

The student movement in Europe in the 1960s gave rise to a renewed interest in activity theory. Our decision to discuss the general history of activity theory and its connections to the events and the consequences of both the Russian Revolution and the student movement is not arbitrary. Authoritative historical analysis also refers contextually to both events. In the well-known book *Age of Extremes,* the historian Eric Hobsbawm (1995) writes, "If there was a single moment in the golden years after 1945 which corresponds to the world simultaneous upheaval of which the revolutionaries had dreamed after 1917, it was surely 1968, when students rebelled..., largely stimulated by the extraordinary outbreak of May 1968 in Paris, epicenter of a Continent-wide student uprising" (p. 298). The year 1968 is merely emblematic; it actually represents a period of about 10 years of social and political awakening of young generations until the mid-1970s.

In these years between the late 1960s and 1970s, activity theory was introduced in the West. Progressive academics like Urie Bronfenbrenner, Jerome Bruner, and Michael Cole brought the works of the founders to American academic circles. In the same years, a number of politically motivated activists from Italy, Germany, Holland, and Japan went to Russia to study with Luria, Leont'ev, and their colleagues. Because of its split society, Germany, in particular, became a crucial entry point for activity theory in the West. East Germany was an official part of Marxist ideology and published German translations of the work of Leont'ev, Luria, Davydov, and others. These translations made their way to the West, exposing a larger number of people to these foundational works. At the same time, Nordic countries were also experiencing a similar political and social awakening of a new generation of both students and young scientists.

Again, activity theory is one that develops as an integral part of the historical turmoil in which activity theorists live. Perhaps today's movements advocating global justice, the rights of ethnic minorities, and ecological sustainability will be the ground for the next generation of activity theorists. The identity of activity theory stands on the ability of those who work within this framework to establish fruitful connections between the classic heritage of the theory, present societal challenges, and orientations toward the future. As Engeström wrote (1999a), "Activity theory has the conceptual and methodological potential to be a pathbreaker in studies that help humans gain control over their own artifacts and thus over their future" (p. 29).

ENGESTRÖM'S WORK AS A PROMOTER OF THESE DIALOGUES

We identify four main phases in Engeström's development as an activity theorist.[1] These cycles are interrelated and their historical boundaries are not well defined: (1) the European student movement of the 1960s and the discovery of activity theory; (2) the study of instruction and the turn from school learning to workplace learning; (3) developmental work research and the theory of expansive learning; and (4) the formation of activity-theoretical communities aimed at changing societal practices.

At the end of the 1960s and during most of the 1970s, Engeström produced a set of works stemming directly from his participation in the student movement. In particular, he wrote his first book (Engeström, 1970), *Education in Class Society: Introduction to the Educational Problems of Capitalism* (in Finnish). The book is a strong critique of education in a capitalist society written from the point of view of a rebellious student, and there is no reference in it to activity theory. Through these intense years of the student movement, Engeström came to the realization that he was not providing an alternative to what he was criticizing. However, he found an alternative during this period in the form of activity theory.

---

[1] The source of the material in this section is a set of interviews with Yrjö Engeström and other information collected by Annalisa Sannino with the support of a Fulbright Scholarship in 2002–2003 at the Laboratory of Comparative Human Cognition, University of California, San Diego.

Engeström's search for pedagogical ideas emanated from the Soviet Union and East Germany, most notably Leont'ev's *Problems of the Development of the Mind,* published in East Germany in 1973 (Leontjew, 1973), and Davydov's *Types of Generalizations in Instruction,* which was available in East Germany in 1977 (Dawydow, 1977). Reading Davydov led him to Il'enkov's essay on the dialectics of the abstract and the concrete, which was published in Germany (Iljenkow, 1975). This first phase of investigation culminated in Engeström's (1979) thesis, *The Imagination and Behavior of School Students Analyzed from the Viewpoint of Education for Peace* (in Finnish), in which he first makes extensive use of activity theory. This empirical study documents the work of nearly 2,000 students who wrote essays on war and violence. At this historical moment, peace movements were very strong, especially after the Vietnam War, and there was sense of urgency in articulating the need for disarmament and a change in the relations between East and West. Engeström wrote his book with the conviction that the education of students as promoters of peace requires a deep understanding of students' representations of war, peace, and violence. This study reinforced his initial frustration at not being able to provide tangible alternatives to the instructional practices of that time.

The second phase of Engeström's development as an activity theorist was an intense period starting at the end of 1970s, in which he devoted his work to the study of instruction with the explicit aim of promoting changes in school practices. Specifically, he attempted to change school instruction by bringing Davydov's ideas to politically and pedagogically radical Finnish teachers. A key text in this period is a chapter in the 1984 book *Learning and Teaching on a Scientific Basis,* which Enström edited with Mariane Hedegaard and Pentti Hakkarainen. However, this work with teachers and Davydovian teaching experiments also renewed Engeström's original frustration with the difficulty of influencing school practices. The result of one of these experiments inspired by the work of Davydov was published in a chapter in Finnish with the title *Developing Theoretical Generalization in Instruction: An Example from History Teaching* (Engeström, 1982). The paper demonstrates that Davydov's principles of instruction aimed at theoretical thinking can be successfully implemented in small-scale experimental curriculum units in Western school practice.

In this period there emerged a new interest in workplace learning and human resource development in organizations. Teaching aimed at developing high-level theoretical thinking remained at the core of research interests, including Engeström's studies of work. His first work-related study was concerned with janitorial cleaning, which was considered to be the occupation with the lowest prestige in Finland. The main motivation for studying the work of cleaners was to demonstrate that this work is creative and has an intellectual basis, and to show the possibilities of development. This study of cleaners (Engeström & Engeström, 1984), published in Finnish, is significant in a number of ways, most notably as the first empirical interventionist study, which led to the formulation of a methodology of developmental work research (for a summary of the study in English, see Engeström & Engeström, 1986).

The third phase in Engeström's work concerns the birth of developmental work research, conceived in parallel with the elaboration of the theory of expansive learning. From 1986 to 1989, Engeström led a study with the primary health care practitioners and patients of the city of Espoo, where patients were facing excessive waiting times before receiving health care and a lack of continuity of care. In this study, Davydov's ideas that had been originally applied in experimental schools were used to investigate/implement radical change at work. When practitioners, with the help of researchers, transform their own work, a new kind of learning emerges. This is the type of learning, brought to fruition, that Davydov (1990) called learning activity – learning that can rarely be observed in schools. Engeström's main argument in *Learning by Expanding* (1987) is that this kind of learning can be seen in full maturity in the transformation of work.

In *Learning by Expanding,* we also see Il'enkov's influence on Engeström in his adoption of the concept of contradictions. The triangular model of activity systems (Engeström, 1987, p. 78), present in embryonic form in early texts (Engeström, 1983; Engeström, Hakkarainen, & Hedegaard, 1984), was further theorized within the development of the theory of expansive learning. The visual representation of the triangle was a way to condense and convey theory in research collaborations with practitioners. Thus, the triangle emerged as a tool designed to destroy the myth of directness in learning and teaching, and to overcome the dualism in existing traditional theories based on subject–object, learner–knowledge, and individual–environment relations. Significantly, the triangular representation is a direct result of the researcher's dialogue with practice. It is important to note that in Engeström's study of cleaners (Engeström & Engeström, 1984), Vygotsky's simple triangular representation was successfully used as a basis for making the distinction between object and tool. This use of the basic triangle was possible because the cleaners Engeström studied worked mainly alone in the evenings in offices. Issues of community, rules, and division of labor in their work were all but nonexistent. In health care settings, in contrast, these issues appeared to be dominant.

A fourth phase of Engeström's work can be characterized as an ongoing effort to initiate communities into the use and development of activity theory for changing societal practices. By 1982, an informal group of activist researchers who worked in various kinds of practices related to human resource development was established in Finland. In addition to Engeström, members of this group included Ritva Engeström, Kirsti Launis, Rejio Miettinen, Kari Toikka, and Jaakko Virkkunen. The group continued to exist informally until 1994, when the Center for Activity Theory and Developmental Work Research was founded at the University of Helsinki.

Beginning in 1989, Engeström also collaborated with Michael Cole, who directed the Laboratory of Comparative Human Cognition (LCHC) at the University of California, San Diego. His experience at LCHC as well as his efforts to bring together scholars who worked within activity theory inspired the creation of the research center in Helsinki. Engeström traveled extensively in the 1980s, especially in Germany, where he met Georg Rückriem, who was working on the translations of Leont'ev's works. Engeström suggested the idea of a conference in which scholars within Germany and elsewhere could gather to discuss ways of influencing human practices on the basis of activity theory. Subsequently, Rückriem started organizing the first conference of the International Society for Cultural Research and Activity Theory (ISCRAT), which took place in 1986. In an effort to disseminate research work and to create a forum for scholarship on cultural-historical activity theory, Engeström suggested the creation of the journal *Mind, Culture, and Activity,* which was originally published as the *Quarterly Newsletter of the Laboratory of Comparative Human Cognition* by Michael Cole and colleagues.

In 1995, Finland was struggling to overcome an economic recession, as were many other countries. The problems of the Finnish economy, however, were also connected with the collapse of the Soviet Union, which had been Finland's main trading partner. Companies were under economic pressure and needed to find short-term solutions to the crisis. Developmental work research was formulated in terms of a long developmental cycle of interventionist work lasting 3 to 5 years (Engeström & Engeström, 1986). Companies in these years could not afford to engage in this kind of transformative venture. The intervention methodology of the Change Laboratory, as compressed cycles of transformation within the broader frame of developmental work research, was elaborated to meet the needs of these institutions.

The main influence of Engeström's work on society has occurred through the research projects and partnerships of the Center for Activity Theory and

Developmental Work Research. The center initiated direct partnerships with organizations in, for example, heath care, occupational health, and vocational education. The work performed at the center inspired the emergence of similar institutions, such as the Centre for Sociocultural and Activity Theory Research at the University of Bath in the United Kingdom, the Centre for Sociocultural and Activity Theory Research at the University of Oxford in the United Kingdom, and the Center for Human Activity Theory at the University of Kansai in Osaka, Japan.

This brief historical account of Yrjö Engeström's work illustrates the development and application of activity theory through the life of an activity theorist. For Engeström, as for the founders of activity theory, theoretical developments require activist involvement in concrete human practices. In constant dialogue with the activity-theoretical classic heritage – in particular that of Vygotsky, Leont'ev, Ilyenkov, and Davydov – Engeström's work addresses the pressing societal challenges of change and learning in work activities.

PART ONE

UNITS OF ANALYSIS

2

Cultural-Historical Activity Theory and Organization Studies

FRANK BLACKLER

What is the appropriate way to evaluate a significant corpus of work in the applied social sciences? One way of considering Engeström's contribution would be to review his version of activity theory, his methodological approach, and his research studies, and to compare his work with related contributions. Such an approach is generally thought to be the essence of academic commentary, and in what follows I will include some comments of that kind. I shall argue, however, that Engeström's work should also be considered in a broader context. Cherns (1979) first pointed out that developments in the applied social sciences are only partly driven by advances in theory and methods; developments are influenced also by changing social priorities and shifting values. Extending Cherns's point, I take the view that applied social science work needs not only to be responsive to emerging concerns but also to contribute to the ways in which issues are understood and addressed.

ORGANIZATION STUDIES

I work in the field of organization studies, also known as organization theory and organization behavior, and it is from this perspective that I approach Engeström's work. Formal organizations are a distinctive feature of modern societies, and it is impossible to understand the nature of contemporary human activity without some appreciation of them. The field of organization studies has developed in a very different way than activity theory, and to introduce my comments I need to say something about this field and to sketch out its achievements and shortcomings as I understand them.

Organization studies emerged as a specialist field as a result of the explosion of interest in "management" that has occurred in recent decades. As I comment later in the chapter, early research in the subject was concerned with the changing nature of work and the relationship of bureaucratic structures to organizational effectiveness. Although the range of issues associated with the subject has grown considerably in recent years, the topic of change has once again been attracting a lot of interest. A recent overview of relevant research, *The Oxford Handbook of Work and Organization,* edited by Ackroyd, Batt, Thompson, and Tolbert (2005), illustrates the point. The book includes sections on the changing nature of organizations, technologies, and the division of labor, contemporary issues in management theory, and the changing nature of occupations. Along with many other commentators, including Engeström, writers contributing to the Ackroyd et al. collection are agreed: Within developed economies, work organizations are changing. As I note later, the research they review suggests that such changes are indeed significant, although it suggests also that the extent and rate of change have been less dramatic than some journalistic commentaries would have us believe.

Organization studies have attracted researchers from many traditions – positivism, social constructionism, critical realism, action research, and ethnomethodology among them – and also researchers who have had very different interests and agendas, from those who wish simply to discover what is happening in organizations, to managers and management researchers who want to find out how they might be run more effectively, and to self-styled critical theorists who are seeking to develop a more detached analysis of the role of organizations in contemporary societies. Organization studies do not, certainly, constitute a unified discipline. The field's short history has been characterized by profound disagreements about what the appropriate foci of the subject should be, and how they should be researched and theorized.

Another collection of essays recently published, *The Oxford Handbook of Organizational Theory,* edited by Tsoukas and Knudsen (2003), explicitly set out to review such debates and assess the general status of organization theory given the high levels of disagreement within it. This collection includes, among others, groups of essays on organization theory as science, on the ways scholars have theorized organizations, on policy matters, and on the future of organization theory.

Readers of the Tsoukas and Knudsen volume could be forgiven if, perhaps, they found themselves wondering whether organization studies have become terminally self-absorbed. However, ever since Burrell and Morgan's (1979) assertion that organization theory is underpinned by competing and incommensurate paradigms, workers in this field have been acutely aware of the relevance of broader epistemological debates in the social sciences to their field. Not that everyone has agreed with Burrell and Morgan's view that fundamental disputes are inevitable; Pfeffer (1993, 1995), for example, famously lamented the lack of a shared focus and suggested that exaggerated disagreements were both delaying progress and diminishing respect for the subject area. Yet despite his intervention, it is clear that the area of organization studies continues to be highly contested. Czarniawska (2003) neatly summarized what has been happening. She pointed to the various rhetorical styles associated with leading contributors: the "scientistic" (her example was James Thompson), the "poetic" (Karl Weick), the "revolutionary" (Gibson Burrell), the "philosophical" (James March), the "educational" (David Silverman), and the "ethnographic" (John Van Maanen). Czarniawska did not lament such diversity of style in principle but concluded that style has, for some people, become the message. In that event it is no wonder that discussions between different "schools" have so often degenerated into argument.

Organization studies are certainly not unique in having strong internal disagreements. Relevant to a discussion of the relevance of Engeström's work is the question: How did this particular field become so fractious? Barley and Kunda's (2001) discussion of the history of work studies and Starbuck's (2003) discussion of the history of organization theory both make similar points about this: that at the time when the area was growing rapidly, important foundational issues became obscured. Barley and Kunda made the point by noting how early studies of work and organization, such as those of Dalton (1950), Walker and Guest (1952), Gouldner (1954), and Blau (1955), were all tightly linked to the study of work practices that were emerging in the postwar years. These detailed studies were very well done. Because of that, and because the nature of work was to remain relatively stable through the 1960s and 1970s, later researchers found that they had the freedom to move away from concrete, situational studies of work to more abstract analysis. Survey methods and systems analysis became popular during this period, and *organizations* as (it was assumed) rational, bounded, purposeful, and sovereign entities became the main unit of analysis, with *management* considered to be the foundation of effective organization. Starbuck's commentary focused on how it was that social scientists who had been interested in the theory of bureaucracy were to become involved in the study of organizational effectiveness. Economic and social changes in the first half of the 20th century stimulated a coming together of these themes, he showed. But when, in the late 1960s and beyond, management schools expanded and the number of organizational academics increased, researchers found that it was advantageous for their careers if they decided for themselves what was important, perhaps proposing a new approach or opening up a new area of inquiry. Through the 1980s and 1990s subtopics proliferated, as did specialized journals, professional subdivisions, and theoretical schisms. As a result, during this period many academics turned away from the practical issues that had stimulated the development of their subject in the first place.

The drift to abstract theorization and specialized areas of interest has had its downside for sure, but nonetheless organizational researchers have produced some good work in recent years. This is illustrated by Ackroyd et al.'s handbook, mentioned earlier, which reviews research on the changing nature of work and organizations. Overall the volume suggests that although variations across countries exist, nonetheless a broad convergence has developed about the way organizations should be managed. For example, across the world a heavy emphasis is now placed on the doctrine of "shareholder value." Such a development has been accompanied by moves toward deregulation and heightened levels of competition, and many employers have adopted practices intended to foster employee commitment by introducing flatter hierarchies, internal teamworking, and external networking. Interestingly, however, there has also been a contrasting trend. There has been a marked increase in the use of outsourcing contracts and of techniques to monitor employee performance; the autonomy of professionals has been eroded; and many employers are investing less in employee training. Job insecurity has grown, the power of trade unions has declined, and new inequalities have developed.

The epistemological debates that were the starting point for Tsoukas and Knudsen's handbook have produced some interesting outcomes as well. In his conclusion to that volume, Tsoukas (2003) offers an assessment that, I would estimate, echoes the views of many involved in the field. Organization theory, he concluded, has limited its focus by concentrating too much on formal organizations and by falsely assuming that these are both solid and enduring. As an alternative, he suggested, organizing processes should be placed center stage. An individualistic bias in the subject, present in much Western thought, has led to an underestimation of the sociality of organizing. Dichotomies that have been common in management theory (e.g., structure vs. process, routines vs. creativity, stability versus change) have not proved helpful either. Above all, Tsoukas emphasized, it is a mistake to conceptualize formal organizations as abstract systems; rather than engaging in a fruitless search for the abstract, the timeless, and the universal, organizational research should turn once again to the concrete, the timely, and the local.

ENGESTRÖM AND ORGANIZATION STUDIES

In recent years activity theory has received some attention in organization studies, but it remains poorly understood and is still a specialized, marginal area of interest in this field. Nonetheless, Engeström's work is clearly relevant to the subject. Regarding research on the changing nature of work, through references to Victor and Boynton (1998) especially, Engeström has repeatedly emphasized the growing importance of nonhierarchical ways of working. His occasional comments on, for example, Sennett's (1999b) concerns about the personal and social disruptions associated with contemporary capitalism and Giddens's (2000) "runaway objects" demonstrate a concern with the ways in which periods of change can overwhelm those involved. Unusual for a social theorist, Engeström is concerned not only to describe but also to intervene. His interest in collective development has involved him in detailed studies of particular activities and the tensions they embrace, and the use of such data to support a process of reflection and experimentation. In this he and his colleagues have produced an impressive corpus of detailed studies highlighting various unfamiliar organizational processes, which he has variously dubbed "the horizontal dimension of expansive learning," "knotworking," "mycorrhizae activities," and "collaborative intentionality capital." The relevance of Engeström's work to important theoretical controversies in the field is also clear. For example, his version of activity theory provides a strong account of agency by featuring the dynamics of relations between individuals, collectivities, objects, and language. This has enabled him to develop powerful critiques of contemporary approaches as diverse as actor network theory and discourse analysis. Indeed, his general approach is very much in accord with suggestions, touched on earlier, that rather than the abstract organization being taken as the central unit of analysis in organization studies, the detail of situated practices should be featured.

The significance of Engeström's work for organization studies is summarized, I suggest, in the following three points:

1. His approach suggests that in place of the assumption that the objectives of an organization are the key to understanding it, it is more useful to prioritize the notion of objects of activity.

2. His approach suggests that rather than working with organizations as the core unit of analysis, it is more helpful to work with the idea of the activity system as the core unit.
3. Engeström's theory of collective learning emphasizes the significance of a situated approach for intervention and the role that social science research can play in turning ideas into practice.

In the following three subsections I develop each of these points.

The Object of Activity

In introducing a discussion of the relevance of Engeström's work to organization studies, it is interesting to compare his approach with the approach associated with the Tavistock Institute of Human Relations in London. Unlike universities in Britain, the Tavistock Institute receives no earmarked funds from government to support its scholarly work; since its foundation shortly after the Second World War, the Tavistock has supported itself mainly from income generated by consultancy work in organizations. The ideas that members of the institute developed to support this work were unusual in a number of respects. First, their interest in organization theory began in the 1950s, many years before the growth of academic university departments with an interest in this area and many years before the huge growth in the consultancy industry. Second, the package of ideas they pioneered has continued to be developed to the present day. In certain respects their approach is very different from Engeström's – most obviously in the central part that psychodynamic theory plays in their thinking. But in other respects there is a commonality of interest between the two orientations. Like Engeström, workers from the Tavistock Institute place heavy emphasis on the transformative nature of work, the need to conceptualize how social and technical factors interact, and the centrality of intervention research. Nonetheless, examination of how their approach differs from Engeström's goes a long way toward illustrating what is distinctive about his approach.

The notion of "the primary task" in Tavistock thinking is the nearest term in organization studies to activity theory's "object of activity." The idea of an organization's primary task was first proposed by workers at the institute in the late 1950s. As discussed by Miller (1993), the principles that guided their work then were, first, the analysis of organizations as "open-systems," taking inputs from their environment, transforming them, and exporting back finished products or services, and second, the application of psychoanalytically informed approaches to group behavior, in particular Bion's (1961) insight that as a workgroup addresses its overt tasks it is, at the same time, dealing with related anxieties. Hirschhorn (1999) explained:

> In the Tavistock tradition we understand an organization by first identifying its primary task. We ask, what is this organization set up to do, how is it organized to accomplish this objective, and what unconscious dynamics limit or distort its members' abilities to do their work? (p. 5)

Surprisingly perhaps, given the centrality of the notion of the primary task to the Tavistock's approach, ambiguity and controversy have been associated with the term since it was first proposed. Though it was initially defined by Rice (1958) as "the task an organization was created to perform," Rice was soon to modify his approach to suggest that the primary task was "the task an organization must perform to survive" (Rice, 1965). Some sociologists of the period thought the term was poorly thought through anyway, suggesting that it encouraged the "reification" of organizations and that it was overly prescriptive (Silverman, 1968, 1970). However, issues of definition were not the main concern for the Tavistock workers. What mattered to them was how useful the notion could be in helping their organizational clients reflect on what they were doing in new and productive ways. As Miller and Rice (1967) explained, the notion of an organization's primary task is

> essentially a heuristic concept, which allows us to explore the ordering of multiple activities (and of constituent systems of activity where these exist). It makes it possible to construct and compare different organization models of an enterprise based on different definitions of its primary task; and to compare the organizations of different enterprises with the same or different primary task. (p. 25)

Lawrence and Robinson (1975) distinguished between an organization's "normative" primary task, that is, its formal or official task; its "existential" primary task, that is, the task people in the organization believe they are carrying out; and finally its "phenomenological" primary task, that is, the task that can be inferred from organizational practices and of which people may not be fully aware. More recently Zagier Roberts (1994) and Obholzer (2001) related the idea of the primary task to the notions of "strategy" and "mission," very popular terms in management circles at the present time. Zagier Roberts argued that when an organization's external environment changes, it may become necessary for its primary task to be redefined, and Obholzer (2001) argued that it was critical that senior leaders keep the concept "uppermost in the minds of all members of the organization" and ensure that it is "constantly reviewed in the light of the external environment," with the "functioning, structure and staffing of the organization" being changed as the primary task is changed (p. 199).

I mentioned earlier that workers at the Tavistock Institute incorporated psychodynamic ideas in their general approach, and a brief comment on this side of their work will be helpful. Their insight was that an organization's primary task may itself generate anxieties and that the way people cope with such feelings can systematically divert their efforts from the task. Miller and Gwynne's (1974) intervention in a home for incurables illustrates the approach. In studying what the primary task of the care home might be, they discovered that the professionals working there held different views. Some believed that their work should be guided by what Miller and Gwynne called a "warehousing" approach; that is, they should "look after patients and prolong their lives." Others, however, favored what Miller and Gwynne called a "horticultural" approach; that is, they should "encourage patients' personal development and independence." Miller and Gwynne concluded that each of these approaches oversimplified a difficult situation and was functioning to protect the caregivers in the home from the inherent anxieties of their work. Thus, the "warehousing" rational allowed workers to deny the distress their patients might feel from a sense of helplessness and futility, whereas the "horticultural" rational allowed them to deny the distress patients might experience as a result of their declining physical and mental states. They suggested how a new, more complex but more realistic primary task could be articulated.

As I hope these comments demonstrate, workers at the Tavistock developed quite a sophisticated and pragmatic package of ideas to guide their intervention work. Their notion of primary task provided a way of debating core objectives; their emphasis on systems thinking was ahead of its time; their interest in how task anxieties can distract people from their priorities remains distinctive. But it needs to be said, too, that in other respects their approach is somewhat conventional: They take the organization as the central unit for analysis; goals and objectives are thought to be relatively malleable; and they anticipate a key role for managers in reviewing established objectives in the light of changing circumstances and deciding what changes to the organization should be made.

Like the Tavistock workers, Engeström emphasizes the practical, transforming nature of work, but because he does not start from either an organizational or a managerial perspective, his approach differs significantly from theirs. Uniquely, activity theory prioritizes the thing or project that people are working to transform. Outcomes, too, are featured, but unlike the Tavistock's approach, practices are not divorced from objectives. Indeed, the notion of the object of activity invites a situated analysis of the activity that is under way – a level of analysis that, as we have seen, is often overlooked in more abstract studies of organizations. Note that whereas the Tavistock workers can assume there is or should be a reasonably straightforward relationship between the primary task of an organization and the values it expresses, Engeström's theory maintains that the values embedded in the object of activity are a contradictory unity of use value and exchange value. Others in organization studies have recognized that tensions in organizations are inevitable. Engeström, however, does not focus just on how different points of view or interpretations can be resolved or tolerated; his approach features how contradictions are at the heart of human activity and invites inquiry into how, in the past, these have been resolved through practices and how, in the future, they may be addressed anew.

For newcomers to activity theory, the notion of the object of activity is unfamiliar and may not be easy to understand. Indeed, the term is complex; objects of activity need to be understood as simultaneously given, socially constructed, contested, and emergent. Objects of activity also provide the basis for theorizing motivation, a point clearly captured by Engeström when he noted that objects of activity are best regarded as

> a project under construction, moving from potential raw material to a meaningful shape and to a result or outcome. In this sense the object determines the horizon of possible goals and actions. But it is truly a horizon: as soon as an intermediate goal is reached, the object escapes and must be reconstructed by means of new intermediate goals and actions. (Engeström 1999c, p. 65)

The complexity of the term should not be thought of as a shortcoming of activity theory, however. Rather, it both reflects and reveals the complexity of human activity. When it is applied to organizational analysis, it can be said that organizations coalesce around objects of activity that are partly shared, partly fragmented, possibly contested, and certainly emergent, and because objects of activity are likely to be rooted in multiple activity systems, they may not be at all easy to change in the short term. Engeström's message to organization studies is: Take objects of activity seriously. Rather than follow the organization and its prescribed objectives, he urges, "follow the object," "give objects a voice," "expand the object." These suggestions are made in an article I discuss later (Engeström, Engeström, & Kerosuo, 2003) and in other publications (Engeström, 1999d; Engeström & Blackler, 2005;

Engeström, Puonti, & Seppänen, 2003) where he discusses, respectively, the relevance of the object of activity to analyzing teamwork, examples of expanding objects, and the life history of objects.

It is interesting that, in recent years, a number of commentators who are closely associated with the Tavistock's approach have voiced criticisms about the way the idea of the primary task has been used. Dartington (1998), for example, objected to the way that both Zagier Roberts and Obholzer equate the term with the idea of an organization's "mission." In organizations that are founded on a moral purpose, he argued, there will be strict limits on the changes that can be made to the primary task. Accordingly, the primary task should be defined as the task an organization needs to address "if it is to continue *as itself,* and not be transformed into something quite different" (p. 1497). Hirschhorn (1999) accepted that, in times of change, many organizations need to confront choices about their primary task, but he pointed out that the stress and uncertainty involved in devising new strategies had been overlooked by Tavistock workers. Difficult choices of this kind can lead to vacillation, denial, and a failure to decide; accordingly, he suggests that rather than placing the notion of primary task center stage, interventionists should encourage their clients to focus on the primary *risk* they must confront. Finally, Armstrong (2005) noted also that the primary task is an instrumental notion based on a conception of external goals and that it does not capture "the journeying" toward them; rather "the journeying is simply read back from the end result, as if, for example, the object of a game were only to win" (p. 129). Armstrong maintained, however, that it is practice that "breathes life into the organization" (p. 131). Leaders, he argued, should encourage people to recognize the internal goods of their practices. From the sense of identity this can provide, people are likely to be "less fearful of the risk of discovering something new" (p. 116).

Note that, in various ways, these more recent debates within the Tavistock community all focus on the relevance of emotional issues – anxiety around the challenges of the primary task; the importance of established values; the worry associated with fundamental choices; the importance of a "secure base" from which new uncertainties can be approached. A consistent theme in the Tavistock work is to find ways of helping clients understand how feelings can hinder effective action even without those involved being aware of the problem. Engeström's priorities are emancipatory as well, but his approach is very different. Although there has been some discussion in activity theory circles recently about the emotional aspects of objects of activity, Engeström himself has not explored such matters. As I note later, he has continued to emphasize activity theory's insight that behavior is influenced "from the outside" by tools, signs, and cultural, social, and organizational factors, and to explore what might be done to help people "re-mediate" their activities for themselves.

The Activity System

Perhaps Engeström's most important contribution to activity theory has been his suggestion that rather than the socially mediated individual being taken as the basic unit of analysis, the historically located activity system should be the fundamental unit. While featuring the crucial link between subject and object, this approach features the essentially social nature of activity and the centrality to it of durable cultural artifacts. The object of activity as a "horizon of possibility" is, in Engeström's approach, theorized as a collective project that is stabilized by shared tools, signs, and procedures. Particular actions need to be analyzed in the context of this longer-term historical dynamic. Further, as noted already, Engeström emphasizes the tensions between use value and exchange value, and he stresses that activity systems not only are stabilizing but also produce disturbance.

Not everyone interested in activity theory accepts Engeström's theory of activity systems (compare Engeström, 2000a, with Bedny & Karwowski, 2004a). Nonetheless, the criticism leveled by Thompson (2004), that Engeström's approach in general, and my use of it in organizational analysis in particular, involves a "drift" away from the immediacy of particular co-constituting relationships toward detached, abstract representations of experience, is mistaken. Engeström's general model includes the terms "community" and "system" certainly, but its purpose is not to support a general and abstracted account of organizations. Engeström locates agency in a mix of relationships centered on objects of activity and, true to the origins of activity theory, he features the ever-present tensions that are at the heart of this dynamic. Note also that central to Engeström's orientation is the insight that although it is individuals who experience the dilemmas, contradictions, and performance shortcomings of the systems of activity they work within, solutions can be developed only collectively. Moreover, his model of activity systems does not accept the traditional lines that are drawn between event and context. One of the major achievements of his empirical work is, I believe, his explorations of how agency is distributed and his demonstrations of how, through relevant mediating factors, agency can be variously located in individuals, in formally appointed functional groups, as well as in the spontaneous communications and improvisations that can occur in loose networks of concerned people. The approach is highly relevant to the analysis of formal organizations: Agency is distributed across the sometimes overlapping and sometimes distinct activities of individuals, departments, organizations, networks, and institutions.

It seems to me that, from an organizational perspective, important points of interest and debate concerning Engeström's account of activity systems are as follows:

1. *The emphasis on practices.* Engeström's focus on the detail of purposeful activity resonates with the suggestion that organizational researchers need to move away from a search for the abstract so that they can, as Barley and Kunda (2001) put it, "bring work back in." As I have already noted, Engeström himself is very interested in the changing nature of work, in particular in the dynamics of fluid, informal, object-centered interactions. In Engeström (2006c) he speculates that important, if not dramatic, changes are afoot; developments are taking place, he suggests, that require a shift away from terms such as "control," "occupational communities," "latent dilemmas," and "stories" and their replacement by notions of swarming, "mycorrhizae" associations, dynamic contradictions, and multiple instrumentalities. There is much that is interesting here, but it is difficult to gauge how widespread such trends really are. I suspect that Engeström's approach has been steered more by a wish to explore exciting new forms of human agency and to demonstrate the relevance of his style of analysis to these than by a serious intention to chart the changing nature of work and organizations. Drawing as it does from a range of resources relevant to understanding the changing nature of work, the Ackroyd et al. (2005) volume mentioned earlier suggests a more well rounded picture of what appears to be happening. If Engeström has tended to feature interesting new developments in the world of work at the expense of what might be described as the more dismal continuities that are to be found there, he is by no means alone in that. In principle, however, there is no reason that, applied to the study of work and organizations, activity theory needs to concentrate merely on the unusual or exotic. In a study I undertook of changes in a high-technology firm a few years ago, I found Engeström's general model very useful as a way of depicting contrasting epochs of activity in that organization, and the tensions and uncertainties that had driven their development (Blackler, Crump, & MacDonald, 1999). Such an approach could be very helpful in other studies of the changing nature of work.

2. *Relations to institution theory.* There is a case for suggesting that activity theorists could extend their analysis of the cultural roots of practices by contributing to current discussions about organizational institution

theory. It can be very helpful for analytical purposes to treat organizations, or subsections of organizations, as activity systems in their own right. However, practices in an organization need also to be located within their broader context – the practices of a medical doctor, for example, need to be analyzed in the broad context of how medical practice has been conceptualized and has been organized in the society he or she is working in, as well as in an analysis of the particular arrangements that have emerged in his or her work organization. The branch of organization studies that explores such matters, institution theory, views organizations as social entities embedded in "fields" of beliefs and conventions (Scott, 2001). In recent years there has been growing interest in how institutional frameworks can be changed. A recent study of my own followed a failing attempt to introduce a new series of beliefs into services for vulnerable children and families living in a deprived area of England (Blackler & Regan, 2006). My conclusion was that theories of institutional change inspired by Foucault and also by Giddens that are popular within organization studies at the moment completely failed to anticipate a major feature of this episode, namely the muddles, misunderstandings, false starts, and loose ends that accompanied the attempt at change. Conventional theories of institutionalization emphasize the importance of the internalization of values, but the problems of this case arose from the difficulties participants had in externalizing their ideals into new routines and procedures. This aspect of collective learning is a feature of Engeström's analysis.

3. *Artifact re-mediation.* In developing this point, as I have already noted, Engeström has placed a strong emphasis on the role of artifacts in mediating activity. Since the advent of actor network theory (Latour, 2005), sociologists have shown much interest in the social role of material objects, but Engeström does not treat objects as "actants." In the Vygotsky tradition his concern has been the instrumentality of mediating artifacts, and he has demonstrated how mediating artifacts influence behavior. Some time ago Zuboff's (1988) landmark commentary on how the skills of "being there" were being displaced by what she called "informated" work environments triggered an awareness among organizational scholars of the way new technologies can change the character of an organization's activity. It is no accident, indeed, that activity theory has attracted a strong following in the area of technology design. But what has been distinctive in Engeström's own work on such matters is the way he has consistently concentrated on the significance of "bottom-up" re-mediation. Uniquely he has emphasized how, through their collective development of the tools they use, people can themselves invest their activities with new meanings.

4. *Linguistic re-mediation.* Engeström has acknowledged that the accent on artifact mediation in his early studies led to a relative neglect of social and organizational factors, that is, in the rules, community, and division of labor shown in his general model of activity (Engeström, 1996b). Certainly, different means of mediation can be expected to act in concert, and a change in one may well require changes elsewhere in the activity system. In recent years, though, the issue that has attracted more attention has concerned the relative emphasis that should be placed on material versus linguistic mediation. In his early empirical studies, Engeström demonstrated rather little concern with language; in recent years, however, the relevance of language to organization studies has attracted widespread interest. In his commentary on the development of organization studies touched on earlier, for example, Tsoukas (2003) suggested that a suitable motto for organization studies now should be: "Don't search for the logic of organizing; look for the discursive practices involved in organizing" (p. 619). Taylor and Van Every's (2000) theory of communication *as* organizing has, indeed, pursued exactly that agenda. Developing their approach, and familiar with activity theory's notion of the object of activity, Taylor and Robichaud (2004) have explored how, through conversations, people "coorient" themselves both to the object and to each other. It is the way roles and relationships are created as part of this process that allows Taylor and his co-workers to equate communicating with organizing. Part of Taylor and Robichaud's analysis explored how people draw on past meanings to explain current activities and relationships; analyzing a film of members of a management team meeting to discuss strategies for their business, they speculated that the interplay of different systems of meaning in an organization can trigger a process of change that is, essentially, unpredictable.

In contrast, Engeström does not equate communicating with organizing; rather, he equates practice with organizing, and his interest in talk is subordinate to his interest in practical actions. Nor does he conceive of change as an essentially random process; his interest in language is subordinate to his interest in how people can participate in the development of their activities. Although Engeström has not, as far as I am aware, studied management teams as they engage in strategy review discussions in quite the way that Taylor has, nonetheless, drawing from his work in a medical context (Engeström, 2004), he has developed a general model that is directly relevant to such a project. His focus was on what is necessary to turn plans into practices; managing as designing, he argued, requires a merging of "paradigmatic language," "experiential language," and "interpretative narratives." Exactly how the ambiguities, conflicts, surprises, and frustrations of such a process might best be dealt with remains, however, the subject of future research.

Collective Learning

In an introduction to a collection of papers by various researchers at his Helsinki research center, Engeström (2005b) commented on how his approach differs from one recently proposed by Flyvbjerg (2001). Inspired by Aristotle and Foucault, Flyvbjerg had argued that rather than being approached in a detached, rationalistic way, social research should be managed as a pragmatic, context-dependent, and ethical activity. Engeström acknowledges similarities between activity theory's approach and the approaches Flyvbjerg favors. But as he points out, the differences between his proposals and those Flyvbjerg developed is revealing. Flyvbjerg advises researchers to ask: Where are we going? Who gains, who looses, by which mechanisms of power? Is this desirable? What should be done?

Regarding the first of these questions, Engeström pointed out that in many situations the direction an organization is taking may be ambiguous or remain contested, so the question "Where are we going?" may be difficult to answer meaningfully. Flyvbjerg's second question is clearly drawn from his emphasis on Foucault's interest in power and governmentality. Engeström notes that Flyvbjerg's third question, like the first, may be either difficult to answer or premature; certainly this will be the case when there is some uncertainty regarding the direction of development. Finally, judging by Flyvbjerg's own research of a town planning project, Engeström comments that his fourth question appears to be an invitation to the researcher to feed back his or her research findings to those involved. That idea is clearly a good one and can stimulate informed discussion of important issues; yet, Engeström pointed out, Flyvbjerg appears to overlook the point that in many situations what should be done may not be the same as what actually can and will be done.

Engeström's alternative questions are: Where do we come from? What are the tools and signs that are available for different participants, and how are they used to construct the object of activity? What are the inner contradictions of the activity? What can and will be done?

These questions draw their inspiration from activity theory's emphasis on historicity, its emphasis on the power of instrumentality, and the driving dynamic of internal contradictions. Critically also, note how Engeström's understanding of the researcher's role extends beyond Flyvbjerg's. He does not accept the distinctions that are normally drawn between pure and applied research or consultancy. Engeström's view is that it is essential that researchers not rest content merely to pass their research findings back to those who are affected by them, but that they remain active in helping to turn new ideas into practices. His disagreement with Flyvbjerg on this point echoes criticisms he has made of Argyris, Putnam, and Smith's (1985) "action science" – another approach that is very familiar to organization scholars. Argyris's approach, he pointed out, encourages researchers to help people recognize basic, but unquestioned assumptions that guide their practices, but it fails completely to explore how people do, or do not, turn such insights into new practices (Engeström, Engeström, & Kerosuo, 2003).

In organization studies there has been extensive discussion about the "relevance" of organizational research in recent years. For example, there has been a strong advocacy of the importance of "evidence based management" (Pfeffer, 2007), a perspective that has been sharply countered by objections that the approach is misconceived (Learmonth & Harding, 2006). Others have called for an independent and "critical" field of organization studies (Alvesson & Willmott, 1992), an outlook that has, in turn, been severely criticized because of its antiperformative stance (Fournier & Grey, 2000). Engeström's theory provides a highly challenging, well-worked-out alternative to both such approaches. Pointing out that solutions imported to an organization from outside or imposed from above are unlikely to work, he grounds his approach in detailed studies of situated practices backed by a clear appreciation of the driving significance of the object of their activities for those involved (Engeström, 2000c).

The project discussed in Engeström, Engeström, and Kerosuo (2003) (see also Kerosuo, 2006) provides a clear example of his approach to intervention research. The project was intended to overcome the difficulties of providing coordinated care for chronically ill patients with multiple illnesses. It drew from an earlier project by Engeström in a hospital for children where attempts had been made to address similar problems of coordination by the introduction of a "care agreement" – a record of the overall plan of care for each patient and a statement of how different care providers would contribute to it (Engeström, Engeström, & Vähäaho, 1999). The hope in that case had been that, as a result of the care agreement, medical practitioners would constantly be reminded that they were interacting with patients who had multiple problems and that their contributions had to be conceived within this broader context. Referring to the care agreement Engeström noted:

> The new instrumentality was supposed to become a germ cell for a new kind of collaborative care in which no single party would have a permanent dominating position and in which no party could evade taking responsibility over the entire care trajectory. The model implied a radical expansion of the object of activity: from singular illness episodes or care visits to a long-term trajectory (temporal expansion), and from relationships between the patient and singular practitioner to the joint monitoring of the entire network of care involved with the patient (socio-spatial expansion). (Engeström, Engeström, & Kerosuo, 2003, pp. 290–291)

As Engeström et al. go on to discuss, their work on services for chronically ill people with multiple ailments adopted the same approach. Early research on this project assembled data that were to act as the foundation for a Change Laboratory intervention, following the general format that has become associated with Engeström's work (Engeström, Virkkunen, Helle, Pihlaja, & Poikela, 1996). A series of such workshops was arranged for a core group of practitioners, plus other health care professionals who were directly responsible for the care of patients whose experiences were to be discussed at the meetings. One or two health care managers also usually attended, as did the patients whose cases were to be discussed.

Engeström noted that a typical workshop would start with a video presentation prepared by the researchers that included extracts from an interview with the patient, clips from recordings of the patient's medical consultations, and extracts from interviews with health care professionals responsible for the patient's treatment. Next the doctor mainly responsible for his or her care would introduce the patient to the group and outline the treatment regime and timetable. Discussions then followed about how the patient's problems should be interpreted, about the flow of information relevant to his or her case, and about the division of care responsibility. Problems were noted. The relevant doctor would introduce the care agreement that had been formulated with the patient, and Engeström reports that sometimes quite detailed changes were made regarding both plans for the specific case and more general issues. Finally, the researchers asked those present to summarize what had been achieved and agreed upon. Over the course of the project, the researchers and core workshop members redesigned the care agreement form and relevant supporting documentation.

The workshops were videotaped, and analysis suggested that, typically, four types of talk took place within them: a jointly told story about the case under review; joint decisions about actions that needed to be taken quite soon; summaries to model the patient's overall situation and any general implications it might suggest; and the emergence of the patient's perspective as a voice in its own right alongside those of the medical professionals. Engeström, Engeström, and Kerosuo (2003) present some examples of conversations to illustrate each of these aspects. The examples they provide of the modeling stage illustrate how involved they, the researchers, were in developing a workable version of the care agreement. Indeed, at the conclusion of the article they observe how, in studies of this kind,

> researcher-interventionists make themselves contestable and fallible participants of the discourse, which means that their actions also become objects of data collection and critical analysis. (Engeström, Engeström, & Kerosuo, 2003)

After the project was completed, senior managers in the health service resolved to introduce the new care agreement forms throughout the whole health care system in Helsinki. However, Kerosuo (2006) reported that this had not actually been done. She does not detail exactly why. She does note, though, that a major outcome of the workshop series was that participants were both willing and able to produce ideas about how the discontinuities of care they were discussing could be overcome. Nonetheless, she says:

> Their suggestions remained captive at the local practice level because the link between developing health care practices and inter-organizational intervention remained weak. Repairing the disjunctions in inter-organizational health care is a complex challenge, requiring solutions that involve multiple providers and high levels of organizational and professional involvement and learning. No doubt these challenges necessitate new approaches to organizational development and new approaches to educating health care providers. (Kerosuo, 2006)

Reflecting on this case, I propose that points of particular interest and debate for organization studies suggested by Engeström's approach to intervention research include the following:

1. *Re-mediation for system change.* The terms under which any research project is commissioned are likely to limit what is possible, and one does what one can, given the opportunities that can be arranged. However, it seems to me that if, in this case, it really was hoped that established practices would be transformed by the introduction of a new approach to recording treatment plans, the expectation was unrealistic. There are multiple mediations

in all complex systems of activity, a point that Engeström has emphasized himself. The point resonates with an observation that organization change theorists have long emphasized: Fundamental shifts in practices must be encouraged over time and in multiple ways. Discussions between professionals at the form-filling-in stage would have been an important occasion for learning certainly; this was the case at the workshops. But how powerful a written agreement about such discussions might subsequently be is another question altogether.

Indeed, it would be very interesting to learn more about how Engeström and his colleagues would retrospectively assess their learning from this project. As already noted, some years ago in reviewing some of his early projects, Engeström (1996b) noted how a heavy emphasis on instrumental mediation had led him to neglect social and organizational factors. In a presentation of a later project (Engeström, 1999c), he reflected back on the point, noting that when new procedures are integrated with a new division of labor, the resulting development is far more robust than would otherwise have been possible. Kerosuo's comments, noted earlier, on the case discussed here suggest that the key lesson of this project might be that in complex organizational settings, integration of that kind can be very difficult to achieve.

It is interesting that in a recent paper Engeström, Kerosuo, and Kajamaa (2007) compared the long-term change trajectories of two other health service organizations in Finland over a period of years. Their findings echo the insights of classic longitudinal studies of organizational change well known to organization theorists: Periods of organizational change are likely to be punctuated by periods of stability; discontinuities can occur over time, but continuity is possible (Child & Smith, 1987; Hinings & Greenwood, 1988; Pettigrew, 1985). Not all expansive learning will take place through the adaptation of existing organizations and institutions; sometimes old organizations need to go and new ones developed. But to the extent that expansive learning can and does happen in such settings, my suggestion is that the theory of expansive learning needs to be extended to help people better anticipate and manage the complex dynamics of organizational change. To pick up a point I made earlier, activity-theoretical studies of senior management teams would be of considerable interest in this respect.

2. *Content versus process in intervention research.* Engeström's Change Laboratories involve the simultaneous use of video recordings of actual practices, interviews, and other relevant data, historical analysis, the modeling of the activity system, and an exploration of its inner contradictions. I have no doubt that they provide a uniquely powerful forum for collective

reflection and development. The approach is quite structured, though, dependent as it is on well-crafted research input and the active involvement of researchers during the meetings. These aspects of the approach may, I suspect, limit the effectiveness of this form of intervention. In the case discussed here it may well have been that the researchers had obtained such a high degree of insight into the problems of cross-agency working that their input to the design of the care agreement form was indispensable. Or perhaps the researchers were hired explicitly to design the form; these things are not altogether clear. However, much of the literature on planned organizational change suggests that rather than seeking to provide clients with technical solutions to the problems they face, interventionists can reap long-term advantages by standing back from the detail and setting out to help clients manage the development process for themselves.

It would also be interesting to know whether in the case discussed here participants were encouraged to begin mobilizing themselves to address not just specific ideas for change stimulated by their reviews of patient experiences, but also the organizational development and educational issues that, looking back, seem necessary. One wonders what those involved in the workshops *currently* think could have been done then, or might be done now, to move their suggestions for change forward. The re-mediation of social and organizational factors can challenge institutionalized power structures; perhaps that is why the process can stretch the imaginations of researcher and client alike.

SUMMARY AND CONCLUSION

At the start of this chapter I suggested that one way of evaluating a significant corpus of work in the applied social sciences is to compare it with related approaches. I began by outlining the field of organizational studies, commented on some of its strengths and weaknesses, and noted how Engeström's approach resonates with calls for organizational theorists to stand back from abstracted theory and to feature the concrete, the situated, and the timely. I compared Engeström's orientation with the approach associated with the Tavistock Institute of Human Relations. Through the notions of "object of activity" and "activity systems," his approach provides a conceptual toolkit that is especially helpful in analyzing both the overall character and the details of practices. His emphasis on the object of activity provides a way of conceptualizing collective intent. His idea of the activity system provides a way of conceptualizing distributed agency. His emphasis on internal contradictions offers an account of the pressures and opportunities for collective development. His approach to research envisages a role for the social researcher not only in problem analysis but also in problem solving, solution implementation, and change evaluation.

At the beginning of the chapter I also suggested that it was important that applied social scientists both respond to changing perceptions of social problems and seek to influence debates about what is important. Engeström's empirical work is outstanding in the contribution it makes to an understanding of unfamiliar but perhaps increasingly important forms of object-oriented activity. My own view, however, is that it is less in such specifics and more in its general orientation that Engeström's work may have its greatest impact. His work is a reminder of the Marxist ambition for the self-determination of human history. Engeström's theory is unique in the analysis it offers of how groups, organizations, and institutions might more actively influence their own social forms. There is a great deal that can be done to develop and extend these ideas. Points I would especially emphasize from my earlier comments are the need to develop an agenda for intervention work that is driven by a recognition of the realities of hierarchy and disadvantage as much as by a vision of dynamic new forms of working; the need to explore more extensively the nature of social and organizational mediation from an activity theory point of view; and the need to develop forms of intervention that do not require the social scientist to act as expert adviser. The achievement of Engeström's theory, indeed, is the strength of the foundations it has provided for further analysis, research, and intervention.

3

Uses of Activity Theory in Written
Communication Research

DAVID R. RUSSELL

Documents largely organize the activity of the modern world and – a forteriori – the postmodern world, with its reliance on hyper*textual* networks. Writing is arguably the most powerful mediational means for organizations and institutions, and writing-in-use in organizations has become an object of research in the past 25 years in North America, with applications in a number of fields, primarily organizational (business, technical, and scientific) communication and education (Bazerman & Russell, 2003). In these fields, analysis of writing-in-use is often crucial for planning interventions to improve students' literacy, at all levels, or to improve organizations' communication, through document design and document management, or what has come to be called information design and information management.

This tradition is largely separate from literary or, indeed, applied linguistic research, though both have influenced it (Bazerman, 1997; Russell, 1997b). Instead, it grows out of a U.S. tradition of rhetorical analysis applied to texts, particularly the concept of genre as social action (Miller, 1984, 1994), with deep roots in Schutz's phenomenological analysis of typification (Schutz & Luckmann, 1973). I will refer to it as writing, activity, and genre research (WAGR). Sociological studies of science and technology were the original impetus (Latour & Woolgar, 1979; Merton, 1968), along with studies of orality and literacy, particularly studies based on Vygotsky's theory (most importantly, Scribner & Cole, 1981).

Empirical and historical research on written communication in this tradition has from its inception in the early 1980s found cultural-historical

---

I wish to thank the two anonymous reviewers of this chapter for their very helpful comments.

activity theory (CHAT) useful. CHAT, in various versions, has been influential because other approaches to written communication (e.g., cognitive psychology, applied linguistics, and cultural studies) have deep theoretical and methodological limitations in studies on writing-in-use within – and among – organizations and institutions. In CHAT, broadly conceived, context is not separated from activity, or from texts, which are seen as tools for the mediation of activity. In this sense, CHAT allows for wider levels of analysis than the dyad, common in much conversation analysis research, or reader–writer interactions per se, as in reader response criticism and critical discourse analysis. And it eschews the Cartesian split between mind and world, texts and context, which is common in cognitive research on written communication (Russell, 1995, 1997a; Russell & Yañez, 2003). CHAT, in principle, does not privilege one medium over another, as all are viewed as mediational tools. Because of this, it is possible to discern the relationship among tools in various media within and among organizations and their subjects.

Finally, CHAT provides for a mesolevel of analysis between microlevel phenomena (including discourse) and macrolevel generalizations common in the ideological analysis of cultural studies and many forms of sociological analysis (e.g., Parsonian social forces). This allows for a more nuanced analysis of organizations and practical interventions to improve organizational communication or pedagogy. Many CHAT and WAGR studies do so through ethnographic and case study methods, as both are interested in looking at change over time rather than developing a theory of language-in-use.

CHAT-influenced WAGR goes on in a very wide range of areas, but in this chapter I will not try to represent that range of theorizing and research on writing, activity, and genre. Instead, I will focus on work closest to my own: that in higher education, workplace studies of organizational communication, and relations between the two. I will pass over a huge number of studies of elementary and secondary education, well represented, for example, by Lee and Smagorinsky (2000) and many who do workplace and higher-education studies that take other approaches to CHAT, many of whom are discussed in Bazerman and Russell (2003).

While CHAT approaches have in general been highly influential, Engeström's systems version of CHAT, using an expanded version of Vygotsky's mediational triangle as a unit of analysis, has not been widely taken up by WAGR research, and where it has, it has usually been as another way of theorizing the social dimensions of activity, along with distributed cognition, community of practice, and so on (Dias, Freedman,

Medway, & Paré, 1999). This perhaps springs from the importance of genre in WAGR. Genre in WAGR is an overarching theoretical concept, a unit of analysis in its own right, conceived as *genre as social action*. By looking at genres as intertextual and hypertextual systems, WAGR constructs a concrete analysis of writing-in-use not only as tools and rules, in actions and operations that stabilize-for-now (Schryer, 1993) behavior in far-flung organizations and help explain institutional change and collective learning, but also as systems, at the level of activity. And particularly in its theory of genre, WAGR has over the past 25 years made a contribution to CHAT approaches to studying organizations (Bazerman & Russell, 2003; Russell & Bazerman, 1997).

My own work, like that of others whom I'll refer to, has used Engeström's expanded version of Vygotsky's mediational triangle as a unit of analysis alongside genre as social action to put the two in productive tension, to seek a synthesis – certainly not yet achieved, perhaps not possible, but nevertheless useful. I offer this chapter not as a resolution but as a way to identify influences, clarify issues, and continue to engage in dialogue.

Beginning in the mid-1990s, Engeström's (1987) elaboration of Leont'ev's (1978) activity system gave some of us doing WAGR a way to articulate the social systematics of textual circulation networks and their contributing role in accomplishing communal work – as well as impeding or transforming work through dialectical contradictions. Indeed, in the concept of dialectical contradictions, Engeström's approach to CHAT also offered fresh elaborations of Marxian notions of work and learning. Engeström's developmental approach suggested ways to trace how people and their writing practices change, individually and collectively, as they move within and among various social practices, theorized in terms of activity systems. Perhaps most importantly, this unit of analysis has been developed recently in terms of multiple and interpenetrating contexts, polycontextual systems of activity – the "third generation" of activity theory research, as Engeström (2001) has called it. This has proved helpful for understanding written communication in modern organizations, because they are so often linked intertextually in interdisciplinary and interorganizational networks or, more recently, "knotworks" (Engeström, Engeström, & Vähäaho, 1999).

I have found that Engeström's systems version of activity theory offers insight into the central problematic of my research: how university students learn to write specialized discourse and write to learn specialized knowledge. This involves several disciplines and requires a theory that will cross disciplinary lines to answer a fundamental question: How can one analyze in a principled and systematic way the macrolevel social and political structures (cultural studies) that affect the microlevel actions of the teaching and learning (educational psychology) that students and teachers do with texts (applied linguistics) in education systems – and vice versa? The activity system offers a useful heuristic for explaining how doing school, doing work, and doing the other things (political, familial, recreational, etc.) our lives are made of are woven together through genre as social action.

GENRE AS A UNIT OF ANALYSIS

Since the mid-1980s, WAGR has developed the concept of genre as social action in order to analyze the role of documents and artifacts in various media in organizational change and learning. The WAGR concept of genre as social action began not with Bakhtin's notion of genre, though this has proved very influential, but with Alfred Schutz's phenomenological concept of *typification* (Schutz & Luckmann, 1973). Carolyn Miller (1984, 1994) introduced the concept of genre as "typified rhetorical actions based in recurrent situations" (1994, p. 31). Genre is seen not as formal features or as packeted speech (Wertsch, 1994), but as typified actions that over time have been routinized, "stabilized-for-now" (Schryer, 1993) in ways that have proved useful in the activity system. Put simply, a genre is the ongoing use of certain material tools (marks, in the case of written genres) in certain ways that worked once and might work again, a typified, tool-mediated response to conditions recognized by participants as recurring. Discursive actions are not seen, in Bakhtin's metaphor, as voices ventriloquized from and contributing to social languages, but rather as speech acts (Austin, 1962; Searle, 1969), utterances that perform actions in practical activity (Bazerman, 2004).

Thus, genres are more than categories of tools classified according to formal features. They are traditions of using a tool or tools, "forms of life, ways of being, frames for social action" (Bazerman, 1994, p. 79). A genre conveys a worldview – not explicitly, but by "developing concrete examples" that allow participants "to experience the world in the genre's way" (Morson & Emerson, 1990, p. 282; Spinuzzi, 2003, p. 42). Genres allow subjects to *recognize* the activity and the appropriate actions in the presence of certain constellations of tools – marks on surfaces and other material phenomena. And genres make it possible to act with others over time in more or less but never entirely predictable ways, individually, collectively, and institutionally. Thus, the theoretical concept has proved useful in written communication studies at the level of the activity system(s), as well as the levels of actions and operations, to use Leont'ev's (1978) terms.

This formulation of genre as social action differs in important ways from the concept of genre that Engeström's group developed in the mid-1990s. Engeström takes issue with the fact that major linguistic approaches to discourse-in-use separate discourse from object-oriented productive activity (a critique that WAGR largely shares). He and his group developed a framework for analyzing discourse-in-use (Engeström, 1999b). R. Engeström (1995) in particular has synthesized Bakhtin's (1987) language theory and Leont'ev's (1978) three-level analysis of joint activity. Bakhtin's concept of "social languages" corresponds to the level of collective activity, analyzed in terms of activity systems. Bakhtin's "voice" corresponds to the level of specific action. Bakhtin's "speech genre" corresponds to the level of unconscious operations.

In WAGR research, by contrast, genre can be analyzed historically at the level of the activity system, as well as at the level of operations. Bazerman's (1988) study of the "genre and activity of the experimental article in science" over two centuries is perhaps the most obvious example. He shows how the activity of science shaped and was shaped by the primary genre that scientists evolved, through their discursive and practical actions, for sharing and verifying their findings. Similarly, Bazerman's (1999) study of written communication in Edison's long career and beyond analyzes the development of institutions to create and extend worldwide the technology of the electric light. Other relevant examples include Russell's (2002) study of the evolution of genres of student writing in U.S. higher education, Yates's (1989) study of industrial communication in the 19th and early 20th centuries, and Spinuzzi's (2003) study of 30 years of traffic mapping.

Genre as social action can be analyzed not only at the level of unconscious operations or activity system(s), but also at the level of conscious action, as an array of strategies or tactics from which participants may "consciously select, interpret, produce and use" in goal-directed actions (Spinuzzi, 2003, p. 46). Studies of tools-in-use show actors consciously selecting, rejecting, and abandoning genres in the course of their work, individual and collective (Schryer, 1993; Spinuzzi, 2003). Moreover, genres must be learned, potentially passing from the level of action to operation and back. Newcomers to an activity must come to perceive how others are using the tools and use them in similar ways in order to perform actions that coordinate with others' actions. In time newcomers may – or may not – operationalize those actions. The ways of writing of experienced insiders in a profession, for example, may become so routine that they come to seem natural. In this sense, genre helps account for social-psychological stability, identity, and predictability in organizations or, indeed, broader social formations as unconscious operationalized actions.

Genres are also central to object formation, transformation, and maintenance of activity systems. As Engeström (1999b) says, "The object is an enduring, constantly reproduced purpose of a collective activity system that motivates and defines the horizon of possible goals and actions" (p. 170). But the object of activity can be seen to attain its stability, reproduction, and continuity through genres, the mutual recognition necessary for joint action to occur over time. And when the object is contested (offering potential for change), it is against the landscape of existing genres.

Genres are also deeply involved in the construction of motives. Genres are, in a sense, classifications of artifacts-plus-intentions. They enact social intentions, offering ways of using tools to accomplish collective activity. As Miller (1984) argues, "What we learn when we learn a genre is not just a pattern of forms or a means of achieving our own ends. We learn, more importantly, what ends we may have" (p. 165) in collective activity. A genre offers not only a landscape of possible action, but also a horizon of potential motives or direction (Bazerman, 1994; Bazerman, Little, & Chavkin, 2003). In this sense, genre provides a way of including motives in the analysis of activity. As such, genres are crucial links between subjects, tools, and objects. In this way, WAGR addresses motive directly, where it is only implied in Engeström's unit of analysis, though it is central to Wertsch's (1994) version of activity theory.

To take a contemporary example, when one recognizes a document as a U.S. Internal Revenue Service tax form (Bazerman, 2000), it is clear that one is defined within a bureaucratic identity of financial calculations, obligations, specific deadlines, and places for submission – and ultimately complex regulations, legal sanctions, and enforcement procedures. It is also clear what actions and tools are salient and irrelevant within the time-space landscape the genre invokes. Yet "no matter how constrained by forms, conventions, regulations and sanctions, the tax form becomes the scene of struggle between compliance and each individual's desire to protect personal financial interests," a way of aligning or contesting motives in relation to the activity system of U.S. government tax collections (Bazerman et al., 2003, p. 459). A genre, particularly a written genre, crystallizes the motives of participants and makes possible certain kinds of interactions while making others more difficult, though never impossible. A genre calls forth certain actions or, for some participants, operations with certain tools at certain times and places.

"In short genre recognition attunes us in deep and complex ways as to what to make of the utterance" (Bazerman et al., 2003, p. 456). In this sense, WAGR differs from other theories of genre in emphasizing the positive valence of genre, as a landscape for action, rather than its limitations or regulation of actions, and calls attention to the strategic agency of participants, who further their interests through mutually recognized, genred action within moments of utterance, though always constrained by the degree of congruence in their understandings and always open to difference. Indeed, genres facilitate improvisation and innovation, marking out the expectations against which innovation is perceived as such and not as meaningless nonsense, in much the way the chordal and melodic structure of a tune facilitates jazz improvisation (Schryer, Lingard, & Spatford, 2003). And even when, or perhaps especially when, participants are at odds, they must have or develop a socially shared repertoire of genred actions to achieve understanding, coordination, and cooperation – to meaningfully disagree over time. As Bazerman (2006) puts it, genres are

> ways of seeing what acts are available that are appropriate to the moment as you see it – what you can do, what you might want to do. For example, you may perceive a moment in a disagreement as offering possibilities of either a rejoinder or an apology. Your motives, goals, plans will take shape within those two constructions of potential action. You would not even consider appropriate filing a legal brief – and if somehow you found a motive and means to pursue that path, that would radically change the nature of the situation and your counterpart's set of genred options. (p. 221)

Organizational change – as distinct from organizational drift or chaos – involves the construction and mutual construal of new routines, norms, interactional rules, and the operationalizing of actions in new genres or old genres appropriated for new purposes. Organizational learning does as well, and it might be thought of as the development by participants of genre knowledge (Berkenkotter & Huckin, 1995). Genres provide mutual recognition of the object in both its concrete and abstract manifestations and orient participants to it. As such, genre can be an important unit of analysis for understanding how organizations change or remain stable. Voices arise more immediately from genres than from the broader social languages; and genres are what structure the cooperation/co-construction of communication through mutual recognition.

ACTIVITY SYSTEMS AND GENRE SYSTEMS

In complex activity systems, there are typically many written genres, which participants use together to structure and change their interactions. WAGR has developed the concept of *genre systems,* or, in Spunuzzi's (2003) formulation, genre ecologies, to understand how genres, particularly written ones, work in and between complex organizations. Bazerman (1994) defines a genre system as "interrelated genres that interact with each other in specific settings" (p. 80). In a genre system, "only a limited range of genres may appropriately follow upon another," because the conditions for successful coordinated action are conditioned – but never finally determined – by their history of previous actions (p. 80). For participants, these written genre systems are more salient than social languages or particular voices, because they are more permanent over time and mobile through space. Beyond a particular moment analyzed, multivoicedness is more than voices; it depends on texts that mobilize actors across activity systems in mutually recognized and acted-upon genres. For example, IRS tax form 1040 is intertextually linked to other documents in other genres, in a taxpayer's files, employers' files, bank records, government regulations, tax laws, accounting standards, addresses, calendars, and so on, and to material property (real estate, factories, farms, etc.) and concrete actions (buying, selling, renting, theft, gambling losses, etc.) that those documents in various genres represent.

What Engeström's unit of analysis has done for WAGR is offer, first of all, a heuristic for describing the social systematics of textual circulation networks and their contributing role in accomplishing communal work. His seven-part triangle diagram of the activity system allows for an analysis of fundamental elements of interaction among people and their tools that organize the joint activity.

Because of the division of labor within and particularly among activity systems, not all of the participants must appropriate (learn to read/write) all of the written genres. Participants at some more or less stable positions within the systems interact in ways that make it more likely they will use certain genres and not others at certain times. Participants from different activity systems or different locations within the division of labor do not have to learn one another's social languages to achieve coordination when the interactions are mediated by tools in genres that they come to mutually recognize. Indeed, participants are not typically aware of social languages, as R. Engeström (1995) points out. But to achieve coordination across boundaries, participants must recognize the genres that shape the co-construction of meaning. Again, in research on interactions among activity systems, it is not the social languages through which either moment-to-moment coordination or historical development goes on. It is through the genre systems.

Second, Engeström's (1987) intermediate theoretical tool of dialectical contradictions has been useful in understanding genre systems. It provides a fresh elaboration of Marxian notions of work and learning, connecting alienation produced by contradictions to psychological double binds. Moreover, it provides a way to connect immediate microlevel disturbances, breakdowns, and conflicts with macrolevel, historically developed contradictions and the potential of such disturbances to produce new forms of activity. It is in relation to genres that disturbances and breakdowns in communication are manifest: Someone has violated or bent the communicative norms; some condition has exposed the genres as needing attention – promoted them to the level of action, in Leont'ev's (1978) terms. Indeed, what is most interesting and important about genres always only stabilized-for-now is this positive, agentive aspect: that subjects recognize disturbance and change in relation to them. Genres' potential for change is as crucial to understanding organizations as is their structuring of actions and activity systems over time.

Systems of typified written communication allow participants in one or more activity systems to coordinate activity through mutual recognition of the possibilities for action. Through these stabilized-for-now genres, the boundaries and interactions between social practices – social structures – are in part maintained and power exerted. But genre systems also reveal loci of discoordinations, breakdowns, power asymmetries, and sharing, and so on, within and among activity systems.

Third, what Engeström (2001) calls the "third generation" of activity-theoretical research theorizes multiple interacting activity systems and boundary crossing and the related concepts of polycontextuality and knotworking. This notion of interlocking activity systems suggests the particular importance of textually mediated interactions, as these tend to be crucial to coordinating disparate activity systems over time and space (Engeström, Engeström, & Kärkkäinen, 1995). Organizations that interact over time and at a distance are ordinarily accomplished in large part through interlocking systems of written communication: printed forms, records, genres of e-mail, and so on. Boundary crossing occurs in more than isolated moments; it tends toward systematicity, toward mutually intelligible communication at a distance in longer timescales, where boundary crossing is more than a foray. By understanding the systematicity of written communication, we can make sense of communication across boundaries, not only how boundaries emerge in zones of proximal development, but also how they are sustained, evolve, or collapse. WAGR has grappled particularly with this problem, and Engeström's theory of multiple, interacting activity systems has often been useful.

Fourth, Engeström's concept of learning by expanding (1987) can be seen in terms of expanding involvement in a system of genres. Students or newcomers to an organization learn new genres as they widen their communicative interactions. In my reading of the literature on writing-to-learn in higher education (Russell, 1997a), for example, I chart the genre system of university cell biology as it intersects with other activity systems and then trace the developmental pathways of students in the activity systems of specific courses in cell biology discussed in the literature on writing-to-learn. Similarly, Spinuzzi (2003) traces genres through organizations to understand organizational learning. Engeström's notions of polycontextuality lie behind both analyses.

These four influences of Engeström's activity system are evident in some recent WAGR studies of genre systems of higher education, which connect the work of formal schooling to the work of researchers and practitioners in the disciplines and professions toward which students are at least officially headed. In a series of studies (Russell & Yañez, 2003; Yañez & Russell, in press) we traced how students in a history course came to recognize and appropriate, or not, genres of academic history in relation to genres of other activity systems, such as journalism and popular history. These studies draw not only on classroom discourse, interviews with students, and teachers and the written documents that mediate classroom interactions, but also on genres of other activity systems – departmental and institutional discourse within formal schooling and genres of historical writing beyond it, scholarly and popular. These studies aim at understanding the contradictions within and between the activity systems of professional history and higher education, as well as the ways students experience these as double binds within the activity system of the specific classroom. Genre systems analysis traces the historical origins of the contradictions between schooling and professional work and between disciplines, and the discoordinations and disturbances in specific classroom learning owing to them. Genre systems shape the motives and identities of participants, as well as their texts, and mark out the dimensions of expansive learning, for both students and teachers, showing possibilities for re-mediating teaching and learning.

Another problem in WAGR and in many of Engeström's developmental work research studies involves the breakdowns and discoordinations within or among participants in different organizational locations acting in different timescales. Engeström, Puonti, and Seppänen (2003), for example, in their study of the spatial and temporal expansion of the object in postmodern work in organic farming, white-collar crime, and medical care systems, examine "subjects moving in space from one space to another and establishing trails that could be followed again, both by those subjects and others. Trails make an *emergent knowable terrain*" and call for "looking closely at the formation of such terrains" (p. 184). What Engeström, Puonti, and Seppänen call for is very much like what WAGR does, though WAGR theorizes those "trails" as stabilized-for-now written genre systems, intertextually linked. This genre system marks out the landscape of action and links the nodes of the knotworking. Such genre analysis looks not only at the formation of these trails but at their development or degeneration over time. It charts horizons into which the object has expanded already though existing genres and the territory into which it may expand. For literate organizations, the expansive reach of the actual or potential object can be traced by following the written genres. Genre systems provide the skeleton of the structure of modern activity systems, visible through genre systems analysis.

For example, Spinuzzi (2003) develops the concept of genre systems as *genre ecologies* to understand the activity of traffic workers using a database of accident records over 30 years, as it changed from paper maps to web-based GPS databases, and involved a range of stakeholders from different activity systems. He traces breakdowns and discoordinations using the activity system as a top-level unit of analysis, but then uses genre systems or ecologies to analyze the meso- and microlevel interactions. By tracing connections among genres, Spinuzzi shows how differences in the parent activities "manifest themselves through destabilizations at all levels" (p. 50). Macrolevel contradictions (and the activities in which they evolved) "engendered mesolevel discoordinations between specific genres originating in different activities. Since the genres retained their orientation to their originating activities, [workers] conflicted in their problem-solving strategies, cultural assumptions, and ideologies. Workers thus encountered micro-level breakdowns as they attempted to use these discoordinated genres to mediate their work" (p. 50). Similarly, a reciprocal discoordination from micro- to macrolevels is possible, putting activity systems in a constant state of flux or disequilibrium "as systematic destabilizations at each level reverberate across the other levels" (p. 50). Other examples include Winsor's (2003) study of engineers, technicians, machinists, and managers writing in a heavy-machinery engineering center over 5 years, and Smart's (2006) study of the genre systems coordinating work in a central bank over a decade.

CONCLUSION

Engeström's unit of analysis, the activity system, then, has been useful in some research in WAGR – not surprising, perhaps, as much of Engeström's research, like WAGR, takes organizations as its primary research object and attempts to explain change and stability in these dynamic contexts historically and developmentally. Moreover, both traditions of research share the motive of producing well-running organizations (and ethical, socially responsible, and humane ones), where effective learning occurs. But Engeström's activity system plays out rather differently when it is used with the unit of analysis of genre as social action to trace how documents come to be and come to be used in organizations. This theoretical difference is perhaps not unrelated to the difference between Vygotsky's recommendation of the word – discourse – as a unit of analysis and Leont'ev's (1978) use of activity as a unit of analysis. Engeström's theory and methods continue to poses challenges and possibilities. Writing research in professional communication and education often resembles developmental work research in that a consultant-researcher takes an active role and includes a range of stakeholders in developing re-mediated activity. User testing has moved from a cognitive theoretical set and laboratory methods to new, more collaborative versions of user-centered design, with analysis of problems in situ over a more extended time frame. The goal is to avoid the "victimhood trope" of much user-centered research and to empower a wider range of participants by providing useful theoretical tools and developing them for re-mediating work practices and organizations (Spinuzzi, 2003).

Similarly, in educational research, interventions to improve student writing and learning in the disciplines increasingly involve teachers and departments collaborating with writing researchers to change pedagogical practice by re-mediating instruction and curriculum (Russell, 2007). For example, in the field of chemistry, Carter (2004) and his collaborators used activity theory to develop Labwrite, an online tool to help students understand scientific method by connecting laboratory practice and lab report writing. In addition, Engeström's activity systems analysis is being taught directly as a theoretical tool for helping students understand the circulation of discourse in genres of professional communication (Kain & Wardle, 2005).

Engeström has for nearly two decades provided a number of us doing WAGR with a robust, flexible, and ever-evolving theory of social-psychological and cultural activity. His vision of research that is responsive to the complexities of human life – practical and ethical – in its immense diversity has driven written communication research to seek new solutions to problems that were not addressed previously. That vision is not of a magic formula for decoding behavior but a challenge to engage theory with human problems over time, to mark out expansive possibilities, to test them, and to critically evaluate them in ways that cannot be generalized in neat ways but that generate new theories and new solutions.

4

On the Inclusion of Emotions, Identity, and
Ethico-Moral Dimensions of Actions

WOLFF-MICHAEL ROTH

With *Learning by Expanding* (Engeström, 1987), the development of cultural-historical activity theory entered a new phase. The book articulated a variety of structural aspects that researchers using cultural-historical activity theory might look for when attempting to analyze concrete human praxis. These aspects are captured emblematically by a triangular representation that has been a main scaffold for many scholars in their effort to understand a theory quite alien, in its dialectical foundations, to that of Western theorizing. Yet some elements of it have not yet come to be appreciated. Thus, to understand practical activity and the participative thinking that accompanies it requires understanding "the regulating effect of emotion" (Leont'ev, 1978, p. 27), because the "objectivity of activity is responsible not only for the objective character of images but also for the objectivity of needs, emotions, and feelings" (p. 54).

Many scholars have focused only on the structural aspects of activity, its systemic dimensions (Roth & Lee, 2007). These scholars have not taken into account the agentive dimensions of activity, including identity, emotion, ethics, and morality, or derivative concepts, such as motivation, identification, responsibility, and solidarity – all of which are integral to concrete praxis and its singular nature. These "sensuous" aspects of activity come into focus only if the whole activity – not only its structural but also its agentive dimensions – is analyzed. Theorizing the sensuous aspects of human labor was central to Karl Marx and to the sociocultural and

Grants from the Social Sciences and Humanities Research Council of Canada and the Natural Sciences and Engineering Council of Canada supported this study. I am grateful to Leanna Boyer, Stuart Lee, and Yew Jin Lee for their assistance in collecting the data in the fish hatchery. I am thankful to the hatchery management and individual staff members for having allowed me to do this research in their midst.

cultural-historical psychological work done in his wake by Lev S. Vygotsky, Alexander Luria, and Alexei N. Leont'ev, among others.

I was encouraged by Yrjö Engeström during a recent workshop to consider integral aspects of human activity such as emotion; hence, much of my recent work has focused on the question of how relevant aspects of activity can be included in the theory he offered and promoted during his career. In this chapter, I provide an extended case study to make the case for including in activity-theoretical studies these sensuous aspects of human activity and to exemplify how researchers can obtain relevant data. I do so as a way of encouraging researchers to include in their research dimensions that are not salient in the triangular representation developed so far, such as identity, emotion, and ethico-moral aspects. This then allows us to draw on Engeström's work in new ways, that is, as an inclusive framework.

ETHNOGRAPHY OF THE WORKPLACE

My study of fish hatcheries was part of a larger project concerned with the economic difficulties experienced by the inhabitants of single-industry villages and towns on the Canadian East and West Coasts. These single-industry communities – focusing as they do on fishing, forestry, and mining – have been subject to enormous changes as a function of changes in the economy and the accelerating depletion of the natural resource on which their economies are based. My part of the larger project was focused on salmon hatcheries. The federally funded Salmon Enhancement Program has been created to boost salmon stocks through the breeding and release of several species, including chinook, coho, and steelhead. As a result, salmon stocks are thought to have increased or at least to have maintained their current levels and thereby provide economic opportunities for commercial fishermen, aboriginal tribes, sports fishers, and the various spin-off service industries (e.g., outfitters, hotels, restaurants, and boat rental businesses). Salmon enhancement, therefore, is a major form of activity on the Canadian West Coast, closely tied to other systems that depend on its production. Over a 5-year period, I conducted, together with several graduate students, a study of one salmon hatchery and the associated scientific laboratories. We used apprenticeship as an ethnographic method by engaging in the work process, which allowed us to come to know and understand this activity system in a concrete way.

Work in the hatchery is determined by the seasonal patterns of the salmon species' growth during the early life stages and the return of the adult salmon, after between 2 and 5 years in the ocean, to spawn and die. Some time in the fall, the salmon return and enter the hatchery, where the females are killed and opened to remove the eggs; the males are bent backward ("cracked") so that the milt squirts out to be gathered in small containers. Batches of eggs are mixed with batches of milt and then placed on incubation trays. Once hatched, the alevins live off their yolk sacks until these are used up, at which point the animals enter the fry stage and are transferred to ponds (Fig. 4.1), where they are fed until they are ready for release into the wild. The period of outdoor rearing differs among the species, ranging from 2 months for chinook (raised to about 5 g) to 12 months for coho (raised to about 20 g) and steelhead (raised to about 80 g). Each fish culturist is in charge of a brood from the very beginning ("egg take") to the release date.

Located in a valley near a pondlike widening of the river, with a view of the surrounding mountains, the hatchery is situated in a forest opening (Fig. 4.1) cleared for the hatchery when it was established in its current place in the 1970s. Much of the piscicultural work takes place outside, though each fish culturist has an office, where records are kept, books and other work-related resources are stored, a computer with an Internet connection is available, and so on. The fish culturists, managers, and temporary workers enjoy working here and indicate –in both formal and informal

Figure 4.1. The outdoor setting of the work in the hatchery.

situations – that they would not want to work elsewhere. They always point to the outdoor environment and contrast it with what they consider the unbearable nature of "nine-to-five office work."

In the course of this 5-year study, I collected data both as a contributing participant in the major daily and seasonal tasks at the site and as a mere observer of events. As part of my research agreement with the hatchery, I helped with various tasks that had to be done on a daily, weekly, monthly, and even yearly basis. By working as an apprentice in the hatchery and thereby contributing to the realization of its object/motive, I got to know the hatchery activity system from the inside, including the sensuous aspects of the work not detectable through observation alone. As a helper, my goals were therefore defined by the task and the motive for an activity; in this case, reflecting on a day's work constituted a means of collecting informational sources. At other moments, I engaged in observation and recording. In this mode, the data sources include observational field notes, videotapes of everyday activities, recorded and transcribed formal interviews, photographs, documents, scientific and mathematical representations, and various other notes and reports created and used as part of the daily work in the study site. The two forms of ethnographic work – that of participant-observer and that of observing participant – provided different perspectives on, and constitute complementary ways of experiencing the productive work in the study site.

As part of my participant-observer role, I recorded people at work or while they explained aspects of their tasks, sometimes in their offices, sometimes in other locations, such as the wet laboratory or during a break from fieldwork (e.g., sampling dead fish, catching salmon in other river systems, sampling in the estuary). As emotional states expressed themselves in their voices (Johnstone & Scherer, 2000), I digitized the sound tracks to make them available to prosodic analysis, that is, to the analysis of speech dimensions such as intensity, pitch, and speech rates. The PRAAT software, which is available for a variety of platforms, can be used to plot and calculate average parameters, including pitch, speech intensity, energy and power, and spectral distributions; speech rates can be determined from changes in the temporal distribution of syllables (Fig. 4.2). For example, the articulation of "if you look at" corresponds to the averaged values of speech intensity and pitch (Fig. 4.2, right). On the other hand, the utterance "way low" (Fig. 4.2, left) is much lower in speech intensity (each 3 dB is a doubling of intensity) and pitch, which is heard as disappointment.

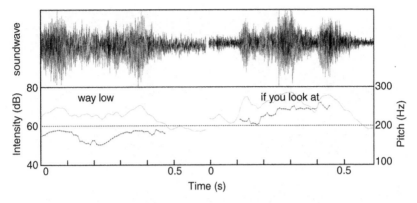

Figure 4.2. Disappointment co-expressed by pitch levels.

SENSUOUS ASPECTS OF WORK

Although *Learning by Expanding* clearly highlights the sensuous nature of human activities, much of the literature does not include this aspect in its analyses. This is also, and perhaps especially, the case in workplaces such as fish hatcheries. The work in the hatchery is sensuous in that, in the production of releasable coho smolt, the fish culturists have to exert themselves in a form of work that frequently is very physical. Thus, fish culturists and temporary workers expend a lot of physical energy even when they use machines and tractors – for example, for transferring coho at the alevin or fry stage to a concrete raceway or holding pond (Fig. 4.3a) or while feeding the fish in the earthen ponds (Fig. 4.3b). Especially toward the end of the rearing period, the person responsible for feeding coho has to finely scatter 200 kg of feed per day, temporally distributed so that none of the feed sinks to the pond bottom, where it would spoil and become a cause of disease. It is hard and time-consuming labor, so that the hatchery managers normally hire additional temporary workers, freeing up regular staff members to complete other required jobs. Nevertheless, those who work in the hatchery enjoy both its physical aspect and the beauty of the surrounding landscape; they do so to such an extent that they are willing to put up with tensions and a variety of problems ("crap") in exchange for being able to work there.

The nature of the work generally has a positive emotional valence – a concept central to Holzkamp's (1983) categorical reconstruction of the human psyche. Other aspects arising, for example, from the labor situation – layoffs, relations with managers – may have the converse effect, mediating

Figure 4.3. The physical nature of the work in the hatchery.

the emotional valence of the work in a negative way. Thus, there were times in the hatchery when the general mood expressed during gatherings – for example, during breaks, at lunch, or in the course of work requiring larger groups of individuals – clearly was negative, as expressed in the conversational topics and in voice parameters (Roth, 2007a). The poor relations between the two managers and some of the employees began to affect the emotions of other employees as well and thereby mediated the collective work in the hatchery. That is, an increasingly negative collective mood mediated the emotions of others, who thereby further lowered the collective mood. One of the five fish culturists in particular was resigned to simply completing his eight-hour day, during which he located himself as far away as possible from the places frequented by the managers. For example, he collected data on fish away from the hatchery or did enhancement work on some lake or in a different river system. He also arrived much earlier in the morning than others, thereby avoiding those contacts that lowered his emotional state. As a consequence of the negative emotional valence of his work, he stopped conducting experiments, for which he had become well known, and thinking up innovations as he had done in the past and for which he was recognized at a national award ceremony. He had gone from giving "300 percent" to the hatchery, and realizing himself in his work, to "doing my eight hours."

Pisciculture has many other sensuous aspects. For example, fish culturists closely observe fish behavior when they feed the animals, looking out

Figure 4.4. Erica's careful inspection of each fish.

for signs that the fish are swimming sluggishly or not feeding as much as they ought to. Experienced fish culturists develop almost personal relationships with their fish populations and frequently talk about what the fish tell them ("I listen to the fish"; "The fish tell me when they have had enough"). When fish culturists such as Erica take samples to measure mean weight and mean length, they handle and inspect each fish from all sides (Fig. 4.4), looking for abrasions, diseases, or signs of aggression among fish (e.g., "nibbles"). Because of this close work with individual fish, the fish culturists can, merely by inspecting a fish, determine with great accuracy its condition coefficient. The condition coefficient K_c is calculated by means of formula (1), which Erica uses in her spreadsheet:

$$K_c = \frac{w * 100}{l * l * l} * 1000 \tag{1}$$

The literature indicates that a value of $K_c = 1.00$ corresponds to a healthy salmon, apparently independent of the species; in a normally distributed population, this value varies for individual fish. The fish culturists have developed such an understanding of and eye for their species that they can determine immediately whether a particular fish is below or above the ideal value and, in fact, determine the K_c within 1 or 2% accuracy.

Throughout my ethnographic study, it was evident that emotions were integral to the work. For example, fish culturists always worry about the brood or population in their charge. They tend to talk about the fish as if these were their children. Fish culturists closely monitor the number of dead fish ("morts") collected and counted each day. They monitor the amount of feed they spread per day and week to determine whether the fish are hungry. The timing of release of the fish population may be crucial, but there are no "hard" data on when precisely to release the fish; each year, the differences between the assessments of correct timing made by fish culturists and managers have stirred emotions. Fish culturists have developed a sense of when this should be, based, for example, on the movement of fish populations toward the lower parts of the pond, on the increased silvery aspect of their scales, which has thus far been dark, and sometimes on increased mortality. Although fish culturists are responsible for all aspects of a particular population until its release, the hatchery managers make the decision about the precise release date. In general, they use scientific publications or reports as resources.

With regard to the timing of the release of the coho that Erica had taken care of for several years, the managers used the results of a study conducted in a very different river system and selected a particular month and day independent of the recommendations of the responsible fish culturist, often supported by several other colleagues. One year during my stay, all of the fish culturists were upset because the mortality among the three coho populations (totaling about 900,000 fish) had increased to 2,000 deaths per day. Although other indicators pointed toward release – the fish were silvery and gathering at the pond outlet – the hatchery managers maintained the a priori fixed release date, which ultimately resulted in the deaths of nearly 30,000 fish over a 2-week period. Most fish culturists, even though they were not responsible for the coho, were angry with the managers for not releasing the fish despite the signs and high mortality. This emotion, in turn, mediated the workers' participation in the hatchery work.

EMOTIONS IN ACTION

Erica was afraid that she had not reached the target of 20 g average weight per coho. She was taking a final sample before the official, management-ordered release date. Erica did not like sampling, because each time the fish are removed from the earthen pond (Fig. 4.1) with the dip net, they are stressed. The fish are stressed even more when handled physically (Fig. 4.4) or when one of their lateral fins is cut for identification purposes. The fish are especially stressed during the sedation procedure, which requires their placement in a holding container with water in which a certain amount of carbon dioxide has been dissolved. There are other methods for sedating fish, but these are even more intrusive and stressful; furthermore, the fish culturists do not like using the most widely used sedative, MS-222, because of possible carcinogenic effects on both fish and humans, who grab the fish from their container. As the veterinarian explained, stress is cumulative at both the individual and collective levels of a fish population. Each time a fish is handled, its chance of survival is lowered and, with it, the survival of the population as a whole. This knowledge mediated Erica's emotions during this work. On the one hand, she continuously improved her practical understanding of the fish and fish culture, as well as her model of the fish population, with each sampling episode and each population she raised. On the other hand, she felt bad about having to stress the fish.

Throughout the sampling episode, during which Erica handled 100 fish, she looked at groups of about 20 collectively and inspected each fish individually (e.g., for cataracts) in addition to measuring its length and weight. Leanna, a member of my research team, joined the sampling process, taking on the jobs of reading the weights off the digital scale of the electronic balance and entering the data (length, weight, abrasion to left [L], right [R], or both eyes [LR]) on the spreadsheet. The spreadsheet was already set up to calculate average values in the course of data entry.

Erica frequently glanced at subsamples of fish collectively (Fig. 4.4); watching in this way and looking at the distributions of weights and lengths of a sample enabled her to develop highly evolved interpretive skills. She could now look at a distribution and understand what a particular sample looked like on average (e.g., "There are long skinny ones and short fat ones, but few in the middle"). Thinking aloud while observing the current subsample (Fig. 4.5), she reminded herself and the others present that the veterinarian had recently described the population as "looking good." Erica generally expressed sadness and disappointment when a subsample seemed below target, and expressed joy and excitement when the sample met or exceeded expectations. She expressed emotions as she measured the length of each fish, inspecting it closely (Fig. 4.4), and placed it in the water-filled dish on the scale. For example, when she had measured a particularly short specimen of low weight, Erica (E) commented, with low voice intensity, much lower than normal, "Way low" (Fig. 4.2), and then added almost inaudibly, "Darned" (Episode 1).[1] This

---

[1] In the transcriptions, I use the following conventions:

[beginning of overlapping talk or gesture;

] end of overlapping talk or gesture;

= equal sign at the end of one turn and at the beginning of the next indicates latching turns; that is, there is no gap between the two speakers;

(1.32) elapsed time in hundreth of a second;

Figure 4.5. Erica articulating the veterinarian's positive assessment of the coho salmon.

was an expression of her anxiety that the fish population might be short of the target weight:

EPISODE 1

01. E: <<p>↓^way ^low>. (1.08) <<pp>darned>.

Throughout the sampling episode, pitch and speech intensity are consistently down when any fish are below the target value but are in the normal

:: lengthening of the preceding phoneme, approximately one-tenth of a second for each colon used;
.,;? punctuation marks that indicate characteristics of speech production, such as intonation, rather than grammatical units of language;
↑↓ shifts to higher or lower pitch in the immediately following utterance part;
^ˇ movement of pitch (F0) in subsequent word downward, up–down, down–up, and upward;
<<p> >, <<pp> > changes in speech parameters: piano (low volume) and pianissimo (very low volume).
WELL upper case is used to indicate sounds louder than the surrounding talk;
.hhh inbreath; without the dot, hhh indicates outbreath;
(stay?) word(s) within parentheses followed by a question mark indicate uncertain but possible hearings;
(()) comments and descriptions;
84 dB speech intensity in decibels (dB);
320 Hz pitch (F0) in Hertz.

range for other fish. On the other hand, there are expressions of joy – indicated by such parameters as descending pitch contour, increased mean pitch, wider pitch range, increase in high-frequency energy, and greater speech intensity (New, Foo, & De Silva, 2003). The changes in emotion expressions are exemplified in Episode 2, which begins when Erica comments on one fish looking "okay" (turn 01), which can be heard as "okay, but not great" (see lower than normal pitch), and then continues when she bursts out with an expression of joy when she sees the measurement results of a specimen meeting expectations (turn 05). Other participants are the researcher-helpers Leanna (L) and I (M).

EPISODE 2

01. E: this size looks okay. ((188–172 Hz))
02.   (0.91)
03.   one ˙twenty nine ((72–77 dB, 187–268 Hz))
04.   (4.68) ((E inspects fish, puts it on scale; L enters data))
05.   HEHA:::. ((85.8 dB, 465–277 Hz)) (0.25) WHOO:: ((86 dB, 600 Hz))
06.   (0.94)
07. L: heha
08.   (1.22)
09. M: is this what you want? twenty grams?
10. E: ^i=want ((196–229 Hz)) twenty ((211–229 Hz)) grams ((220–194 Hz)).

The changes in pitch level are dramatic between turn 03, which represents normal range, to turn 05, in which the joy is expressed. Here, the pitch level doubles and even triples, curbing downward toward the end, and the speech intensity increases more than eightfold, all of which are indications of joy, which any culturally competent person can hear in Erica's voice. The power-in-the-air produced during the utterance of turn 03 ($2.41 \cdot 10^5$–W/m^2) increases to about sixfold ($14.0 \cdot 10^5$– W/m^2) and sevenfold ($17.9 \cdot 10^5$–Watt/m^2) in turn 05 for the "HEHA:::" and "WHOO::," respectively.

In Episode 3 Erica and Leanna had finished a batch of about 20 coho and were waiting for a second batch to be tranquilized in the carbon dioxide bath. Erica was eager to know the average weight and asked Leanna, who had been entering the data on the spreadsheet, to read off the requested value. Leanna cackled and then turned toward the monitor to seek the value. Erica read a value, 18.75 cm, and then produced a loud and high-pitched "No," which expressed her disappointment and fear (turn 05); she then addressed the computer, database, and values, asking them to "go over [the 20 g target value]."

EPISODE 3

```
01. E:    'whts the average. ((80 dB))
02.       (0.97)
03. L:    uh HA ha HA .h
04.       (0.81)
06.       u::::[:::::::::]
05. E:    [eighteen point seven five]? ((84 dB, 320–400 Hz)) u ^NO:[::: ]((85
          dB, 560 Hz))
06. L:    [<<p>some][what less>]
07. M:    [no that's ] because of the outlier, fifteen
08.       (0.16)
09. E:    go:: (bi:s?) O::Ve::R.
10.       (0.79)
11. L:    <<p>ya know> lots to go. he ha he.
```

The disappointment and fear are detectable to the other two individuals present, who attempt to mediate the impact this fact had on Erica. Thus, both Leanna and I attempt to mediate the "bad" intermediate value that is considerably below the desired target value, thought to provide the best survival conditions for the coho on their journey through the river and estuary and into the ocean. In my utterance, there is one explanation for the low value – one fish in particular, weighing only 15 g, pulls the average down (turn 07). Leanna, too, suggested that there are many more specimens to come ("lots to go" [turn 11]), implying that the larger number of specimens will mediate the overall effect the one measurement will have on the average. Both utterances are spoken at the lower ends of normal pitch ranges and with subdued intensity, both speech features that have a calming effect on individual and collective emotion and express empathy and solidarity.

AN INCLUSIVE WAY OF THINKING ABOUT
ACTIVITY THEORY

In the two preceding sections, I provided some case material on the sensuous nature of activity generally and on the emotions that arise at work particularly. Yet the emotional aspects of work are seldom captured in activity-theoretical studies. Whereas some scholars have developed A. N. Leont'ev's work toward an understanding of individual subjectivity and consciousness (Holzkamp, 1983), most Western researchers have not concerned themselves with Engeström's discussion of this aspect of work and have largely studied the structural dimensions of activity. I do think of human activities in terms of the mediational triangle Engeström proposed, but think about it *together with* the sensuous nature, emotive, identity-related, and ethico-moral dimensions of human actions and activities that currently are not highlighted in this representation. If we do not think about these dimensions together with the triangle, then we lose the link between emotion and emotional valence and participation in activity, concretely realized in and through specific goals. That is, neither the collective dimensions of motive setting nor the individual dimensions of goal setting and conditioning of operations are linked to emotional valence, the ultimate mediating moment of an activity system.

Clarifications

To use cultural-historical activity theory to analyze the productive work in the fish hatchery, different levels have to be distinguished: activity (e.g., "enhancing salmon stocks"), action (e.g., "feeding fish"), and operation (e.g., "flicking hand to get the feed to spread"). Following Leont'ev (1978), activity theorists explicitly have written about the dual existence of the object. But it is not only the object that exists in two ways: the activity system as a whole both embodies material aspects and exists in consciousness. The subject, the conscious means of production, community, division of labor, rules, and object, exist as objectively experienced societal and material structures in the world that other actors can use as resources in their actions. But all of these also are moments of consciousness. Thus, the activity system represented in Figure 4.6 not only refers to the

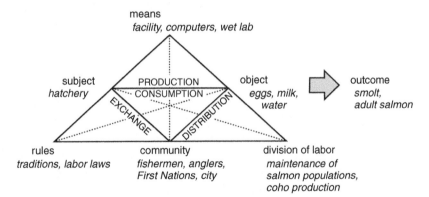

Figure 4.6. Representation of one concrete realization of the activity of salmon enhancement.

material aspects of the different moments but also, on a second level, refers to consciousness – the subject is the subject of consciousness just as the object is the object of consciousness.

The generalized structure of the activity of fish hatching is represented by the standard mediational triangle (Engeström, 1987, p.178). This activity (Fig. 4.6) can be realized in various ways – in fact, my research shows that there are different species raised in federally funded fish hatcheries in British Columbia. The practices differ among hatcheries, too; and so do the means of production and even the community. At a collective level, the products of the labor in the hatchery are *exchanged* with others in the community, where the products of labor come to be accumulated and *distributed* differentially as a function of the division of labor.

In my study of the fish hatchery, I specifically investigated one concrete activity system, that is, one concrete realization of a general possibility of contributing to the maintenance of society and its relations to the natural world. To get the work done in this activity system, specific individuals formulate and accomplish goals such as feeding; the action *feeding* realizes this goal, and the realization depends on a choice Erica makes between using the scoop and using the mechanical sprayer (Fig. 4.7). Observing the person in Figure 4.3b even from afar, everyone in the hatchery – in fact, every fish culturist and anyone else knowledgeable about fish culture – knows not only what is happening but also what goals are realized in the process. That is, the action observable is a patterned behavior specific to the community; it is a practice. The mediational triangle for concrete actions exhibits both mediations: the means (scoop, sprayer) are characteristic of the community in which everyone recognizes an action as something he or she might be doing as well. "Thus the action has double significance not only because

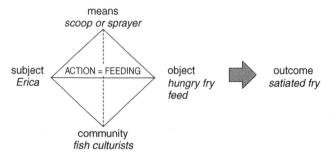

Figure 4.7. Erica's action of feeding depending on a choice between the use of a scoop and the use of a sprayer.

it is directed against itself as well as against the other, but also because it is indivisibly the action of one as well of the other" (Hegel, 1977, p. 112).

Actions are important for further theorizing in cultural-historical activity theory. The level of actions is precisely the one at which other moments of activity, including emotions, identity, and the ethico-moral dimensions of work, can be linked to the existing framework.

Emotions

Something unique about human agents is that they do not exist merely as bodies among bodies: as phenomenological philosophers have shown, human beings exist in sensuous flesh and blood. Only because human bodies are endowed with senses do they have the capacity to make sense. Thus, conscious goals are set because of the payoffs they promise; positive outcomes – successes, expansions of action possibilities and control, and goal realization – have positive emotional valence; failures – decreasing action possibilities and loss of control – have negative emotional valence that human agents consciously avoid. Thus, we can understand why the fish culturist resigned himself to doing an eight-hour job and sought out tasks that decreased the possibility of interactions with the managers, something associated with negative valence. Every face-to-face meeting between him and the mangers in fact further lowered his emotional state.

Both levels of emotion also mediate Erica's intermediate and long-term goals. For example, she frequently chooses to feed with the sprayer, a device she had traded for fish feed with another hatchery. She does so because of health considerations: using the device decreases stress and strain on the throwing arm and therefore the risk of injury, which, as a prospective by-product of her work, has a negative valence. Others in her hatchery look at the machine with suspicion; rather than use it, they continue to throw feed; they consciously choose the scoop as their tool.

The object of *this* activity system is the production of a healthy population without losses; a measure of health is the average condition coefficient, a variable that is calculated using the size and weight of the fish. A healthy population at release time is associated with positive emotional valence, whereas an unhealthy, underweight, or fat population is undesirable and has negative emotional valence. Erica frets when she takes the last sample, because she considers the outcome a measure of her success in having met the target. Other aspects of the activity that have negative valence are forms of waste (money, feed) or injury, disease, and other stresses on the fish population. Sometimes multiple goals compete: Knowing more about the fish population has a positive valence, but sampling the coho population has a negative valence, because it constitutes a stress factor that decreases health and survival. Here, the former goal wins out because in the long run it is expected to lead to better understanding and ultimately greater success.

Sense mediates the long-term payoffs that might be expected from the conscious evaluation of goals. But human beings also are subject to a complex mix of bodily states – physical, biochemical, and physiological – that mediate and condition goal setting and goal realization in operations. These bodily states are experienced, in part, as emotions (Damasio, 2000). Being in a serene setting, having a positive relationship with nature, and working outdoors have positive valence, which mediated the choice of all full-time and part-time staff members to work at the fish hatchery; and working there mediated the emotive states in a positive way.

At the lowest level of analysis, unconscious or nonconscious operations, emotions also mediate what a person does. That is, the same bodily states that a person experiences as emotions also, by their very nature, constitute the context that determines the form of the operations that the body produces. On days when a person feels elated and "emotionally charged," what she does in the hatchery and how she does it are different than when a person feels emotionally drained. These emotional states also, and importantly, mediate face-to-face interpersonal transactions; and these transactions mediate current emotional states (Turner, 2002).

During my stay in the hatchery, Erica was laid off. Erica's layoff and the effect it had on her mediated the transactions during breaks and over lunch; as a result, the general mood among the fish culturists generally declined. The face-to-face meetings between Erica and her managers became more difficult as a result of the way she felt; and each time she met with one of them, her emotions were negatively affected. More and more so, meetings with the managers had come to have negative emotional valence, as Erica "knew" beforehand that she would feel worse.

Identity

We are what we do. Or rather, in and at work, human beings concretely realize their goals in outcomes or products, which therefore come to embody an aspect of the person – the agents *exteriorize* and *estrange* themselves in the products of their labor. Watching Erica from afar, other fish culturists know that this is an accomplished and knowledgeable person feeding the fish. On the other hand, time and again, knowledgeable fish culturists have pointed out to me that this or that temporary worker does not knowledgeably feed the fish, a fact for which they can give specific evidence upon inspecting the pond – for example, unused feed on the bottom. Therefore, just from the way a person feeds, established fish culturists can identify the person as either a knowledgeable or not so knowledgeable fish culturist. Here, aspects of identity are constructed on the basis of the actions of feeding and outcomes – feed on the bottom of the pond, too much or too little feed used. Thus, Erica is known beyond the immediate boundaries of the hatchery as a very knowledgeable fish culturist. Moreover, every knowledgeable fish culturist can see in her actions a "300% committed" and "motivated" fish culturist. That is, from the material relationship between the subject and object in Figure 4.7, others in the fish culturist community can make attributions about the identity of Erica.

Erica was laid off because she had filled a position temporarily vacated by a person with tenure. When budget cuts forced the tenured person to return to his original workplace in the hatchery, he displaced Erica. This had a tremendous impact on her emotions, as the workers in her husband's company had simultaneously gone on strike. Erica and her husbsand were considering selling their house because of the lack of income. These threats influenced what Erica was doing and how she was doing it. Thus, whereas she normally was a highly conscientious fish culturist who apparently attended to everything, there were repeated instances when she forgot to feed the fish or to take care of other aspects of her work. Others could see how distraught she was in the way she did her job. Erica frequently was on the edge, expressed in sudden shifts in pitch levels, and she spoke in a higher key, expressed in the overall shift of her base pitch by nearly 40 Hz (Roth, 2007a). Others in the hatchery attributed these changes to Erica's identity, allowing them to make statements about who she is and how she feels. That is, actions and outcomes make apparent to others both their goals and emotional states; and these actions and the outcomes in which the acting subject concretizes an aspect of herself are used in turn to construct aspects of the agent's identity.

Ethico-Moral Dimensions of Actions

The model represented in Figure 4.7 also allows us to think about and theorize ethico-moral dimensions of work that generally remain unarticulated and undertheorized because researchers focus on the epistemic and technical aspects of actions and not on their effects (Roth, 2007b). This restriction to the epistemic and technical dimensions of actions detaches answerability from the richness of life attested to in praxis: "I cannot include my actual self and my life (*qua* movement) in the world constituted by the constructions of theoretical consciousness in abstraction from the answerable and individual historical act" (Bakhtin, 1993, pp. 8–9). A theoretical world of conceptual knowledge and technical skills thereby comes to exist separate from my unique being and from the ethico-moral sense of acting. As a result, people generally become indifferent and fundamentally predetermined and determinate beings.

If, however, actions are theorized together with their effects, such as in speech act theory (Austin, 1962), then the ethico-moral dimensions of work can be theorized within third-generation cultural-historical activity theory. The intentions a fish culturist expresses in and through her actions can be compared with stated or unstated ethico-moral principles, such as the principles of stewardship and care. Thus, Erica's peers recognize her as a morally principled person, because she has not slacked off, despite having received a layoff notice and despite her strained relations with the managers, who apparently favored less experienced and knowledgeable persons. Others, too, recognized the ethical principle of care and stewardship concerning the fish population that had been assigned to her. That is, every competent fish culturist could see that she "did the best for the fish" and "gave 300%," and this even after she had received the layoff notice.

TOWARD AN INCLUSIVE UNIT OF ANALYSIS

In this chapter, I have presented an extensive case study that shows the emotional, identity-related, and ethico-moral aspects of human activities that often are not addressed in activity-theoretical studies. Needs, emotions, and feelings – which exist at both the individual and collective level and, in fact, stand in a constitutive relation – mediate the goals and frame the operation-determining conditions. That is, in a strong sense, without articulating and theorizing needs, emotions, and feelings, we are hard pressed to arrive at more than a reductionist image of activity generally, and concrete activity systems such as the hatchery I studied particularly. Only by including these needs, emotions, and feelings do we capture the activity system as a whole, that is, as intended by cultural-historical activity theory since its inception. In writing this chapter, I hope to encourage others to include emotional, identity-related, and ethico-moral aspects of activity in their studies. The clear distinction between the activity and action levels allows us to link collective needs and emotions to the former, and individual needs, emotions, and feelings to the latter. The two levels of study are articulated in Figures 4.6 and 4.7, respectively. The study of goals, actions, and concretely achieved outcomes provides us with the resources for articulating and theorizing emotions, identity, and the ethico-moral moment of human praxis. In some activities, such as environmentalism or "charitable work," the ethico-moral dimensions are already available at the collective level, because the explicit motives and goals of the activities have to do with assisting others and humanity as a whole.

PART TWO

MEDIATION AND DISCOURSE

5

Mediation as a Means of Collective Activity

VLADISLAV A. LEKTORSKY

Yrjö Engeström has elaborated a very interesting and fruitful variant of cultural-historical activity theory, which he and his collaborators successfully use in analyzing and solving concrete problems in developmental work research. The activity approach and activity theory in different forms have been very popular among Russian psychologists and philosophers for many decades. Although in Russia a lot of research in different human sciences has been carried out in the framework of cultural-historical activity theory, many of its key ideas continue to be insufficiently elaborated, it is given different interpretations, and there are discussions about the meaning of its basic tenets.

In recent times some scholars in Russia and other countries have begun to criticize the activity approach and its results. I think that the results of Engeström's research are important in the context of contemporary discussions about the possibilities of activity theory. In this chapter, I will try to analyze the place of Engeström's variant of activity theory among other variants. In this connection, I will try to elucidate some key notions of the activity approach, first of all those of mediation and subject. Specifically, I will analyze reflective mediation as a means of changing collective activity.

ACTIVITY

It is important to stress that the idea of activity was first introduced in philosophy and subsequently in the human sciences as a means of overcoming the Cartesian opposition between the subject and the object, between the "inner" world of consciousness and the "outer" world. This became possible in the context of the projective-constructive attitude, which has been specific to European civilization since the 17th century. In the ancient Greek picture of the world, technical activity, producing artificial objects, did not have any relationship to the cognition of natural objects, because natural and artificial processes were considered to be different. The rise of modern science eliminated the principal difference between these processes. The idea that human beings could have genuine knowledge of only those objects that they themselves had made became popular. The German idealist philosophy of the early 19th century (Fichte, Hegel) espoused the idea of activity as creation of the world of objects by the Transcendental Subject, Absolute Ego, or Absolute Spirit. These philosophers accepted Kant's idea about the construction of the world of experience by the Transcendental Subject and at same time rejected his idea concerning the existence of an outer reality as the "thing in itself." According to Fichte and Hegel, there is nothing immediately "given," not only in the sphere of "outer" objects, but also in the sphere of empirical consciousness. All phenomena, objective and subjective, are constructed, mediated by spiritual (cognitive or mental) activity. It is senseless to speak about reality beyond the system of such activity.

Marx, who was a genuine heir of this tradition, managed to overcome its subjectivism. The starting point in understanding a human being for Marx was not the activity of consciousness – empirical or transcendental, individual or absolute – but real empirical activity, practice, transforming real natural and social surroundings. It is not individual, but collective social activity. The activity of an individual and individual consciousness derive from collective activity. The latter presupposes interindividual relations, interaction, and communication – hence the very important role of human-made things, which mediate all human relations and, in this process of mediation, participate in creating specific human features.

Nevertheless, the opposition between the "inner" and the "outer" worlds, between "immediately given" and mediated phenomena, remains a problem for many philosophers and scholars. The understanding of the phenomena of consciousness as something immediately given in the acts of introspection is shared not only by phenomenologists but also by some representatives of contemporary philosophy of mind and cognitive science (Searle, 1990). Different philosophers and scholars (pragmatists, operationalists, epistemological constructivists, social constructionists, etc.) used the activity approach as a means of overcoming this opposition, but it was given different interpretations, and at the same time it could not resolve some problems and created other ones.

It was Lev Vygotsky (1978) who elaborated the theory of the cultural mediation of higher psychic functions, using some principal ideas of Marx.

Communication between the child and the adult, using such human-made things as language signs and creating intrapsychic processes, was at the center of his studies. Many scholars think that it is possible to consider Vygotsky's conception as the first variant of cultural-historical activity theory. But Vygotsky himself did not speak about activity theory. Moreover, some of his pupils (A. N. Leont'ev, P. I. Zinchenko, and P. J. Gal'perin) and other psychologists (S. L. Rubinstein) criticized him for not taking into account the role of practical activity in the process of mediation. Nevertheless, there is no doubt that Vygotsky's ideas are at the base of all contemporary variants of activity theory.

The first variant of psychological activity theory was elaborated by the famous Soviet psychologist A. N. Leont'ev, who was a pupil of Vygotsky. According to Leont'ev (1978), activity consists of actions, the latter of operations. Activity presupposes a corresponding motive, which coincides with an object of activity; actions are aimed at concrete goals; and operations are connected to certain tasks. These relations are flexible: An action can become an activity, a goal can transform into a motive, a task can become an operation, and so on. According to Leont'ev, it is important to understand actions as deriving from the whole process of activity, because a meaning of an action is dependent on its role in activity. A lot of research was carried out within this framework by Leont'ev himself and by his pupils. Leont'ev stressed that activity should be understood as a collective formation. But at the same time the problems of activity as a collective process, presupposing interactions and communication between different participants with different positions, were not investigated in a practical way in the framework of Leont'ev's theory. In reality, the activity of an individual and individual actions and operations were at the center of this research. Vygotsky understood the importance of the problems of collective activity and stressed the collective character of the primary forms of psychological processes. But he studied mainly the process of communication between adults and children.

The group of Russian psychologists who were disciples of A. N. Leont'ev, headed by V. V. Davydov, began to study collective activity in different forms (Davydov, 1988, 1996). They have showed that to understand collective activity in terms of actions, operations, motives, goals, and tasks is not enough. It is also necessary to take into account the values and norms of activity. According to Davydov, internalization can be understood as a mode of individual appropriation of forms of collective activity. Davydov and his followers, notably V. V. Rubtsov (1991), have discovered several types of collective subjects of learning activity on the basis of their psychological and pedagogical experiments. But collective activity can also presuppose constant communication between participants as a necessary condition. This case is especially interesting. In a series of experiments it was shown that the abilities of self-control and self-reflection in the process of learning activity can arise only if children extract themselves from the situation of interaction with an adult (in this case with a teacher) and begin to cooperate with each other. The latter presupposes the distribution of different positions, an agreement among them, the discovery of their differences, and by such means the discovery by a pupil of the existence of a position for him- or herself.

Another variant of activity theory was formulated by the Soviet philosopher and methodologist G. P. Shchedrovitsky (1995). It is distinct from Leont'ev's theory and from the work of Davydov and his followers. For Leont'ev and Davydov, activity was a means of understanding psychic phenomena and creating some of them, for understanding a personality. For Shchedrovitsky, activity was to be understood as a collective process, and an individual subject was interesting only as a function of collective activity. According to Shchedrovitsky, collective activity is a definite system that in particular includes a goal, tasks, methods, procedures, initial material, and outcomes. He was not interested in what processes are going on in the "inner world" of consciousness, what personality is, or what an individual subject is. In other words, his theory is not psychological. Its aim is to understand collective processes and to project new kinds of activity. The General Theory of Activity (the name Shchedrovitsky gave to his theory) has been adopted by a number of specialists in the spheres of projective organizational games and design, and has created a whole movement that continues to develop in Russia and is connected to the solution of concrete problems (Rotkirch, 1996).

Yrjö Engeström says that he himself uses Vygotsky's principal ideas and proceeds from the theory of Leont'ev. I agree with him on that point. At the same time I would stress that Engeström's ideas are essentially original. They contain a new conception of activity, a new understanding of its structure, and they are used to solve new problems (Engeström, 2005a). For Engeström, activity is a collective process. Building on collectivity as the main feature of activity, Engeström offers a new model of activity. The important components of the structure of activity are division of labor, community, rules, subject, and object. Mediating artifacts are also an important component – their role is emphasized not only by Leont'ev but also in the work of Davydov and in Shchedrovitsky's scheme of collective activity. Engeström interprets collective activity as a system, as does

Shchedrovitsky. But for Engeström this system should be seen in relation to other activity systems and interpreted as multivoiced, including a community of multiple points of view, traditions, interests, and interactions between participants. Engeström's idea of the central role of contradictions as sources of change and development of activity systems is very important and fruitful. I find also that the idea of the possibility of expansive transformations in activity systems is very stimulating. Engeström has been elaborating his theory in connection with its application to concrete problems in the field of developmental work research. I think that this indicates that the theory is promising.

In this context I will take up two notions that are important for the elaboration of activity theory, used by Engeström and discussed by philosophers and psychologists in Russia and other countries. I refer to the notions of subject and mediation.

SUBJECT

It has been argued that the notion of subject is not necessary for activity theory. This was, for example, the opinion of Shchedrovitsky, who wrote about activity without a subject. I cannot agree with this idea. Activity has its bearer. If it is a collective activity, there is a collective subject. If it is activity of an individual, there is an individual subject. In both cases, a subject is not something that generates activity from the outside. The subject is activity itself, considered from a certain point of view.

Without the activity of individuals, a collective activity is impossible. Activity is a specific kind of entity that can be understood with the help of an analogy. If we study, for example, a water wave, we should take into account that its movement is possible only owing to the movements of separate particles interacting with each other and transferring movement from some particles to others. But the interactions of these particles are not the same as the wave movement. Similarly, collective activity cannot exist without individuals participating in it. An individual can influence collective activity, but only by connecting with it and participating in it. Individual actions are not completely determined by collective activity. An individual is a free being, pursues his or her own goals, forms his or her life projects, can cease to follow existing norms and rules and suggest some other ones. To predict the behavior of an individual is more difficult than to predict the behavior of a social group; indeed, sometimes individuals cannot predict their own behavior. But they cannot have norms and rules of activity that are only theirs. These norms and rules will always be shared by a number of people.

Collective activity and mediation are crucial for understanding an individual subject. Mediational means exist in a field that is, on the one hand, external to each individual and, on the other hand, presupposes the activity of individuals. It is beyond the border of mine and not-mine. There is a lot of interesting research in Russia on how conscious individual processes are generated in the processes of activity. Nevertheless, I think that many problems in this field have not been solved. An individual subject cannot be dissolved into the system of collective activity. The individual is a specific system of its own. The problems of the relationship between conscious and unconscious processes, of the existence of free will, and of the nature of the ego continue to be discussed in philosophy, psychology, and cognitive science. Activity theory suggests an interesting way to approach these problems. But it does not have a ready and easy solution.

For classical philosophy and the human sciences, the existence of the subject and "the inner world" is an immediate and indubitable fact. The existence of the outer world and another subject is a problem. How is the outer world possible? How are other minds possible? How can we know the outer world? How can we know other minds? How can one's inner ideas be known by another? These questions have been discussed for several centuries. From the point of view of activity theory, consciousness and "the inner" are social and cultural constructions and exist first of all in forms of collective activity. For activity theory there is another question: How is the subject possible?

The classical philosophical opposition of "the inner" and "the outer" has been overcome from the point of view of activity approach. Nevertheless, the idea of "the inner world" is very important in cultural and social contexts. The subject as the unity of consciousness, the unity of an individual biography, and the center of making decisions can exist only as the center of "the inner world." But the appearance of "the inner world" is possible only when the idea of "the inner" arises in culture, in other words, when it is realized in forms of collective activity. This means that there may exist cultures and forms of activity, including forms of communication, where the subjects have no feelings of the ego and "the inner world."

The ego of an individual subject may be understood to be a complicated, changing, and somewhat problematic formation. It has different layers, which sometimes are interpreted as different egos, engaged in communication with each other and formed in different kinds of activity and in different relations with other people. Ego identity can be confused and fragmented. Thus, an individual subject can be understood to be a collective entity, as a kind of collective subject. A specific feature of such a collective subject is that it is embodied in a single physical body, and has a unity of consciousness and a central ego, regulating activities of different subegos. In cases of multiple personalities, a central ego is absent, so several egos coexist in the same body. In philosophical literature, the possibility that the same ego may exist in different bodies is being discussed. In any case it is clear that the traditional understanding of an individual subject should be revised. This is an urgent challenge, particularly with respect to popular ideas of the practical transformation of individual bodies through genetic engineering and electronic devices. Activity theory has not dealt with the latter ideas until now.

There is also an idea that the notion of a collective subject can be avoided. Some people think that even if one accepts collective activity, one does not need to agree with the existence of a collective subject. For example, Karl Popper wrote that it is impossible to understand the process of the development of scientific ideas if one analyzes the processes in the mental sphere of an individual subject. The development of these ideas goes beyond the minds of single individuals. It is not a subjective process, but an objective one. So according to Popper it is not necessary to refer to individual subjects when one investigates the development of scientific thinking. He concludes that it is necessary to eliminate the notion of a subject in the analysis of cognitive processes. In this connection, he formulates his project of "epistemology without a cognizing subject" (Popper, 1975).

In reality, analysis of such a specific kind of collective activity as cognition is impossible if one does not use the idea of a collective subject. Cognition as a collective process can be understood only if one takes into consideration specific features of a collective subject that is the bearer of scientific cognition. In such a case it is a scientific community adhering to a certain scientific paradigm, or research program, or research tradition. Different collective subjects in science have different programs of collective cognitive activity. The development of scientific ideas can be understood as the development of relations between these collective subjects, including their competition and struggle, but not as relations between pure objective ideas, as Popper thought. The same can be said about other kinds of collective activity.

It is important to stress that a collective subject is an active agent. It is similar to an individual subject in certain respects: It has its own aims, interests, memory, and norms. Individual subjects, participating in collective activity, feel that they belong to a collective entity with which they identify themselves. Thus, collective responsibility becomes possible. Specific "we" feelings arise. Engeström (2005a, pp. 89–117) presents an interesting analysis of collective intentionality. There are reasons to think that the "ego" feeling arises later than the "we" feeling, as the former derives from the latter (Searle, 1990). This concerns both phylogenesis and ontogenesis. For example, relations between a baby and a mother are not those of two individual subjects but of a specific dyad, a kind of a collective subject.

On the other hand, there are differences between an individual subject and a collective one. A collective subject is normally not embodied in a single body. It cannot be considered an ego or a superego, although some writers think that it can be understood as a kind of a person. The "we" feeling exists only in the minds of individual subjects, participating in a certain kind of activity. Because a collective subject cannot exist independently of individual actions, it can disappear if individuals decide to stop fulfilling a collective activity that is connected to a certain collective subject.

Collective subjects can be very different. They can be social institutions or more or less constant social groups. They can be organizations or temporary groups that have definite goals and that disappear when these goals are achieved. They can be associations of several groups. Relations between individual subjects participating in collective activity can also be different. Individual subjects can adhere to strict rules or can imitate some patterns of activity. They occupy different positions, have different individual life projects, different plans for fulfilling certain common tasks.

Engeström (2005a, pp. 97–100) has analyzed interesting kinds of collective activity systems that exist without a center. One may think that in such cases it is senseless to speak about collective subjects. I think that collective subjects exist in any and every case of collective activity. It is important to take into account that a collective subject is not necessarily a center that governs activity. It is a bearer of rules and norms of activity, of its object and means of mediation. In contemporary cognitive science some researchers have begun to elaborate ideas about the so-called extended subject, which includes various artifacts. These researchers try to understand cognition as a collective process of interaction among individual subjects. These attempts may be interpreted as steps toward the idea of a collective subject (Clark, 1998, p. 49; Clark & Chalmers, 1998, pp. 7–19).

MEDIATION

In Russia some philosophers and psychologists (Rubinstein, Brushlinsky, and Slavskaja, among others) have criticized Vygotsky and Leont'ev's activity theory for a narrow and one-sided understanding of relations between activity and inner psychic processes. The critics target the idea of the generation of inner psychic processes through internalization of outer actions and activities. They stress that the idea of internalization does not take into consideration the creative nature of human activity. According to them, internalization can explain only the learning of some simple habits, but it does not help us to understand genuine relations between the "inner world" of a subject and outer activity. I agree with this criticism. In reality, internalization and externalization presuppose each other and are two sides of activity, as has been shown by Engeström (2005a, pp. 25–26). Internalization or externalization can prevail in different phases of the process of activity. But they constantly accompany each other.

If internalization is assimilation by an individual subject of certain kinds of activity, it can be realized only by means of some external mediated actions. Some followers of activity theory (e.g., Gal'perin) interpreted the forming of specific human psychic mechanisms as the result of the internalization of outer actions, their transfer into "an inner space." But it is not clear how, according to this conception, "an inner space" arises, because the process of transfer presupposes the existence of the latter. In reality, the "inner space" of consciousness is a result of individual appropriation of certain kinds of external collective activity. So we may say that the so-called inner space first exists in outer, external actions as a part of collective activity. Internalization is impossible without participation in external mediated activity.

There are different kinds of externalization. It can comprise simple reproductive actions, and it can involve the creation of new products, new ideas, even new standards, rules, and norms of activity. But as some researchers (in particular, Zinchenko, 2006a) have shown, simple reproduction is impossible, because every case of application presupposes taking into account new circumstances, so it presupposes a kind of creativity. Not only does every creative action transform something in the outer world, it at the same time forms new features of personality, in other words, forms a subject. But if every action presupposes something creative, then every action of externalization is at the same time a process of internalization. Such an understanding of human activity corresponds to Marx's (1976, p. 4) interpretation of praxis as the co-occurrence of changing the surroundings and changing one's change.

Some scholars in Russia criticize the idea of mediation because from their point of view it presupposes the existence of activity. But the point is that mediation is not something that is imposed on activity from without. Activity exists only as mediated. This is its specific characteristic. As means of mediation are human-made things, things that refer to another person, communication is foundationally included in the process of activity. If individual behavior is not mediated, it is not an action understood as a part of activity. Means of mediation can be different: tools, instruments, domestic utilities, sign systems. When a baby cannot speak, he or she participates in a shared activity with a mother, and this activity is mediated by different things, including toys. These things play a role as means of communication, of a certain "practical language." So communication exists in every kind of activity, also before a baby learns a spoken language.

Some contemporary followers of Vygotsky think that it is possible to study mediating processes without taking activity into consideration. In reality it is impossible to understand mediation and its different modes if one does not take into consideration the connection between definite modes of mediation (e.g., definite signs and sign systems) and the corresponding activity, as only this activity gives meaning to the means of mediation. The same thing that is used as a means of mediation has different meanings and mediates different processes if it is used in different kinds of activity.

REFLECTIVE MEDIATION AS THE CREATION OF NEW ACTIVITY

Some actions can be re-mediated and as a result become different ones, generating new actions and even a new kind of activity. This is a process of re-mediation, of the replacement of an old mediation by a new one. Re-mediation can be understood as a process of reflection. I would like to give an example of such a process from the history of science. This example is borrowed from an article by the Russian philosopher Rozov (1981, pp. 78–94).

Toward the end of the 18th century, the French physicist Charles Augustin Coulomb tried to answer questions arising in the theory of elasticity, in other words, within the framework of a certain collective scientific activity. In his research he managed to discover the dependence of the angle of a thread's turn on the quantity of the acting force. But when he discovered this dependence, he reflected on the results and reinterpreted them, in other words, re-mediated them. He understood that they can be interpreted as answering [fundamentally different questions, which did not initially arise in the process of the collective activity in the framework of which the results had been obtained]. The new question was: What is the quantity of force if we know the angle of turning of a thread? In other words, he discovered a method of measuring force on the basis of which he made a corresponding device – a turning balance. He began to use the device for measuring forces in different fields, including the interaction of electrical charges. So the discovery of Coulomb's law was not a result of searching for an answer to a question about the character of the interaction of electrical charges. This question did not arise in the framework of the previous collective activity; it was an unexpected consequence of the solution to a different task. Coulomb's actions were reinterpreted, in other words, were given a new mediation, and as a result became other actions, generating another collective activity: research in the field of the theory of electricity. Reflection on individual actions as a kind of re-mediation generated a new kind of collective activity.

In philosophy there are different interpretations of relations between reflection and its object, understood as individual consciousness and individual and collective activity. There is an idea that acts of reflection on the states of individual consciousness do not change the object of reflection. This is an old idea concerning the possibility of introspection that was criticized but that nevertheless has followers even now among philosophers, psychologists, and cognitive scientists. It seems that introspection is simply a fact of consciousness. But its understanding creates a lot of philosophical difficulties, as an act of introspection is involved in a state of consciousness and changes it.

Some philosophers think that reflection cannot be a mode of awareness of what is there, as it always destroys its object and creates something new. Sometimes it is suggested that all reflection is a kind of self-deception. This was the position of Sartre, for example, who described self-reflection as self-deception (Sartre, 2000, pp. 95–101). I think that there are cases of self-deception and that this a real philosophical problem, but I cannot agree with the idea that every reflection is a kind of self-deception.

Finally there is a very popular conception according to which there is no object of reflection. The followers of this conception, mostly among post-structuralists and postmodernists, think that in the strict sense of the word reflection is impossible. What seems to be reflection is really only generating new activity. From this point of view, reality in any sense does not exist; it is a construction in the process of communication. According to this conception, mediation is not a very good term, as it is possible to mediate only something existing. Thus, it would be better to speak simply about social construction (Gergen, 1999). I think that accepting this point of view leads to paradoxes. Construction presupposes the existence of some real matter that can be an object of constructive activity.

In discussing these positions I would like to use the important ideas Engeström (2005a, pp. 150–170) puts forward in a chapter entitled "Activity

Theory and the Social Construction of Knowledge: A Story of Four Umpires." Engeström analyzes three epistemological conceptions – naive realism, constructivism, and social constructionism – and shows that none of them can explain a concrete case in a certain collective activity. The need to change collective activity arises as a result of the existence of inner contradictions in a system, a certain degree of inner tension. Reflection is a mode of comprehending these contradictions and understanding possibilities of changing activity within the framework of the same system by way of a new mediation. But it presupposes that reflection takes into account the history of a system – the principle of historicity is one of the main principles of cultural-historical activity theory, as emphasized by Engeström. In other words, reflection as a new mediation is necessary for changing activity, for generating and constructing something new. This theory is used by Engeström in the elaboration of an interventionist methodology, aimed at generating new kinds of practice. But such generation is possible only when reflection can comprehend real contradictions in an activity system and understand the real possibilities of its changes.

I share this conception, which I call "constructive realism" or "activity realism." Constructive realism proceeds from the idea that human relations with the outer reality are mediated by a system of collective activity. Objects of activity are not simply real entities, but those real things, processes, events, natural and social, that are involved in the system of activity. At the same time, collective activity is a real system with its own structure, history, and laws of expansion and transformation. This system cannot exist without the activity of individuals, their actions and acts of communication, but it cannot be reduced to the latter, as the principal features of a system of activity do not depend on them. I think that the conception of constructive realism is very close to that proposed by Roy Bhaskar (1977) and also to the ideas of Rom Harré (1984, 1986).

Reflection as an act of individual consciousness does not necessarily change its object. For example, when individuals reflect on their personality and as a result do not like themselves, it changes something in them. Something like an identity crisis may arise. But this does not necessarily mean that the personality changes. The latter presupposes a new kind of mediation, a new interpretation, constructing a new project of individual life and generating new activity. If these do not happen, an individual identity crisis cannot be solved. It is necessary to stress that a new kind of mediation can solve an individual identity crisis only if it takes into account the real life of an individual, his or her real history, his or her past. In psychology, it is a known fact that individuals construct their memory, forget things, give a new interpretation to recollections, and so on. They can have false recollections. But that does not mean that there is no principal difference between false and true recollections. The invention of the past, a false memory, can seem to help for a short time, but usually it leads to serious problems and conflicts, although some followers of social constructionism among psychologists and psychotherapists assert that all of them are social constructions, and the real past doesn't exist (Hacking, 1995).

So research as a kind of reflection on human activity can change its objects. But this can happen only when there is not only research, but also a project of changing the existing activity and generating a new one. This means that human beings who are the object of research, as a kind of reflection, accept the results of research and suggested modes of transforming the activity, make a new mediation of their activity, and so change it. If the results of research are unknown to human beings who are under investigation, or if they do not accept these results, or if a researcher cannot suggest any project for generating new activity, the object of research does not change. Research as activity is different from the activity that is the object of investigation. On the other hand, in some cases if people accept the results of research and suggested projects of changing their life, they may re-mediate their activity and create something that is not only new, but has no real connection to their past.

Cultural-historical activity theory has very good prospects. The work of Yrjö Engeström has convinced me about that. There are a lot of problems that have not been investigated with the help of this theory, especially in the field of the philosophy of mind, cognitive science, and psychology. But from my point of view it is possible to develop the theory and to generate new ideas within its framework.

6

Digital Technology and Mediation:
A Challenge to Activity Theory

GEORG RÜCKRIEM

No societal development within the past 50 years or so has been more fierce or far-reaching than that related to information and telecommunication technology. The digital technology on which it is based has penetrated every societal process and every societal activity system. It not only laid the foundations of the World Wide Web, including its derivations, but built a new global network of communication systems.

No matter how we may judge the consequences of this technical development, we cannot but concede that digital technology has entered most things in everyday life, and it increasingly determines the activity of people even if they avoid using it. In more general terms, it has become the basis of an emerging globalization process that is not only economic but cultural, not only universal but irreversible. There is nothing outside it. Reality itself has changed fundamentally.

Amazingly, most of the scholars committed to either cultural-historical psychology or activity theory do not deal with digitalization. Or at least they underestimate its revolutionary quality and so fail to prove their concepts and methodology. Clearly, when Vygotsky, Leont'ev, and Luria built the foundations of their approach, computers did not exist, and digitalization was not at stake. But does this fact justify the contemporary reserve? I am convinced that digitalization marks a twofold – methodological and theoretical – problem for activity theory, possibly the most difficult challenge it has been confronted with. In the following, I will therefore deal with such questions as the following: Is the current activity-oriented concept of mediation, with its notions of tool, symbol, and artifact, still sufficient for an adequate understanding of the societal and individual importance of digital technology? Is it adequate to deal with the epistemological quality of a "leading medium" as if it were just a material object or a tool and to subordinate it to a socioeconomic theory with its traditional categories of use value and exchange value? Can the consideration of mediatedness be restricted to just activity systems *within* societies, neglecting the mediatedness of society *as a whole*? Is activity theory able to reflect on its own mediatedness and, in particular, its dependence on what media theorists call "the Gutenberg galaxy" (McLuhan, 1962)?

I'll try to find answers to these questions by analyzing as an example the work of one of the best-known activity theorists at present. But my approach is based on theoretical premises that have to be explained first. I try to meet this requirement by discussing three hypotheses:

1. *We are witnessing a revolutionary transformation without really noticing it.* We should therefore put more attention to specific disciplines such as media theory and history of media, the former investigating the fundamental process of mediatization as such, the latter doing concrete research on which medium is functioning as the determining factor in characterizing a given epoch (and ours in particular) as a whole. In doing so, media history is reconceptualizing our historiography, constituting a new history of societal and cultural formations. From this point of view, global digitalization and networking represent the specific "leading" and epoch-making medium of our present time and provide totally new and rather inexhaustible potentials to human practice, bringing about new notions and self-identifications to specify an emerging societal formation, such as information society (Giesecke, 1998), media society (Flusser, 1998), network society (Castells, 1996), knowledge society (Willke, 2001), and meaning society (Bolz, 1993).

2. *The solutions of the problem of mediation, developed by Vygotsky and Leont'ev, are historically determined.* They belong to the worldview of the "Gutenberg galaxy" (McLuhan, 1962); that is, they depend on printing as medium. This sets limits on the thinking of Vygotsky and Leont'ev. The way of thinking that corresponds to the medium web in the information society is neither historically nor theoretically accessible to them.

3. *The distinction between medium and means of mediation can be made only if the problem of mediation is seen historically.* The concept of mediation, which is fundamental to activity theory, has to be conceived as a historically specific solution to the general problem of mediation, in order to not only see the potentialities but above all to accept the limitations of this historical solution. It is "a difference that makes a difference," as Bateson (1972, p. 453) put it. But this difference has to be made.

I should once more stress that my point is theoretical, not empirical. I try to focus on a new theoretical approach – media theory and media history – that is suitable for questioning not only the fundamentals of activity theory but its existence as a whole. And I'll try to point out and explain a possible interface between media theory and activity theory, which seems to be the concept of "medium" and which I think is as important as it is fruitful.

My questions are: First, what are we talking about? Second, what is Engeström's point of view? Third, what are media theory and media history about? Fourth, what are the solutions of Vygotsky and Leont'ev about? Finally, what conclusion is to be reached about the dependency of activity theory on book culture and its failure to notice that dependency?

WHAT ARE WE TALKING ABOUT?

Clearly, everybody knows about computers, but most people still think of a computer as that box we can carry around, and find it difficult to understand the Internet as computer because it cannot be seen or touched or localized. Although it is based on those 13 mighty servers, it is nothing but a communication system, which has even changed its quality within the past 10 years. In the beginning, the Internet – retroactively called Web 1.0 – was a sort of one-to-one (e-mail) or one-to-many communication device (Web pages). Today communication technology has reached the level of many-to-many communication (blogs, Wikis, and other new interactive media), now called Web 2.0 or social software, which makes it possible to communicate and collaborate in networks globally and unlimitedly. There is no telling how things will turn out. The whole extent and the consequences of the emerging, globally spreading transformation processes are not yet known, nor are they even foreseeable in any detail. Clearly, knowledge and collective knowledge work will be freed from any current technical limits and normative limitations. There is no doubt that the new social networks of Web 2.0 not only organize life online but also have a serious impact on real life, bringing about "ubiquitous computing" and the "disappearance" of the computer into the background (Weiser, 1991, pp. 94–104). Weiser's early vision is even surpassed by the automatic monitoring technology using transponder chips based on RFID programs (called the "Internet of things" and already realized by all big shopping centers and supermarkets) and by its linking up with the NFC technology of mobile telephones developed through a collaboration of Sony, Philips, and Nokia. In the meantime, Tim Berners-Lee published RDF as the first standard of Web 3.0, also called the "Semantic Web" because it enables machines to "understand" and to interpret by automatically linking up Web contents with the help of special programs for "meta-tagging" semantic data. It can be argued that the emerging Web is one in which the machines talk as much to each other as humans talk to machines or other humans.

There are still no perceptible limits on the invention of new forms of networking, and surprisingly new forms of applications emerge every year. And if we can believe futurologists and media theorists, these processes mark just a transitional period. The unbelievable speed of change seems to indicate that they are right.

Owing to inadequate concepts, activity theory fails to perceive the material reality of the global networks that make possible these forms of networking, going far beyond mobile technology and Internet 1. The correct functioning of those services is controlled by automatically working protocol systems. They guarantee that all kinds of existing networks, especially corporate and organizational intranets, can be globally linked and expanded to extranets of any range, such as the existing global networks of finance, trade, health, sports, traffic, and standardization, which Willke (2001, p. 70) calls "lateral world systems." They have been built and financed by big players and financially powerful syndicates, but they operate automatically. There is no way to characterize those communication networks adequately in terms of subject, action, or activity, let alone goal or motive. They do not link up "things or beings," but combine "the pure contingency of possible ways into self-weaving networks of communicative relations" (Willke, 2001, p. 78), whose rate of emergence, speed of development, and rate of use increase exponentially (Kelly, 2005). The global networks are material but not objects; they are media for autonomously communicating systems but not identifiable tools or artifacts to any individual or collective, although they are of the utmost importance to every individual activity or collective activity system.

To me these facts give reason to ask: Can those automatically and independently functioning technical systems still be called activities or activity systems? Are they really just tools? And whose tools? Is there any identifiable individual or collective subject of those systems? Is it adequate to look for a motive or a goal within automatic processes? Or in more general terms: Can activity theory and its methodology still be applied to a digitalized reality?

WHAT IS ENGESTRÖM'S POINT OF VIEW?

Looking at the work of Yrjö Engeström while asking these questions, I must at first note that among all third-generation activity theorists he clearly is one of the most sensible researchers, concerning the perception of current societal changes, and certainly he is the most productive among them, if we consider his efforts to bring activity theory up to date. This is reflected in his numerous proposals for further development of the basic concepts and in his innovations in the extension of the methodology of activity theory. He is one of the outstanding representatives of the "multivoicedness" approach among activity theorists. There is no doubt that Engeström focuses more strictly and more concretely on emerging problems in different societal sectors than most of the activity theorists do, and unquestionably it is he who made activity theory a successful intervention strategy. In spite of all this, the idea of the epoch-making global impact of information and tele-communication technology and its resulting societal transformations is not included in his interventionist methodology.

To give an example, Engeström refers in one of his recent publications (2005a, p. 99) to the description of a spontaneously emerging communi-cation network (Rafael, 2003), which, being realized only with the help of mobile technology and without any stabilizing institutional or organiza-tional background or stable center respectively, nevertheless was aimed at a common end: the downfall of President Estrada of the Philippines. Rheingold (2002) used this example to discuss his concept of "smart mobs" in order to explain their fundamental part in "the next social revolution." To Engeström, however, the existence of "smart mobs" seems to be a single phenomenon and just a motive for reflecting on the possibility of intro-ducing new system-like concepts such as "*collective* intentionality," "*dis-tributed* agency," and "object-oriented *inter*agency" into his intervention research without changing his methodology or dealing with Rheingold's results. Engeström no longer refers to the abundance of data or impressive descriptions of digitalization processes in Rheingold (2002) or to his idea of an emerging social revolution.

Today, however, "smart mobs" are not a single phenomenon but mold our everyday life, although the public media report almost exclusively only the most spectacular political Weblog campaigns. The more than 200 mil-lion blogs worldwide are able to produce seismic communication waves whose reverberations not only reach the classic media scene but strongly affect public opinion in the Internet. Although these networks can hardly be controlled by a fixed center, they "have actually the power to mobilize at any time millions of people" (Friebe & Lobo, 2006, p. 171). The new underly-ing communication system is the most rapidly growing technical system in human history. It creates a fusion of technique and society and merges those forms of transformation that Rheingold and so many others write about.

This argument is also true concerning "smart artifacts" or "smart environments." Because of their inherent digital technology, they are perceived as "knowledge based." But there is no hidden subject inside, no motive, no intentionality. It is only their knowledge-based capability to function as independent systems that makes them smart, as Willke (1998) argues. He proposes that digital technology must be understood as embedded in every product, and even in human labor itself, as a "knowledge foundation." "Organized knowledge labor" should be considered to be a totally new force of production whose results are "intelligent" products and "intelligent organizations," the latter characterized by a self-increasing recursiveness in using and generating knowledge, that is, learning. Thus, knowledge becomes a critical resource and is already the most important factor in societal reproduction, even more so than land, capital, or labor. To Willke, "knowledge society" means, therefore, a radical new form of global socialization, which makes possible new forms of self-creation and self-definition for individuals.

Most activity theorists are not aware of the importance of these transformation processes or at least do not assess them adequately. Even Engeström deals with them rather as one would with rare, bizarre, or difficult to comprehend phenomena, although they have long been pervasively present. Engeström's (2005a, pp. 116–117) proposal, to characterize such smart mobs as "interagency," is an interesting attempt to capture a system that demonstrates neither individual, institutional, or organizational contours nor any personal continuity to tie it into any kind of intentionality. It is a system that does not have any temporal consistency but rather is fluid and exists only because of the networking of participating individuals. Since activity theory is basically tied up with the concept of a subject of activity, it is more than difficult to combine the above-mentioned "very temporary organizational forms" – as Engeström (2006b, p. 8) describes those independently functioning systems – with a kind of "collective intentionality." To Engeström, these "swarm" or "amoeba" organizations are rather exotic appearances anyhow. He focuses instead on "partnership" and "alliance formations" as forms of collaborative work that he calls "knotworking," the characterization of which, however, corresponds to a great extent to what is normally called "networking" (Engeström, 2005a, p. 98; 2006b, p. 6).

Engeström speaks of "infrastructural entities," which "seem to be utilities rather than utensils, media rather than means" (Engeström, 2005a, p. 50), but he does not reflect on the concept of medium. He writes on "co-configuration work" (Engeström 2005a, p. 437) in order to find a new "framework for such a reintegration of organization, work, and learning" and "to capture the emerging possibilities and new forms of learning." He identifies co-configuration as a historically new type of work, and he defines it most interestingly using concepts such as "adaptive customer-intelligent products or services," "mutual exchange between customer, producer, and the product/service combinations," "active customer involvement," and "mutual learning from interactions between the parties" (Engeström, 2005a, pp. 438–439). These concepts, however, show that co-configuration is possible only on the basis and under the conditions of global digitalization. Co-configuration has been produced by digitalization and it is fixed to it. It first emerged within the computer world in work with beta versions of software, to configure user-oriented combinations of hardware, or to shape and adjust software and its applications according to a particular user's needs. It was through the experiences of this field that the traditional concepts of producer and consumer or producer and user lost their fixed meaning and began to dissolve. The ongoing debate on these concepts is nowhere more fierce and passionate than within the world of new media. The dissolution process of those concepts and their traditional norms and rules – concerning intellectual property, copyright, and authorship – is increasingly vivid because of the consequences of Web 2.0. It is therefore actually impossible to analyze adequately the emerging new forms of work or learning outside digitalization. To discuss co-configuration without mentioning computers and the Internet is like studying the results without considering the causes.

Of course, Engeström is absolutely right, when he – under the rubric "mediation as a key" – finds it "somewhat amazing that in the recent theoretical discussion concerning the concept of activity, very little attention is paid to the idea of mediation" (Engeström, 2005a, p. 28). That is a correct balance, indeed, and therefore Engeström is also right when he calls the idea of mediation "the first prerequisite for any fruitful elaboration" (p. 28). Much more important, however, is the emphasis that characterizes the underlying theoretical understanding. It ought to be said: Mediation is *the* key! Engeström does not consider the Internet as *the* key, that is, not as a medium, but as an instrument. Asked about the importance of new media, he answered, "The internet is a useful instrument, that's all. ... It is useful the same way like books or other means. ... I can't see any revolutionary impact in it" (Lompscher, 2004, p. 292). In his methodology, the Internet never appears as an explanatory principle but as a tool or "instrumentality" only.

Even in his recent paper on "mycorrhizae activities," Engeström (2006b, p. 32) refers to digitalization just as *"technology"* and fails to reflect on the mediational relationship between this technology and the mycorrhizae activities that would not and could not exist without this technology as their basis. He focuses on mediation by "integrated toolkits," "tool constellations," or "configuration technologies," "which includes fitting together new and old tools and procedures" (Engeström, 2007a, p. 33) – that is, methodologically speaking, nothing radically new, but more of the same. Consequently, remaining within the boundaries of a traditional worldview, he seeks an alternative to the "promises of bandwidth revolution" in the *objects* only (Engeström, 2006b, p. 34) and fails to notice that the object has been changed by a new medium. "Again, digital networking technologies are important in the formation of these forms of knotworking and mycorrhizae. ... But they are tools, not the object" (Engeström, 2006b, p. 37).

Engeström's understanding of the problem of mediation remains within the framework of the classical authors and alternates between Vygotsky's and Leont'ev's version of how to solve the problem of mediation. In consequence, Engeström refers to collective activity systems embedded in capitalist societal structures as described by historical materialism. His methodology does not allow him to interpret the Internet as a basic transformation factor, let alone as a framework for perceiving our present reality as a qualitatively new emerging societal formation. Because there is no theoretical possibility for distinguishing between different dominating media, Engeström is hardly able to tell the difference between activity systems determined by an old medium and those processes formed by a new medium. That means that he deals with local changes and limited developments of activity systems within the boundaries of a society coined by a traditionally perceived dominating medium. In consequence, he analyzes emerging communication processes in terms of old socioeconomic concepts. He studies modern Web-based activity systems under pre-Web conditions, which might have been effective for understanding the epoch of industrial society, but not for considering the entirely new forms of their mediation mentioned earlier. His intervention strategy does not provide him with an adequate instrument to differentiate between traditional changes and emerging revolutionary transformations and their specific problem structures.

Relying only on the Vygotskian concept of mediation, activity theory cannot really approach the historically new and basic societal transformations that determine the framework of the entire societal reality. When trying to do it nonetheless, Engeström encounters difficult problems with his concepts, because these concepts stem from a time when there were no computers and no networks. They cannot be applied to today's problems without discontinuities, contradictions, and distortions or without running the risk of mistaking one's own contradictions for objective problems. This does not mean, however, that Engeström's numerous projects or his intervention strategy in particular are unproductive efforts. On the contrary, in times of transformation they are even necessary, as will be shown later in the chapter, but they fall short of their real possibilities.

WHAT ARE MEDIA THEORY AND MEDIA HISTORY ABOUT?

One of the most interesting living scholars doing research in the tradition of McLuhan is the media theorist and media historian Michael Giesecke (1998, 2002, 2006). I condense the theoretical guidelines of his voluminous historical research on media as follows.

1. There is no information between systems without medium. Every new medium gives rise to a new epistemology, and this again leads to the discovery of new worlds. New worldviews emerge, and the position of humans in relation to the world gets reformulated.

   Each epistemology is the epistemology of a period within the development of media. (Postman, 1988, pp. 36–37)

2. This is true of individual and social systems. They cannot communicate without a medium, taking communication in a much broader sense then just interaction.

3. Every medium, necessarily based on a specific technology, determines the information itself, the information process, and the processors' communication potentials and possibilities as well.

   It would be naive to assume that what had been expressed in a certain medium could also be expressed in any other medium without changing considerably its meaning, its structure, and its value. (Postman, 1988, p. 145)

4. Every culture gives preference to a certain medium to define its own cultural identity. This medium becomes the dominating medium integrating every other existing medium into a kind of medium constellation. Therefore, owing to the preferred medium

   to any given culture only very specific types of information are actually real; all the other information is either not even perceived or brushed aside as illusions, dreams, fantasies, infernal stuff, or whatsoever. (Giesecke, 2002, p. 239)

5. Depending on the given leading medium, the understanding of what could be an object, a tool, or a helpful instrument changes. Forms and functions of tools and instruments as well as the social rules of their application and use depend on the given medium and its information and communication systems (Giesecke, 2002, p. 290). Every leading medium constellation produces its own typical practices and products, activities and cooperation forms, its means, tools, and advice as a medium between humans and the environment. Symbolically generalized communication media emerge to steer the communication between individual and social systems, such as power, law, money, and knowledge.

Even the defining characteristics of what is human move and slip. (Giesecke, 2002, p. 290)

6. This basic impact of media on speech and thinking, on feeling and knowledge, on perception and cognition, esthetics, epistemology, social rules, and ways of reflecting on the world gave media historians the impetus to discuss cultural history as a genealogy of leading media and media formations, such as oral, scriptographic, typographic, and electronic or digital cultures.

7. The methodological problem of analyzing the present as determined by digitalization and networking as leading media is that there is "no point of view from the outside." In each case the respective ideas of description depend on the chosen point of view (Giesecke, 2002, p. 280). But trying to understand the currently emerging information society and its fundamental transformations by analyzing the current use of computers is like coming to a conclusion about a person's vocational future from the heartbeat of an unborn child in the womb of an expectant mother (Giesecke, 2006).

The full understanding of the current technological revolution would require the discussion of the specificity of new information technologies vis-à-vis their historical ancestors of equally revolutionary character, such as the discovery of printing in China in the late seventeenth, and in Europe in the fifteenth century. (Castells, 1996, p. 31)

8. Giesecke's work centers on this comparison and draws conclusions concerning our present network society by analogy with book culture. Analyzing the print medium, he argues that unbelievable obstacles and barriers were cleared away to push through the typographic communication system. All linguistic conditions were completely

restructured, Latin lost its monopoly, new standardized national languages with specific oral and scriptural forms emerged, the status and function of dialects within the hierarchy of languages changed fundamentally, age-old religious myths were replaced by new ones, social norms valid for thousands of years were smashed, even the self-image of the individual was thoroughly revised (Giesecke, 2006).

New religiousness, enlightenment, democracy, and industrialization – everything has been given a push, accelerated and perfected by this medium. Each field of life has been made scriptural and is controlled by bookish knowledge. (Giesecke, 2002, p. 227)

9. For Giesecke, this applies also to production. McLuhan (1962) called Gutenberg's invention the basic form of any further mechanization. Several other historians of technology argue that the principle of Gutenberg's mold returns in every machine, up to the modern age. Giesecke concludes that without the printing machine, indefinitely producing identical, perfectly fitting pieces, neither industrial mass production nor the market economy and its distribution mechanisms would have been possible (Giesecke, 2002, p. 225; 2006). Disagreeing with historical materialism, he is convinced that

the typographical technology is the prototype of the production technology of the industrial era. (Giesecke, 2002, p. 229)

10. To make things absolutely clear, Giesecke emphasizes that the privileging and accelerating of a new medium, in those days and as well as today, depend basically on the potential, viability, and power that people expect from it in realizing their social utopias. In other words, a medium is a catalyst, not a cause.

In order to become a catalyst of social transformations a medium has to draw social attention and to attract social projections. The more total the demand for those projections is – it could also be said: their megalomania is – the more important the catalytic effects on societal transformation will be. (Giesecke, 2002, p. 156)

11. But there are always different competing technologies with different promises of sense and value. This forces them to initiate a predatory competition by developing sense-building processes and forming new semantic systems and ideologies. Because of the heavy cultural losses that unavoidably accompany a new medium, cultures are forced to justify their self-definition by depreciating the old media and glorifying their own aims and goals, and by making mysteries of their historical outcomes and achievements as if they

were unchangeable human characteristics and mark the pinnacle of human development.

12. The failure to scrutinize the mysteries and ideologies of the book-printing culture has an adverse effect on the critical analysis and shaping of the potentialities of the new medium. Giesecke (2002, pp. 223–257) describes eleven such myths and mystifications. I will merely mention the most interesting ones concerning my theme:

   - The myth of rational linguistic information processing: Logical thinking and reason are more important and valuable than emotional intelligence.
   - The myth of one "true or objective reality."
   - The myth of history being a steady linear process of accumulating knowledge.
   - The myth of early cultures being "natural" and "direct," that is "nonmediated" and therefore minor, primitive, or inferior, whereas books and reason are identified and privileged as "real" culture.

All these myths are specific to book culture and its "imperialistic" medium and cannot be found in any earlier leading media formation.

13. In every new media formation, the sheer reproduction of the programs of a declining formation cannot by any means uphold the achievements of the old medium; the latter is condemned to fail in the face of the new challenges (Giesecke, 2002, p. 227, p. 274).

14. In order to take these challenges we have to see through the myths, to understand their dependency and to grasp their historical necessity. That is the only way to get along with the problems of transformation processes, that is, with the coexistence of different leading media, such as books and networks, both of which are still competing for privileged and generalized positions.

WHAT ARE THE SOLUTIONS OF VYGOTSKY AND LEONT'EV ABOUT?

Looking at cultural-historical psychology from this point of view, I begin with Vygotsky's (1997b) solution, which I first describe in his own terms. His model of mediation is discussed in detail in Engeström's (1987) *Learning by Expanding*. It is therefore sufficient to recall that Vygotsky put a third item into the scheme of stimulus–response, an auxiliary stimulus mediating between subject and object. The third item was still a kind of stimulus, but a stimulus of its own, an artificial stimulus, an instrument to mediate human and nature. Using tools, originally serving to control other humans, now in order to control themselves, human beings became aware of themselves, and so freed themselves from the determinism of nature. That was the meaning of mediation. This intellectualization of behavior by mediatization marked a difference between "lower" ("natural," "rudimentary," "primitive," or "elementary") and "higher" ("artificial," "complex," or "instrumental") forms. The deciding factor of the difference is its new, specific stimulus–response relation (Vygotsky, 1997b, pp. 53–54). While the lower forms are totally determined by immediate stimulation, the basic characteristics of higher forms consist in "*autostimulation,* the creation and use of artificial stimuli-devices and determining one's own behavior with their help" (Vygotsky, 1997b, p. 54). In the course of social life, humans created the most complicated systems of psychic communication without which labor activity would be impossible. Among other psychological tools, the most adequate means for psychic self-regulation are signs, language, and written text in particular. Signs are historical and societal both in origin and in function. They come from the history of culture and serve initially as means of communication, means of influencing other humans.

> The means of social contact are thus also basic means for the formation of the complex psychological links that emerge when these functions become individual functions and grow into a personal style of behavior (Vygotsky, 1997a, p. 96).

From this point of view Vygotsky expresses his "basic genetic law of cultural development":

> Every function in the child's cultural development appears twice: First, on the social level, and later, on the individual level; first, *between* people (*interpsychological*), and then inside the child (*intrapsychological*) (Vygotsky, 1978, p. 57)

Considering Engeström's reception of Vygotsky's concept of mediational means and its transformation into "mediational artifacts," it should be added that Vygotsky certainly spoke of "psychological tools," but most prominently he used the concept of sign instead. He rejected the identification of tool and sign, and even explicitly criticized the subsumption of tools and signs under the concept of "artifact" (Vygotsky, 1997b, p. 61).

> The tool serves for conveying man's activity to the object of his activity, it is directed outward, it must result in one change or another in the object, it is the means for man's external activity directed toward subjugating

nature. The sign changes nothing in the object of the psychological operation, it is a means of psychological action on behavior, one's own or another's, a means of internal activity directed toward mastering man himself; the sign is directed inward. These activities are so different that even the nature of the devices used cannot be one and the same in both cases. (Vygotsky, 1997b, p. 62)

The basis of any analogy between tool and sign is their mediating function only. Vygotsky's point is that tools and artifacts are not psychic phenomena!

Vygotsky did not explain where the subject's capacity for self-stimulation by external stimuli came from. But he was aware of the problem and sharply, even gruffly, denied the simple attempts of his ideological enemies to walk off with the problem by sheer deduction from dialectical or historical materialism or even from the economic categories of *Capital*:

> The *direct* application of the theory of *dialectical materialism* to the problems of natural science and in particular to the group of biological sciences or psychology is *impossible,* just as it is *impossible to apply it directly* to history and sociology. ... Like history, sociology is in need of the intermediate *special theory* of historical materialism which explains the *concrete* meaning, for the given group of phenomena, of the abstract laws of dialectical materialism. In exactly the same way we are in need of an as yet undeveloped but inevitable theory of biological materialism and psychological materialism as an intermediate science which explains the concrete application of the abstract theses of dialectical materialism to the given field of phenomena. (Vygotsky, 1997a, p. 330)

Unfortunately, Vygotsky was unable to realize this program of a metatheory that possibly could have explained the coevolution of systems and media. Nevertheless, he seemingly speaks with Giesecke's words when he depicts the effects of a leading medium on individual and social systems, saying that the introduction of psychological tools "modifies the entire course and structure of mental functions" (Vygotsky, 1997a, p. 85).

Although Vygotsky was sure of this fundamental fact, he acknowledged only two kinds of media: natural and artificial. This is exactly the pattern of thought we know from the myths of book culture. Correspondingly, Vygotsky saw written text as the decisive divide separating the primitive epoch of humankind from that of civilization (Vygotsky, 1997b, pp. 131–148). Lack of contact with the European book society was "primitive." This bias is visible also in Luria's expedition to Uzbekistan and its assessment by Vygotsky (Van der Veer, 1996; Van der Veer & Valsiner, 1991, pp. 251–253).

Also, the last of the aforementioned myths of the book culture, the linear understanding of history, is typical of Vygotsky, as can be shown with one more example, namely Vygotsky's (1994) essay "The Socialist Alteration of Man." Vygotsky distinguished between "primitive man" and "modern type" of man, describing a transition to the formation of a new type of human being in communist society. According to Vygotsky, the transformation would finally be realized by mastering not only psychic processes but all functions determined by human nature, and so finally by learning to consciously restructure even the "biological organization" of man. The linearity of thinking is obvious. What is changing is the form of behavior from direct to mediated, and the volume of conscious behavior from mastering the psychic to even mastering the physical processes. All this was seen as an effect of mediational means that would remain equal. Their form was irrelevant; only their function was important.

Vygotsky's theoretical framework assumes book culture and printing to be leading media. In this respect, we can describe this model of mediation as essentially unhistorical. At any rate, because of its dependence on the old leading medium, it can hardly serve as an adequate instrument for grasping the emerging new leading medium and for conceptualizing modern intervention strategies.

LEONT'EV'S SOLUTION OF THE MEDIATION PROBLEM

For Leont'ev, the problem of mediation was not sufficiently solved by Vygotsky. He clearly followed Vygotsky in supposing that the mediatedness of the relationship of humans with the world marks the peculiarity of being human. He also accepted the mediating function of signs;

> The sign mediates the consciousness, because the sign has meaning.... *Sign is what matters.* (Leont'ev, 2005, p. 451)

On the other hand, Leont'ev criticized Vygotsky – very early indeed – for taking signs and meanings as means of mediation that could not be questioned. Leont'ev's argument was that as long as the origins of signs and meanings cannot be explained, their emergence and function remain restricted to the social, more precisely linguistic, communication:

> Consciousness is a product of linguistic, actually of mental interaction. (Leont'ev, 2005, p. 457)
>
> The social mind [determines] the personal and the personal mind determines the social. (Leont'ev, 2005, p. 325)

This means, according to Leont'ev, that Vygotsky's solution to the problem of mediation ends in circular reasoning, much as in "the classical circle of French sociologism" (Leont'ev, 2005, p. 459):

The society influences the human being, and the human influences the society. (Leont'ev, 2005, p. 325)

According to Leont'ev (2005, p. 459), this conclusion meant for psychology "an affirmation of exactly that *cultural*-historical theory" that would be indefensible from the point of view of historical and philosophical materialism:

The history of consciousness joins only with the history of the societal mind, not with the material history of society, only cultural-historical facts prove to be determinant. (Leont'ev, 2005, p. 459)

Leont'ev preferred an alternative solution. Instead of sticking to linguistic interaction as the only mediating entity and thus considering the word a "demiurg" of consciousness, he suggested inquiring into "what stands behind interaction" (Leont'ev, 2005, p. 325). "Behind" the linguistic communication stands only the material activity itself (p. 247):

Vygotsky's thesis that consciousness is a product of the child's linguistic communication on the condition of his or her activity in relation to the surrounding objective reality, thus has to be reversed: The child's consciousness is a product of his or her human activity in relation to the objective reality, which takes place on the condition of speech, of linguistic communication. (Leont'ev, 2001, p. 304)

Leont'ev's experiments in Char'kov led to the conclusion that the appropriation of a meaning resulted not from communication but originally from the child's external activity with material objects in cooperative interaction. Thus, Leont'ev replaced the formula subject–sign–object with the formula subject–activity–object. This had consequences. The object now appeared twice: first, as a thing and then as a mediational means of activity. The tool concept lost its special Vygotskian function for four reasons:

1. Human activity is object oriented from the beginning. "The expression 'objectless activity' is devoid of any meaning" (Leont'ev, 1978, p. 52).
2. The mediating object appears either as a tool or as a goal or a motive of activity, according to its status within the system of an activity. "Objects themselves can become stimuli, goals, or tools only

in a system of human activity; deprived of connections within this system they lose their existence as stimuli, goals, or tools" (Leont'ev, 1978, p. 67).

3. The nature of tools is not psychic. "Obviously, a tool is a material object in which are crystallized methods and operations, not actions or goals" (Leont'ev, 1978, p. 65). This is true of all human tools; they are objectifications of operations.

4. Consciousness "is not the only existing, only possible, only imaginable form of psychic reflection" (Leont'ev, 2005, p. 443). Every human activity is mediated by psychic reflection, that is, by internal activity that has the same structure as external activity. Therefore, the "activity that is internal in its form, originating from external practical activity," cannot be separated from the latter "but continues to preserve an essential, twofold connection with it" (Leont'ev, 1978, pp. 61–62).

Tracing mediating reflection back to material activity and genetically explaining reflection by activity itself rendered superfluous the immediate internalization of mediational means by communication and thus avoided the intellectualization Leont'ev saw in Vygotsky's work. But this caused a new form of immediacy between activity and consciousness. Leont'ev (1981) solved this problem with the help of his strict historical analysis in *Problems of the Development of the Mind*. The central outcome of this book, with respect to our problem, is the difference between "reflection *within* activity" and "reflection *as* activity" (for a logical-systematic reconstruction of Leont'ev's theory, see Messmann & Rückriem, 1978, pp. 80–133):

> The animal's activity, that links it *in practice* with objective reality, is understandably basic in this complex unity of reflection and activity; psychic reflection ... is secondary and derivative. (Leont'ev, 1981, p. 160)

On the basis of this assumption, Leont'ev formulated his own "basic law" of practical activity hurrying ahead and reflection lagging behind:

> The evolution of animals' reflection of their environment ... , as it were, lags behind the evolution of their activity. ... The development of the form of psychic reflection is thus ... a step downward shifted in relation to the evolution of the structure of the animals' activity, so that there is never a direct correspondence between them (Leont'ev, 1981, pp. 195–196).

He, of course, then faced the same problem as that already pointed out in Vygotsky's case: the exigency of a philosophical foundation for his assumptions. In an unpublished manuscript, Leont'ev explicated his understanding of Vygotsky's claim for a psychological materialism:

> The philosophical issue of consciousness has to be distinguished from:
>
> A. the issue of societal consciousness and
> B. the issue of the consciousness of societal man.
>
> The first is the subject of analysis of the historical sciences, of historical materialism. The second is the subject of psychology. (Leont'ev, 2005, p. 443)

And once more he repeats:

> This means: The theory of consciousness is necessarily a subject of psychology, but by no means does it and may it coincide with the theory of consciousness of diamat [dialectical materialism] or histomat [historical materialism]. To substitute psychological, that is, concrete scientific assumptions on consciousness by epistemological assumptions or by assumptions of historical materialism is grossly erroneous (Leont'ev, 2005, p. 444)

But Leont'ev held that psychology could achieve its scientific assumptions *within the framework* of historical materialism only, because it was the only way to argue for activity as an explanatory principle.

In reconstructing the genesis of consciousness, Leont'ev resorted to speech and, in attempting to explain the emergence of speech, harked back to gesture and "kinetic speech." He treated both as independent media that are not identical with labor (Leont'ev, 2005, pp. 241, 251, 263) and actually develop side by side in coevolution. However, monism forced him to deny this idea and to eventually subordinate gesture and speech to labor. Even though he occasionally conceded that "the appearance of phonetic language was a revolution" (Leont'ev, 2005, pp. 475, 481) and that written speech "together with book printing" transformed into one of the most important, even "predominant form[s] of human speech" and thus into "a capacious creative power" (Leont'ev, 2005, p. 481), such appreciation remained accidental in the end. Thus, Leont'ev only indirectly affirmed Giesecke's argument:

> Modern book cultures tied "intrinsic," "true" information to human consciousness and gave to linguistic-conceptual knowledge a virtually absolute power over other, "inferior" forms of information. (Giesecke, 2002, p. 78)

Leont'ev (2001) focused on a "general psychology" only, which in itself had no need for a historical observation of itself. In describing the history of the psyche he therefore inevitably switched to the method of historical materialism, in other words, to a stance that regards activity and labor as identical. His periods of historical structures of consciousness match the well-known periodization of societal labor. The phase of "primitive, integrated" consciousness (Leont'ev, 1981, p. 245), not yet separated into external and internal or practical and mental activity (manual and mental labor), was followed by the phase of "disintegrated," that is, class, consciousness, characterized by alienation of personal sense from societal meaning, and finally by the phase of "reintegration" with its new relation between sense and meaning and with "a new psychological structure of consciousness" (Leont'ev, 1981, p. 268), caused by the liberation of human labor through communist society. But, according to Leont'ev, "class consciousness" is "*societal* consciousness" and thus is explicitly the subject of historical materialism, *not* of psychology. The reception of Leont'ev's work up to now systematically ignores the fact that, according to Leont'ev, activity and labor are not identical, and all categories of general psychology – activity, action, operation or motive, goal, condition or sense, and meaning– cannot be grouped together with, deduced from, or replaced by the categories of historical materialism or even the concepts of political economy:

> Due to the existing relations between these sciences, which reflect the objective relations between their objects, such a substitution would make the psychology of consciousness not only lacking in substance [meaningless], but would restrict the potential for a further full development of the other sciences of consciousness. (Leont'ev, 2005, pp. 444–445)

Nevertheless, since Yudin's essential and useful distinction between activity as an object and as a principle of explanation (Judin, 1984; Yudin, 1978), which has been grotesquely misunderstood by Kozulin (1986) and taken as a fundamental methodological criticism, it has been rather common to argue that Leont'ev's psychology and activity theory are one and the same. Actually that is by no means correct, and Yudin's distinction is very helpful in making that clear. Indeed, the object of *psychology* is, according to Leont'ev, activity. But that can be legitimized only within the framework of a *philosophy*, using activity as an explanatory principle. This is exactly Vygotsky's "psychological materialism" (Vygotsky, 1997a, p. 331;

see also Keiler, 2002) as a philosophy or worldview, as Leont'ev expresses in an unmistakably clear way in his famous letter to Vygotsky:

> Today the developmental logic of the system of C[ultural] P[sychology] makes it necessary to focus on the issue of philosophical understanding of its basic concepts and principles (Divergence between the actual content of analysis and the level of development [degree of understanding] of its philos[ophical] foundations, of its underlying world view. . . .)
>
> This task ... cannot be accomplished by adapting the C[ultural] P[sychology] to the "standard", in other words, it may not be *mechanically* squeezed into this or that philos[ophical] context. – It is by itself a *philosophical* system (a *psychological philosophy!* – a world view!). (Leont'ev, 2005, p. 224; emphases in original)

In sum, Leont'ev, too, did not get beyond the limits of the leading medium. He remained – at least in his works before 1960 – within the boundaries of the book-printing medium.

LEONT'EV'S APPROACH TO INFORMATION TECHNOLOGY

In his first publications about the psychological meaning of automatically controlled machines, Leont'ev came to a point of view that even at the time was much more open to digitalization than are the arguments of many contemporary scholars (Leont'ev & Panov, 1963). Above all, in his assessment of the psychological consequences, he freed himself of all restrictions of historical materialism and focused exclusively on the psychological components of activity and the possibility of their technical modeling.

According to Leont'ev, tools are externalized operations. This understanding lends the tool a conceptual extension far beyond Vygotsky's idea. On the one hand, to Leont'ev even computers are "just a technical means, ... a method to realize the productive activity" or " 'algorithmized' and 'automatized' actions." On the other hand, he considers computers to be "objectified *human functions*" (Leont'ev, 1964, p. 17). In operations "only those interrelations of the action structure have been retained and fused which replicate the objective relations of the objective conditions of their accomplishment" and therefore "as such can be uncoupled from man." Thus, "the forming of operations, metaphorically speaking, equals the death of formerly inventive actions" (Leont'ev, 1964, p. 18). In other words, such actions may in principle be modeled technically. So Leont'ev did not balk at the then-revolutionary consequence that today remains frightening to many of his colleagues:

> What today appears to human thinking as a not-to-be-formalized creative action could tomorrow already be changed into an operation. Thus, there are no limits to the development of always "smarter" machines. (Leont'ev, 1964, p, 19)

Hence, according to Leont'ev, all existing barriers to the technical modeling of actions are temporary. When he was asked to assess the limits of capability of computers, he always spoke of "presently *really existing* automatic machines" (Leont'ev, 1964, p. 5) whose "actual success ... lies ahead in the near future" (Leont'ev, 1964, p. 7; see also 1966, pp. 36–43; 1968, pp. 36–322; 1970, pp. 3–12; 1977, pp. 172–181; Leont'ev & Lomov, 1963, pp. 29–37).

Surprisingly, Leont'ev had already in the 1960s enunciated the idea that is customarily associated with McLuhan, namely that man by means of tools "by which labor is carried out, generates in a way new organs," which "he adds to the vital organs of his body" and thus overcomes "the biological idleness of his natural organs, powers and abilities" (Leont'ev, 1964, pp. 10–11). Very much like McLuhan in his comment on the socialization process of people by media, Leont'ev writes:

> While learning to use tools man subordinates his motions to the societally evolved system of operations, which is materially ingrained in them. The tool changes the behavior of people, it builds new abilities in them. (Leont'ev, 1964, p. 11)
>
> What machines contribute to human activity by their work at the same time gives rise to the emergence of new abilities of man – of new functional systems of his brain, which appear like the 'mobile physiological organs' (Uhtomski) of those abilities. (Leont'ev, 1964, p. 19)

Leont'ev obviously supposed that with machines – seen as technically modeled former human operations – quasi-human "organs" are built and located on the outside – much as the brain today no longer serves the function of information storage to the extent that it used to because we can relocate our memory in a computer. Although Leont'ev viewed the state of affairs of the digitalization development rather skeptically, he anticipated the technical modeling even of brain functions, which today is available to anyone who has an Internet account and adequate media skills. Software developments of Web 2.0, such as social bookmarking and socially interactive memory stores, combine the memories of people concerning a special class of objects and make the combination available to everybody, much like a collective brain.

This characterizes, although only in general and implicitly, the basic dependence of consciousness as a totality of human potentialities on the actual social-historical system of human "tools." Even though the explicit concept of "medium" is still missing, Leont'ev's approach to computerization provides us with nothing less than a compatible and extremely important interface with actual media theory and media history, respectively, despite the understandable lack of concrete ideas of qualitatively new human abilities coming from the new medium and of their effects on societal practice. This lack is understandable, inasmuch as these developments will actually be manifested first by the societally general acquisition of the operative potentials of Web 2.0.

BACK TO ENGESTRÖM

Engeström makes use of both Vygotsky's and Leont'ev's models of mediation – more, however, of Vygotsky's than Leont'ev's. He does include in his theorizing some basic concepts of Leont'ev's activity theory, but neglects Leont'ev's distinction between psychology and historical materialism and the difference between the societal and the social nature of activity. Because of his special focus on collective activity systems, he identifies activity and labor – the latter being for him "the mother form of all human activity" (Engeström, 1987, p. 66) – and includes the categories of Marx's political economy – production, consumption, and distribution – as components of his psychologically oriented structural scheme of collective activity (Engeström, 1987, p. 78). In consequence, the contradiction between use value and exchange value, concepts of Marx's political economy, seems to be more fundamental to Engeström than is Leont'ev's psychological contradiction of societal meaning and personal sense.

Engeström seems to fail to take notice of Leont'ev's explicitly repeated emphasis on the strictly systemic nature of the components of individual activity. Instead, he stresses their hierarchical structure and so turns them into an ontological understanding. The psychological meaning of central concepts such as "subject" and "intentionality" inevitably slips into a sociological understanding of activity. The same happens with the concepts of "tool," as well as with "instrumentality," understood as a system that includes multiple cognitive artifacts and semiotic means that form a dense mediational setting. There is no theoretical understanding of why and how this complexity has been formed as an independent system and got to be more than an augmentation of the same.

Engeström, like Vygotsky and Leont'ev, comes rather close and much closer than many other activity theorists to a media-theoretical and media-historical understanding. But refraining from taking "the last step" he – like his predecessors – runs into problems with history. Vygotsky and Leont'ev referred to cultural tools as a specific repertoire and considered this as a whole. They both failed to conceptualize this wholeness as a consequence of a specific historical medium. Although they clearly saw that what Vygotsky called higher psychological functions depend on the existence of school as a societal medium, they did not understand that "low" and "high" or "primitive" and "advanced" are nothing but assessments based on the ontological generalization of a given historical medium. Although Leont'ev sometimes admitted the relative independence of speech from practical activity (Leont'ev, 2005, pp. 334–335), the consequences of this admission remained undiscussed.

In terms of political theory, it is ideological thinking to consider one's own way of thinking the only truly human way. In terms of media history, the equivalent is perpetuating and imposing an old medium on new phenomena. Engeström steers clear of that problem, but only by avoiding the periodization of societal formations in principle. To him historicity seems to be just the trajectory of developmental expansive cycles of activity systems (Engeström, 2005a, p. 32). But since he cannot acknowledge digitalization as a medium of societal transformation, the argument of societal transformation does not even exist as an idea. So Engeström is forced to consider the existing societal formation as the only possible one. At any rate, there is no discussion of the consequences of Web 2.0 as societally relevant changes, such as "crowd-sourcing" or the consumer as producer, the customer as distributor, the client as co-developer, and so on, which are widely discussed as ongoing processes of a revolutionary transformation, although, of course, not always in the sense of political economy or historical materialism.

To understand the limitations and differences of Vygotsky and Leont'ev concerning the problem of mediation – which are taken up again by Engeström himself and by his "third generation of activity theory" – it seems appropriate to argue that each generation of activity theory has thus far moved within a closed space of thinking that is finally based on the same fundamental problem of mediation, whose origin is historically far beyond the activity theory of the 20th century. This historical constellation fixed a boundary on the perception of the evolution of media, a boundary that restricts the attempts of modern activity theory to gain dependence and to re-adapt its methodology.

CONCLUSION

Activity theory in its basic structure depends on book culture but does not notice this dependency because of its lack of adequate instruments. During the ongoing transformation processes, we are still forced to stick to the epistemological and theoretical structures of book culture: "Such an anachronism is rather unavoidable" (Giesecke, 2002, p. 301). Following the period of "multivoicedness" of activity theory, we are entering a new phase. What we need now is a boundary crossing between activity theory, systems theory, and media theory. Activity theory should not stay in its closed space of thinking and only look "through the window" (Engeström, 2005a, p. 59) at the societal transformations taking place outside it. Activity theory should leave behind the conditions of that bygone or at least passing cultural historical formation and reformulate itself.

Clearly, Vygotsky could not be expected to have considered this issue, nor possibly did Leont'ev, given the ideological circumstances. But living activity theorists should very well be able to do so. If they don't want to lose touch not only with the ongoing societal transformation but with scientific research and theoretical developments, they ought to do so.

My conclusion therefore is short: To create a developmental strategy that is able to analyze and support transformation processes between the old and the new leading medium, I propose that instead of asking only, "When is a tool?" (Engeström, 1990, p. 171), we should ask, "Tool or medium?"

7

Contextualizing Social Dilemmas in Institutional Practices: Negotiating Objects of Activity in Labor Market Organizations

ÅSA MÄKITALO AND ROGER SÄLJÖ

In sociocultural and activity-theoretical perspectives, institutions are understood as communities of practice with intermediary functions; they regulate and handle conflicts and dilemmas between individuals and collectives in society. How institutional actors deal with such dilemmas, and what consequences their activities will have for the collective as well as for individuals, are important issues to explore (Engeström, 2005a; Engeström & Toivianen, in press). Through their rules and practices, institutions act as arbiters of opportunity, making decisions about how certain situations are to be interpreted in an ambiguous world of complex social activities (Mäkitalo & Säljö, 2002a). One interesting feature of such communities is how they accommodate the emergence of tensions and conflicts that challenge the institutional order and established practices. In this chapter we primarily address the notion of community in this sense, with a focus on how institutional agency is constituted at the local level.

A historically significant conflict in society is that between labor and capital. Many of the institutions that are responsible for health care, social welfare, or taxation, for instance, directly or indirectly intervene in such matters when making decisions as to whether individuals and groups are entitled to certain benefits. In times of societal transformation and changes in production, tensions may emerge in the labor market concerning the obligations and entitlements of workers and employers. During such periods of transformation, institutions have to respond to new challenges coming from the outside. The dramatic increase of reported illness, which

---

This research was funded by the Swedish Research Council. The authors are members of the Linnaeus Centre for Research on Learning, Interaction and Mediated Communication in Contemporary Society (LinCS).

in Sweden and other countries has been a matter of public debate over the past decades, represents one such challenge. In the following, we will analyze the local discussion of this dilemma and the discursive formation of it as it enters two institutional settings responsible for taking action. The two communities we followed represent the parties in the labor market: trade unions and employers, respectively.

Analytically, we will address the question of how a complex, highly contested social dilemma (Billig, 1996) is *locally constituted as an object of institutional activity,* that is, how it becomes part of an institutional order (Smith, 2005), which has no ready-made strategy for dealing with it. When a dilemma that is new to an institution arises, discursive work by the participants is necessary. The issue has to be negotiated and strategies articulated in order for it to become manageable and "fit into" established patterns of discourse and institutional accountability (Hall, Slembrouck, & Sarangi, 2006). The challenge, as we will show in the following, concerns how institutionally established categories and ways of arguing need to be reconsidered and transformed into new strategies and activities. In such processes, what Engeström (2007c) refers to as "stabilization knowledge" has to play a role, but there is also a need for "possibility knowledge" that can serve as an element of conceiving viable future strategies. In the following, we will give a brief introduction to the social dilemma addressed in our empirical study.

BURNOUT, STRESS, AND LONG-TERM SICK LEAVES: ACCOUNTING FOR A SOCIAL DILEMMA

"Burnout" and various kinds of "fatigue syndromes" have caused concern in the public debate. Such metaphors are commonly used by people sharing experiences in everyday life, in self-help groups, and in patient organizations (Bülow, 2004). In scientific discussions, however, where a more critical attitude to language is expected, there have been intense debates over the question of whether or not these conditions qualify as "real" ailments. Thousands of studies of burnout in fields such as neurobiology, psychiatry, occupational medicine, psychology, and the history of ideas have been conducted, and about 130 symptoms and factors have been used to characterize the syndrome and to explain it. Schaufeli and Enzmann (1998, p. 12) conclude that "these factors are interrelated and do not operate independently from each other. In one way or another all the factors are aspects of a global economic, social and cultural transformation process that has affected society as a whole."

In scientific argumentation there is, it seems safe to say, no consensus about what constitutes burnout. Many even question its existence as an identifiable condition. Such argumentation about the essence of a matter is characteristic of what Billig (1996) refers to as a social dilemma. But, regardless of the essence, or whether burnout "really" exists or not, it does appear in the public debate, and in that sense it will have political, social, and material consequences. Institutions need to deal with burnout as a social fact; that is, they have to constitute it in discourse because it is of importance for their community. Politicians, health care staff, representatives of public and private health insurance agencies, employers, and trade unions are but a few of the stakeholders who encounter burnout as a practical and institutionally significant concern.

PUBLIC ATTENTION AND POLITICAL ACTION TO REDUCE LONG-TERM SICK LEAVES

The negative consequences of "burnout" for the individual, the workplace, and society as a whole have been publicly discussed since the mid-1980s in Sweden. Around the turn of the millennium, the debate reached a peak, and the issue emerged as a significant societal problem. The media frequently reported dramatic examples of people who "gick in i väggen" (literally, "walked into the wall"), who suffered from "extreme fatigue," "memory loss," "apathy," and similar symptoms. The consequences were also obvious from the statistics, which showed a rather dramatic increase in people on long-term sick leave. The political debate turned to the economic and social consequences of the problems of poor health in Swedish society. The government, and the minister of working life at the time, pointed to the workplace as having a central role in attempts to reduce these kinds of health problems. Consequently, the issue of the increase in long-term sick leaves was framed as a problem of the organization of work, and it was argued that it needed to be handled primarily by the parties of the labor market:

> Regardless the cause of a sick leave, it is from work you are on sick leave, and it is to work you are returning. (Minister's speech at the Social Insurance Assembly in 2004)

In the government's strategy, two issues were pointed out as significant:

1. Measures to *prevent* health problems in working life
2. Measures to create possibilities for those on sick leave to *return to* work

Resources were directed to union representatives responsible for safety and health issues and to projects at the regional level promoting health at the workplace. Employers, on the other hand, were obliged to account for sick leaves in their annual financial reports and to take on greater economic responsibility for people on sick leave. This should provide visibility to the problem and incentives for efficient action. Employers were also obliged to conduct a rehabilitation inquiry for every person on sick leave and to attend so-called check meetings in which the employee, the health insurance officer, and the physician who signed the sick leave certificate participated.

In the following, we will analyze how this particular dilemma is picked up locally and how the actors, when attempting to meet these political expectations, constitute it as an object of activity. We have observed discussions in two settings:

1. A trade union initiative launching a mentor project to deal with this issue
2. Representatives of employers from three companies engaged in a joint project to prevent poor health

Our analysis has thus focused on how institutional categories (Mäkitalo & Säljö, 2002b) are used in defining the dilemma in institutional terms, and whether existing categories are transformed to accommodate the tensions and challenges at the local level. Our questions can be formulated as follows:

1. What terms and thematic patterns are used in discussing the dilemma generally?
2. What institutional categories become productive in dealing with the dilemma locally?
3. What rhetorical tools are used in constituting the issue in locally relevant terms?

INCREASES IN POOR HEALTH: ENCOUNTERING THE DILEMMA IN LABOR MARKET ORGANIZATIONS

Initially, the discussion in both communities focused on understanding the increase in sick leave and the causes of this development. It incorporated a moral dimension of who was to blame and who should be held responsible. In neither community did such discussions result in any consensus. The participants seemingly passed from one argumentative premise and position, and from one thematic pattern (Lemke, 1990), to another without noticing such shifts in how they discussed the issue. Their attempts to find a cause of the problem always ended up in cul-de-sacs. Participants often ended the discussion in resignation, with a collective sigh and a general comment to the effect that "that's what the world is like."

However, since the actors at this local level were concretely responsible for dealing with the issue and knew they were accountable for taking action, they sooner or later needed to address the immediate problems of how to handle sick leaves and sick leave compensation, how to organize rehabilitation programs, and so on. Such discussions were couched in terms of how the actors were to respond rhetorically to the concerns of important stakeholders to whom they were accountable within as well as outside their own community. In the following we will give examples of how this discursive work unfolded in the two settings.

CATEGORIZING LONG-TERM SICK LEAVE IN TRADE UNION DISCOURSE

In the trade union discussions we documented, local, regional, and central representatives participated. The regional and central representatives have administrative roles and are responsible for the strategic work of the union. They started a mentorship program with the explicit aim of decreasing the number of people on long-term sick leave. They were also in charge of the meetings. In the mentorship program, the local representatives were encouraged to actively involve politicians, employers, and employees in their area in a common effort to do something. The local representatives are employed by the municipalities and work part time for the union. They are the representatives to whom members normally turn when contacting the union. The data used in the following were gathered on two different occasions. The first was a meeting about two months into the program. The second was a two-day conference, where the work during past months was discussed alongside questions of how to continue.

The talk within the institutional frames of the labor union is from the beginning characterized by discussions about responsibilities, and it is carried out largely in moral and ethical terms. The discussion addresses their duties as union representatives and how far their responsibilities and concerns should extend in relation to members. The core problem is articulated and dealt with by means of a distinction between the institutional categories of what should be classified as "work-related" and "non-work-related" problems, respectively. This difference can be viewed as a tension in the system, in the sense that it is very difficult to be clear-cut about this point. Are non-work-related health problems something the union and the employers should assume responsibility for? And there is, of course, also the intriguing issue of how one decides whether a health problem is work related or not in a specific case.

In this first example,[1] we show how the necessity for action is formulated by trade union representatives in terms of their responsibilities vis-à-vis members. The natural focus for trade unions in any kind of discussion is the well-being of members. It is their best interest that is the raison d'être of union work. But the limitations of the union's responsibilities toward members also have to be handled. After all, a labor union has its primary source of legitimacy in issues that concern the workplace, and it cannot assume responsibility for all spheres of the lives of members. Deciding exactly how to draw the line when discussing a dilemma of this kind is difficult. As we enter the conversation, one representative (Karl) has just told a story about a situation in which he faced a member threatening to commit suicide. The example serves as an illustration of the problems of deciding how far the responsibilities of the union should extend.

EXCERPT 1

320. RITA: you're on to something important here ( ) that not everything *is* work related ( ) and ( ) it may sound a bit harsh ( ) but sometimes we have to learn to limit our areas of responsibility ( ) I mean when to take action and what we actually can do something about ( ) it's also important to be able to support members and that's what I mean. It can be difficult to meet them when they threaten to take their lives ( ) and it might be for completely different reasons than those connected to work ( ) how do we talk to them? I think <u>everyone</u> ( ) at least among us in the Southern District will discuss this.

---

[1] Transcript legend:

(( )) Comments on nonverbal contributions, clarifications, and other interpolations
( ) Untimed audible pause
(1.5 sec) Timed pause
, Continuing intonation
? Question intonation
Underline emphasis
– Cut-off sound, interruption
Italics within quote marks Enacted speech

Rita, regional representative of a district, uses the distinction between work-related and non-work-related causes for sick leave to frame the discussion. She brings up the core question of their responsibilities toward members as union representatives. In this discursive work, the issue of how to categorize sick leave cases is central, and the distinction is introduced as an indirect suggestion to help define a limit to their responsibility in relation to members. Setting boundaries is a sensitive matter for a number of reasons. For instance, at the workplace Rita and the other participants in this discussion are both colleagues and union representatives of their members. So how do they handle this?

EXCERPT 2

322. ULF:	yeah I sort of agree with you but I can also feel the way Karl expressed it when I start to think about our task ( ) how far do our responsibilities extend? and I think it's important with guidance in terms of *"this is what you're supposed to take care of –*
323. RITA:	m
324. ULF:	*but not this"*
325. RITA:	m
326. ULF:	*"take care of this but learn to say no, this is not –"* so it – it would be great if we could have this basic –
327. RITA:	well yeah I think you should be careful though in producing a manual but I also think this which I attempt – we attempt to do also concerns what attitude I have and how much of my person I engage in this ( ) that is which part of me as a professional – I do this professionally so to speak

Ulf continues discussing the problem (lines 322–326) in terms of what their responsibilities include, that is, how much they should engage in members' problems. His argument is also an uptake of an earlier discussion initiated by Karl about the need for professional advisers. Ulf frames his statement as a wish for such advisers to set the limits on their responsibilities. What he is saying is that they need to learn how and when to say no to requests. This, in our terms, concerns the concrete question of how to categorize cases of long-term sick leaves. Rita does not believe in the usefulness of a written manual (line 327). Instead she refers to the decision of creating such definitions of the responsibilities for trade union representatives as an issue of professionalism. From an analytical perspective, this discussion illustrates tensions in the constitution of the object of activity.

The difficulties of formulating the task and deciding what falls inside or outside the local responsibility can be seen in the light of another significant party and adversary absent from the discussion. The voice of this other party, the employers, must be anticipated by the union representatives in their strategic formulations for future action (Bakhtin, Holquist, & Emerson, 1986; Billig, 1996). Arguing for, or against, a certain contested issue is a dialectic process that presumes at least one defined "other" (Smith, 2005). For the union representatives, defining their task only in relation to union members is insufficient. To position themselves discursively as union representatives in this situation, the issue needs to be related to the third party in the ongoing debate about the dilemma of long-term sick leave.

DEVELOPING A STRATEGY: ANTICIPATING EMPLOYERS' ARGUMENTS

The categorization of long-term sick leaves into work-related and non-work-related leaves, respectively, is also used as a resource for framing the next piece of interaction. In the preceding excerpt, the participants focused their attention only on dilemmas they faced in relation to members. The next excerpt shows how the mediating role of union work, by necessity, also involves another party, the employers. As we shall see, the anticipation of the employers' arguments provides a framework for distinguishing the premises for and principles of the union more clearly.

EXCERPT 3

338. BENGT: regarding the issue of what's work related and non-work related ( ) it seems the employer wants to do less and less about what's <u>not</u> work related but they still as far as I know have the responsibility for rehabilitation ( ) so where is our boundary then?

339. RITA: m

340. BENGT: I mean the member, the individual, is just an individual in need of support in general I mean (3 sec) <u>can</u> we draw a line ( ) where we're fellow beings? (3 sec)

342. URBAN: you seriously don't mean that if you hear someone has broken a leg we're supposed to say *"– we don't care about you,"* we still need to be of help that's what <u>I</u> think, but to answer your question

343. BENGT: yeah

344. URBAN: it can be equally difficult for <u>that</u> individual to come back
                 to work as it is for someone who ( ) you don't mean, if I
                 understand you, that we should ignore you just because you
                 didn't break your leg at work ( ) but <u>that's</u> how the employer
                 argues in their runthrough with the health insurance office
                 ( ) at every work site they find out <u>just</u> whether it is caused
                 by work or not, and it just sounds in a way like ( ) if it doesn't
                 depend on work ( ) we don't have to care

345. RITA: m

346. URBAN: but ( ) in our municipality ( ) we have our policy to inform
                 the individual when there's a rehab meeting that the
                 union participates in ( ) so we have turned this around so
                 to speak, now you have to make clear from the beginning
                 if you don't want your union representative present.

Again, we can see how the distinction between work-related and non-work-related sick leave is used as a resource to frame the discussion about how far the responsibilities of the union extend. Bengt (line 338) for the first time points to the employers' use of the distinction, and he wonders where the "boundary" is to be drawn by the union. When suggesting that employers do not take full responsibility, Bengt implies that the union needs to engage regardless of the distinction and whether a sick leave period is work related or not.

By pointing to the fact that the employers are accountable for rehabilitation, the question of what task they as union representatives have is brought to their attention (line 338). Without some kind of working definition of the problem, or where the problem lies, there is no way to articulate strategies for future action. When the claim is made that the employers do not take full responsibility, the positioning and the arguments of the employers are invoked in their own discussion of responsibilities. As Urban engages in the discussion, he articulates how the employers usually argue (line 344). At this point it suddenly becomes obvious to the participants that the distinction they have been using up to this point really serves the interests of the employers rather than the interests of their members. This is a turning point in the discussion. The distinction they have been using to talk about limiting their responsibilities toward their members is no longer seen to be valid. Rather, they need to take the opposite stance.

Urban now emphasizes his claim about the employers' arguments and lack of responsibility for individuals, by giving an example from his professional experience (line 344). Bengt and Urban claim that the members must be considered to be in need of support irrespective of the causes of their difficulties. In continuing to characterize the employers as untrustworthy in this matter, Urban describes how the local union in his municipality decided on new procedures for the rehabilitation meetings to confront such challenges (lines 346). This strategy implies that the member (often in a poor condition and in a vulnerable position) does not have to actively ask for support from the union during rehabilitation meetings. As the trade unions were not included as an obligatory party in such meetings, their presence was dependent on their members actively asking them to join. With the union representative present at every meeting of the rehabilitation group, the interests of the member will be looked after.

By discussing the dilemma in relation to another party, the union representatives found a way of articulating their strategies and accountability. The trade union, in this case, noticed that a task and responsibility have been given to employers by the government. Their strategy was to engage in this activity to actively support their members in the particular institutional setting where important decisions are made.

ACCOUNTING FOR LONG-TERM SICK LEAVE: EMPLOYERS' DISCURSIVE WORK

In the following we will address a discussion of the same dilemma among employers' representatives from three large Swedish companies. The common project they engaged in, referred to as the Health Company, was launched for the purpose of reducing the number of stress-related ailments at work. The transcripts used in the following are from a group discussion at a conference arranged in June 2004. We will first provide a sample of the employers' conversations regarding the responsibility for government-sponsored rehabilitation of employees whose illness is long term. We do so to demonstrate the relation of these opposing stances, which, though different, are both couched in terms of moral accountability. It is clear in the employers' discussions that they mediate the concerns of several stakeholders: the owners (shareholders) of their companies as well their employees.

378. KRISTER: maybe this group shouldn't work as much, maybe this is about the way of looking at how efficient or capable you need to be in order to be regarded as healthy and fit for work ( ) to even get a chance

379. LARS: mm but no one argues like you in this society, that kind of reasoning doesn't exist

380. MANY: no

– – – – –

403. KRISTER: this is also a question of values ( ) to be able to <u>not</u> work a
                 hundred per cent and that would still be okay
404. MARIA: yes that's how one should argue in some kind of humane
                 terms, but there's a catch in this ( ) and it's business
405. KRISTER: mm
406. MARIA: companies need to show results and that's when it really
                 becomes – so very short-sighted, we have to take a long
                 term view on this work
407. KRISTER: mm
408. MARIA: that's why Ingvar Kamprad ((the founder of IKEA))
                 never listed his company on the stock exchange, 'cause
                 you can't work long term, but we can't really question
                 that can we?
409. MANY: no ((laughs))
410. MARIA: we can sit here on our humanistic horses but there is a
                 harsh economy ruling it all
411. KRISTER: but long term sick leaves are also costly
412. MARIA: yeah so then we're back to the calculations
. . . .
438. MARIA: we mustn't forget that the individuals who are sick
                 are not just bad people. Our problem is that our <u>best</u>
                 employees are the ones who suffer from psychosocial ill-
                 ness, those are the ones at risk and we really want them
                 to stay with us ( ) they are psychologically exhausted but
                 we don't want to get rid of them, we need to see the signs
                 at an early stage
439. MANY: yes absolutely

As we can see, the employers do not disregard the problem and the need
for rehabilitation among employees on long-term sick leave. Krister, for
instance, argues that the problem perhaps lies not with the group of employees on long-term sick leave, but rather with what it takes to be regarded as
being fit for work (lines 378 and 403). Lars, however, points to the fact they
must be able to address other stakeholders through their argumentation,
implying that no one would respond to such an argument (line 379). Maria
then distinguishes what is reasonable in terms of human values from what
is reasonable in terms of "a harsh economy ruling it all" (line 404). In this
manner, two thematic patterns that rely on different premises are brought
into the deliberations. Maria addresses the issue of being accountable to
stakeholders (shareholders and potential investors), who have a decisive
influence on their activities. In making both of these lines of reasoning relevant, she uses the distinction between a short-term and a long-term view

(lines 406 and 408) to differentiate between them. It is in this mediating role that they have to find a strategy for dealing with the new dilemma. Their increased responsibility for rehabilitation will create strains on the productivity of their companies, and the results of their actions will have to be accounted for in their annual financial reports.

DEVELOPING A STRATEGY: ARGUING
THROUGH CALCULATIONS

The employers, just like the union representatives, have to transform their general discussions into manageable, concrete decisions. As they do this, a major challenge is to succeed in addressing and convincing their organizations of the measures that have to be taken. Early in the discussion, one of the participants talks about this issue in reference to the subtitle of their recent report:

> 221. KRISTER: the report we just received, I don't know who came up with the subtitle ((others laughing)) but as an old mathematician I like to think about what it actually says ( ) that productivity is inversely proportional to sick attendance ( ) the more people attend work while sick, the less productive the company will be ( ) so this is a way to argue to teach our organizations and employees

This way of reformulating the traditional argument, that sick *leaves* are costly and have a negative impact on productivity, as sick *attendance* is also costly and has a negative impact on productivity challenges the stabilization knowledge (Engeström, 2007c) and inspires the group to define their task. They still need to account for absence caused by illness in their annual reports, but the work they engage in locally is the task of producing possibility knowledge (Engeström, 2007c), that is, formulating strategies and arguments useful for promoting health. In order to gain support for this kind of argumentation in the company, they claim that models are needed:

> 306. KRISTER: it's for all the measures we take, 'cause it might be easy to say that we can see this person is feeling better, but what we gain in terms of money is very hard to show, I think we need to improve here, we need to find some useful models for doing that

The dilemma, as addressed locally among the employers, is clearly articulated by this utterance, and it is couched in economic terms. What the participants need to engage in is an old argumentative tradition, where the use of economic categories is a core vehicle (Hopwood & Miller, 1994). The institutional practice of accounting, and its generic language, is at the core of all companies, and it provides tools necessary for most economic activities. This is what gives it validity for the three companies. As these arguments are institutionalized, they can be used without further explanation, which also shows how well coordinated and aligned the participants are across the companies in their strategies of dealing with health accounting. We will show how this kind of argumentation unfolds:

259. MARIA: I think the issue of the annual health statement is really interesting

260. MANY: yes

261. MARIA: but here we go blank ( ) we talk about accounting but we're far behind in models of calculation

262. KRISTER: exactly

263. MARIA: we should be ahead instead, be able to calculate instead

264. MANY: ((expressions of agreement))

265. KRISTER: instead of accounting for illness we do health accounting

266. SOME: mm

267. KRISTER: didn't the company have a, what was it called? staff annual account ( ) it's actually a better word ( ) it was about the same they had it but it was removed, but I agree with you that it's too late, annual reports summarize the last year but we need signals earlier to be able to take action earlier

268. MARIA: it's important with annual reports, but we need to be able to show what we are doing now

269. MANY: exactly, yes

270. MARIA: a model of calculation with a forecast

Their argumentation in economic terms is twofold: It is something they may use retrospectively to account for their actions (line 268), but it may also serve as a strategic tool, prospectively, in arguing for new measures to be adopted within their organizations (lines 263, 268, and 270). As their priorities and concerns are articulated and agreed on at the general level (i.e., calculating for the future rather than just accounting for the past), there is a platform for the discussion to continue. They now move on to the concrete question of how such an argument could be rhetorically crafted, and here they provide examples:

276. LARS: what's it gonna be, if you put it in concrete form *"if we keep the level of absence due to illness two per cent lower the company will earn thirteen million crowns"*?

277. MARIA:	yeah, something like that
278. LARS:	to be able to <u>show</u> the organization
279. MANY:	yeah
280. LARS:	I usually say "*in the profit and loss account, salary costs are by far the largest entry ( ) but how much do we work on it? If we buy a machine or invest in a building, we scrutinize everything in detail, but how often do we look at the item which drives the company ahead?*" ( ) and then make up a calulation model as you propose?
281. KRISTER:	yeah
282. LARS:	'cause okay "*if we do this we will reduce our costs this much and it doesn't cost us as nearly as much*"
283. MANY:	exactly
284. LARS:	"*we actually reduce costs*"
285. KRISTER:	it's really to be able to say for instance that: "*– we save one of our co-workers from absence due to illness*" or "*– if we arrange a programme including thirty co-workers it's enough if just one of them doesn't get sick for us to profit from this project*" we need to find some ratios to use in everyday argumentation

As we can see, these examples of formulations address sick leaves in terms of the category of reducible costs (lines 280, 282, and 284) as well as in terms of what is gained (line 276) or saved (line 285). The arguments are rhetorically crafted in hypothetical and strategic terms ("if … then" formulations). By using the relevant institutional language, the participants try to signal to their organization that they know about the prerequisites of doing business, and the arguments are formulated to move the organization to action in relation to this critical issue.

CONCLUSION

In this chapter we address the issue of how an ambiguous, highly contested societal issue and dilemma is discursively transformed into objects of institutional activity by two main parties to the labor market (trade unions and employers). In responding to the government's policy, both of these communities had to assume a key role in handling the problem. The aim of our study has been to analyze the local discussion of this societal dilemma and the discursive formation of it, as it becomes a problem in local institutional settings. The issue had to be negotiated and strategies for future action were articulated in both settings. In order to achieve this, the participants had to make the dilemma "fit into" established patterns of discourse and institutional accountability (Hall et al., 2006). We have seen some thematic patterns at work in both discussions. However, the participants did not invoke scientific argumentation in discussing these health issues. Rather, the thematic patterns they used were of a sociological, economic, humanistic, and moral nature.

Trade union discourse was predominantly couched in moral and ethical terms. It concerned the obligation of trade union representatives to members, and how far their responsibilities should extend in relation to those members. Their traditional argumentation, where the categories of work-related and non-work-related illness constituted core elements, was transformed, and the articulation of a strategic position for future action was made possible as they addressed and anticipated the argumentation of the other party, the employers. In this sense, it was clearly in dialogue between people with opposing stances that this position was reached. The discourse of the employers was predominantly couched in humanistic and economic terms. The categories "accounting" versus "calculating" were effectively used as tools to shift the discussion into strategic terms, defining the task as one of developing models for calculation and forecast that would be useful as argumentative resources within the organization. Through the reverse argument that productivity is inversely proportional to sick attendance (rather than sick leave), their strategy became one of formulating arguments for developing relevant measures of health.

Institutional categories were in this sense used and attended to as powerful tools for future action. At the local level, such tools are not as fixed and ready-made for use as they may seem. As we have noticed, they can become discursive tools for change if they are used in novel, yet recognizable and accountable ways. As such they may have both constitutive and directive functions in defining objects of institutional practice. In both settings, the local transformation and articulation of the dilemma as an object of institutional activity clearly needed to take account of local needs, as well as institutional relevance and ways of arguing. As the interaction unfolded, the participants anticipated the response from the "other" when discussing what impact their arguments could have (Linell, 1998; Potter, 1996). This included anticipating attempts that would undermine their arguments on future occasions.

PART THREE

EXPANSIVE LEARNING AND DEVELOPMENT

8

The Concept of Development in Cultural-Historical Activity Theory: Vertical and Horizontal

MICHAEL COLE AND NATALIA GAJDAMASHKO

Throughout his career, Yrjö Engeström's work has been characterized by his ability to bridge theory and research originating in Russia with similar work from Western Europe and North America. In this regard, he has been prominent in Finland's historical role as a mediator between these differently organized and oriented competitors on the world stage.

In this chapter, as part of the celebration of Yrjö's career, we address the issue of theories of human development as one strategically promising site for East and West to learn from each other, to find their common origins, to evaluate their divergences, and to create understanding across the borders of Russia and Eastern European countries, on the one hand, and those dominated by the West, including Western Europe, on the other. This is a propitious time for such an effort because there has been an unprecedented flow of ideas in recent decades across the divides of former Cold War adversaries; this has provided new and promising opportunities to synthesize common understandings and to better locate fundamental issues where it appears that there are disagreements that need to be understood and, perhaps, resolved.

As vast as it is, the topic of human development cannot be given an exhaustive treatment in a single chapter, so we have decided to organize our discussion through an exploration of an issue that Engeström raises in his *Learning by Expanding* (1987) – the question of "purpose," or teleology, in development. That discussion will also bring us to related issues that Engeström (1996a) makes in his provocative article "Development as Breaking Away and Opening Up." That essay, framed as a challenge to Vygotsky and Piaget, discusses the ways in which development entails destruction of the old as part of the creation of the new, the relationship of individual development to changes in the environment, and the individual's relationship to that environment.

THE PROBLEM OF TELEOLOGY IN HUMAN DEVELOPMENT

In the context of a discussion about Vygotsky's concept of the zone of proximal development, Engeström (1987, pp. 171–172) quotes from an article by Peg Griffin and one of the present authors, then comments on the apparent lack of follow-through with respect to the point being made. We wrote:

> Adult wisdom does not provide a teleology for child development. Social organization and leading activities provide a gap within which the child can develop novel creative analysis. ... a Zo-ped is a dialogue between the child and his future; it is not a dialogue between the child and an adult's past. (Griffin & Cole, 1984, p. 62)

Engeström then commented:

> Inspiring as this conclusion is, it is difficult to avoid the impression that the authors themselves, not to mention other researchers, have only started to consider its implications. This is evident in the inconsistency between the conclusion cited above and Cole's formulations in other publications. An article in the recent fine volume edited by Wertsch (1985) is a case in point. Here, Cole speaks of the zone of proximal development exclusively in terms of "acquiring culture," never in terms of creating it. (1987, p. 171)

Engeström hit on a point of ambiguity that not only is in Cole's work, but also differentiates the cultural-historical theorizing of Vygotsky and his colleagues from that of many North Americans who use their ideas. To clarify the issues involved, it will be helpful to stop and consider more carefully the use of the term "teleology" in the quotation from Griffin and Cole in relationship to phylogeny, cultural history, and ontogeny as understood within the cultural-historical tradition.

The *Oxford English Dictionary* defines "teleology" as the "doctrine or study of ends or final causes, esp. as related to the evidences of design or purpose in *nature*" (our emphasis). One of the dictionary examples of a 19th-century use of the term is taken from an article by G. J. Romanes, a famous early scholar interested in animal behavior: "Teleology in this larger sense, or the doctrine that behind all the facts open to scientific enquiry ... there is 'Mind and Will' as the ultimate cause of all things ... does not fall within the scope of scientific method."

We have emphasized the term "nature" in the definition of teleology because we believe that although human immersion in culture is a natural phenomenon that should not be explained in terms of a supervening

Mind or Will (e.g., a supernatural agent), we also believe that questions of purpose, goals, functions, values, and so on are central to understanding the cultural medium that sustains human life and the crucial role that the cultural medium plays in development. Hence, we must distinguish between what has here (following Vygotsky) been termed the cultural and the natural if we are to untangle questions of teleology in human life.

Such an effort is very much a part of the cultural-historical tradition on which both we and Engeström draw. As Wertsch (1985) has emphasized, a basic assumption of the cultural-historical approach to human psychological processes is that it insists on the principled importance of studying behavior in the process of change on several different timescales: the history of the species (phylogeny), the cultural history of the social group (cultural history), the history of the experiences of each individual child (ontogeny), and the micro-history of events that are the immediate context of the child's life (microgenesis). It is also assumed that human beings occupy a species-specific ecological niche within nature – the artifact-saturated world that is the product of prior human activity, what Lotman (1988) referred to as the semiosphere and what cultural-historical psychologists refer to as culture (Cole, 1996; Zinchenko, 2006b).

With respect to phylogenesis, we take no exception to Romanes's prohibition of teleological explanation. Evolution is, to be sure, a process of the random creation of genetic variations, combined with the process of natural selection, "preservation of favourable variations and the rejection of injurious variations" (Darwin, 1859, p. 81) such that the favorable variations increase in frequency within the population in the next generation. To attribute a "higher purpose" to this process has no place in scientific explanation. However, the situation with respect to cultural variation is different in principle; it is Lamarckian, in the sense that the useful discoveries of one generation are passed directly to the next, a conclusion that follows ineluctably from the very definition of human culture (e.g., as the socially inherited body of past human accomplishments that serves as the resources for the current life of a social group ordinarily thought of as the inhabitants of a country or region: D'Andrade, 1996).

Rephrasing D'Andrade's generally accepted notion of culture indicates that it represents the species-specific environment of human life that is constituted of the accumulated *artifacts* of prior generations, extending back to the beginning of the species (Cole, 1996; Geertz, 1973; Ingold, 2000; Leont'ev, 1981; Luria, 1979; Sahlins, 1976). From the perspective shared by Engeström and ourselves, an artifact is an aspect of the material world that was incorporated into goal-directed human action at a prior time in such a manner that it facilitated achieving the person's goals or purposes in the given time and circumstances. It then survived into the present as the embodiment of a series of successful refinements in the course of subsequent goal-directed human actions.

An important consequence of artifact (cultural) mediation of human actions is that by virtue of the changes wrought in the process of their creation and use, artifacts are *simultaneously ideal (conceptual) and material,* and, of special importance to the present discussion, they are infused with human purposes, human reasons. The properties of artifacts were at the center of the work of the Russian philosopher Evald Il'enkov (1977a, 1977b), who argued that "in being created as an embodiment of purpose and incorporated into life activity in a certain way – being manufactured for a *reason* and put into *use* – the natural object acquires a significance. This significance is the 'ideal form' of the object, a form that includes not a single atom of the tangible physical substance that possess it" (quoted in Bakhurst, 1990, p. 182).

From this perspective, the artifacts that constitute culture-as-medium are different in principle from the material world of the larger ecosystem that existed before the appearance of *Homo sapiens* and that continues to exist as its macroenvironment (albeit in forms that have themselves been changed as a consequence of human activity). The environment into which children are born is different from the natural or material world; it is a culturally organized world that envelops the developing child, and that cultural world is saturated with purpose.

This teleological role of culture in human development is emphasized by V. P. Zinchenko (2002), who, drawing on the work of the poet Osip Mandelshtam, writes that

> culture can be viewed as an "inviting force," or a challenge, rather than merely a familiar surrounding. Culture often engulfs a person, though it can push a person away. A human being is free to accept or reject the invitation, the challenge. The challenge consists in the "difference of potential" that exists between ideal and real forms. If the person accepts the challenge, then she or he masters and appropriates ideal forms and may even transcend them. In this process, these ideal forms turn into personal/individual real forms. The latter, in their turn, can and should be able to generate new ideal forms ... which contribute to the whole "body" of ideal forms. In the absence of this dynamism, the development of culture itself would stop (p. 5).

Hence, insofar as the conditions of development are organized with respect to the *cultural environment* and children are dependent on adults for their own survival, adults do indeed provide the (cultural-historical) teleology for their children's development. But culture, being itself the cumulative transforming actions of prior generations on an ever-changing natural environment, cannot provide any ultimate teleology for human development, as both Engeström and Zinchenko make clear.

Considerations of Timescale

In order to dig more deeply into the apparent contradiction that Engeström noted between the idea that parents do not provide the teleology of their children and the idea that interaction with adults is essential to the process of human development, it is helpful to consider the relative timescales of phylogeny, cultural history, and ontogeny, as well as the principles that govern change in each domain.

With respect to phylogeny and cultural history, D. P. Barash (1986) makes clear the linkage between cultural change and teleology when he writes:

> Culture can spread independently of our genes and in response to conscious decisions.... Natural selection does not involve any conscious choice on the part of those genes and gene combinations that experience maximum reproductive success. By contrast, culture often proceeds by the intentional selection of specific practices from among a large array of those available. In this sense, then, it is "teleological" or goal directed in a way that biological evolution never is. (p. 47)

In a complementary manner, Stephen Jay Gould (2007) noted:

> Change in this Lamarckian mode easily overwhelms the much slower process of Darwinian natural selection, which requires a Mendelian form of inheritance based on small-scale and undirected variation that can then be sifted and sorted through the struggle for existence. (p. 546)

The massively different timescales of phylogenetic and cultural change were also commented on by Lumsden and Wilson (1983), who suggested that phylogeny and culture are held together by an unbreakable but elastic leash:

> As culture surges forward by means of innovation and the introduction of new ideas and artifacts from the outside, it is constrained and directed to some extent by the genes. At the same time, the pressure of cultural innovation affects the survival of the genes and ultimately alters the strength and torque of the genetic leash. (p. 60)

It should be clear from the foregoing considerations that correctly bracketing or parsing the Darwinian and Lamarckian features of human development is a formidable problem. The teleological (cultural) system as an encompassing medium of human life is a relatively recent phenomenon in the history of animal evolution, one that generally changes rapidly with respect to phylogeny, but (ordinarily) slowly with respect to human ontogeny.

As a consequence of the simultaneous influence of these different timescales, it is important to consider the shifting relations between the phylogenetic, cultural-historical, and ontogenetic domains depending on the age of a particular child. At the moment of conception, children are bequeathed a particular phylogenetic history. Although their specific biological makeup as they grow will depend on subsequent encounters with the intrauterine and postnatal environments they encounter (mutation-inducing radiation or neuron-destroying alcohol are but two of the many *cultural* products that can change a to-be-child's biological makeup), for all practical purposes, the phylogenetic *history* of developing children is invariant throughout their lifetime. The situation concerning cultural history depends much more on the time and place a child is born. During a good deal of human history, it appears that cultural change is glacially slow in many locations. Generations of people could live in what seemed from our current perspective to be a constant cultural environment. At other times in some places (points of historical transition such as the rise of city-states in the Euphrates Valley several millennia ago or the rapid changes associated with industrialization in 19th-century Europe and North America or any locale subject to rapid ecological change such as those caused by volcanic activity or disease-engendered crop failures), cultural change appears to be relatively rapid.

The rate of cultural change in any given society and the demographic composition of the group with respect to age both have an obvious impact on intergenerational relations and, hence, on the extent to which the cultural knowledge of adult generations is likely to provide a reasonable teleology for the children growing up at the time. In times and places where cultural change is relatively slow (so-called cold societies; Levi-Strauss, 1962) and where, often, mortality is such that children are particularly vulnerable, the part of the life span in which the cultural knowledge of adults provides a teleology for more junior members of the society is likely to be considerable. We need think only of the well-known fact that, in such societies, great respect and power is invested in the older members of the group who have the greatest accumulation of knowledge with which to address (the relatively few) apparently novel problems that arise for group members. By contrast, in "hot" societies, which are characteristic of many parts of the world at present, it is a commonplace that, despite their relative longevity, old people are "fogies," unable to text-message or set the controls on the electronic devices in their homes and unable to use their past experience as a reasonable facsimile of "wisdom" that the young are likely to believe important. Consequently, in such societies, the point in ontogeny where the "culturally given" embodied in the practices and power relations among people ceases to provide a teleology for social life and the valorization of cultural innovation relative to cultural memory occurs much earlier in ontogenetic time. However, because at whatever rate cultural innovation occurs, it is to some extent constantly transforming while maintaining the cultural medium of the group, in this sense it continues to act as a teleology for the development of its members, albeit under changed social and ecological conditions and for lesser or greater parts of the ontogenetic life cycle.

DEVELOPMENT AS BREAKING AWAY AND OPENING UP

With these considerations in hand, we now examine ideas put forth by Engeström (1996a). Engeström uses Peter Hoeg's 1994 novel *Borderliners* as a thought experiment on which to base his challenge to Vygotsky, Piaget, and us. Briefly, this novel follows the lives of three youth who attend an elite boarding school, the purpose of which is to create perfectly socialized, well-adjusted adults through a carefully designed and structured regimen of carefully organized activities, both in the classroom and in the daily routines of the school. Each of the youths has had a troubled path: One is described as having no parents and experiencing difficulties in the institutions he was placed in; one has lost her parents to illness and suicide; one has killed his parents. Finding each other in their shared marginal histories, they collectively investigate the socialization regime into which they have been placed in order to understand why they are there – what the adult purpose is in placing them there. In the process of their investigations, they illustrate the three major and unappreciated principles of development that Engeström (1996a, p. 126) wishes to emphasize:

1. Instead of just benign achievement of mastery, development may be viewed as a partially destructive rejection of the old.
2. Instead of just individual transformation, development may be viewed as collective transformation.

3. Instead of just vertical movement across levels, development may be viewed as horizontal movement across borders.

BENIGN MASTERY AND DESTRUCTION OF THE OLD

Engeström's (1996a) basic point with respect to this issue is that "both Piaget and Vygotsky, as most other theories of development, depict development essentially as progression from a limited toward a broader and more inclusive mastery over the environment and the self. As such, development is a positive process" (p. 128). In Hoeg's story, the positive features of development described in the preceding section are accompanied by a number of painful and destructive events, including the death of one of the protagonists and various kinds of less drastic destruction, both to persons and property.

There can be little doubt that developmentalists generally focus on the new, the novel, and the more inclusive and power-enhancing side of the dialectic of development, although there are many well-known phenomena in normal development in which the losses associated with the gains are prominent and often noted. The ability to acquire one's native language, for example, is accompanied by the loss of the ability to make phonetic discriminations that are essential to acquiring other languages (Ravier-Gaxiola, Silva-Pereyra, & Kuhl, 2005). The achievement of walking is associated with a wide range of new and positively valued changes: Children no longer need to be carried in many circumstances; the accompanying increase in their manual skills means that they can feed themselves. On the other hand, while celebrated, the advent of language is also accompanied by unwelcome forms of personality change characterized by noncompliance of the sort that gives rise to the notion of the "terrible twos."

But it is especially in the transition from childhood to adulthood, a transition that is identified as a specific, qualitatively distinct stage of development by both Vygotsky and Piaget, that psychologists are most likely to emphasize intergenerational conflict, changes in both the behavior and personality of the developing young person that are perceived by adults as destructive (e.g., high levels of behavior considered criminal or immoral, high suicide rates). And it is also in the passage from childhood to adulthood that cultural creation is likely to be most prominent, giving birth to the new while diminishing, if not extinguishing, the old. In this regard, it is significant that the young people in Hoeg's story have entered this transition period.

It is easy to agree with Engeström on the double-sided nature of developmental change, which helps us to attend to aspects of the "breaking away/opening up" dynamic that might be obscured as a result of the reigning cultural ideology. For example, it helps us to note that while in some cultural circumstances it may be considered a bad thing when small infants are difficult and vociferously demanding (such children are less likely to exhibit "secure attachment," which is predictive of smooth social relations and cultural achievements in later life; Johnson, Dweck, & Chen, 2007), in circumstances of severe economic privation, such behaviors may be the best predictor of continued life (De Vries, 1987). Or it might help us to keep in mind that adolescents have historically been among the leaders in a variety of social movements seeking social change (Sherrod, Flanagan, Kassimir, & Syvertsen, 2006).

INDIVIDUAL AND COLLECTIVE TRANSFORMATION

Engeström (1996a) begins his discussion of this challenge to Vygotsky and Piaget by declaring:

> Developmental theories are about individuals. Even Vygotsky, a champion of the social and cultural in developmental psychology, did not conceptualize development as transformation of human collectives. For him, development required social interaction and collaboration, but it was the individual child who actually developed in the collaboration. (p. 128)

There is little doubt in our minds that given psychology's historical focus on "the individual," developmental psychologists have generally focused on "individual children who actually developed in the collaboration," as Engeström suggests. It is a genuine challenge to focus simultaneously on individuals and the social groups of which they are a part. However, we need not be restricted to fictional accounts of individual and collective development for data on this issue. Both in theory and in practice, developmentalists have long stressed that the developmental changes manifested by a child are reciprocally related to changes in the child's environment, that one cannot occur without the other.

Vygotsky himself was mindful of this principle. For example, in one of his essays on children's development at different stages of life, Vygotsky (1998) wrote:

> We have studied inadequately the internal relation of the child to those around him, and we have not considered him as an active participant in the social situation. We admit in words that it is necessary to study the personal and the environment of the child as a unit. But we must

not think that the influence of the personality is on one side and the influence of the environment, on the other, that the one and the other act the way external forces do. (p. 292)

Moreover, some contemporary scholars working within the cultural-historical tradition have quite explicitly conducted their research following the principle that because all individuals are simultaneously and necessary members of a social group, developmental changes must occur simultaneously on both planes of analysis. Barbara Rogoff (2003), who also decries the failure of many developmental psychologists to consider jointly developmental changes in children as both individual and social, quite explicitly adopts the view that "development is a process of *people's changing participation in sociocultural activities of their communities*. People contribute to the processes involved in sociocultural activities at the same time that they inherit practices invented by others" (p. 52).

Greenfield and her colleagues (Greenfield, 1999, 2004) have documented this process in their studies of developmental change that occurs in rural Mayan families in central Guatemala. From at least the time they are toddlers, female children are present along with older kin when cloth weaving is occurring. A great deal of their learning takes place through a process akin to Lave and Wenger's (1991) notion of "peripheral participation," in which the forms of their activities change as they come to take over greater responsibility for the weaving process, a complex accomplishment that requires various qualitative changes in their behavior of the sort that Engeström, in concert with Vygotsky and Piaget, considers a hallmark of developmental change. But the "target child" whose development a psychologist might focus on is very clearly not the only one who is undergoing development; so are other members of the group. When a child shifts social positions to become responsible for the production of cloth on the loom, older members of the community, no longer responsible for this activity, may be "relegated" to new roles as caretakers of infant newcomers to the community or may acquire new capabilities as healers and caretakers.

This same line of research also implicates cultural-historical change in the process of ontogenetic change. Rogoff et al. have consistently found that when young women have had several years of schooling, the pattern of participation and modes of learning in joint activities with their children changes. When engaged in joint activities with their children, they are less likely to share collectively in many parts of a task and instead subdivide the children into dyads or to work as singletons, in which case the linkage between developmental changes in individual children's behavior is less visibly linked to changes in the collective (Rogoff, Correa-Chávez, & Cotuc,

2005). Patricia Greenfield (2004) has observed similar phenomena, in which changes in economic activities associated with new economic practices and the spread of schooling engender changes in mother–child interactions that affect both the developmental trajectories of individual children and the trajectory of development of interpersonal interactions within the group.

Unfortunately, such phenomena are obscured in a good deal of developmental-psychological research because so much of it takes place in public institutions, often relying on psychological testing procedures that provide a kind of tunnel vision about the ways in which individual and collective change are intimately connected. Long ago, A. N. Leont'ev (1981) noted that when children begin to attend school and acquire a new developmental status, one sees not only changes in their orientation to, and means of dealing with, the academic tasks assigned to them in school. At home younger siblings must learn to inhibit their behavior so that the schoolchildren will have the requisite quiet time to do their homework (itself a qualitatively new form of behavior) and even their parents orient to them differently, changing their modes of behavior to help create the new sociocognitive space that the children's new developmental status requires.

VERTICAL VERSUS HORIZONTAL DIMENSIONS OF DEVELOPMENT

Engeström's (1996a) final challenge is stated in terms of his concern that "exclusive concentration on the vertical dimension of development requires closed boundaries, elimination of horizontal movement across social worlds" (p. 129). "The challenge to developmental theory," he writes, "is to account for such processes of boundary crossing" (p. 130).

We believe that this concern should, indeed, be included in any theory of development that considers culturally organized human activities to be a fundamental unit of analysis, just as it is a fundamental unit of human experience. However, in counterdistinction to the first two challenges Engeström posed, in this case we believe that developmentalists have been more cognizant of the issues than Engeström has given them credit for.

In a tradition that reaches back at least to the classic work of Barker and Wright (1954) on the social ecology of childhood development, the relationship between "vertical" development (as indexed by any number of cognitive abilities, involvement in socially valued economic activities, etc.) and horizontal development has been an important theme. For example, Barker and Wright documented a marked increase in the range of settings that children living in the U.S. Midwest participated in that coincides with the transition to middle childhood, increases in the transition to adulthood, and lasts until old age, paralleling a variety of changes in psychological abilities ordinarily considered along a "vertical" dimension.

Psychological anthropologists have also studied this emphasis on the importance of the range of activities that children engage in as it relates to their intellectual development. For example, Sarah Nerlove and her colleagues (Nerlove, Munroe, & Munroe, 1971) studied gender differences in the range of activities that 5- to 8-year-old rural Kenyan children engaged in and related it to performance on tests of spatial ability. In general, boys spent more time in a range of settings distant from their homes than girls did, and boys in general scored better on the tests of spatial thinking. However, in (the less frequent) cases where girls spent time away from home, they performed better on the spatial tests than boys, implicating the "horizontal" range and location of activities as the critical variable in "vertical" development.

This same line of evidence clearly points to the role of adults in organizing the development of children according to *their own* teleology. In fact, Beatrice Whiting (1980), who was a pioneer in the study of the role of culture in human development, linked Engeström's emphasis on the horizontal dimension of development to our point that adults' beliefs do indeed provide a cultural teleology for their children's development in clear terms: She argued on the basis of her massive research on children's lives in many parts of the world that "the mother and father's greatest effect is in the assignment of the child to settings that have important socialization influences" (p. 97). "... Many of the age changes that have been reported in the literature on child development may be the result of frequenting new settings as well as gaining new physical and cognitive skills" (p. 111).

IN PLACE OF A CONCLUSION: NICARAGUAN SIGN LANGUAGE AS A REAL-LIFE CASE STUDY

In a well-known essay, Vygotsky (1978) proposed that "the acquisition of language can provide a paradigm for the entire problem of the relation between learning and development" (p. 89). In seeking to bring together the different threads of the current discussion, we will follow Vygotsky's lead and use the historically unusual case of the development of sign language at a school established in Nicaragua in 1979 (Helmuth, 2001; Senghas, Senghas, & Pyers, 2005).

In the 1970s, the Nicaraguan government set up the first school for deaf children. These children were brought to the residential school from villages all over the country. They arrived being able to use only "home sign," a rudimentary form of signing idiosyncratic to each of the children and their immediate social group. At the most, home sign shows only the most rudimentary, "resilient" forms of language, or protolanguage (Goldin-Meadow, 2002). The curriculum at the school was focused on teaching the children to acquire spoken language by acquiring the ability to read lips and to read and write in Spanish. However, outside of the classroom, the children began to create new hand gestures. Over time (which in this case means over 25 years, during which many new children came to the school) new generations of children were exposed to the social practices, the vocabulary of signs increased dramatically, and there emerged a system for stringing signs together to form longer utterances – a grammar.

Three facts concerning this process are of particular interest for the present discussion. First, this language was created without a ready-made model to learn from, "on the school bus and in the play yard" as one of the researchers put it. Second, when a new cohort of home-signing children came to the school, the sign language they encountered in their social interaction with the "idioculture" of the children attending the school was akin to a pidgin language. They not only acquired this pidgin language, but also invented new and more complex linguistic forms, refining and systematizing the forms they initially encountered, so that what initially was akin to a pidgin language began to evolve into a more complex form of signing, akin to a creole language. Third, the language change over successive generations was not the result of innovations by the oldest students but the *youngest* ones.

We need not get into controversies about the significance of these findings for debates about whether or not children have an innately specified language module that causes the development of the Nicaraguan sign language. Clearly, humans have a special proclivity to interact with each other through language; moreover, contemporary students of language evolution make a strong case, à la Vygotsky, that language evolution is driven by the need to create and sustain culture, which is the essential adaptive medium of human life (Christensen & Kirby, 2003).

What makes the case of Nicaraguan sign language so relevant to our discussion of Engeström's ideas about development is that it brings together concerns about conditions under which culture does or does not provide a teleology for development in ways that link directly to the idea of development as opening up and breaking away. At the Nicaraguan school for deaf children, the cultural environment arranged by the adults was *clearly not adequate* for the children. As many have noted, socialization practices that restrict deaf children's access to language to lip-reading generally fail, and even for those few deaf people who become relatively proficient lip-readers, their language and their cognitive and social development are slowed down and limited (Padden & Humphries, 2005). By contrast, children who acquire a mature sign language such as American Sign Language, as part of the everyday cultural practices of the social group into which they are born, show perfectly normal development.

In the framework of the current discussion, it seems clear that we can consider dysfunctional the initial conditions that the children encountered when they were removed from their homes and put into a strange social environment. The culture of the school embodying the adult "teleology" for the children was the intended medium for their development. However, the fact that the children did not spend all of their time in the classroom, and could organize their own interactions with others who shared their biological capacities in the gaps between adult-controlled, orally mediated activities, made it both necessary and possible for them to start "breaking away and opening up" early in life.

We have not seen recent reports of changes in the schooling practices of the adults at this school, but earlier reports (Helmuth, 2001) indicated that the new linguistic practices of the children have had an effect on the practices of the hearing adults, who have started to use the children's sign language (now referred to as Nicaraguan Sign Language [NSL]). Consequently, this unusual case supports Engeström's emphasis on the way in which such breaking away opens up new possibilities not only for the principal characters themselves but for their social group as well.

To return to the case of well-established cultural systems, such as those that serve as the context of children's development in most parts of the world most of the time, the language and culture of the adults is, generally speaking, adaptive and hence can serve for a time (how much time depends on the stability of the overall ecology that gave rise to the culture in place at the moment) as a cultural teleology nurturing children's development. In such conditions, not only the children but also the adults can be lulled into believing that they really do know what is best for the children – which way "is up." In such conditions, it is not until they reach adolescence that most children discover that a lot of the seeming sensibleness and power of adults is a partial sham in need of repair, which is why the innovation and breaking away are not seen in such populations earlier. Such innovative changes, with their destructive as well as constructive consequences, as we have argued earlier and as Engeström emphasizes, are always there. It is just that they have been rendered invisible by their very ordinariness. Like fish in water, adults in relatively stable cultural circumstances fail to see the medium that sustains their life. Unlike fish in water, human children, in acquiring the competencies to propagate the life of their social group constantly change that medium as a condition of maintaining it.

Many years ago, the embryologist Charles Waddington (1947) asserted that every new level of development is a new relevant context. Although seemingly far distant from Waddington in the focus of his interests in development, Yrjö Engeström's ideas seem to be fully compatible with Waddington's formulation. If we think about development during the embryonic period, each of Engeström's key formulations concerning developmental principles can be seen to apply.

9

Two Theories of Organizational Knowledge Creation

JAAKKO VIRKKUNEN

LEARNING WHAT DOES NOT YET EXIST

In the mid-1990s knowledge management became an important area of business management studies (Swan, Robertson, & Bresnen, 2003). Ikuro Nonaka and Nobuko Takeuchi set the scene for much of the later discussion in their seminal book *The Knowledge Creating Company* (1995). The authors quote Herbert Simon's (1986) definition of the task of modern organization theory:

> A major target for research in organisations today is to understand how organisations acquire new products, new methods of manufacture and marketing, and new organisational forms. This is the unfinished business that Chester Barnard left for us. (Nonaka & Takeuchi, 1995, p. 50)

According to Nonaka and Takeuchi, it is even more important to understand how organizations create the new knowledge that makes innovations possible.

After reviewing how knowledge creation has been dealt with in different traditions, they conclude:

> Even though many of the new management theories since the mid-1980s have pointed out the importance of knowledge to society and organisations in the coming era, there are very few studies on how knowledge is created within and between business organisations. At the core concern of these theories is the acquisition, accumulation, and utilization of existing knowledge; they lack the perspective of creating new knowledge. (Nonaka & Takeuchi, 1995, p. 49)

Eight years earlier, Yrjö Engeström's book *Learning by Expanding* (1987) had been published, with the following blurb on the back cover:

Traditional learning theories regard learning as a process of acquisition and reorganisation of cognitive structures within the closed boundaries of given tasks or problem contexts. This kind of learning is incapable of meeting the demands of complex social change and creation of novel artefacts and social structures. On the other hand, traditional conceptions of development picture expansion as an uncontrollable, spontaneous phenomenon. This study presents a conceptual framework for a theory of expansive learning activity that transcends both traditional forms of thought characterized above.

The two books have different backgrounds. Nonaka and Takeuchi approach the problem of knowledge creation from the perspective of business management, whereas Engeström takes the point of view of actors involved in a joint activity. Their views on the current challenges of learning theory are, however, strikingly similar. Both theories have arisen from discontent with the preoccupation of mainstream learning research with existing knowledge. Both view knowledge creation as concept formation and highlight both horizontal and vertical dialogue in it. They share the objective of creating a theory that promotes the understanding of creative, practice-related learning processes.

Yrjö Engeström discusses the relative merits of these theories in explaining knowledge creation in his study of innovative learning in work teams (Engeström, 1999e). In this chapter I will compare the view of concept development put forward in these two theories from a broader epistemological perspective. I thereby hope to make visible the importance in the theory of knowledge creation of a historical approach and the concepts of *inner contradiction, object of activity and knowledge,* and *generalization.*

The original publication of the theories led in both cases to a great number of studies applying the theory. Here, however, I will focus on the original formulations and their underpinnings. I will first briefly introduce the theories and then compare them with respect to how they conceptualize the unit of analysis of knowledge creation, what they understand knowledge to be, how they describe the process and dynamics of knowledge creation, and finally, how they assess the possibilities of supporting and enhancing it. I will concretize the comparison by reinterpreting one of Nonaka and Takeuchi's examples in the light of the two theories.

THE TWO THEORIES

Nonaka and Takeuchi are management scientists. They see their theory as a further development of the resource-based approach to business strategy (Prahalad & Hamel, 1990; Stalk, Evans, & Shulman, 1992). In addition to this, they lean on the Japanese intellectual tradition that highlights the oneness of humanity and nature, body and mind, as well as self and other, by focusing on action in the world rather than cognizance of it. They contrast this tradition with Cartesian rationalism, which, according to them, still largely characterizes Western thinking. The inspiration and empirical substantiation of their theory are based on extensive case analyses from large Japanese companies. The theory comprises both a model of the process of organizational knowledge creation and a theory of enabling conditions for knowledge creation in organizations.

Yrjö Engeström's work in the 1980s on the possibilities of changing and developing professional practices took him quite a long way from mainstream pedagogical research and brought him into the arena of collective learning and the creation of new forms of work activities. He published his theory of expansive learning in *Learning by Expanding* in 1987 as a synthesis of several lines of theoretical and methodological thinking inspired by the classics of cultural-historical activity theory. The theory also owes much to Karl Marx's economic theory of the basic contradictions in capitalism, as well as his idea of the historical socialization of forces of production, in other words, the progressively deepening division of labor, the tightening of interconnections between productive activities, and the increasing importance of scientific knowledge in production (Marx, 1973, pp. 705–706, 750; 1977, p. 1024). In line with the interventionist research methodology of developmental work research, which he also developed in *Learning by Expanding,* Engeström puts these theoretical ideas to practical use in the pursuit of changing societal activities.

THE UNIT OF ANALYSIS AND DEVELOPMENT OF KNOWLEDGE CREATION IN THE THEORIES

Nonaka and Takeuchi see the development of new products as the core of organizational knowledge creation, but they analyze it in the broader context of business strategy as a process of forming and generalizing new business concepts. Thus, the basic unit of their analysis is this process of product and business concept formation within a firm. Within this unit, they focus on the interaction between *knowledge-creating entities:* individuals, groups, organizations, and interorganizational relationships as well as the related *tacit and explicit forms of knowledge* and the dynamic interaction and transformations between these forms.

Engeström, on the other hand, elaborates on Leont'ev's (1978) idea that the basic unit of human concept formation is a historically evolving system of object-oriented societal activity. Activities are delimited by their objects. The object of an activity is, on the one hand, something given, something material or ideal with which the actors are interacting. On the other hand, it is a special cultural interpretation and construction of what is given and a projection of what the givens can be made into with the help of available means. In the latter sense it is the societal motive for collaborative activity. The generally available cultural means of understanding, interpreting, and transforming the objects of societal activities bridge different local activity systems. An activity is thus at the same time a specific local system and an instance of a type of activity as a general cultural phenomenon.

Both authors relate knowledge creation to the conceptualization of objects of productive activities, that is, what is dealt with and produced. Nonaka and Takeuchi take the object of knowledge creation and the knowledge-creating entities as given. Engeström, on the other hand, highlights the coevolution and mutual determination of the elements of an activity system. This difference reflects the basic interests of the theorists: Nonaka and Takeuchi study knowledge creation as a means of business competition, whereas Engeström is interested in revealing realistic possibilities for emancipation and agency.

THE VIEW OF KNOWLEDGE IN THE TWO THEORIES

Nonaka and Takeuchi (1995) define knowledge as *"a dynamic human process of justifying personal belief toward the 'truth',"* highlighting the processual aspect (p. 58). Knowledge is created dynamically in social interactions among people. By sharing knowledge, people construct a social reality, which in turn influences their judgment, behavior, and attitudes. In order to go beyond Cartesian rationalism, the authors lean on Polanyi's (1958) idea that human beings create knowledge by involving themselves with objects, by "indwelling" them. To know something is to create its image or pattern by tacitly integrating particulars. Indwelling breaks the traditional dichotomies between mind and body, reason and emotion, subject and object, knower and known. Tacit knowledge comprises the individual's images of reality, and his or her visions for the future as well as concrete know-how, crafts, and skills. It is therefore bound to the person and the situation and is hard to transfer. Transferable and manipulable explicit knowledge is created by externalizing tacit knowledge. In highlighting the tacit–explicit dichotomy, the authors posit the internal–external dichotomy as essential in knowledge creation.

Engeström's concept of knowledge is based on the Vygotskian idea of tool use as the prototype of human knowledge and tools as physical embodiments of practice-relevant generalizations. According to this view, the development of knowledge is based on the dialectical interplay between generalizations and the processes of their creation and use in man's practical activities (Leont'ev, 1990). These ideas make it possible to abandon the traditional Cartesian assumption about the opposition between the internal and the external worlds, and to replace it with a model in which the important opposition is the one between generalized representation (tool/concept) and the process (tool/concept creation and use), irrespective of whether they are internal or external.

Following L. S. Vygotsky and V. V. Davydov, Engeström distinguishes between everyday concepts and scientific concepts. The former are created by classifying things on the basis of their external similarities and differences and the latter through an analysis that establishes systemic functional relationships between externally different objects and the origin of such relationships. The appropriation of a theoretical concept requires its abstract basic idea first to be learned and then to be concretized step by step through its application in more and more complex situations. Scientific concepts assume meaning and substance from everyday generalizations, and spontaneous everyday generalizations are restructured in interaction with scientific concepts (Vygotsky, 1986, pp. 1481–1449). A generalization can exist in many forms, as tacit or explicit knowledge or in the form and principle of a tool or technical system.

The idea of concepts as generalizations highlights the importance of their relative explanatory power. Engeström's idea of expansive learning is not fully understandable without the Marxian notion of the historical socialization of labor. Each step forward in this historical process means that the objects and systems of productive activities in society become more complex and intertwined. New concepts and forms of knowledge that have more explanatory power than the previous ones are needed in order to master the expanded objects of human activities and the increasingly complex and tight interrelationships between activities.

THE PROCESS OF KNOWLEDGE CREATION

According to Nonaka and Takeuchi, the articulation of tacit mental models is a key factor in the creation of new knowledge, the dynamics of which are based on discrepancies between tacit images and explicit concepts as well as between different views. New knowledge is created in cycles of conversions of knowledge along two dimensions, which they call *epistemological* and *ontological,* respectively. The former refers to the articulation and explication of tacit knowledge and the transformation of explicit into tacit knowledge, whereas the latter concerns knowledge-creating entities (who knows, who has the knowledge, to what extent the knowledge is shared). They suggest that knowledge is, in a strict sense, created only by individuals, but knowledge creation can be organizationally amplified. In cycles of knowledge creation, one person's tacit knowledge is transformed into another person's tacit knowledge, tacit knowledge is articulated and transformed into explicit knowledge, pieces of explicit knowledge are combined, and explicit knowledge is turned into new tacit knowledge (Fig. 9.1). Externalization, the conversion of tacit into explicit knowledge, is the key to knowledge creation because it creates new explicit concepts through the sequential use of metaphor, analogy, and models.

Successive cycles of knowledge creation form the five phases of organizational knowledge creation, which starts from the sharing of tacit knowledge and proceeds through its articulation and the forming of explicit concepts to the justification and evaluation of the explicit concepts in the organization in order to determine whether or not they are worthy of pursuit. Following its approval, in the fourth phase the new concept is converted to an *archetype* in the form of a prototype, an operating principle,

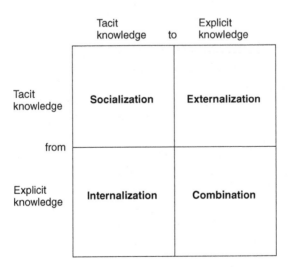

Figure 9.1. The four types of knowledge conversion and the corresponding types of knowledge (Nonaka & Takeuchi, 1995, pp. 71–72).

a novel managerial system, or an innovative organizational structure. Finally, in the fifth phase the knowledge is cross-leveled to other units of the organization, consumers, and affiliated companies.

Engeström's theory also highlights the role of collective reflection triggered by discrepancies in individuals' views and understandings. However, he locates the dynamics of knowledge creation not primarily on the level of representations, but rather on the level of contradictory forces within human activities. The *primary contradiction* within activity systems is between the use value and the exchange value of its elements. When the activity and its context change, the system moves from a relatively stable state first to an unarticulated "need state" and then to a stage of increasingly acute *secondary contradictions* between some elements of it. Secondary contradictions push the system farther and farther away from a quasi-stationary equilibrium, eventually to a bifurcation point at which a new solution is necessary.

Engeström applies A. N. Leont'ev's idea of motivation in his theory. According to Leont'ev, a need does not create a motive for an activity; it only motivates a search for an object that would meet the need. When such an object is found, it becomes a motive. Thus, an increase in the instability and in the number of problems in the activity system leads the actors at some point to a need state, and to making conscious efforts to analyze the causes of the problems and to find a new object for the activity that would meet the need created by the evolving inner contradictions. In the midst of regressive and evasive attempts to solve the problems there emerges the novel "germ cell" of a new object of the activity, which promises to resolve the aggravated inner secondary contradictions. If that idea or prototypic new solution gains momentum, it is turned into a model that is enriched through the design of corresponding new tools and patterns of interaction. When the new model is implemented in practice, contradictions emerge between the new and the old elements of the activity. In the working through of these *tertiary contradictions,* the designed or given new model is gradually replaced by another new one, firmly grounded in practice through the resolving of the contradictions between the given new and the existing forms of the activity. The change of activity, however, leads to *quaternary contradictions* between the central and the neighboring activities. Figure 9.2 depicts the phases of this cycle of expansive development in an idealized and simplified form. The two-headed arrows signify the iterative, nonlinear character of the process.

Because generalizations exist not only in human minds but also in forms of material tools and organizational structures, expansive

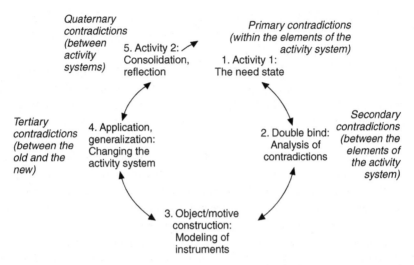

Figure 9.2. Phases of a cycle of expansive development (Engeström, 1987, p. 189).

learning is a complicated historical process involving the transforming of an institutionalized form of social practice. During this process, individual and collective learning, cognitive development, and the development of new artifacts and organizational arrangements interact. The expansive transformation of an activity system may comprise several smaller cycles of expansive learning through which partial solutions are created.

Nonaka and Takeuchi base the phases of knowledge creation on transformations of the form of knowledge. They do not include the need state or the change of activity in the knowledge creation process proper, but focus on the creation, justification, and leveling of new product and business concepts. In Engeström's theory the dynamics and phases of the cycle of expansive learning are demarcated through a change in the type of contradiction, which then becomes central in the new phase of the cycle and defines the current challenges of learning and the further creation of knowledge. He criticizes Nonaka and Takeuchi's way of founding their cyclic model on modes of knowledge representation and of leaving aside problem formation and goal setting, as well as the use of the new knowledge in transforming practice (Engeström, 1999e, p. 380).

SUPPORTING KNOWLEDGE CREATION

Nonaka and Takeuchi do not see any way of influencing knowledge creation directly and instead identify five enabling conditions. The first of these is *organizational intention*, a vision of what kind of knowledge should be developed, and the second is *autonomy* in individuals and groups. Then there is *fluctuation* and *creative chaos*, which create "breakdowns" of routines, habits, and cognitive frameworks, and present the members with a challenge and the opportunity to reconsider their fundamental thinking and perspectives. Uncertainty, as well as interpretative equivocality created consciously by the management, may trigger reflection in the members and a search for new ways of thinking. The fourth enabling condition is *redundancy*, in other words, the existence of information that goes beyond the immediate operational requirements of the present work of the organization's members. The fifth condition that helps to advance the knowledge spiral is *requisite variety*, internal diversity in the organization that matches the variety and complexity of the environment.

One way of managing creative chaos is through *middle-up-down management*. According to this model, top management articulates the vision or dream of the company, while frontline employees down in the trenches look at the reality. The gap between the dream and the reality is narrowed by middle managers who mediate between the two by creating middle-range business and product concepts.

As Engeström sees it, knowledge creation and expansive learning may become a conscious collaborative activity, beginning when individuals question the accepted practices and concepts. This could then gradually expand into expansive learning activity, in which the actors jointly inquire into the root causes of problems in the current activity system and transform it expansively in order to avert the threat of crisis. This activity is carried out through individually and jointly taken epistemic actions such as questioning the prevailing practices and ideas, analyzing and modeling the systemic causes of problems, modeling the new object and form of the activity, and implementing the new model in practice (Engeström, 1999e, pp. 383–384).

The practitioners need intellectual and practical tools for taking epistemic actions and creating new concepts. *Springboards* are "facilitative images, techniques or socioconversational constellations (or combinations of these) misplaced or transplanted from some previous context into a new, expansively transitional activity context during an acute conflict of a double bind character" (Engeström, 1987, p. 287). Nonaka and Takeuchi, (1995, p. 12) present, in their case analyses, a number of interesting examples of what Engeström would call springboards. For instance, the design group in Honda used the biological idea of evolution to create the idea of a new car type. *Instrumental models* such as exemplars or prototypes, classifications, procedural rules, systemic models, or a germ cell model of the basic contradictory relationship of a system may be used, as are conceptual tools produced in research and development activities as well as models arising from more advanced forms of the same activity. These different kinds of intellectual tools are useful when applied in a *multivoiced discussion*, in which "all the conflicting and complementary voices of various groups and strata in the activity system under scrutiny shall be involved and utilized" (Engeström, 1987, p. 316).

The researcher following the interventionist research methodology of developmental work research helps the practitioners to take the necessary epistemic actions and to engage themselves in expansive learning activity. The researcher, together with the practitioners, produces data that helps them to question the current practice and to analyze it systematically in order to reveal the historical and systemic causes of current problems. The researcher also helps the actors to model the main inner contradictions in the current activity system. He or she helps the practitioners to find a "springboard" for locating cultural resources and using them in developing a new model for the activity and to transform the activity through the experimental application of new tools that concretize the created new model.

The two theories give different pictures of agency in knowledge creation. Nonaka and Takeuchi's theory ascribes it to project teams organized by middle management in order to reconcile general management's visions and frontline workers' knowledge of the daily realities. Engeström's theory, on the other hand, postulates the historical possibility that the actors involved in a productive activity distance themselves from their daily activity and become engaged in joint learning activity in order to create the knowledge needed for transforming the activity expansively and using the new knowledge for carrying out the transformation. This historical possibility can be realized through the intervention methodology of developmental work research, with which the practitioners can be helped to become a collective subject of knowledge creation and a collective agent of the expansive transformation of their activity system.

AN EMPIRICAL CASE VIEWED THROUGH THE LENSES OF THE TWO THEORIES

To further elaborate on the differences between the two theories I will, in the following, present a shortened version of Nonaka and Takeuchi's (1995, pp. 95–123) description of the development of the Home Bakery product in the Matsushita Electric Industrial Co. and then interpret it in the light of the two theories.

Matsushita's Home Bakery was the first fully automatic bread-making machine for home use when it was introduced in 1987. The process that led to its development began in the 1970s. At that time Matsushita's operational profitability had diminished because the market for household appliances had matured and new low-cost competitors had entered it. In reacting to these challenges, the management announced a three-year plan to increase the competitiveness of the firm's core businesses and to assemble the resources required to enter new markets.

Matsushita produced home appliances in three divisions: the Rice-Cooker Division, which made microcomputer-controlled rice cookers, the Heating Appliances Division, which used induction heater technology in the production of hot plates, oven toasters, and coffeemakers, and the Rotation Division, which made motorized products such as food processors. The three divisions were united in a Cooking Appliances Division in May 1984. During the next two years the new division's profitability increased because excess capacity was eliminated, but its sales kept on declining and people began to question the benefits of the integration. The situation created a sense of crisis in the Cooking Appliances Division. The different traditions and expertise embedded in the previous divisions made mutual communication within the new one difficult, however.

The new division sent 13 middle managers to a 3-day retreat to discuss the current situation and future direction. They came up with the idea of guiding a group of diverse individuals toward one goal. In order to find the new direction, a planning team was sent to the United States to observe trends in the daily lives of Americans. The team observed that women were working outside the home, and therefore home cooking was increasingly simplified and diets had become poorer. The group concluded that the same development would probably also take place in Japan. They thought that women working outside the home would appreciate an appliance that could produce delicious and nutritious food easily. The idea was crystallized in the paradoxical combination of two requirements: easy and rich. Not long after the planning team returned to Japan, another firm proposed an automatic bread-making machine. The Matsushita people immediately saw that this product would meet the easy-and-rich requirement and also allow the division to combine its diverse areas of expertise.

The product development team specified the product features and produced the first prototype. This did not meet the requirements, however.

One of the key problems was finding the right way to knead the dough. In order to do this, a software developer went to learn kneading from a famous baker. He studied thoroughly how a good baker kneaded dough and invented the concept of "twisting stretch" to describe the right movement. After that invention, the product development team was able to create a prototype that functioned adequately; the product was transferred from the laboratory to production and commercialization, and new persons were involved in the project. The success of the Home Bakery encouraged the firm to develop a number of other "rich-and-easy" products. Later, the more general concept of "human electronics" was derived from the "rich-and-easy" concept as the general line of Matsushita's products.

Nonaka and Takeuchi interpreted the initial crisis in the home appliance divisions as *creative chaos* that created enabling conditions for knowledge creation. The situation prompted individuals' *intention* and the need to develop a new kind of product that would combine the knowledge of the previous three divisions. In their view, the integration of the departments created further enabling conditions: *requisite variety* and *redundancy of information.*

Management and production in the home appliance divisions are, in terms of expansive learning, different although closely related activity systems (the data do not allow us to depict the network of related systems in more detail). As far as the home appliance production activity was concerned, the integration of the divisions was an externally induced change that aggravated the need state, created by the maturation of the markets, into a double-bind situation dominated by contradictions between the old objects of activity, on the one hand, and the new community (the new integrated division), on the other, as well as by the management's directive to enter new markets.

According to both theories, the crisis situation simultaneously incorporated the need for change and new elements that could be used as resources in creating it. As Nonaka and Takeuchi see it, the middle managers' retreat was an attempt to mobilize and share the participants' tacit knowledge. In Engeström's thinking, however, the object of an activity resides between the producing activity and the using activity. Therefore, it is understandable that the sharing of tacit knowledge between the home appliance producers did not lead to a breakthrough and that that was achieved only when the planning team traveled to the United States to analyze the situation of potential users. The trip could be seen as a springboard for finding a new object and a new motive for the home appliance production activity.

It is also important to recognize that the expanded redefinition of customer need was formulated by identifying an inner contradiction in the client activity of providing food for the family at home. The "easy-and-rich" concept represents the two elements of this contradiction: "rich" corresponding to the values of traditional housewives and "easy" to their current reality of working outside the home. A tool for making families rich food easily would be an object that would meet the need created by the historically evolved inner contradiction of family life and would therefore create a motive for acquiring such a tool.

When the new generalization concerning customer need was created, the first object to meet this need, the automatic bread machine, was found relatively easily. It could satisfy the customer's need as well as the division's need for integrating its separate areas of technological expertise in a meaningful way. Therefore, it became the germ cell model of the new object and the motive of the integrated home appliance production activity.

Nonaka and Takeuchi saw the bread machine as an archetype of a new concept that combined previously existing areas of knowledge. They did not explicitly state what the newly created knowledge was actually about, however. According to Engeström's theory, the new concept did not just comprise knowledge about how to make a bread machine; it also concerned the kind of object that could meet customers' and the division's current needs and help them resolve the historically evolved contradictions in their respective activities.

According to Nonaka and Takeuchi's theory, this process involved two cycles of knowledge creation. The first one began with the sharing of tacit knowledge among the members of the product development team and proceeded to an explication of the product features that were then crystallized in an archetype (the Home Bakery prototype), which was evaluated against the easy-and-rich concept. As the prototype failed to meet the requirements, a second cycle began with the software developer's studies of kneading, in which he acquired the tacit knowledge of the baker and explicated it in the concept of "twisting stretch." This process continued with the creation of the second prototype, which was again justified in terms of the easy-and-rich concept.

Nonaka and Takeuchi do not include the analysis of U.S. family life and the reconceptualization of clients' needs in the process of knowledge creation proper, and they characterize the easy-and-rich concept as "organizational intention." This interpretation overlooks the important generalization concerning clients' needs inherent in the concept, which is hardly reducible to an explication of the tacit knowledge of the product development team members – or of U.S. housewives. It required a historical analysis of changes in family life. Nonaka and Takeuchi's theory of articulation and explication does not allow for specific epistemic actions of knowledge creation or for the specific tools and methods used in them. The conceptualization of clients' needs was based on taking a step over the boundary of the Matschusita organization and into the world of potential clients. It was this step that led eventually to a new relationship between the division's activity of producing tools for food making and the housewife's activity of feeding her family.

Nonaka and Takeuchi assume that the process of knowledge creation ended when the archetype of an easy-and-rich product was made and the concept was abstracted into "human technology." The transfer of the product from laboratory to production and commercialization was not part of it. According to Engeström's theory, however, this transfer would have started the fourth phase of the expansive cycle, during which the old and new elements in the production and commercialization activities would collide, thereby creating the need for further elaboration of the new form of production and marketing based on the more complicated product that integrated several technologies. Engeström's theory would further predict that before Matsushita's new product concept was fully realized in all retailing channels and the whole network of concerned organizations, the contradictions between the company's traditional way of working and the new approach would have to be overcome creatively.

Nonaka and Takeuchi do not deal directly with the question of the explanatory and generative power of knowledge. Their case description nevertheless convincingly demonstrates the great explanatory and generative power of the easy-and-rich concept. What gave this generalization its explanatory and generative power? They do not ask this question, but they do hint at a response. According to Leont'ev (1990) the proper content of a generalization can be revealed only through an analysis of the process of its creation. "Easy-and-rich" was based on the planning team's historical analysis of the development of family life and the recognition of a historically evolved contradiction within it, as well as on a general principle of resolving the contradiction: an easy way of making rich food. The later formulation of "human technology" seems to be the result of the abstraction necessitated by the diversity of activities in the corporation. It does not convey the generalization of customer need, and therefore a motive for production, as the easy-and-rich concept did, but defines a type of technology.

IS THERE DIRECTION IN KNOWLEDGE CREATION?

Nonaka and Takeuchi, in their theory of middle-up-down management, discuss the vertical dialogue between general management and frontline workers mediated by middle management. In the context of concept formation, they also describe how different areas of expertise are combined to create a new product concept. They go on to discuss the horizontal cross-leveling of new knowledge from unit to unit and highlight the development of explicit, transferable knowledge.

These could be seen as three complementary directions of what Marx termed the historical socialization of forces of production: the vertical socialization that takes place as the centralization of decision making, the systemic socialization that is the integration of specialized activities and forms of knowledge in order to master complex problems and objects of activity, and the horizontal socialization in the tightening of the exchange and transfer of ideas and material between local actors (Virkkunen, 2006b). According to Marx (1973, pp. 705, 750; 1977, p. 1024), an essential aspect of this development is the increasing use and importance of general scientific knowledge in production, knowledge that is progressively more context independent.

On the global level, the historical socialization of forces of production seems to proceed in waves of transformation triggered by technological revolution (Freeman & Louçã, 2000). At present, the emerging digital information and communication technology is fueling a great leap in the socialization of human activities, leading to the integration of functions and ever more complex and tightly interconnected systems of human activity. The knowledge management discourse is an offspring of this historical transformation: the socialization of forces of production increasingly involves the deeper division of labor, as well as broader and intensified exchange in the production of knowledge and learning (von Hippel, 2005; Zuboff, 1988). There is an increasing need not only for theoretical generalizations and scientific knowledge in productive activities, but also for new kinds of platforms and instrumentalities for integrating various forms of scientific and technological knowledge in order to master increasingly complex objects (Keating & Cambrosio, 2003).

A fundamental difference between the two theories is in their relationship to historical development. Although topical, Nonaka and Takeuchi's theory is ahistorical in the sense that it abstracts from the historical changes and specificities of forms of knowledge creation. Engeström, on the other hand, focuses on the historical change of forms of learning and elaborates a hypothesis of a historically new form, a work community's expansive learning activity. In my own work, I have followed that line and have tried to conceptualize the ongoing historical transformation of forms of work-related learning and the practical possibilities of making collaborative learning activity an integrated part of work practices (Virkkunen, 2006b; Virkkunen & Ahonen, 2004).

10

Contradictions of High-Technology Capitalism and the Emergence of New Forms of Work

REIJO MIETTINEN

The idea of contradictions as a source of change and development is central to the dialectical tradition in philosophy (e.g., Wilde, 1989). The idea also plays a constitutive role in Yrjö Engeström's theory of expansive learning and the methodology of developmental work research (DWR). The triangle of an activity system would be a truncated model without its connection to historical change, which is analyzed in terms of the contradictions of activities in capitalism. Recently Engeström (2008a) pointed out, "If activity theory is stripped of its historical analysis of contradictions of capitalism, the theory becomes either another management toolkit or another psychological approach without potential for radical transformations" (p. 258). With his comments on a critique of the ways of using the model of an activity system (Engeström, 2006d), he reminds us of the key contribution of Il'enkov to activity theory, namely the idea of "objective dialectical contradictions as the motor of self-development in real systems" (p. 3).

The concept of contradiction was developed in *Learning by Expanding* (1987, chap. 2) in two ways. First, the inner contradictions of school activity, of work activity, as well as of science and art in capitalism are delineated. Second, the concept is elaborated and made operative for empirical research through its relation to the model of an activity system, to the cycle of expansive learning, and to the methodological cycle of DWR. As a result, four types of contradictions are defined. In this chapter I will focus on the relationship between two of them, the primary contradiction (between the use value and the exchange value) and the secondary contradiction (between the elements of activity systems). I think this relationship is important for the identity and methodology of DWR. Besides, it has remained theoretically somewhat unarticulated.

I will proceed as follows. I first briefly present how the primary and secondary types of contradictions are defined by Engeström. Second, I will have a look at how these contradictions have been used in empirical studies of DWR by using the studies of his research group on health care work as an example. Third, I will discuss the forms that the contradiction between the use value and the exchange value takes in the latest phase of capitalism, which I call, following Haug (2003), high-technology capitalism. Linux, Wikipedia, and Synaptic Leap are used as examples of the Internet-mediated and use-value-oriented general intellect that directly challenges the logic of capitalist value production.

DEFINITION OF THE CONCEPT OF CONTRADICTION IN EXPANSIVE LEARNING

According to Engeström (1987, p. 82), the basic inner contradiction of human activity is its dual existence as the total societal production and one specific production among many. Any specific production is at the same time independent of and subordinated to the total societal production. This contradiction acquires different forms in different socioeconomic formations. In pre-capitalist society, it takes the form of direct personal suppression by force exercised by slave owners or feudal lords (Engeström, 1987, p. 83). In capitalism, the contradiction assumes the form of commodity, the contradictory unity of the use value and the exchange value: "All things, activities and relations" become saturated by the dual nature of commodity – which, accordingly – penetrates all corners of the triangular structure of activity (Engeström, 1987, pp. 84, 112; see Figure 10.1).

The two poles of the contradiction in each of the elements "suggest two alternative competing strategies both for management and the trade unions," exemplified by the strategy of the "unmanned factory" and the strategy of "skill-based production" (Engeström, 1987, p. 112). The sociological qualification research of the 1970s and 1980s showed that, instead of there being any linear trajectory, the development of worker qualifications was contradictory: The strategies of both de-skilling and re-skilling were adopted in the implementation of automation technology (Toikka, 1984). Because of the increasingly societal nature and internal complexity of work processes, there are "gray zones" in work activities where nobody actually masters the activity as a whole. That is why actions must increasingly be transformed with respect to the changing object and motive of a given activity by the people who participate in that activity. A new kind of activity, learning activity, is needed to accomplish this.

Engeström (1987) further develops the concept of contradiction in two ways. First, he connects it to concepts taken from psychology. The

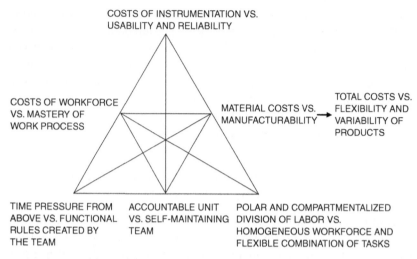

COSTS OF INSTRUMENTATION VS.
USABILITY AND RELIABILITY

COSTS OF WORKFORCE
VS. MASTERY OF
WORK PROCESS

MATERIAL COSTS VS.
MANUFACTURABILITY

TOTAL COSTS VS.
FLEXIBILITY AND
VARIABILITY OF
PRODUCTS

TIME PRESSURE FROM
ABOVE VS. FUNCTIONAL
RULES CREATED BY
THE TEAM

ACCOUNTABLE UNIT
VS. SELF-MAINTAINING
TEAM

POLAR AND COMPARTMENTALIZED
DIVISION OF LABOR VS.
HOMOGENEOUS WORKFORCE AND
FLEXIBLE COMBINATION OF TASKS

Figure 10.1. The primary contradictions of modern work activity (Engeström, 1987, p. 113).

double bind, a term originally coined by Bateson (1972), is introduced as "a contradiction which uncompromisingly demands qualitatively new instruments for its resolution" (Engeström, 1987, p. 175). The concept of the zone of proximal development is defined in terms of a double bind, a type of aggravated contradiction "potentially embedded in everyday actions" (p. 174).

Second, he defines three other types of contradictions that are related to the successive phases of the expansive change of activity systems (Fig. 10.2). The primary contradiction is connected to the first phase of the cycle ("need state") and secondary contradictions to the second phase (double bind). Secondary contradictions are between the elements of activity systems (or "constituents of the central system"). The tertiary contradictions between new and old follow the fourth phase (application of the new model), and the quaternary contradictions (between the activity and other activities) follow the fifth phase, consolidation. The three latter types of contradictions may be regarded as developmental forms of the primary contradiction.[1]

---

[1] "Contradictions are traced back to the primary inner contradictions characteristic of all objects and activities in capitalist society" (Engeström, 1990, p. 255). "It [primary contradiction] evolves and takes the form of specific secondary contradictions as the activity system interacts with other activity systems" (Engeström, 2005a, p. 181).

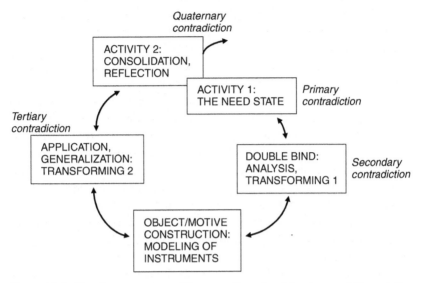

Figure 10.2. The phase structure of the zone of proximal development (Engeström. 1987, p. 189) or the cycle of expansive transition (p. 322).

In the methodological cycle of expansive developmental research (Engeström, 1987, p. 323), the corresponding five phases are characterized from the point of view of interventionist research. The first phase in the methodological cycle is designated the "phenomenology and delineation of the activity system" (p. 334), and the second, "analysis of activity" (p. 335), which is composed of three kinds of analysis: object historical, theory historical, and actual empirical. An outcome of these analyses is "a hypothetical picture of the next, more advanced developmental form of the activity system" (p. 335). This hypothesis includes an instrumentality, a new solution to the contradictions of an activity system. The ultimate aim of the analysis "is to make the participants, the potential subjects of the activity, themselves face the secondary contradictions. In other words, the analysis functions as a midwife for bringing about a double bind or at least a grasp of the double bind in the form of intense conceptual conflict" (p. 335).

CONTRADICTIONS IN STUDIES OF HEALTH CARE WORK

In the following, I will use two studies by Engeström and his research group on health care work as an example of the use of contradictions in empirical research: the work done at the Leppävaara health center in the

1980s (Engeström, 1990; Engeström, Engeström, Helenius, & Koistinen, 1989) and at the children's hospital in Helsinki in the 1990s (Engeström, 1999c, 2000a). Since more than a decade lapsed between the two studies, they reflect changes both in the research object – the patients and the health care system – and in the methodology of DWR.

In the Leppävaara study, the primary contradictions of health care center work are presented "in the form of dilemmas within each of the components of the triangle" (Engeström, 1990, p. 92). The three secondary contradictions all "originate in the object component, indicating that the patients' novel problems and demands are the factor that initially brought about these contradictions." These contradictions were initially identified and formulated as an outcome of historical analyses of both the Leppävaara health station and primary-care practice in Finland (Engeström et al., 1989), as well as based on rich empirical data on the daily work at the health center (see Figure 10.3).

The secondary contradictions were (1) the contradiction between the novel object represented by the patients' changing problems and the traditional biomedically oriented conceptual and communicative instruments at the doctor's disposal; (2) the contradiction between the novel object and

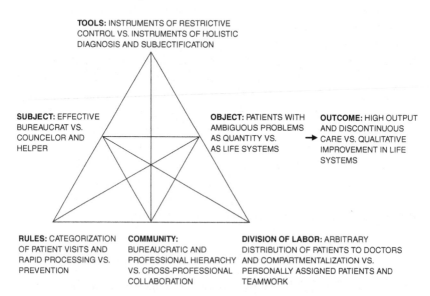

Figure 10.3. Inner contradictions of the work activity of general practitioners at the health center (Engeström, 1990, p. 93).

the administrative rule separating rapidly conducted urgent consultations and regular consultation with appointments, each with different criteria of access; and (3) the contradiction between the novel object and the division of labor whereby patients were arbitrarily distributed to doctors in the health center (Engeström, 1990, pp. 90–92; Engeström, 1991a, p. 276).

A new model of activity and a solution to these contradictions consisted of the introduction of multidisciplinary teams and population responsibility: A geographical area and its population were assigned to each doctor and each team (Engeström, 1991a, p. 281). Corresponding changes were accomplished by rules and instruments, including an interaction-oriented PC database for the teams.

After the Leppävaara study, considerable change took place in Finnish society and the health care system. The incidence and significance of chronic illnesses (such as asthma, diabetes, and heart disease) increased. On the other hand, the diversity of care providers dramatically increased as a result of both specialization and changes in the organization of care (Kerosuo, 2006, pp. 57–69). The problem of and a strong demand for cost efficiency emerged. These changes are clearly seen in the way the contradictions became defined in the children's hospital, in which the patients often had chronic multiple illnesses (Fig. 10.4).

The three secondary contradictions of the care work in the children's hospital study (Engeström, 2000a, p. 965) were (1) the contradiction between the chronic patients with multiple problems and the critical path based on

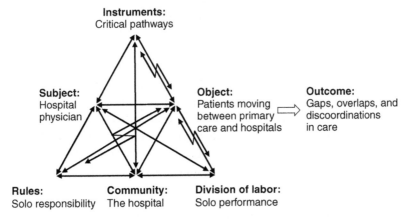

Figure 10.4. The contradictions in the activity system of the children's hospital (Engeström, 2000a, p. 965).

the assumption that a patient has a single diagnosis; (2) the contradiction between the multiple-diagnoses patients and the rule of solo responsibility, according to which each physician is alone responsible for the care of his or her patient; and (3) the contradiction between the multiple-diagnoses patients and the solo performance without collaborative negotiations about the course of care (division of labor).

In another article (Engeström, 2001), the contradictions in children's hospital care activity are analyzed from the point of view of the three activity systems involved in the care of the patient: the family, the health care center, and the children's hospital (p. 145). The change in the contents of secondary contradictions in the two studies reflects the expansion of the research object. The unit of analysis changed from one activity system to networks of activity systems (or the multiorganizational field) and to the idea of "following the object" across organizational boundaries, in the case of the children's hospital patients' care trajectories.

These contradictions in the 2001 article were as follows: (1) In both the hospital and the health center, "a contradiction emerges between the increasingly important *object* of patients moving from the primary care and hospital care and the rule of cost efficiency implemented in both activity systems. This contradiction expressed itself also as a tension between the health center and the hospital. (2) A contradiction also emerged between the new object (patients moving …) and recently established tools, namely the care relationship in primary care and critical path in hospital work, and (3) in the activity system of patient's family between the complex object of multiple illnesses and the largely unavailable and unknown tools for mastering the object (Engeström, 2001).

The solution suggested was a care agreement practice in which the primary-care health center, the children's hospital, as well as the patient and the patient's parents together formulate a mutually acceptable care agreement. In it a plan for care and the division of labor between care providers is defined. This instrumentality has also been introduced in social work in Finland, where many help providers (in social work, youth work, mental health and drug services, etc.) work with people with multiple problems. In this way, the analysis of the contradictions in one study not only supplies a blueprint for a local solution, but contributes to a wider understanding of the contradictions in the social sector and possible ways of solving them.[2]

---

[2] However, it can be asked to what extent the definition of the secondary contradictions of separate activity systems suffices to make sense of the evolving contradictions in a network of activity systems (Engeström, 2001).

Two observations can be made about the definitions of the contradictions in the two studies. First, three functional types of secondary contradictions were seen between (1) object and the means, (2) object and the rules, and (3) object and the division of labor. These types tend to dominate the empirical studies of DWR in general. This raises the question of why the subject and the community are not involved in the definition of secondary contradictions. Second, the primary contradictions within the elements of activity were presented in graphic form only in the first study. In addition, the relationships between primary and secondary contradictions were not explicitly discussed, even if, as in the 1990 article, primary and secondary contradictions are presented in the same graphic representation. The reader may surely infer the relationship. A contradiction "between administrative efficiency and patient-oriented quality of care" (Engeström, 2005a, p. 115) is visible, for instance, in the rule of cost efficiency and looms behind the introduction of critical patient paths. This contradiction is also discussed when the implementation of new tools (such as medical records) is analyzed. A problem may arise if the summary presentation of the secondary contradictions, analyzed in the second phase of the intervention cycle, remains the only or dominant way of dealing with contradictions. It cannot substitute for an analysis of how the contradictions are evolving during the process of expansive transformation or even during the intervention process. Although these changes are addressed in the change accounts, such analyses are seldom supplied by the articles based on the DWR studies.

The contradictions of capitalism as a source of change in work activities need to be analyzed on at least two levels, as Engeström did in *Learning by Expanding*. On the one hand, we need analyses of the development of capitalist production and social institutions in order to recognize the primary contradictions in the elements of a local activity system. The development of new forms of contradictions in capitalism may be only partially or in a preliminary way expressed in a specific activity system. That is why the comparison of many empirical studies can contribute to a more profound analysis of the evolving contradictions of a field of activity. On the other hand, the recognition of contradictions presupposes an analysis of what is happening in other productive activities and institutions (such as intellectual property right regimes) of capitalist society. Such an analysis is important for constantly reconceptualizing the "gray," contradictory zone of threats and emancipatory possibilities in the development of work.

Such an analysis is also important for two other reasons. First, if empirical studies of local activity systems focus on the secondary contradictions distinct or abstracted from the primary contradiction, the approach is subject to criticism, in that it tends to degenerate into a version of adaptive systems theory or a version of the situated social practice approach, which is losing its radical potential (e.g., Avis, 2007). Second, an analysis of the contradictions of capitalism is also important to avoid linear visions of the development of the organization of work, exemplified by the "right path" suggested by Victor and Boynton (1998). I am fully aware that an attempt to analyze these contradictions in a short essay is limited, but it is meant to be a call for further contributions to an issue vital to activity theory.

THE CONTRADICTIONS OF CAPITALISM AND THE CONSTITUTION OF THE "GENERAL INTELLECT"

The recent development of "high-technology capitalism" (Haug, 2003) has interestingly re-actualized the famous passage on the inner contradiction of the capitalist production in Marx's *Grundrisse* (1973):

> But to the degree that large industry develops, the creation of real wealth comes to depend less on labor time and the amount of labor employed than on the power of agencies set in motion during labor time, whose "powerful effectiveness" ... depends ... on the general state of science and the progress of technology, or the application of this science to production.... In this transformation, it is neither direct human labor he himself performs, nor the time during which he works, but rather the appropriation of his own general productive power, his understanding of nature, of its mastery over it by virtue of his presence as social body – it is, in a word, the development of the social individual which appears as the great foundation stone of production and wealth.... As soon as labor in the direct form has ceased to be the great well-spring of wealth, labor time ceases and must cease to be its measure, and exchange value [must cease to be the measure] of use value.... With that, production based on exchange value breaks down, and the direct material production process is stripped of its form of penuries and antithesis, (pp. 704–706)

In this passage, the application of science and technology to production challenges and ultimately will replace the exchange-value-oriented forms of organizing production. "The general productive power" (the application of science and technology to production) is realized only by individuals as parts of the social body: The socialization of production calls for a means of interaction through which the richness of specialized human capabilities is mobilized in design and production.

What is interesting in this vision are the keen connections between the development of science and technology (and industry), the development of individuals, the organization of work, and political institutions and democracy in capitalist society. The metaphor of "general intellect" is used by Marx (1973, p. 706) to refer to the accumulated collective cultural-cognitive-technical potential of production (Haug, 2003, p. 45). The general intellect is mobilized for production (turned into a force of production) only by individuals' use of that diversified potential together (as a "presence as social body"). On the one hand, "the development of the social individual as the great foundation stone of production and wealth" means access to and individually partaking in the developing "general intellect." This corresponds to Marx's anthropology, in which "species being" (*Gattungswesen*, human essence), that is, the potential to develop individual capabilities, depends on the possibility of such participation through creative work, which is also a key issue of democracy.

On the other hand, Marx states that the institutions and social organizations of capitalism must be transformed to make possible the use of the general intellect as a force of production. The institutions of capitalism, such as markets, hierarchy as an organizational form of production, and the systems of intellectual property rights evidently do not satisfactorily support the formation and uses of the general intellect. New nonmarket and nonhierarchical forms of organization are needed that allow the development of individual capabilities and call for trust-based collaboration, and that favor the exchange of knowledge and understanding between the participants in the general intellect. This is a formulation of how new use-value demands of production (based increasingly on the general intellect) challenge prevailing forms of production and institutions of capitalism, including the power relationships in production.

Owing to the increased significance of knowledge and technology, the present society and economy have been generically characterized as a knowledge society (Böhme, 1998), a knowledge economy (Powell & Snellman, 2004), or an informational network society (Castells, 2000). Haug (2003) speaks about high-technology capitalism to avoid the intellectualist overtones of the concept of (scientific) knowledge. To concretize this position, I will discuss some interdependent recent developments of capitalism: the increased significance of science and technology in production, the sophistication of the needs of consumers and users of production, and the changes in the intellectual property right regime.

In addition, I suggest that the breakthrough of the Internet in the 1990s both invigorated the forms of socialization that were already developing independently of it and made possible the emergence of new forms of distributed production, as exemplified by Linux in software development,

Wikipedia in cultural production, and Synaptic Leap in molecular biology. Here I agree with Nick Dyer-Witheford (1999, p. 192), who suggests that the creation of universal communication networks is instrumental for the formation of forms of general intellect that also constitute viable alternatives to capitalism.

ALTERNATIVES TO EXCHANGE-VALUE-ORIENTED FORMS OF ORGANIZING WORK

There is a growing agreement that the traditional forms of organizing economic activity, that is, markets and hierarchy, no longer work when knowledge and the capacity to innovate become central sources of competitiveness. Attempts have been made to characterize the new, emerging form of organization: network (Castells, 2000; Powell, 1990), distributed creation (Boyle, 2003), commons-based peer production (Benkler, 2006), co-configuration (Victor & Boynton, 1998), collaborative community (Adler & Hecksher, 2006), and knotworking (Engeström, 2005a). These different terms represent different aspects of the ongoing transformation of the forms of the organization of work. I will use the concept of network in this chapter because it has been seriously regarded as an alternative to the capitalist forms of organizing production (Benkler, 2006; Castells, 2000; Weber, 2004).

Market and hierarchy are forms of organization in which the product primarily appears as an exchange value. In a hierarchy, the exchange value is present as a demand of cost efficiency, which is realized through a vertical and horizontal division of labor, exemplified by the Taylorian planning of work. The separation of designers and producers prevails: The production process is planned at the higher levels of the hierarchy, and standards are used to control the production process. The communication and collaboration related to the shared object – the product (its design and usability) – remain marginal. Price mechanism and bargaining are central in the market – control and following the orders of management are central in hierarchy. A network, on the other hand, is a form of collaboration and communication in which the use-value qualities of the products, that is, their usability and the complementary knowledge and capabilities needed to achieve them, are at the forefront. The more they are ignored, the more they are expressed later as disturbances in the market and the hierarchy.

The so-called free and open source development model of software production (FOSS) has been regarded as a paradigmatic case of a network organization and distributed work (Moon & Sproul, 2002). Linux kernel development is the best-known example of this model. The core of the community comprises Linus Torvalds and 121 maintainers, who are responsible for Linux's modules. In addition, several thousand user-developers participate in the reporting of bugs and in the writing of new pieces of code (Lee & Cole, 2003). This kind of distributed creation is not controlled by an innovator; developers on the periphery select the problems and improvements they want to work with.

Free source code (freely available on the Internet) is essentially connected to usability. Access to source code makes it possible for users to change it to conform to their specific needs. In the open developmental model, users (those able to write code) are developers and are motivated by the need for a useful tool for themselves. In addition, a user can ask for instructions and advice from other users. Consequently, the more users a network has, the more value it has for a user. The open development model is also said to offer advantages over the closed, in-house model of software development (Moon & Sproul, 2002). Eric Raymond (1999, p. 43) suggests that the reason is the "Delphi effect": The variety of skills, the uses for the software, and the working environments of the contributors add extra value to the quality of the code.

The open development model of free software is an example of a use-value-oriented network that has directly emerged from the needs of the complex product and from the possibilities provided by the Internet. The model developed as an alternative to a closed, proprietary mode of software production (as exemplified by Microsoft). In recent years, firms have started to utilize the open development model either by releasing their source code, inviting users' contributions, or by joining open development projects. A key question in the near future will be what combinations of hierarchical or market-oriented organizations and open development communities will emerge and whether the open source development model can preserve its identity and principles in community–firm hybrids (Weber, 2004).

INTELLECTUAL PROPERTY RIGHT INSTITUTIONS AND THE "INTERNAL CONTRADICTION OF A KNOWLEDGE SOCIETY"

The leading thesis of knowledge society theorists is that knowledge, high technology, and innovation have become decisive factors in the economic competition among market firms. Some well-known proponents of the knowledge society theory and the so-called enterprise university have suggested that the private ownership of knowledge is the greatest institutional innovation of the past century (Etzkowitz & Webster, 1995). Since the 1980s, the sphere of what can be patented has been enormously enlarged to include such entities as cells, tissues, plants, animals, genes, business models, and teaching methods (Jaffe & Lerner, 2004). On the other hand, knowledge is a paradigmatic case of the "public good"; that is, its availability to one consumer is not diminished by its use by another. It is therefore not suitable at all for exchange in markets, where scarcity is the premise. This is why knowledge has to be made a marketable commodity through copyrights and patents. Many economists and students of property rights see here the central emerging contradiction of high-technology capitalism.

Representatives of academic science have defined this contradiction between commodification and open, critical science: "Knowledge society incorporates the internal contradiction between knowledge, which as cultural capital is common property, and the knowledge economy, which is based on the privatization of knowledge" (Böhme 1998, p. 461). Many scholars have concluded that the increasing private ownership of knowledge already impedes communication among researchers, the availability of new knowledge, and innovative activity (Heller & Eisenberg, 1998; Nelson, 2001). They think that the culturally cumulating nature of knowledge, the extensive use of prior cultural resources, imitation, and the combination of the ingredients of culture in creative work (or "the standing on the shoulders of giants" effect) demand a strong public domain able to keep knowledge freely available (Benkler 2006; Cohen, 2006).

In the FOSS model, licenses based on the copyleft principle, as exemplified by the *general public license* (GPL), are used. They allow users to use, modify, and further distribute code. Richard Stallman (2002), founder of the Free Software Foundation and GPL, explains the idea of the copyleft as follows:

> So we needed to use distribution terms that would prevent GNU software from being turned into proprietary software. The method we used is called *copy left*. Copy left uses copyright law, but flips it over to serve the opposite of its usual purpose. Instead of a means of privatizing software, it becomes a means of keeping software free. The central idea of copy left is that we give everyone permission to run the program, modify the program, and distribute the modified versions – but not permission to add restrictions of their own. (p. 20)

Stallman finds two foundations for the copyleft method. First, as a result of digitalization and the emergence of the Internet, the cost and time of reproducing and transmitting knowledge have decreased to almost zero.

Second, patents are incompatible with the incremental or culturally cumulative nature of software design. Stallman (2002) explains, "When you write a program, you are using lots of different ideas; any one of them might be patented by somebody.... So there are possibly thousands of things ... in your program, which might be patented by somebody else already. This is why software patents tend to obstruct the progress of software – the work of software development" (p. 105). Stallman challenges the prevailing institutions of intellectual property rights by referring to economic reasons (the cost of the reproduction and transmission of digital products), the rights of users in an information society, as well as to the use-value demands of software production.

INTERNET-MEDIATED DISTRIBUTED WORK, USERS, AND THE DEMOCRATIZATION OF INNOVATION

Market and hierarchy are undermined by the increasing sophistication of consumers (Adler & Hecksher, 2006). First, consumers move beyond mass-market consumption and increasingly look for customized products. Second, business-to-business markets have greatly expanded, and the customers in these markets are often knowledgeable and demanding. Even the traditional hierarchical enterprise giants have had to adapt to these changes. IBM, for instance, provides solutions to customers' problems by providing a tailored mix of products and services.

In this reorganization of producer–user relationships, information technologies play a significant role. Zysman and Newman (2004) analyze how digital tools and the Internet affect firms' value creation: "A fundamental feature of the digital era is that analytic tools of database management permit the consumer community to be segmented into sub-components, each with distinct needs and wishes" (p. 19). Market segmentation and product versioning can be extended to the individual level. For example, when I order a book from Amazon, the display immediately suggests to me other books related to the contents and topic of the book ordered.

In his book *Democratizing Innovation*, Eric von Hippel (2005) suggests that open source development anticipates and expresses an ongoing development toward user-community-based innovation. The emergence of the Internet and new tools based on information technology, such as CAD (computer-aided design), databases, and platforms, have made this development possible. The heterogeneous needs and capabilities of users can be mobilized to contribute to the design of new products. According to von Hippel, firms will increasingly externalize the development of ideas and prototypes to user communities and will appropriate the results in their business without owning them. Red Hat, the vendor of Linux distributions, is a successful example of this business model. By the democratization of innovation, von Hippel means two things. First, users can increasingly participate in innovation. Second, the products developed in user communities better meet the individual needs of citizens as well as concerns for welfare.

The open development model can evidently be transferred outside the sphere of software production. An example of this is Wikipedia, an encyclopedia established in 2001 that is developed and maintained by users. In 2003, the English Wikipedia included some 130,000 entries. By the end of the summer of 2007, the number of entries reached 2 million. Unlike traditional encyclopedias, it is quickly and constantly updated, and entries include recent review articles. This remarkable innovation was constructed outside the markets and convincingly demonstrates the strength of Internet-mediated distributed creation. It is an example of the workings of the "general intellect." The Web pages of Wikipedia indicate that 67,000 active contributors are working on the articles.

The open development model is also spreading to biology, bioinformatics, and biomedical research (Deibel, 2006). An example is Synaptic Leap, "a network of online research communities that connect and enable open source biomedical research," founded in 2005. The communities involved (the malaria research community and the community for schistosomiasis) aim to develop proteins for medicines for "severely underresearched tropical diseases where the for-profit incentives are falling short." The goal is to establish an alternative to the commercial development of pharmaceuticals.

CONCLUSIONS

Marx anticipated in *Grundrisse* that the production of exchange value would create new use values (e.g., science-based technologies, such as the Internet) that would challenge the prevailing forms of production and the property right institutions of capitalism. The production and use of these new use values assume, to paraphrase Marx, a form of "general intellect" and will be realized by "social individual." Internet-mediated distributed work activities and the externalization of innovation to user communities, as exemplified by Linux, Wikipedia, and Synaptic Leap, can be seen as steps toward such a general, distributed intellect. Likewise, the care agreement practice introduced by Yrjö Engeström's group can be seen both as an alternative to exchange-value-oriented forms of health care and a potential step toward a general distributed intellect. As Nick Dyer-Witheford (1999, p. 4) has suggested, the internal contradiction of capitalism will assume the form of a "contest for general intellect." It is an open question whether new forms of work will develop as robust alternative forms of production within capitalism, or whether they will gradually be fused with or subsumed within the demands of value production.

11

Spinozic Reconsiderations of the Concept of Activity: Politico-Affective Process and Discursive Practice in Transitive Learning

SHUTA KAGAWA AND YUJI MORO

In this chapter, we attempt to articulate and expand the concept of activity by applying Spinoza's idea concerning human collective activeness. Though rarely discussed in an activity-theoretical research context, Spinoza's idea, we believe, has multifaceted implications for advancing and supplementing the concept of activity. Among these, we will focus on three. First, concerning the ontological articulation of the concept of activity, we will briefly discuss the connection between Spinoza and Vygotsky. Second, we will, on the basis of Spinozic anthropology, focus on what is called politico-affective process in human local interaction. Third, we will discuss discursive practice, a form of activity in Spinozic anthropology, and, specifically, its significance in the transitive learning process of student nurses.

PRIMORDIAL ARTICULATION OF THE CONCEPT OF ACTIVITY

It is widely held that the historical origin of activity theory was German idealist philosophy and that the activity concept was fully developed in Marx's writings, with the concept being introduced to psychology by Vygotsky (Davydov, 1999b; Engeström, 1999a; Kasavin, 1990; Lektorsky, 1999; Tolman, 2001). As it is rare for Spinoza's ideas to be regarded as a philosophical foundation of activity theory, it seems rather strange for a scientific explication of the activity concept to draw on the ideas of Spinoza, who has been depicted as a "god-intoxicated" pantheist.

However, Spinoza has unquestionably been an extremely influential philosophical source of activity theory, as evidenced by the wide-ranging impact his work has had on the philosophical founders of activity theory, particularly on Marx. Yovel (1989) points out that "the actual presence of Spinoza in Marx surpasses his direct mention by name" (p. 79). Il'enkov (1977a) appreciated that Spinoza was one of the great thinkers of the pre-Marxian era, and the influence of his ideas on subsequent dialectical thought can hardly be exaggerated.

Vygotsky (1999, p. 105) admired Spinoza's teaching on emotion as "a turning point of the whole history of psychology and its future development," and Spinoza's influence on Vygotsky was far reaching and formative. Van der Veer (1984) identifies three ideas in Vygotsky's work that are inspired by Spinoza, namely (1) intellectualism, (2) monism, or determinism, and (3) intellectual tools. The most decisive impact of Spinoza on Vygotsky is seen in monism, or determinism, which enabled Vygotsky to develop "dialectical psychology," which synthesizes antagonistic tensions in psychological thinking. "Dialectical psychology proceeds first of all from the unity of mental and physiological processes. Because for the dialectical psychology mind is not, in the words of Spinoza (1955, p. 128), something that is situated outside nature or as a kingdom within the kingdom, it is a part of nature itself, directly linked to the functions of higher organized matter of our brain" (Vygotsky, 1997a, p. 112). Vygotsky applied this monistic principle of dialectical psychology to various domains, including the resolution of tension between explanatory and descriptive psychology (Vygotsky, 1997a, p. 316), developmental explication of the interrelationships between the affects and the intellect (Vygotsky, 1997a, p. 103), and the genetic and ontological solution of the dualism of mind and spirit (Vygotsky, 1999, p. 198). Vygotsky's dialectical psychology criticizes the notion of a separate psychological process constructed by Descartes. Derry (2004) focuses on the relationship between free will and intellect. The common notion of free will refers to free choice and the absence of constraints, which mirrors the modern notion of the free actor constructed by Descartes's separation of mind and body (and material world). Derry (2004) demonstrates that "Vygotsky considered freedom in Spinoza's sense of self-determination as integral to education as specifically human process of coming to be in the world" (p. 119).

As several post-Vygotskians have pointed out (Davydov & Radikhovskii, 1985; Robbins, 2001; Van der Veer & Valsiner, 1991; Wertsch, 1985), Vygotsky's monism can be linked to Spinoza's ontological distinction between substance and attribute. Spinoza (1994) defines substance as what "is in itself and is conceived through itself" and defines attribute as what "the intellect perceives of substance as constituting its essence" (p. 1). Drawing on this distinction, Vygotsky argued that neither mental nor physiological phenomena are substance; both are attributes of the substance.

Spinoza's notion of substance allows a primordial articulation of the ontological aspect of the concept of activity. Spinozic substance fundamentally differs from the substance of Descartes, who treated mind and body, or thought and extension, as distinct substances. Il'enkov (1977a) observed that Spinoza's "simple and profoundly true idea" makes it clear that thought and extension are "not two special objects, capable of existing separately and independently of each other, but only two different and even opposite aspects under which one and the same thing appears, two different modes of existence, two forms of the manifestation of some third thing" (p. 32).

The third issue relating to Spinoza's ontological system is real, infinite Nature, which affords a primordial foundation for the concept of activity. According to Il'enkov (1977a), "Thought [is] a spatially expressed activity" (p. 35). He illustrates the meaning of this with an analogy: "Thinking is not the product of an action but the action itself, considered at the moment of its performance, just as walking, for example, is the mode of action of the legs, the 'product' of which, it transpires, is the space walked" (p. 35).

With the aid of Spinoza's ideas on substance and attribute, Vygotsky succeeded in articulating the ontological status of psychological phenomena and came very close to the notion of activity, "a molar, not an additive unit of the life of the physical, material subject" (Leont'ev, 1980, p. 68).

Spinoza's contribution to activity theory is not limited to the ontological articulation of the concept of activity. In the following sections, we will reconsider the notion of activity by drawing on Spinoza's politico-affective ideas concerning the sociality of the human mind, ideas that have seldom been applied in discussions of activity theory. Specifically, we argue that Spinoza's ideas elucidate the concept of activity, emphasizing the significance of local interactive and affective aspects in learning activity.

COLLECTIVITY IN ENGESTRÖM'S SYSTEMIC CONCEPT OF ACTIVITY

Engeström (1987) attempted to explore the supraindividual, or the social and collective, dimensions of activity, in order to expand the application of the original activity theory. To that aim, he supplemented Vygotsky's (1997a) triangular model of mediation – the somewhat simplistic representation of interdependencies between subject, object, and tool – with three additional components of an activity system, namely community, rules, and the division of labor. Thus, Engeström (1987, p. 78) created a complex and systemic representation of collective human activity that articulates the structural composition of activity, and so brought the aspects of distribution, exchange, and consumption into sharper focus. This systemic representation enabled him to delineate more distinctly the societal and collective levels of the learning process, particularly in organizational changes within the workplace. This also provided tools for interventions in which practitioners in the workplace could utilize this conceptual representation for reflection on their own activities. Daniels (2001) points out that Engeström's attempt to recognize the social allows him to examine the system of activity at the collective and community levels in preference to the individual microlevel. What the social is for Engeström (1987) can be characterized as the collectivity of organizational activity.

To appreciate the significance of Engeström's activity system, two facets of the collective activity system should be distinguished. These two enable us to depict vividly the dynamic nature of the activity system. The first facet of the productive collectivity consists of the developmental forces that drive the transformation of primitive forms of activity into advanced and specifically human forms within Engeström's (1987) historical outline. Human production yields more than the mere reproduction of the subjects and social relations of previous settings. While the productive collectivity results in the surplus that is a condition for human sharing and social bonds, the form of collectivity is transformed through the development of immanent contradictions in production. As a theoretical implication, productive collectivity within the complex triangle model offers a thinking device for probing and specifying various kinds of contradictions in activity systems.

The second facet, namely the multivoicedness of the collectivity, was introduced more recently (Engeström, 1999a) as a conceptual tool that enables the third generation of activity theory to understand cultural diversity inside activity systems and to explicate dialogic interactions among activity systems. The introduction of this multivoiced aspect was motivated by a critique of and reflections on the insensitivity of the second generation to cultural diversity (Cole, 1996). The multivoiced collectivity can shed light on the intercontextual relationships between two or more activity systems.

THE POLITICO-AFFECTIVE PROCESS IN LEARNING

How can the participants within learning settings accomplish collectivity in "the activity of concrete individuals that takes place either in conditions of open association, in the midst of people, or eye to eye with the surrounding object world" (Leont'ev, 1980, p. 69)? We would argue that collective sociality is accomplished through a "politico-affective process" whereby each participant in the learning situation submits to and is submitted to by all other participants. What constitutes the collectivity in learning settings is the dynamism of submission and disobedience among the participants. The term "submission" may seem rather strong, bringing to mind images of social order controlled by force. However, submission is undeniably an omnipresent process in human activity, especially in collective learning activity. For instance, from peer interaction studies, it is clear that peer collaboration sessions do not necessarily have positive effects on post-tests (Tudge, Winterhoff, & Hogan, 1996), as negative effects can arise, in part owing to the dynamics and fluctuations of peer interactions. The determining factor for positive effects can be a child's appreciation of the significance of another child as a model for solving a task. Thus, the participants strengthen affective ties with one another through a submissive process. Peer interaction emerges out of the emotional fluctuation between submission and disobedience (Park & Moro, 2006).

By politico-affective processes, we mean the Spinozic mechanism of encountering individual bodies, through which individuals try to preserve themselves and increase their power of acting. Individual bodies are constrained by their inadequate knowledge of themselves, and through this inadequacy emerges the conflict of affections. The Spinozic individual is not a self-sufficient one. According to Spinoza, no individual person is ever corporeally or psychologically independent. Individual life necessitates the coming together and uniting of individuals. Thus, "if two come together and unite their strength, they have jointly more power, and consequently more right over nature than both of them separately, and the more there are that have joined in alliance, the more right they all collectively possess" (Spinoza, 2004, p. 296). The politico-affective process is a local interactive aspect of an activity system, which develops through the encountering of bodies and represents the gathering of people through the submissive process and the dynamics of affects.

As an illustration of the significance of the politico-affective process, Engeström (1987) cites an episode, recounted in Snyder (1971), of a teacher informing his class at the start of the term that they are expected to be creative and involved. However, after five weeks of creative lessons that differed from normal classroom work, the students realized that the first test was asking for forms of knowledge that could be mastered only through memorization. Betraying his own opening proclamations, the teacher's calls for imagination and creativity were merely part of the empty language game surrounding education. One cynical student remarked, "Okay, if that's the way you play the academic game, if that's what he really wants, I won't make the same mistake again. Next time I'll memorize the key points" (Snyder, 1973, cited by Engeström 1987, p. 130).

In invoking this episode, Engeström (1987) seeks to point out the limitations of the theory of "metacognition." The metacognitive approach has "no awareness of the possibility that the tasks themselves might be inherently contradictory" (p. 129). It accounts only for adaptive selection and cognitive calculations in learning strategies, such as how to obtain a good grade with minimum effort. However, the possibility of the learners themselves reconstructing the activity setting is excluded from the outset.

Another aspect that is ruled out by a metacognitive interpretation of the episode is the feeling that the students might have experienced, whereas Engeström (1987) appreciates the feeling of something missing beyond the game of successful adaptation. The feeling of the students could be interpreted as sadness, according to Spinoza's (1994) anthropology of emotion, which classifies basic emotions into desire, joy, and sadness. Emotion comprises "affections of the body by which the body's power of acting is increased or diminished, aided or restrained" (p. 154). Sadness is "man's transition from a state of greater perfection to a state of less perfection" (p. 311). Following Spinoza, emotion is not an inner mental state. It is an interactive encountering process as well as a process of aspiring to achieve perfection, in which "the greater the joy with which we are affected, the greater the perfection to which we pass" (p. 154).

How did sadness arise in the students? It emerged from the local interaction, or the state of submission between the students and the teacher and the degeneration that led to the students' alienation from the teacher. The teacher's description of the course captured the students' affection so strongly that they willingly submitted to the teacher in their expectations of going beyond mere academic games. However, once the students discovered the hidden agenda of the course, they had to obey the teacher in order to earn credits. This discovery led the students to perceive a decrease in the power of their actions. The sadness appears to have arisen out of their perception of the dynamic shift in submission and the degeneration of the significance of the submission.

To explore the significance of the politico-affective process, the next sections will focus on three interrelated aspects of Spinoza's ideas – "multitude of activity," "constrained forms of individual agency," and "imaginative-discursive practice" – which can potentially explicate the concept of activity. The "multitude" discussed in Spinoza's writings on politics appears to have the potential to bridge the gap between collectivity and individuality within activity theory. Constrained forms of individual agency, or "conatus," serve as a matrix that generates both the inherent deficiencies of individual actors and their relative freedoms. According to Spinoza's insight, these deficiencies yield the inadequate, but practically useful understanding process that is attained through imaginative discursive practices.

MULTITUDE OF ACTIVITY

"Multitude" refers to the dynamism among participants in which the collectivity of activity is driven to function, is maintained, and is shifted to other states. Spinoza does not talk about the collective state from the viewpoint of a contract or a moralistic pact; rather, he defines it in terms of pluralistic potentiality and treats the state that arises as a natural process.

Spinoza (2004) writes: "16. Where men have general rights, and are all guided, as it were by one mind, it is certain that every individual has the less right the more the rest collectively exceed him in power; that is, he has, in fact, no right over nature but that which the common law allows him. But whatever he is ordered by the general consent, he is bound to execute, or may rightfully be compelled thereto. 17. This right, which is determined by the power of a multitude, is generally called Dominion" (p. 297).

What Spinoza is commenting on is state power, but the notion of "multitude," or "mass" (Balibar, 1994), could be advantageously applied to more mundane activity settings, including learning situations. In Spinoza's argument, state power is derived from gatherings of individuals who are constrained cognitively and driven by affections. It could be the multitude that transforms some settings into learning situations in which one participant submits to the other participants out of reliance on the overwhelming power of the other participants or out of some fear of them. Both reliance on and fear of the other participants can lead a participant to an attitude of submission whereby the order of the learning situation is constituted. Spinoza referred to anonymous power as the multitudinous potentiality that is constituted by differences in power between the individual and the rest of the participants (Ueno, 2006). This anonymous power is what leads the individual to submit to the order of the situation.

CONSTRAINED FORMS OF INDIVIDUAL AGENCY

To understand the dynamics between submission and disobedience, as well as the constitution of order within a learning situation, we should apply Spinoza's anthropology, explicated mainly in his *Ethics*. The third part of *Ethics* focuses on ideas about forms of individuality (Balibar,

1994) – how human beings are to behave as individuals. The form of individuality refers both to constraints and deficiencies within the individual and to the activation of the individual's potential in an activity triggered by the constraints.

According to Spinoza, individuals, including humans and nonhumans, are not composed of a substance that is the cause of itself, and they require no other things; rather they are finite modes of being that need to be acted on and are dependent on other beings. However, each individual is a being that brings about some effects and outcomes. Individual finite things have a "conatus," or "the striving by which each thing strives to persevere in its being" (Spinoza, 1994, p. 75). Because each person is an active being that strives to convert his or her latent possibilities into reality, each person "is opposed to everything which can take its existence away" (Spinoza, 1994, p. 75). Thus, the learning situation might be an arena where a number of persons encounter each other and struggle to preserve their being. It is a place constituted by the tensions among the participants that struggle with each other.

These forces make up the multitude in learning settings. The form of individuality, finite and constrained, serves as an ontological background that invites collectivity, power, and submission. It is possible only in fiction that an isolated person approaches nature by him- or herself. "When each man most seeks his own advantage for himself, then men are most useful to one another" (Spinoza, 1994, p. 132). This is the reason that people come together and constitute the collectivity through submission to one another.

IMAGINATIVE-DISCURSIVE PRACTICE

The human process of knowing is also inherently constrained, and such constraint has effects on the practices of emotion and discourse. "In each human mind," according to Spinoza, "some ideas are adequate, but others are mutilated and confused" (Spinoza, 1994, p. 71). The human process of knowing is like knowing only results without comprehending causes. Humans in their finite mode are conscious of their desire, but totally unconscious about the causes of that desire. Metaphorically, man is dreaming with his eyes open (Spinoza, 1994, p. 74).

"The ideas of affections of the human body, insofar as they are related only to the human mind, are not clear and distinct, but confused" (Spinoza, 1994, p. 51). The human body is a complex and multiple composite and is sensitively affected by the presence of another composite body. However, it is impossible for a person to adequately perceive and know about the totality of events that act on the body, for he or she can perceive only part of the totality. The human being, as a finite mode, can only guess on the basis of data from the affected body what is going on around his or her body.

According to Ueno (2006), these constraints and deficiencies drive the emotional process and the submission process. Human beings are full of fear and anticipation because they do not know the causal connections by which an event proceeds, and thus fear and expectation drive them to act without consideration for the causal connections. In learning settings, a participant anticipates the overwhelming power of the other participants and fears it, and then experiences an urge to submit to it.

Another kind of action is also driven by these constraints and deficiencies. It is the imaginative-discursive practice that is driven by the inadequacies of human knowledge. Imagination is one way in which humans perceive and form universal notions "from singular things ... represented to us through the senses in a way which is mutilated, confused, and without order for the intellect" (Spinoza, 1994, p. 48). It is important for Spinoza that imagination is not totally useless; it is partly and practically significant.

Imagination also emerges from "signs," or "from the fact that, having heard and read certain words, we recollect things, and form certain ideas of them, like those through which we imagine the things" (Spinoza, 1994, p. 48). Discursive practice in our everyday learning is based on imagination, which cannot be regarded as adequate knowledge but which is very useful in a practical sense in that it enables humans to speculate about and account for their conduct.

What we have been discussing has implications for the problem of discourse within activity theory. Discourse has been treated as a useful tool for researchers to probe deeply into activity systems, as well as for practitioners to re-mediate people, artifacts, and objects in the systems. On the basis of Spinoza's discussion about imagination and discourse, we may secure an ontological location for discursive practice within activity systems (Engeström, 1999b; R. Engeström, 1995). According to Spinoza, imaginative-discursive practice derives from the existential and epistemological constraints of human beings, and everyday learners struggle to expand their power of action with limited resources of affective and imaginative discourse.

TRANSFER AS DISCOURSE

Activity theorists and situated learning theorists (Beach, 2003; Greeno, 1997; Lave, 1988; Tuomi-Gröhn & Engeström, 2003b; Van Oers, 1998) have repeatedly criticized the theory of transfer based on solipsistic cognitivism and on the notion of decontextualization. For example, Van Oers (1999), citing Donaldson (1978), points out that the development of abstract thinking leading to transfer is not "a process of detachment from conditions that constrain the generality of meaning and actions," that is, decontextualizaton, but is rather "a state of being highly involved in a theoretically construed world, based on explicitly used relations, logical rules, and strict norms of negotiation." Similarly, Beach (2003) argues that "knowledge generalization is never separate or decontextualized from social organization, though it may become distanced from particular social organizations over time" (pp. 40–41), and so it "is best understood as a set of processes that relate changing social organizations and individuals" (p. 41). Emphasizing the failings of transfer theories that treat learning as a process of internalizing portable knowledge in the head of an individual, activity theory formulates learning as changes in the holistic and indivisible relationships among the individual, artifacts, and other people. Furthermore, although Tuomi-Gröhn and Engeström (2003b; Tuomi-Gröhn, 2003) agree with the idea that learning is always embedded in a situation, they criticize theories of situated learning, pointing out that the "locus of learning is still firmly in the individual." They expand the concept of transfer into the realm of interrelations among collective activity systems, proposing the concept of "developmental transfer." According to Tuomi-Gröhn (2003), "Meaningful transfer of learning takes place through interaction between collective activity systems. For example, the school and the workplace may engage in collaborative interaction in which both activity systems learn something from each other. Such transfer takes the form of negotiation and exchange between different cultures" (p. 202).

The attempts of Engeström and Tuomi-Gröhn are very important. However, they leave room for further explication. The central concern for activity theorists, as well as for traditional theorists such as behaviorists, Gestalt psychologists, and cognitivists, seems to be the reality of the transfer process. They investigate the conditions of (non-)transfer, or they ask how we can make transfer really occur. Although these questions are very significant, they are also rather unsatisfactory because they have shed no light on transfer as the discourse that mediates our experiences in everyday learning practices.

Here, we will discuss transfer from a different angle. We suggest that the concepts of transfer held by local actors function as mediating artifacts within an activity system and that transfer discourse organizes people's local actions and activities. Our attempt, based on Spinoza's imaginary-discursive practice, can reveal the meanings and functions of transfer concepts for everyday persons who are themselves actually working with transfer in making sense of their lives.

DISTANTIATION

What kinds of discursive practice do we engage in when we talk about a certain event as "transfer?" When talking about transfer, we engage in the discursive practice of "distantiation," by which we articulate events and identify points of difference and of similarity.

The semantic content of the transfer concept is confusing because its unit of analysis varies considerably among researchers. For instance, Säljö (2003), following Smedslund (1953), depicts the transfer concept as a pseudo-concept. Säljö (2003) proposes that examples of successful boundary crossing are best conceived of as learning experiences at the collective and individual levels, rather than as transfer. How are these learning experiences constructed? Distantiation is to divide the experienced world into more than one element and to combine these elements into some shape connecting them. We will treat these two aspects of distantiation together to signify that people are always pulling apart and rejoining the elements.

The lifeworld surrounding us is seamless and has no lines of demarcation. By distancing work, we articulate parts or elements of the lifeworld spatially and temporally (Fig. 11.1). Spatial distancing involves picking out parts of the lifeworld and making distinctions between them. Through temporal distancing, we compartmentalize "the past," "the present," and

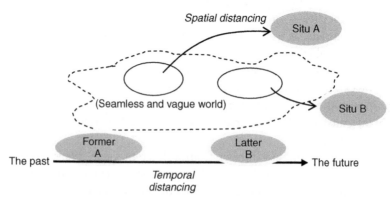

Figure 11.1. Distancing.

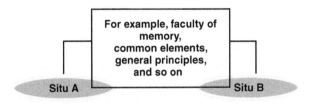

Figure 11.2. Connecting.

"the future" and construct the learning experience through discourse. Connecting is a discursive practice that ensures the continuity between the past, the present, and the future, with the aid of mediating factors, such as the faculty of memory, common elements, and general principles (Fig. 11.2).[1]

When we talk about the learning experience from the viewpoint of transfer, we engage in the practice of discursive work, dividing the world up into various elements and connecting them through some mediating items. Thus, when some researcher remarks that "learning in the prior task will not be made use of in solving the target task" of a transfer experiment, the researcher is doing discursive work, temporally distancing the past learning and the future action and disconnecting them. Similarly, when someone comments that "although Mr. X graduated from the University of Tokyo, X hasn't made a sale yet this month" in a corporate sales department, he is engaging in a distancing practice that is articulating past learning and present action and spatially connecting the college learning with sales. Distancing is followed by the work of connecting in which separated elements are joined together, which ensures a continuity so that knowledge and abilities learned in past situations can be applied to solving tasks in the present situation or learning in the present can later be applied to solving some future task. In this connecting work, a mediating item, such as the faculty of memory, functions as the "glue" that links distanced elements together.

Distantiation, identifying the resemblances and differences between situations, can be derived from Spinoza's (1994) discussion on similarity and the affective process. According to his politico-affective anthropology, human beings are affected in diverse and contradictory ways from the

---

[1] Mediating items such as faculty of memory, common elements, and general principles derive from representative transfer theories in psychology. In addition, there can be others, such as brain functions in brain science.

outside, and try to preserve and increase their power of acting. "Man is affected with the same affect of joy or sadness from the image of a past or future thing as from the image of a present thing" (p. 80). In other words, the human being is searching for and detecting the resemblance between present situations and past (or future) situations, separating them, and reuniting them in imaginative discourse. By finding the resemblance, the individual may have an opportunity to experience joy or an expansion of his or her power of action.

TRANSFER AS CONSTRUCTED REALITY

Talking about a certain phenomenon as transfer is in itself a social practice in which we reconstruct and make sense of our learning experience through distantiation. Transfer might be thought of as an everyday phenomenon in our lives. However, it is a very special one in the sense that it is constituted through practice that makes the transfer "visible" (Wenger, 1990) in focusing and highlighting some aspects of everyday life events that can be variously interpreted.

Let us reconsider the aforementioned "Mr. X," Salesperson X often fails in the sales business, and his colleagues and superiors comment that his business performance is poor, even though he should be very smart because he has graduated from the University of Tokyo. This is a "story" narrated from the viewpoint of transfer that is very akin to the theory of formal discipline, assuming that sales ability can be transferred from the intelligence fostered through intense preparation for the entrance examination of the University of Tokyo.

However, a transfer failure is not the only story that could account for X's unsatisfactory business performance. It is also possible, for example, to account for his difficulties as being related to his personality, in that he is a poor communicator.

Gergen (1999) maintains that we do not picture "value-neutral" and "objective truth" or an "exterior world" independent of people's practice with words. We construct the reality itself with words. For example, the characteristics of an object called "desk" will be expressed in different discursive forms by everyday people, psychologists, physicists, and biologists, even though they all speak of the same object.

Similarly, transfer is not value-neutral and objective truth or given reality that exists before our discursive practice. It is rather *one of the various realities* that is constructed through practice. Although discursive resources can make a particular event visible as transfer, at the same time they can make other accounts of the event "invisible" (Wenger, 1990). Finding the arrangement and the economy between what is visible and what is invisible in discursive work allows us to appreciate the social meaning in the notion of transfer as used in our everyday learning experiences. When someone remarks that Mr. X is not a brilliant salesman, even though he is a graduate of the University of Tokyo, the utterance has a particular meaning and certain implications in the given situation. It can be a kind of "claims-making" (Best, 1987); it can belie the person's envy of graduates of the University of Tokyo, or it can convey some sarcasm toward Japanese society, which places so great a value on an individual's academic career, or it can even be a proclamation of "an exchange value of knowledge" (Engeström, 1987).

DISCURSIVE PRACTICE AMONG STUDENT NURSES

We will now discuss distantiation discourses in our study of the learning process among student nurses during their transition from the classroom to a clinical stage in their basic training (Kagawa & Moro, 2006), and seek to reveal the functions of transfer discourse.

While in the classroom, student nurses believe that the nursing procedures they study in textbooks will be almost the same as those learned in their clinical course and in their practice on the ward. Accordingly, they attempt to apply the procedures to their patients almost exactly as they studied them in their textbooks. For instance, a student (Student A) mentioned in a research interview:

> I attended the classes convinced that the nursing procedures learned in class would be actually performed on the ward just as they were explained in the textbook, because that is all that I know.

And, indeed, in the classroom exercises, we observed that the student nurses tried to faithfully follow the procedures described in the textbook. The learning actions of the student nurses were consistent with their perspective on transfer.

However, after participating in the clinical course at a hospital and encountering the gaps that exist between textbook knowledge and clinical practice, Student A stated, "When I went onto the ward bringing the knowledge learned from the textbook in my head, I later realized that all the things were different from the textbook." The students realized that procedures carried out on the ward must achieve an effective economy of care costs and time. On the other hand, the knowledge taught in the classroom is formal and procedural in nature and seems to be extremely focused on the patients' well-being. These formal procedures appear to be so static that they cannot easily accommodate a patient's medical condition, personality, body features, or economic conditions.

For example, Student B said:

> The textbook is idealistic. The textbook doesn't care about how much money you spend on caring, but, in the clinical course, what we have to first consider is the burden to the patient's family; we try to greatly lessen the burdens on the family and patient.

When asked to comment on the negative aspects of the procedures followed on the ward, Student C replied:

> I couldn't help doubting that nurses are only interested in improving efficiency. I thought it was terrible when they bathe patients in bed using just warm water (without soap) simply to finish the bathing quickly and economically. Because, in the class discussion about bathing, I pointed out that bathing with soap is much more hygienic than with water only.

Experiencing these gaps leads the students to realize that the procedures taught in the classroom are totally different from the actual practices implemented on the ward. This can trap them in a state of conflict that is not easy to resolve, because both approaches can be rationalized. The students appear to modify the significance they attach to textbook knowledge, no longer seeing it as an ideal resource but rather as a mediating artifact that allows them attain a more critical perspective on practice on the ward. They shift to a discursive formation on transfer, which maintains that textbook knowledge learned in the classroom is to be modified in flexible ways that are responsive to the characteristics and conditions of their patients.

This shift between discursive formations can be illustrated by Student D's statement. When asked about the shift in the significance of the textbook after the clinical course, Student D replied:

> Yes, it changed very much. I began to feel slight doubts about the knowledge and procedures in the textbook. In this case, it is good for the patient, but in another case, I wondered whether it might be irrelevant, and so on.

In summary, the discursive practice of transfer consists of two kinds of discursive work. The first is the work of distancing. While in the classroom, the student nurses assumed that the classroom and the clinical course would be virtually the same or that they would at least be able to make a connection between the two situations. In the process of transition, as they identified the gaps and became aware of the differences between the two situations, the nurses began to construct a disconnection.

The second is the work of connecting. Through the disconnection, paradoxically, the student nurses attained some continuity between the different learning situations. On the presupposition of disconnection, they were able to scrutinize the aspects of their actions that remained the same despite the changes and shifts in various elements and units.

We should note that transfer discourse itself is an object of learning. There is a vast range of discursive formations that could be employed in distancing situations and connecting them. A specific transfer discourse may be useful as a resource in a particular situation. However, it may not be as effective in every case of discursive practice. We have to learn which discursive formations are applicable to what kinds of learning that we engage in. And we change transfer discourse as the need arises. Various troubles, conflicts, anger, and joy experienced through access to many materials, and diverse physical and discursive actions function as *energy* changing the discourse. Thus, learning discursive ways to connect situations is a part of "participation in social practice" (Lave & Wenger, 1991).

Generalizing this discussion, we may state that transfer discourse is a resource for learning that directs how learners should act in practice, and it is also what is to be learned dynamically and creatively in practice.

TRANSFER DISCOURSE AS A CATALYST

Metaphorically, transfer discourse may be seen as a "catalyst" that affects relations among activity domains and brings about a novel form of activity. Transfer discourse as a catalyst is well illustrated by the recent boom in brain-exercising games in Japan.

Brain Training is a video game in which players use a console to solve various tasks, such as multiplication, word memorization, and writing and reading of kanji characters. Brain Training, released by a video-game maker, is based on research by the neuroscientist Dr. Ryuta Kawashima, who specializes in brain imaging. According to Kawashima, daily training in such problem-solving activities can help to avert the reduction in brain function that accompanies aging, because these activities enhance blood flow to the frontal areas of the brain cortex as the brain regulates the cognitive functions required by the game activities. We can find a transfer discourse in this brain game boom that connects daily training and the prevention of some future decreases in brain functioning based on a neuroscientific discourse.

Learning research following a nondiscursive research agenda would focus on whether the training in the game really boosts general cognitive capabilities. However, a nondiscursive agenda would veil the sociocultural aspects of this brain game boom. The brain-training discourse forms a novel socioeconomic network. For example, one travel agency has organized a bus tour named "Brain Train Tour," a one-day bus tour for elderly people who are interested in preventing mental aging (Fuyuno, 2007). After being tested for brain age at the start to determine the effects of revitalizing and improving brain age, about 40 participants travel to a scenic rural area, try some handicrafts, eat organic meals, and bathe in hot springs. The organization of and participation in the bus tour is motivated by the discourse on brain training. Transfer discourses thus contribute to the reformulation of activity networks, intermediating scientific, economic, and everyday activities. Alternatively, transfer discourse as a catalyst is a mediating artifact that moves between various people and situations and, in the process, activates their movements, connections, and emotions.

THE POTENTIAL OF SPINOZA'S IDEAS

By applying Spinoza's ideas of imagination and discourse to the problems of transfer, we have reformulated the notion of transfer into discourse practice that intermediates between the various sectors of our daily activities. We have demonstrated the structure of transfer as discursive practice: It consists of the actions of distancing and connecting – the articulation of the seamless world into elements and their subsequent reconnection through mediating commonalities. Transfer as discursive practice is a creative and plastic resource that directs and constrains the actions of learners, and constitutes an economy of the visible and the invisible that highlights some of the commonalities between situations at different times and spaces and provides learners with a future perspective.

The concept of activity itself can be more deeply explicated by Spinoza's monistic ontology of the human mind. The problem of emotion and affect is an urgent issue for activity-theoretical research. Spinoza provides us with a genetic perspective on human emotions in terms of the constraints on human living and the conatus that causes humans to strive against these constraints in their lives. The Spinozic perspective on human emotion can contribute to accounts of the interrelations among human agency, objects of activity, and desire. Moreover, one potential that may enhance the power of the concept of activity would seem to reside in Spinoza's peculiar ideas about the ontology of things. Spinoza's ontology provides us with a symmetric understanding of the unity of person–tool–object of an activity system, in the sense that Spinoza recognizes the conatus as the striving to maintain one's being irrespective of whether one is human or nonhuman. We close this essay by pointing out two theoretical interests that should be cultivated in further research. The first is the connection between Spinoza and Vygotsky. This connection needs thorough probing in order to shed light on not only their textual similarities, but on Spinoza's implicit influence that is not identifiable in Vygotsky's explicit texts. For example, the possibility of reinterpreting the notion of the zone proximal development in terms of Spinoza's politico-affective process seems very intriguing.

The second theoretical challenge is to relate Spinoza's politico-affective notion with recent discussions of the subjective aspect of the object of activity (Kaptelinin, 2005; Miettinen, 2005; Nardi, 2005). Miettinen (2005) discusses the co-formative process of object, goal, motives, and individual capabilities, introducing the Hegelian notion of the desire for recognition. Desire is one of the central notions in Spinoza's affective system. It will be productive and advantageous to establish a connection between Spinoza and the problem of the object of activity.

PART FOUR

SUBJECTIVITY, AGENCY, AND
COMMUNITY

12

From the Systemic to the Relational:
Relational Agency and Activity Theory

ANNE EDWARDS

ERODING WORK IDENTITIES

We live in risky times (Beck, 1992; Friedland & Boden, 1994). The boundaries and certainties that shored up systems from nation-states to professional bodies for the past 150 years are dissolving, leaving individuals feeling exposed and unprotected by familiar and historically grounded practices. New forms of work combining real-time face-to-face negotiations with more distributed connections mean that we are linked as individuals per-haps as never before (Giddens, 1991); and the work systems we occupy are perhaps more open, with, as Sennett (1999a) puts it, "febrile" boundaries and mixed work forms. At the same time, the sequential linearity of early modernism, evidenced in narrative structures that give historical coher-ence to current actions, has been disrupted. For example, people may now need to take into account the narratives of other workgroups as they align their actions across time and space and learn when to interact and when to withdraw.

The workplace is therefore now less likely to be the source of a sustained identity, whether we are victims of short-term contracts (Sennett, 1998), are boundary-breaking creatives (Guile, 2007), or are specialist profes-sionals collaborating on complex tasks (Edwards, 2005). However, as we are propelled forward, sustained more by a sense of our own purposeful agency than by a situated form of professional identity, we are perhaps in danger of revisiting a past that gave rise to the very certainties currently being eroded. As Sennett (1999a) explains:

> The rigid large scale bureaucracies which developed at the end of the nineteenth century provided an institutional architecture in which dependence became honourable, to which the learner could become loyal. Static institutions provide, unfortunately, a framework of daily

trust, a reality which has to be acknowledged in thinking about efforts
in our own time to take these institutions apart. (p. 19)

These organizations emerged to counter the rampant subjectivity that
marked the worst of capitalism. They provided certainty and protection so
that long-term narratives of work life could be projected and achieved. But
Sennett's term "unfortunately" is well chosen. Now in the throes of late
capitalism, we face new challenges of identity and life purpose even in our
working lives. For some the response has been a renewed focus on understanding how place and time intersect to shape our actions (Featherstone &
Lash, 1999) or on local action as sites of personal and social change
(Holland & Lave, 2001). Engeström's contribution to this broad field has
been to take up the challenge of understanding the distributed connections
that shape work identities and actions. His focus is on the nature of work
rather than identity, and his conclusions take us to the collective rather
than the individual. In doing so, they provide a way of thinking about the
risky nature of work that is carried out beyond the safety of established
social practices and perhaps a way of countering rampant subjectivity.

ENGESTRÖM'S NEW CONCEPTS FOR NEW
WORK CHALLENGES

Seeing "the shape and implications of spatio-temporally distributed
work and expertise" as "fragile and open, literally under construction"
(Engeström, 2005c, p. 324), Engeström offers two new concepts that are
potentially capable of reflecting and creating purposeful work under these
conditions. He describes the concepts as "immature" and presents them in
order to open up the field for further theoretical work. Both concepts operate at the level of the collective. First is the idea of "collaborative intentionality capital" as "an emerging form of organisational assets," which makes
collaboration on complex tasks possible beyond organizational boundaries. The second tentative concept, "object-oriented interagency," suggests
a slightly more interactional focus, as Engeström sees it as a form of "connecting and reciprocating" while "circling around a complex object" and
"dwelling in" the object, that is, maintaining a long-term relationship with
it (Engeström, 2005c, p. 333).

Central to both these concepts is the cultural-historical activity theory
(CHAT) recognition that action is object oriented and that our interpretations of the problems, or objects of activity, that we are working on and
trying to transform are shaped by the historical practices of the systems
in which we are operating. First, our interpretations of an object, such as

a work task, are restricted by the system in which it is located. Second, an object may motivate us to react in particular ways by eliciting responses from us that are permissible within particular sets of social practices. Far from being static, these object-oriented systems are responsive to changes in material and conceptual tools, shifts in the division of labor, and so on. Systems are therefore reconfigured as we deal with contradictions that arise in them. Contradictions occur when, for example, current rules restrict the use of new tools and limit our capacity to interpret and act on work tasks in fresh ways. Because systems are dynamic, the object embedded in a system is not static and may be subject to changing interpretations, which, in turn, work back on the system to produce the systemic change that Engeström describes as expansive learning. Although this model originated in work on single systems, the same dynamics may obtain when the same objects are worked on by several systems.

Engeström observes that, in complex work environments, direct connections between workers and those objects that carry the collectively developed object motive of systems, such as illness in hospitals, are often hard to discern. He argues that "human agency gains unusual powers when future-oriented activity-level envisioning and consequential action-level decision-making, come together in close interplay" (Engeström, 2005c, p. 313). Pickering (1993) put the relationship between immediate practices and distant purposes slightly differently, adopting a more individual notion of human agency: "We should see the intentional nature of human agency as itself temporally emergent, albeit on a longer timescale than the details of practice" (p. 598). Both Engeström and Pickering take as given the temporal dimension of intentional action and the way the problems that are being worked on can almost assume a life of their own as they move ahead of us. Engeström, invoking Giddens's (1991) description of the complex "runaway world" of high modernity, labels these problems as "runaway" objects, which call for collaborative and negotiated responses that may not be predictable.

For Engeström, then, human agency is powerful as a set of collective intentions. Both collaborative intentionality capital and object-oriented interagency are offered as ways of beginning to describe what enables the "reaching out" that occurs when people operate across the boundaries of discrete activity systems to work on common objects in distributed activity fields, such as across departments in a hospital. That is, the solution to the workplace dissonances and complex tasks of late capitalism, therefore, remains the collective. For Engeström (2005c), notions of, for example, mutual responsibility and recognition and rewards have "serious weaknesses from the point of view of activity theory" because of their primary focus on individual actors and their limited attention to historicity with "little potential for understanding change" (p. 332).

Engeström takes the tools of activity theory and identifies and describes the challenges of what Blackler and McDonald (2000) have called the "fluctuating collaborative relations" of an increasing amount of work. The analytic tools he has developed in doing so have been generously presented as objects for further work in the distributed field that is CHAT, and we are encouraged to "reach out" and join him in "circling around" the complex object. From my perspective at least, that object is an understanding of agency that doesn't return us to the rampant individualism of early capitalism but that tries to get inside the collective version of agency Engeström has offered, in order to discover what it comprises and how it is achieved. To do this I shall draw on two studies,[1] which focus on the demands of cross-boundary collaborations while working with mobile runaway objects.

THE EVIDENCE BASE

The first of the two studies is the National Evaluation of the Children's Fund (NECF), which was a 39-month government-funded study of a national initiative in England. The initiative aimed at preventing the social exclusion of children and young people by, among other things, enabling interprofessional work in localities (Edwards et al., 2006). The second study, Learning in and for Interagency Working (LIW), was a four-year Research Council–funded study of the learning challenges involved in learning to do interprofessional work, again with vulnerable young people. The studies are located within a current restructuring of services for children and families in every local authority in England that aims at providing integrated systems of care to prevent the social exclusion of vulnerable children and young people.

In both studies we used activity theory to examine how practitioners from different organizations, with different belief systems and priorities, learn to work together to disrupt the trajectories of social exclusion among vulnerable young people. These trajectories are mobile and changing objects of activity, and far from being the "almost human" artifacts discussed by Pickering (1993, 1995), they are certainly capable of biting back.

---

[1] The two studies are the DfES-funded National Evaluation of the Children's Fund (2003–2006) and an ESRC-TLRP Phase III study, Learning in and for Interagency Working (ESRC RES-13925-0100), with H. Daniels, J. Leadbetter, D. Martin, D. Middleton, P. Warmington, A. Apostolov, A. Popova, and S. Brown (2004–2007).

Indeed, the intention is that young people ultimately take control of their own trajectories.

The collaborations of practitioners are fluctuating and often short-lived, as these practitioners move in and out of the lives of children. To take an example of the trajectory of a troubled child at school: The education welfare officer (EWO) may act when the child doesn't attend school, the housing charity worker will come in when her family becomes homeless, and the educational psychologist will make an assessment of her well-being in school. Others, such as teachers, social workers, and mental health workers, may have longer-term relationships with the child and may perhaps be able to "dwell in the object." Potentially at least, these kinds of collaboration are a form of de-centered knotworking, that is, "a rapidly pulsating, distributed and partially improvised orchestration of collaborative performance between otherwise loosely connected actors and activity systems" (Engeström, Engeström, & Vähäaho, 1999, p. 346). It is therefore not the "institutionalised knotworking" that Blackler and McDonald (2000) invoke, as it is likely to involve collaborations outside the safety of practitioners' "institutional shelters" (Sennett, 1999a).

The affective demands of this kind of work are considerable. Not only is it relatively high risk work for relatively low status workers (Edwards, 2004). As Blackler and McDonald observe, "People's imaginations are linked with social and institutional structures." In addition, the new spaces of integrated working have yet to be securely configured as sites of distributed expertise primed to support vulnerable children, and indeed they may need to sustain a degree of latency if they are also to achieve the fluidity and responsiveness that is needed. Although old networks continue to function, new relationships are only just being negotiated, and long-standing ways of categorizing children that are specific to each profession remain located within each institution so that they rarely travel beyond organizational boundaries. Collaboration in some places is a parallel or synchronic "circling around," but much remains diachronic or sequential, with, as one worker put it, the problematic "bits" of children identified and passed from, for example, a teacher to a mental health worker.

In this context, the idea of collaborative intentionality capital as an organizational capacity to reach out and engage with others in order to work on objects that move away as they are being transformed is extremely powerful. Integrated into the social and institutional structures of home organizations, it may reduce the risks of working in those yet to be formed spaces of de-centered collaboration. Levered into the "structures of wanting" (Jensen, 2007; Knorr Cetina & Bruggar, 2002) of organizations where collaboration is essential to functioning, it may help to sustain the identities of workers who are undertaking high-risk work.

But how is collaborative intentionality capital enacted and developed? To answer that question we do need to delve into the miasma of the collective and follow Vygotsky's lead by trying to understand how important cultural concepts, in this case the capacity for being in and part of the collaborative, are incorporated into the individual. This is not a hidebound assertion of the importance of the individual. Rather, it is arguably important for sustaining and re-creating the collective that we understand how people work relationally on complex runaway objects, particularly if we are to get beyond the notion of untrammeled subjectivity as a model of agentic selfhood.

A FOCUS ON THE RELATIONAL

Focusing on the relational as a capacity to work with others reminds us of the moral purposes of working together. From an interactionist perspective, Hicks (2000) has argued that moral projects are curiously absent from studies of social learning. For Hicks, in such projects the self is placed in relation to the intentions of others. She argues that a stronger emphasis on the recognition of the moral aspects of engaging with the sense-making and goals of others can enrich dialogic accounts of learning.

C. Taylor, more obviously, gets to the core of the present discussion to explore a concern with the rampant subjectivities that may emerge in the new spaces created by late capitalism. Identifying the problem to be the overweening selves that are produced by modernity, he asks for a stronger connection of individual selves with the common good (Taylor, 1991) – a cry that resonates with Shotter (1993) in his call for a relational ethics, Earlier C. Taylor had described agency as a capacity to identify the goals at which one is directing one's action and to evaluate whether one has been successful (Taylor, 1977). More recently he has become concerned about an emphasis on individual action at the expense of responsibility to and for others. Hence, one can see a shift to a focus on the relational as an important move in the development of meshes of mutual responsibility and a move from an overly strong focus on the individual.

We can see the beginnings of similar moves in psychology more generally. For the British Psychological Society, 2005 was "the Year of Relationships," signaling that mainstream psychology is at last recognizing some of the methodological challenges posed by the fluidity and flux that characterize late modernity. Goodwin (2005), echoing years of research on social capital

(Field, 2002; Halpern, 2005), explained why, as a psychologist, he studies relationships: "Everywhere, however, we found that close relationships acted as important 'social glue', helping people deal with the uncertainties of their changing world" (p. 615).

Collaborative intentionality capital certainly takes us far beyond notions of "social glue," though currently it eschews, overtly at least, notions of moral purpose and common good. I, too, will walk away from those challenges, leaving them, for example, to Sennett (2003). Instead, I will focus on the capacity to align one's practices with others in order to participate in object-oriented interagency work. To do so I need to turn to the concept of relational agency, which I have developed elsewhere and most extensively in Edwards (2005, in press). Relational agency is a capacity to align one's thought and actions with those of others in order to interpret problems of practice and to respond to those interpretations. Let us see how it is played out and whether it adds to the conceptual field developed by Engeström (2005c).

NETWORKS AND HORIZONTAL COLLABORATIONS

The NECF analyses of partnership working (Edwards et al., 2006) would confirm Engeström's (2005c) observation that, although partnerships and alliances are increasing in number, they are laden with tensions and are extremely difficult to sustain and manage. They would also confirm that the exciting work with runaway objects occurs in more open and loosely linked latent systems where practitioners' expertise is distributed and brought into play when appropriate.

The open systems that we found were often stimulated by what we described during the study as object-oriented "boundary zones" (Konkola, Tuomi-Gröhn, Lambert, & Ludvigsen, 2007), where the priorities of each profession were respected as they focused on the needs of local children. These boundary zones were multiprofessional meetings that operated as springboards for new confidence pathways (Knorr Cetina, 1999), that is, routes taken by practitioners to gain information or support they knew would be useful. New pathways were taken by practitioners as they connected vulnerable children with other specialist practitioners who could also help them (Edwards, in press; Edwards et al., 2006). Practitioners came to these boundary meetings because they were seen as valuable for their own specialist work and for the work of their immediate colleagues. That is, the meetings and the linkages they produced seemed to be offering emergent "structures of wanting" for local interagency collaboration. These seemed to strengthen practitioners' professional identities and capacity for collaboration in the newly emerging "figured world" (Holland, Skinner, Lachicotte, & Cain, 1998) of integrated services. One practitioner explained the value of work in the boundary zone meetings as follows:

> It's about understanding at a deeper level. It's about connections. Maybe you are not sure about the child we are thinking about; but as we talk it through there may be a connection and, if not for that child, maybe for another.

We were careful not to describe these configurations of confidence pathways as networks. They appeared to be quite broadly based, latent, and open – nearer to Engeström's idea of latent "mycorrhizae activities" than visible networks (Engeström, 2006c). They seemed to avoid fossilizing into the old local networks of personal trust that we also observed. These older networks always pre-dated the initiative and, because of their well-worn linkages, displayed very little engagement with the rethinking of practices required by the initiative. In doing so, they very much reflected the conservatism of networks alluded to by Castells (2000). It is important to note that the links in the older, stabilized networks were mainly personal – for example, "I've known Sarah and how she likes to work for years" – and they did not depend on anything approaching the notion of collaborative intentionality capital in their home organizations.

Work arising from the more open and fluid configurations of springboard and pathways was not simply a matter of "knowing Sarah," though at times it helped. Rather, it involved knowing that one's own effectiveness was enhanced when one was working with others. For example, a 7-year-old refugee from Angola was much less troubled at school once an art therapist became involved and the mother received help from a specialist in post-traumatic stress. It was, undoubtedly, possible that the new confidence pathways walked by these practitioners might become as fossilized as the older networks. Therefore, we recommended to the government that it recognize the processes and competences involved in this kind of collaborative work and enable them. Our developmental work research (DWR) interventions (Engeström, 2007d) helped to reveal aspects of what was involved.[2] For example, one practitioner explained that for practitioners

---

[2] DWR is premised on the Vygotskian notion of dual stimulation, which he used to reveal the ways in which children make sense of the worlds they act within: "We simultaneously offer a second series of stimuli that have a special function. In this way, we are able to study the process of accomplishing a task by the aid of specific auxiliary means; thus

multiprofessional work was simply a matter of "adjusting what you do to other people's needs and strengths."

That statement needs some elaboration if we are to understand what was involved in these collaborations and to encourage its widespread application. Analyses arising from development economics, where there is a similar interest in horizontal collaborations at the level of practice, are helpful. Particularly useful is Lundvall's idea of "know-who" as an important aspect of knowledge at work: "Know-who involves information about who knows how to do what. But especially it involves the social capability to establish relationships to specialised groups in order to draw on their expertise" (Lundvall, 1996, p. 7).

Lundvall argues that know-who is embedded and learned in social practices and cannot simply be codified into a register of names. His analysis of know-who as a capacity to "draw on" expertise perhaps resonates more with Nardi, Whittaker, and Schwarz's (2002) notion of networks of expertise as resources to enhance one's own performance than it does with more de-centered notions of knotworking and object-oriented interagency. Nonetheless, it allows us to label and explore the processes of collaboration and indeed how one learns *how to know how to know who.*

It would seem that *knowing how to know who* involves an ability to look outward, an openness to what one sees and a capacity to critically reflect on what might impede object-oriented activity. Some signs of it emerged in the Children's Fund. The springboard boundary zones we saw in the Children's Fund were demanding the ability to look outward with open minds. They led practitioners to work against well-entrenched grains of interprofessional mistrust. As one practitioner put it:

> Social Services could be seen in a very negative way, but because we have had the same person come along every week, people have got to know her. They understand the reasons why they don't do this and why they do that, so they are less likely to be negative about it.

we are also able to discover the inner structure and development of higher psychological processes" (Vygotsky, 1978, p. 74).

The "second series stimuli" offered in DWR are the conceptual tools of activity theory (Engeström, 2007c), which are provided by the workshop facilitators to enable participants to analyze and make sense of their practices, the objects of those practices, and the organizational features that shape them. Evidence of the practices are presented to them by the facilitators, and participants are helped to examine those practices using the tools of activity theory. In doing so, practitioners reveal the conceptual tools they are using as they engage in or hope to develop their work.

Here we can begin to see how *knowing who* functioned as a mediating tool for rethinking collaboration and reducing concerns about the difficulties involved. Elsewhere (Edwards, 2005), I have suggested that *knowing how to know who* is an important part of the repertoire of conceptual tools needed to mediate professional relations across organizational boundaries. It is a precursor to negotiating interpretations of the object of activity and aligning responses to those interpretations.

Knowing how to know who does not simply involve the acquisition of "information about who knows how to do what" so that expertise can be marshaled to respond to a diagnosis made by one professional. The new connections we have observed in both studies resonate strongly with Engeström's object-oriented interagency. They have involved a growing ability to be professionally multilingual, to be able to speak across professional boundaries, and to be explicit about how expertise of different kinds leads to foregrounding different features of a child's trajectory. *Knowing how to know who* therefore includes a capacity for mutuality. It can lead to a form of practice that is enhanced by the interpretations of others and is not simply a matter of coordinating the expertise of others to respond to the interpretations made by one practitioner. An object-oriented, client-centered focus on children's trajectories has seemed to be an important driver for flexible collaborations, as this practitioner explains:

> My point is that you can put a group of people together, but it's about what they do when they get there. Because it just could be regrouping the same people doing the same tasks. But with [name of service] it's the way we work, having people grouped in a particular way to help the service user.

What also distinguished the more advanced forms of collaboration from what was simply boundary crossing to access support was the length of commitment to a constantly renegotiated object of activity that collaboration required. Here we find echoes of Engeström's view that it is not enough to simply connect and reciprocate and that one should also "dwell in" the object. One practitioner described the process in this way:

> It comes down to a seamlessness of service ... in terms of having the same people on a longer period of time to develop trust and gain knowledge and informed ideas about the family, rather than passing them from pillar to post and back again.

We can, therefore, begin to compile some of the organizational and personal features that are starting to contribute to the expansive practice necessary for the prevention of social exclusion. Most important, this practice involves an ongoing interweaving of different professional interpretations of a mobile and transforming object with their responses to it. It is not simply a matter of coordination, brokering, or accessing resources to work on the interpretations of a child's trajectory that has been made by one professional. Expansive interprofessional practice consists of generative, forward-focused negotiations of interpretations and responses. Let us therefore turn to the runaway object that is being encircled and its contribution to the dynamics at work.

THE RESPONSIVE OBJECT

Describing what he meant by "dwelling in the object," Engeström says, "I refer to a longitudinal dialogical relationship with the object that goes beyond 'focussing on' or 'appropriating' the object" (Engeström, 2005c, p. 334). Earlier in the chapter he suggests, "Objects resist and bite back, they seem to have lives of their own" (p. 312). Leaving aside for the moment the fact that the children's trajectories that were the Children's Fund objects literally were "lives of their own," let us explore a little further the resistances and biting back that occur in the kinds of reaching-out practices discussed so far.

As I noted earlier, Engeström takes as given the temporal nature of intentionality and assumes that today's work may be linked to a relatively long-term collective purpose. That is not to say that he is working with an instrumental notion of rational planning. Rather, these precepts are laid out to build a picture of the challenges of mustering the idea of a longer-term collective purpose when working across organizations. One of these challenges is the disruption of more established narratives of practice that might arise.

As we move to less boundaried ways of working, we may find that when these collectively described objects respond or bite back, they may be doing so in unfamiliar ways. For example, a teacher may find he is diverted from his focus on curricula and educational success, because a vulnerable child believes she has the right in a collaborative, flexible, and responsive version of care to focus on what matters to her. That may be a breakup of the family or homelessness, and may require other practitioners to take center stage while the teacher withdraws. The biting back is, therefore, initially felt by an individual. Similarly, although one can see that shifts in the division of labor in a school that allow the teacher to withdraw require a systemic response, those shifts also lead to changes in how the teacher is positioned within the practices or figured world of the school and its collaborating services. That is, expansive learning at the level of the system can also be recognized in the repositioning of individuals and their relationships.

Activity theory adds a great deal to more interactional accounts of these individual identity shifts, as Stetsenko makes clear. In her recent work on Leont'ev's notion of object motive (Stetsenko, 2005), she draws out features of object-oriented action that are relevant to the present argument. She notes the dynamic that exists between object and subject. That is, as we work on an object, the object itself works back on us, having an impact on our subjectivity and how we in turn approach the object. In this transactional relationship between subject and object, we transform the object by, for example, contesting its meaning and understanding it better, and we also transform ourselves.

For Stetsenko, the focus on the transaction between subject and culturally constructed object presents an opportunity to bring human subjectivity into activity theory, indeed a human subjectivity that "is laden with practical relevance and agency" (Stetsenko, 2005, p. 83). Stetsenko's argument is also relevant to understanding relational agency. For example, joint action by two practitioners, such as a school counselor and an EWO on a shared object or problem space such as a child's phobia of school, involves bringing to bear two subjectivities and sets of conceptual tools on the problem and thereby expands interpretations of the problem and the range of possible responses. As one practitioner in a multiprofessional team recently put it in a DWR session, "When two or three of you are working on a child's trajectory as an object, we bring to bear different mindsets."

Stetsenko's work helps us to see that, when the object is expanded through an awareness of these different mindsets, the expanded object, that is, an enriched understanding of the problem space, works back on the mindsets of the practitioners, and these may in turn be enriched by the interpretations of the others. Of course, they may not be enriched. Instead, entrenched views may remain untouched. A better understanding of how aligned action is negotiated and sustained is, I suggest, a useful step toward enabling people to learn how to work together and to learn from doing so. Let us, therefore, now turn more specifically to the idea of relational agency and particularly examine how it might inform the idea of object-oriented interagency.

RELATIONAL AGENCY

In CHAT terms, relational agency is a capacity to work with others to expand the object that one is working on and trying to transform by recognizing, examining, and working with the resources that others bring to bear as they interpret and respond to the object. It is a capacity that involves recognizing that another person may be a resource, who knows how to know who, and what needs to be done to elicit, recognize, and negotiate the use of that resource in order to align oneself in joint action on the expanded object. It is therefore an enhanced version of personal agency that involves looking across organizational boundaries to make possible aligned and mutually supportive action outside the institutional shelters of specialist organizations.

Relational agency thus has some resonance with the work of Hakkarainen and his colleagues on reciprocity and mutual strengthening of competence and expertise to enhance the collective competence of a community (Hakkarainen, Palonen, Paavola, & Lehtinen, 2004). Where it differs is in focusing more directly on the nature of the relationships that comprise a network of expertise. It also connects with Billett's (2006) focus on relational interdependence, by arguing for greater attention to agency in explaining relationships between the individual and the social in working life. Like Billett, it recognizes the importance of preexisting personal understandings gained in other situations in mediating interpretations of new situations and argues for attention to the negotiations that individuals make as they work in and with the social.

It is also closely connected with the ideas of distributed intelligence and distributed expertise. Here the starting point for analysis is not individual cognition, but the resources found outside the individual mind. It recognizes that cultural tools, both material and representational, are loaded with intelligence, which enhances action. Distributed expertise can be seen as a subcategory of distributed intelligence that relates more directly to working practices. A particular version of distributed expertise is to be found in the systemic approaches to enhancing learning developed by Engeström. Engeström and Middleton (1996), for example, describe a CHAT perspective on expertise as the "collaborative and discursive construction of tasks, solutions, visions, breakdowns and innovations" (p. 4) within and across systems rather than individual mastery of specific areas of relatively stable activity.

Relational agency, I suggest, can begin to help us to understand the negotiations and reconfiguring of tasks indicated by Engeström and Middleton, by focusing on the capacity for undertaking these negotiations. It occupies a conceptual space between a focus on learning as enhancing individual understanding and a focus on learning as systemic change and includes both. It fits squarely within sociocultural readings of mind and world, by seeing mind as outward looking, pattern seeking, and engaged with the world (Greeno, 1997, 2006). Furthermore, by including a focus on the mediating function of *knowing how to know who,* it begins to indicate how a more relational form of engaging may be accomplished in both local and more extended configurations of practice.

In summary, the premise set out by Vygotsky and developed over the past 80 years is that we transform the world by interpreting and acting on the basis of our interpretations. Interpreting and responding involve the conceptual and material resources we have at our disposal. In Engeström's development of activity theory, this process occurs at the level of the system. Systems learn, that is, change, through the expansion of the object that is being worked on. The object is expanded when the variety of interpretations that may be available and the contradictions that arise are revealed and explored. The expanded object in turn works back on the conceptual tools, and other features in the system or related systems, and reshapes them.

Relational agency shifts the focus, at least temporarily, from the system to joint action within and across systems and the impact on those who engage in it. In doing so, it attempts to place some focus on the actions of participants in and across systems so that we can recognize how collaboration is accomplished and a capacity for it can be developed.

CONCLUDING POINTS

Explaining that he preferred the idea of "radicalised modernity" to the postmodernity of Lyotard and its lack of faith in humanly engineered progress, Giddens (1991) challenged us to "harness the juggernaut" of the post-Enlightenment to "minimise the dangers and maximise the opportunities which modernity offers to us." He followed that challenge by asking why "we currently live in a runaway world, so different from that which the Enlightenment thinkers anticipated?" – that is, in a world that we cannot predict or control (p. 151).

Activity theory, with its origins in the transforming and improving intentions of Marx and Vygotsky, has been well suited to understanding and supporting humanly engineered progress and, thanks to Engeström, has kept pace with the runaway world of high modernity. The intention has not been to predict and control, but to attempt to minimize the dangers and maximize the opportunities offered by modernity, by engaging in the world. Giddens, like Chaiklin (1993), sees one of the virtues of social science as its capacity to affect the world it attempts to reveal, sending it "spinning ... off in novel directions" (Giddens, 1991, p. 153). Without a doubt, Engeström's operationalizing of Vygotsky's method of dual stimulation in DWR (Engeström, 2007d) is an exemplar without equal of how the concepts of social science can be donated to enable people to harness the juggernaut.

The ideas of "collaborative intentionality capital" and "object-oriented interagency" fit well with the methods of DWR and their focus on systemic change to facilitate reaching out and working with others in this case. The first of these concepts captures the need to anchor organizational flexibility and responsiveness in a long-term sense of commitment and belief; the second usefully labels, from an organizational perspective, what is involved in negotiated knotworking.

But as Giddens explains, "We live in a peopled world" (1991, p. 143) where trust is always ambivalent and where self-revelation, including, I suggest, revealing one's expertise, calls for "reciprocity and support" (p. 144). I wonder whether, in the idea of object-oriented interagency as a way of conceptualizing the unstable knots of knotworking and in the formulation of it as "Dwell in the object, connect and reciprocate across boundaries" (Engeström, 2005c, p. 333), there may be a just discernible shift toward unpicking the peopled world that activity systems comprise.

Within that reading, relational agency is offered here in the same tentative manner in which Engeström presented the two concepts that stimulated the discussion in this chapter. Along with it is, perhaps, the suggestion that it might contribute to unpicking the peopling of the systemic. It would seem that all three concepts are oriented toward preventing a return to the rampant subjectivity that has marked the worst of capitalism, while ensuring that a capacity to deal creatively with the complexity that arises as the juggernaut surges forward is strengthened.

13

Expansive Agency in Multi-Activity Collaboration

KATSUHIRO YAMAZUMI

Yrjö Engeström (1987) developed cultural-historical activity theory and its interventionist methodology in modeling expansive learning in and for the collaborative production of new object-oriented collective activity systems. Engeström's formulation of activity theory has laid the cornerstone of developmental research to reconceptualize humans as creators and transformers. In this way, human agency is a central focus of activity theory.

From the viewpoint of activity and expansive learning theories, the concept of human agency is briefly described as the subject potentialities and positions of creation of new tools and forms of activity with which humans transform both their outer and inner worlds and thus master their own lives and futures (Engeström, 2005a, 2005c, 2006b). The account of new forms of agency in activity theory brings the Vygotskian heritage alive with regard to the future of human freedom (Yamazumi, 2007).

Today, new forms of human activity are experiencing accelerated paradigm shifts from mass-production-based systems to new systems based on interorganizational collaboration, building partnerships, and networking across cultural, organizational, and occupational boundaries. As human activity rapidly changes to partnering and networking among diverse cultural organizations, we need to ask ourselves whether schools and other contexts devoted to learning are equipped to prepare people for such practices. We also need to consider what kind of learning can generate critical and creative agency among learners. Such agency will help

The writing of this chapter was supported in part by a grant from the Japanese Society for the Promotion of Science. The research project on which the analysis is based was developed at the Center for Human Activity Theory, Kansai University, and was partly funded by the Ministry of Education, Culture, Sports, Science and Technology as an "Academic Frontier" project.

people shape their own lives and futures, which are gradually undergoing transformation.

This chapter focuses on new forms of learning that generate new types of distributed, multiple, and networked agency in dialogic, boundary-crossing, and hybridized activity systems. In the following sections, I first discuss an emergent, pedagogical theory of expansive learning. In particular, I focus on new forms of expansive learning with the help of the framework of third-generation activity theory. Drawing on this notion of expansive learning, I show that new types of agency are collaborations and engagements with a shared object in and for relationships of interaction between multiple activity systems. Second, to concretize new forms of expansive agency, I present an example of an expansive learning approach to changing schools by creating networks of learning that transcend the institutional boundaries of the school. Third, I analyze some data and findings from the implementation of a children's after-school learning activity called New School (NS). New School as intervention research aims at developing a *hybrid activity system* among diverse cultural organizations for school innovation. The idea of this intervention is that changing the school is carried out in various networks of learning and hybrid forms of activities. I investigate the dynamics through which the multiple participants and parties involved in the NS project engage in the process of interinstitutional, collaborative learning for implementing new activities. Finally, I discuss a new landscape of agency as expansive phenomena in the field of pedagogical practice on the basis of new practices of creative collaboration between schools, communities, and various organizations outside schools.

EXPANSIVE LEARNING AND AGENCY IN DISTRIBUTED
MULTI-ACTIVITY FIELDS

In 1999 my colleagues and I published a Japanese edition of Engeström's most important work, *Learning by Expanding: An Activity-Theoretical Approach to Developmental Research*, published in 1987 (see Engeström, 1999f). This publication has provided a promising mediating artifact to enact activity theory for both Japanese scholars and practitioners involved in new learning theories in fields of human and social sciences.

In the foreword to the Japanese edition of *Learning by Expanding*, Engeström (1999f) clearly states his work's central thesis:

> *Learning by Expanding* is a book about collective creative activity. My
> thesis is that we as human beings have to become able to transform

our institutions and practices in a way that mobilizes the intellects and energies of all participants from the ground up. Creativity here is understood as involvement in such collective transformation of practices. Although theories of learning have tried to explain enduring changes in human behavior and cognition, they have not addressed the issue of how people can change themselves as they change their circumstances. That is why a new theory of expansive learning is needed. (p. i)

The notion of expansive learning refers to the creation of new concepts and practices for emerging forms and patterns of activity. Engeström (1999f) also suggests looking at emerging forms of expansive learning:

> This book is also about multi-voicedness and building networks between different activity systems. In an increasingly global economy, expansive learning must be studied and facilitated as movement and collaboration across national and cultural boundaries. (pp. i–ii)

This new thesis is associated with the transformative shift to the third generation of activity theory (Engeström, 1996b). Challenged by diversity and dialogue between different traditions or perspectives, the third generation of activity theory has developed conceptual tools to understand dialogue, multiple perspectives, and networks of interacting activity systems. The first and second generations represented by Lev Vygotsky (1978) and Aleksei Leont'ev (1978) were limited in their focus on a single activity system as the unit of analysis of human action and practice. The challenge of the third generation is therefore to expand the unit of analysis to "interacting activity systems with a partially shared object as minimal model" (Engeström, 2001, p. 136).

Since the 1990s, as the historically transitional age continues to move toward globalization in every field of human activity – even if the activity is physically limited to local areas – expansive learning has clearly become increasingly valuable for creating new forms of activities. The world of human activity is increasingly dominated by longitudinal dialogic relationships of collaboration between multiple activity systems. In activity-theoretical terms, these multiple activity systems are engaged by "runaway objects," that is, partially shared large-scale objects in complex, distributed multi-activity fields (Engeström, 2005a, 2005c, 2006b). Although these partnerships and alliances are obviously relevant to rediscovering and expanding use values in the objects of activities, they are extremely difficult to sustain and manage. This is where collaborative learning possibilities and challenges truly become necessary. Such learning can be characterized as interorganizational learning (Engeström, 2001) engaged in the expansive reforging of shared objects and creating new forms of activity between different activity systems.

What type of agency might be urgently required in such a horizontal movement of expansive learning across boundaries? In the new generation of activity theory, this focus on agency must shift to an analysis of a new type of agency in fields of distributed and networked activities. As pointed out by Engeström (2005a, 2005c, 2006b) and Harry Daniels and his colleagues (2005, 2007), this is a transition to object-oriented collective intentionality, interagency, or multiagency studies in distributed multi-activity fields. Such agency generally may be called a new type of expansive agency.

Engeström (2005c, 2006b) analyzes distributed interagency currently taking shape in work organizations, for example, in the expansive learning processes of medical professionals in health care settings. In this empirical case, because different medical professionals across institutional boundaries were involved in the care of chronic patients with multiple illnesses in Helsinki, they needed to solve the contradictions around the patients' complex care trajectories without assigning overview and overall responsibility for them to anyone. Different professionals contributed to the reshaping of their work method toward emerging organizational forms called "negotiated knotworking" (Engeström, Engeström, & Vähäaho, 1999) in "mycorrhizae-like activities" (Engeström, 2006b).

Work activities are becoming increasingly networked, hybrid, and weekly bounded forms of organization. To highlight the importance of horizontal and multidirectional connections in the human lives involved in such historical changes, Engeström (2006b) introduces "mycorrhizae," which are organizing activities oriented toward runaway objects that are seen as an alternative to the "rhizome" proposed by Gilles Deleuze and Félix Guattari (1987). A "mycorrhizae" formation is a symbiotic association between a fungus and the roots, or rhizoids, of a plant. A mycorrhizae formation is "simultaneously a living, expanding process (or bundle of developing connections) *and* a relatively durable, stabilized structure" (Engeström, 2006b, p. 12).

"Knotworking," which is also seen as an emergent form of collaborative work, refers to partially improvised forms of intense collaboration between partners that are otherwise loosely connected but are engaging in solving problems and rapidly designing solutions when required by their common object; in knotworking, there is no fixed center of authority and control. Distributed agency located in knotworking-type formations, which can solve problems and make decisions in situations where the "combinations of people and the contents of tasks change constantly"

(Engeström, Engeström & Vähäaho, 1999, p. 353), is valuable for the movement of changing initiatives from moment to moment and distributed leaderships.

In the third generation and post-generation of activity theory, focusing on reaching beyond and across the boundaries and gaps between activity systems must be acknowledged as a historically new feature of distributed or fractured agency located in the knots or mycorrhizae. Such historicity of agency is currently sought in network organizations where a new type of agency might be visible, required, and emerging. Participants and parties from different terrains involved in the network and beyond organizations seek innovations by collaboration across traditional boundaries. In such organizational forms, the nature of agency, as Engeström (2005c) states, can "connect and reciprocate." This imperative of a new type of agency principally differs from the historically previous forms: "control and command" for management, "resist and defend" for workers in hierarchy organizations, and "take advantage and maximize gain" in market organizations. The efficacy and value of collaboration and reciprocity are missed or limited in both of these forms.

EXPANSIVE LEARNING APPROACH TO SCHOOL CHANGE

Expansive learning in schools (Engeström, 1991b, p. 255) would construct a new, expanded object of learning by connecting the following contexts of learning: the context of criticism (the powers of resisting, questioning, contradicting, and debating), the context of discovery (the powers of experimenting, modeling, symbolizing, and generalizing), and the context of practical social application (the powers of social relevance and embeddedness of knowledge, community involvement, and guided practice). This kind of expansion in the object proceeds to break "the encapsulation of school learning" within the confines of school texts and thus implies a qualitative transformation in the entire activity system of school learning.

This expansive transition toward a new activity system of school learning is itself "a long, distributed process, not a once and for all transformation dictated from above" (Engeström, 1991b, p. 256), of learning through collective and reflective self-organization from below. It is of crucial importance that the collaborative self-organization manifests itself in the "creation of networks of learning that transcend the institutional boundaries of the school," turning the school into a "collective instrument" (Engeström, 1991b, p. 257). In other words, expansive learning for school innovation offers teachers', children's, and participants' learning as collaborative, self-organizing processes for transforming the activity of school learning itself from within.

This kind of learning to transform the school activity system motivates the school community to engage in the following expansive development of school learning: the expansion of the object of school learning to encompass the creation of multiple contexts of learning, the breaking of the encapsulation of school learning, and eventually the formation and creation of collaborative self-organization and advanced networks of learning transcending the institutional boundaries of the school. In this way, people in the school community should be seen as a collective of expansive learners who are willing to make school innovations together and become collaborative change agents by turning their school institution into a collective instrument for them. The expansive learning approach opens up qualitatively new possibilities for a new form of school innovation called "school as change agent." It involves collaborative self-organization and networks of learning for transforming traditional school learning and pedagogical practices.

The essential concern with expansive learning in and for the creation of new forms of pedagogical practices in schools is that people involved in schooling can "design and implement their own futures as their prevalent practices show symptoms of crisis" (Engeström, 1991b, p. 256). The expansive learning approach exploits the actual conflicts and dissatisfactions among teachers, students, parents, and others involved in or affected by schooling, inviting them to join in a concrete transformation of the current practice. In other words, this approach is not built on benevolent reform from above. It is built on facing the current contradictions and draws strength from the participants' joint analysis (Engeström, 1991b, pp. 256–257).

An expansive learning approach in schools is a promising scenario that would evoke and generate the participants' critical and creative agency for school reform as collaborative self-organization from below, creating learning networks transcending the institutional boundaries of the school. This approach is based on bottom-up, reflective communication initiated among people involved in schooling.

The model of expansive learning significantly contributes to the development of pedagogy based on the active societal change agent's role of schools in today's educational research (Yamazumi, 2001, 2005, 2006a, 2007). This also means contributions to discussions of new forms of expansive agency among diverse participants inside and outside schools.

CREATING A HYBRID ACTIVITY SYSTEM IN
AN AFTER-SCHOOL EDUCATIONAL PRACTICE: AN
INTERVENTION STUDY

New School is a children's after-school learning activity project in which the following partners cooperate to create advanced networks of learning: a university, local elementary schools, families, experts, and community organizations outside the school. They are supported in the collaborative effort by the Center for Human Activity Theory at Kansai University in Osaka[1] (Yamazumi, 2006a, 2006b, 2007, in press).

In the NS project, these parties are involved in designing grade-mixed, group- and project-based learning activities. Inspired by everyday practices, the themes of NS activities include eating and cooking, gardening and farming, personal well-being, ecological thinking, and responsibility for the environment and a sustainable future. The activities of the NS aim to develop agentive, critical, and creative learning abilities in the children involved in the project.

In the NS project, activities in which elementary school children are engaged in a fun, creative learning processes on the theme of food are carried out at the center every Wednesday after school (Figs. 13.1a and 13.1c); in addition, children work on a farm and cook in the school's home economics room on holidays (Figs. 13.1b and 13.1d). The NS activities include project-based learning with the support of university students (Fig. 13.1a), rice planting (Fig. 13.1b), digital storytelling (Fig. 13.1c), cooking local vegetables with the support of university students, and inviting high school students within an exchange program between the university and local schools (Fig. 13.1d). In such a hybrid activity, learning networks are created and advanced.

By exposing children to the community activities and productive practices of farmers, agricultural experts, senior nutritionists, and food-related producers, distributors, and social organizations like Slow Food Kobe, NS activities aim to develop project-based learning for children

---

[1] The Center for Human Activity Theory (CHAT) was established at Kansai University in Osaka, Japan, in April 2005 to focus on educational research and development based on cultural-historical activity theory and its interventionist approach to human education, learning, and development. CHAT is involved in a joint research project entitled "International Joint Research in Innovative Learning and Education System Development: The Creation of Human Activity Theory," which is funded by the Ministry of Education, Culture, Sports, Science, and Technology as an "Academic Frontier" Project, 2005–2009. See Center for Human Activity Theory Web site: http://www.chat.kansai-u.ac.jp.

Figure 13.1. New School activities.

whereby real-life activities are synergistically networked through the creation of productive collaboration among multiple parties. A key goal is bridging the gap between the activities of the elementary school and the productive practice of everyday life outside the school.

In NS interventions, new mixed activities are created through broad-ranging overlapping and interconnection between the after-school play activities of elementary school students, the learning activities of university students, and the work of practitioners and researchers. On the basis of the perspective of third-generation activity theory on interacting activity systems with a partially shared object, it is possible to characterize NS as a boundary organization to create an emerging hybrid activity system in which multiple and different activity systems interact and engage together, expanding their own objects and partially sharing a new object.

Hugh Mehan (2007) illuminates and analyzes the interorganizational collaboration in which his Center for Research on Educational Equity, Access, and Teaching Excellence (CREATE) at the University of California, San Diego (UCSD) makes collective efforts to improve the opportunity for low-income students of color to attend colleges and universities by assisting public schools in San Diego in adapting the principles developed at the highly successful Preuss School on the UCSD campus to their local circumstances. He describes how CREATE serves as a mediator between the Preuss School and local schools that are interested in building a college-going culture of learning in order to improve the education of underrepresented minority students.

It is possible to equate the work of NS with a mediating system such as CREATE. Namely the NS project can serve as a mediating system between local elementary schools and expert groups and community organizations outside schools – community activities and productive practices – offering new forms of school learning activity for children, such as "networks of learning" and "school as societal change agent" to schools, and providing a range of resources such as university students and researchers, experts and practitioners outside the school, and physical facilities and equipment for school activities. Figure 13.2 is a schematic representation of NS as a mediating system.

As NS develops, it increasingly mediates the emergence of networked hybridity. Although this hybridity is clearly an important resource for developing new activities, it is also full of tensions and contradictions because it takes shape without standardized procedures and scripted norms. It is insufficient to merely establish hybrid forms of activity. Practitioners themselves should learn new rules and patterns in hybrid activity systems by implementing and expanding them. In the following, I analyze some data and findings from the implementation of NS activities that attempt to cross the boundaries between multiple activity systems.

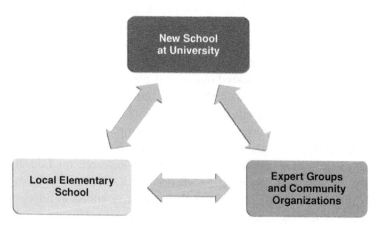

Figure 13.2. New School as a mediating system.

COLLABORATIVE CONCEPT FORMATION FOR
BOUNDARY CROSSING

From July to December 2006, we participated in the NS project while it conducted seven case study sessions to facilitate, support, and follow participant expansive learning in the implementation of grade-mixed, group- and project-based learning activities. Three key groups were involved: Kansai University students, who served as tutors for the children; the research coordinator of the Center for Human Activity Theory at Kansai University, who served as the principal NS practitioner; and the center's researchers, who served as interventionists.

In the sessions, after watching a video of the children's group work and stating the concept for implementing the NS project, the participants offered personal assessments of grade-mixed and group-based learning as an alternative to traditional school learning. Such a learning process involved, first of all, the analysis of contradictions and collective discussions among participants concerning concrete cases that were carefully selected from all videotaped practices and field notes. The intervention here would facilitate, support, and follow cycles of expansive learning by participants: analyzing, reflecting, criticizing, and discussing perceived disturbances and contradictions in their existing work and organizations; modeling and implementing a solution for the new practice; and thus moving into mastering their own models and visions for the community's and organization's future (Engeström, 2007d).

The first case study session was held on July 19, 2006. In NS, 13 children from the third to the sixth grades were divided into three grade-mixed groups as a minimum unit of the project-based collaborative learning. University students were assigned as group tutors. After the participants watched a video during the session, the research coordinator presented her reflections and questions regarding the group organization to the university students, based on her storytelling and sense-making, as follows:

EXCERPT 1

RESEARCH COORDINATOR: Even though it looks as if everything was well organized, I thought that development through group-based learning was stalling. ... If you can only take care of a single child without taking care of a whole group, you can see how far other groups are progressing and will adjust the progress of your group to that. Let's discuss what roles they should play to avoid segmenting the groups. ... To facilitate group-based learning, I think that the division of labor within the groups of children is more important than how the university students directly interact with the children.

Following this assessment, university student 1 started analyzing her own current practice as follows:

EXCERPT 2

UNIVERSITY STUDENT 1: In my group, there are five children, but many of them ask, "Who will do this?" I think we university students did not give enough instructions. Seizi (a sixth-grade boy) often does things properly, but there were times when I didn't know what he should do. I've always thought I need to give more instructions at the beginning.

Participants involved in this series of sessions stood at the starting point of "collaborative concept formation as expansive learning" analyzed by Engeström and his colleagues (Engeström, Pasanen, Toiviainen, & Haavisto, 2005). In other words, they began not only to solve the actual problems of current practice but to form new perspectives to reshape the learning activities in NS by means of mediating between "declared" concepts ("grade-mixed and group-based learning") and "experienced" concepts ("need for children's involvement") and sharing their object of activity. This also entailed the horizontal movement of boundary crossing. "Boundary crossing" refers to work and learning in which actors step outside their customary domains of authority and expertise to find new ideas and solutions together with other actors; boundary crossing typically entails risks and requires efforts at building a shared language between actors (Engeström, Engeström, & Kärkkäinen, 1995; Tuomi-Gröhn & Engeström, 2003a).

However, this movement toward boundary crossing resulted in great tension for the participants. The third case study session was held on September 12, 2006. The principal of the local elementary school, a farmer, a professor of nutrition, and a senior nutritionist were invited to attend. At the session, university student 2, who was charged with being the tutor of a children's grade-mixed group, expressed his hesitation concerning his relations with the children in their project work as follows:

EXCERPT 3

UNIVERSITY STUDENT 2: There are things we must do here, aren't there? I may be wrong in saying "must." Aren't there often times when something is finished, and the children ask, "It's finished. What's next?" If a child is playing around while saying this, I just can't get angry with him. Because he's enjoying himself, and we're outside of school, and children naturally play. So I can't get angry with them. If this were a school, the teachers would say, "Hey!" and become stern.

University student 2 as well as other university students involved in NS were confronted with a situation in which their actions involved an under-explored emotional dilemma, resistance, and insecurity about which would be better, controlling the children or allowing them to play freely. University student 2 commented that because NS is a different place from school, it is hard for him to guide the children's individual behavior apart from the original group work. His statement might be a result of a struggle with the "declared" concept of NS as "fun, creative learning" compared with his perspective of an "experienced" concept. This kind of conflict could also be derived from the contradictions between the different logics of traditional school learning in the school and alternative forms of learning in NS activities (Yamazumi, in press).

From the conceptual framework of activity theory (Engeström, 1987), the contradiction humans face in their activities is viewed as a driving force and as a contradictory motive for development. It involves structural tensions or a "double bind" (that is, situations in which differing messages are received simultaneously; Bateson, 1972) within and between activity systems. These contradictions are faced and identified between "multiple motives embedded in and engendered by their historically evolving communities and objects" (Engeström, 2006b, p. 3).

The contradictions between the logics of the different activity systems obstruct but also energize collaborative change efforts in the NS project as intervention research to create a hybrid activity system for school innovation. To analyze such an initial contradiction in which group-based learning was not taking place as assessed and discussed in the previous sessions, for example, in Excerpts 1 and 2, the university students and the research coordinator jointly examined a typical case, as shown in Figure 13.3, on November 1, 2006. The children and the students discussed a plan to make a final digital storytelling presentation of their entire project. In this case, however, the project was not a group effort, even though it seemed as though the group worked together. The university student-tutor had already written a presentation "script" before the group discussion and assigned roles for the entire process to individual children. Although her intention was to organize the group well, the individual assignments segmented the group. In other words, the group could not act as a whole.

Figure 13.3. University student assigning her script to each child.

After analyzing the contradiction, the university students and the research coordinator began to seek an innovative way to include the children in the case study sessions. They implemented a new way of responding to the children's need for involvement, in particular, the group work initiated by a child group leader, a sixth-grade boy named Kota. As shown in Figure 13.4, on November 8, 2006, they tried to encourage and help Kota (seated at the far right in the photograph) to take a leadership role in the formation of joint learning. In this case, they shifted their instructions from the top-down assignment of prescribed operations to each child toward the children's involvement in and responsibility for the entire group's work.

In the following activity, Kota came into his leadership role to act in concert with the other children in his group. As shown in Figure 13.5, on November 15, 2006, he proposed a division of labor and group collaboration to the other children for making their final presentation by showing them a draft of his proposal on a computer. He invited them to join the presentation: "Look, everyone. Let's see what roles look interesting. Which one do you want to play?" When we observed his agentive leadership in group- and project-based learning, we obviously acknowledged not only his individual development but also the excellent collective development of the group's participants, including the children, the university students, the research coordinator, and the researchers.

Figure 13.4. Research coordinator and university students facilitating child's initiatives as group leader.

Figure 13.5. Child taking the initiative for group- and project-based learning.

Here let me employ a simplified representation of the three transforming configurations in the group work of the children, the university students, and the research coordinator through the NS activities on November 1, 8, and 15, 2006, as shown in Figure 13.6. This figure shows that the configuration of

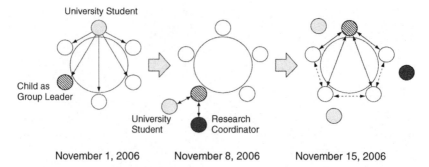

Figure 13.6. Three successive configurations in children's, university students', and research coordinator's group work through New School activities on November 1, 8, and 15, 2006.

their group work changed from *university student assigning her script to each child* (November 1, 2006) to *research coordinator and university students evoking and facilitating the child's initiatives as group leader* (November 8, 2006), to *the child embracing his initiative and leadership role to interact and collaborate with his peers* (November 15, 2006).

Distributed agency emerged expansively. It reshaped the configuration of group- and project-based learning in which the segregated activities of participants were synergistically connected and reciprocated. Such agency would be located in knotworking for horizontal movement on changing initiatives, distributed leaderships, and communicative engagements.

CONCLUSION: TOWARD EXPANSIVE AGENCY IN MULTI-ACTIVITY COLLABORATION ACROSS BOUNDARIES

The NS project is now moving into building partnerships with local elementary schools to create new forms of learning in the schools by discussing with teachers how NS activities can be involved in school innovation itself (Yamazumi, in press). In particular, the purpose of NS's attempt at building partnerships is to offer new forms of school learning activities, such as project-based learning and networks of learning, and to bridge the gap between the activities of elementary schools and the productive practices of everyday life outside the school.

In this multi-activity collaboration, although NS activities have not yet been directly integrated into school activities, the NS and the schools can collaborate in designing and implementing various networks of learning and hybrid forms of activity. Specifically, a joint effort was undertaken between the NS and an elementary school to design and implement third graders' and their teachers' project-based learning unit entitled "A Kansai University Exploration: What Place?" In this project-based learning unit in the fall semester of 2007, the NS invited the third graders to the university and facilitated their group- and project-based learning to investigate such topics as the facilities, equipment, and people's activities in the university that the children were interested in. The university is the biggest neighborhood public community for the children.

By using the knotworking-type formation of collaborative performance, the otherwise loosely connected school and NS can cross boundaries between involved activity systems and expand their willingness to create school innovations together by sharing their object. The knotworking engagements described here are based on the idea of changing the school not from the inside alone but by creating hybrid forms of activity in the community.

Actually, it may remain a form of small-scale expansive learning. The design and implementation of such a hybrid activity system typically entail vulnerability, and require learning how to cross boundaries in building a shared object of school innovation between the actors and activities. As I have analyzed, it is possible to identify crucial contradictions that obstruct the implementation of new forms of learning in hybrid types of activity. Nevertheless, such contradictions also open up and energize collaborative efforts to transform traditional pedagogical practices into new practices of collaboration between schools and outside society, generating new types of expansive agency that would be oriented toward mastering and/or cultivating the runaway object between multiple activity systems. As Engeström (2005c, p. 333) characterizes it, such agency in network organizations might be formulated as "Dwell in the object, connect and reciprocate across boundaries" in relation to a longitudinal dialogic relationship with the expanded, shared object. Such agency might include the will and courage to create innovations so that schools can become collaborative change agents.

14

The Communicative Construction of Community:
Authority and Organizing

JAMES R. TAYLOR

I aim to accomplish two things in this chapter. First, I want to present what I see as the striking similarities between activity theory and our own somewhat different concept of coorientation (see Groleau, 2006, for a contrasting view). Second, and more important, I will delve into where I think our ideas diverge and, indeed, significantly so. I hope in this way to enlarge the dialogue, because taking account of similarities and differences is how we learn. This chapter should thus be read as one more episode in an ongoing dialogue that began more than a decade ago, in Albuquerque, New Mexico.

POINTS OF AGREEMENT

Probably the most important insight that activity theory has emphasized is that, when we turn to examine any segment of behavior, individual or collective, we should bear in mind its embedding in a heterogeneous material, technical, social, and cultural world. It is always tempting for an empirically oriented researcher to focus in on some single aspect of the situation, the discourse of people at work, for example, and in privileging their concentration on that dimension, to set the rest aside as irrelevant to the task at hand. Activity theory rejects, in my opinion correctly, this narrowing down.

My intuition, in this respect, dates from my years as a television producer. In the television studio, the producer was never confronted with a choice of less than two (often three or more) alternative images of the action unfolding before the cameras. One was always a close-up, focused tight in on some detail of the action. Another was called, in the jargon of the trade, an "establishing shot": a wide-angle perspective that took in the whole scene. The single researcher or research team, to me, is like one of those perspectives, selected by only one of the potential camera positions. There are always other, equally valid perspectives that could have, with equal justification, been taken. A problem arises, however, because researchers, unlike cameras, have an ego-stake in the image they are recording. That is, furthermore, not just a personal idiosyncrasy: it is continually being reinforced by the whole teaching, review, and publishing system.

One of the great achievements of activity theory has been to remind us of the need to keep in mind that any system of interaction and performance lends itself to a multiplicity of perspectives. To stick with the television analogy, what the viewer sees as a detached, autonomous stream of images – namely what the producer has chosen to highlight – is in fact a construction, once we factor in the context of production. It is all the elements that the viewer does *not* see, the perspectives that *could* have been privileged – not just the cameras or the cameramen, or even the studio, but the whole institutional embedding of TV that is actually being made present: sponsor, banker, advertiser, the lot – that are being what Cooren (2006) calls "presentified": paradoxically made present in their very absence. It is not merely the TV show that is being put together; the context is itself constructed in and by the same activity, all the way back to society itself.

As Engeström (2000b) has written, the baseball game you are watching at the stadium involves more than the actions of the players. It is the whole institution of the sport, made contingently present, on this day, in this park.

Activity theory has chosen as its fulcrum the subject–object axis, and there again I have always felt comfortable with this manner of conceptualizing this crucial link within standard activity theory. I have more than once cited the characterization of object in Engeström's 1990 book *Learning, Working and Imagining*: "The *object* refers to the 'raw material' or 'problem space' at which the activity is directed and which is molded or transformed into *outcomes* with the help of physical and symbolic, external and internal *tools* (mediating instruments and signs)" (p. 79). This is a definition that retains the crucial distinction between subject and object (Robichaud, 2006) and yet, at the same time, reminds us that both are being co-constructed in the same activity, as their relationship is materialized in the real world, through the mediation of a technology, while simultaneously being symbolically constructed and reconstructed within the domain of language.

My own reading on this concept of the subject–object axis and its systemic dependencies has been deeply influenced by the greatly underrated structuralist theorist Algirdas Greimas (1987; Taylor, 2006; Taylor & Van Every, 2000). The terminology is different, but the central idea of the co-constitution of subjects and object is grounded in the same insight. The subject–object co-construction is the basis of all value, and the motive that justifies intersubjective interaction. All activity is realized in performance, in a mixed environment of "helpers" (*adjuvants,* in the French) who are both material ("tools") and human. Every system of action has within it contradictions that are the potential seeds of its own destruction. To survive means to have learned.

All of this I feel very comfortable with, quite at home. Where I have more difficulty is with an Engeström innovation, the inclusion of a concept of "community." I certainly concur on the importance of community as a factor of systemness. But it seems to me that community has been weakly conceptualized in activity theory: treated as little more than a parameter, rather than being explicitly problematized. For me, as an organizational communication scholar, I am left feeling deeply dissatisfied. So in what remains of this chapter, I will suggest how we might reestablish the balance.

THINKING ABOUT COMMUNITY

Let me begin with a premise: A community is not just part of the background, an enveloping context; it is an *outcome.* Community must be constructed, and in this sense it is *also* the object of an activity. It is, granted, a *given,* but we should also bear in mind that it is equally a *finality* – an end to be accomplished. Community is an instance of that most troubling of mathematical properties – Kurt Gödel's great contribution (Yourgrau, 2005): the reflexive and recursive character of any system of activity that is language dependent, or grounded in communication. To me, the failure to come to grips with this recursive reconstitution of community in the very realization of its activities is the great gap in activity theory, as presently understood.

If community is an object – an outcome of activity – and not just a parameter, then we need an explanation of its construction. It is toward this end that all of my work over the years, as well as that of my closest associates, has been addressed. To do so I have resurrected and refurbished what Newcomb (1953) called "coorientation theory." The rest of this chapter will set out in broad outline the main thrust of the theory, revised to serve as the building block of a conceptualization of community.

Coorientation Theory, My Version

Coorientation theory, like activity theory, takes as a basis the assumption that all constructive human activity has at its core a subject–object relationship, mediated by one form of technology or another (the human body, to begin with). The relationship is realized as a performance, in that the object undergoes a transformation that is the result of the subject's acting on it through whatever means is at his or her disposal. The outcome of the transformation is the creation of *value,* in that the object in its new form is useful in a way that it was not before. I interpret the term "object," incidentally, broadly to include the gamut of purposes to which human activity is typically addressed. The important point is the creation of value.

Because it is useful, and because the subject or agent who transformed it needed to have skill and an access to specialized tools, the artifact – the locus of value – is now, potentially, the object of a transaction, one that brings into a complementary relationship the producer and a user or beneficiary. For the subject or agent, the value derives from the *exchange,* in the form of recompense, in coin or in kind. For the beneficiary, the value is in its subsequent *use.*

I assume that it is this relationship, of agent to beneficiary, in its multifarious variations on a basic theme that is the building block of community. I term this, following Newcomb, an A–B–X relationship (beneficiary–agent–object). The relationship is, it is important to note, triadic, not dyadic, in kind. Dyadic relationships are often privileged by those involved in conversation and discourse analysis, and by theorists of dialogue, as fundamentally discursive. Such a limited, myopic focus has more than once been criticized by Engeström (e.g., 1999b), and I share his view. A and B do not *first* relate to each other in conversation and *secondarily* focus on an object, thematized as a topic of their talk, as too many communication theorists have assumed; they relate to each other, to begin with, *through* their common interest in X. The talk is chitchat; it becomes organizational only in a context of activity. The triad, where activity is concerned, cannot simply be decomposed into dyads; as Caplow (1968) has remarked, "Triads are the building blocks of which all social organizations are constructed" (p. 1).

Nevertheless, the triadic unit always incorporates within itself the potential for contradiction (Greimas, 1987). It may easily mutate from a harmonious two-way exchange – value for equivalent value – into something less socially acceptable. One or the other may lie, cheat, default, or fudge.

To put it in different terms, what was the translation of three into one – a bonding of sociality – can degenerate into two against one: the object monopolized by one at the expense of the other. What should have been an equitable exchange is transformed into something less positive: theft or betrayal.

Here again, I believe the emphasis of activity theory on the potential for contradiction in any complex system of activity is well founded. My own way of conceptualizing this is as an incompatibility of "worldview" (Taylor, 1983, 1993; Taylor & Cooren, 2006; Taylor, Gurd, & Bardini, 1997). The concept of worldview, which derives from earlier work in computer simulation of activity systems, simply incorporates the perception that, in any agent–beneficiary transaction, A and B occupy different universes of time and space, and their purposes are fundamentally divergent in that there would be no transaction without a difference of ownership. The relationship is never – *cannot* ever be – symmetric. It is intrinsically complementary and, as Bateson (1972) argued, therefore has the potential to be "schismogenetic": to dissolve into conflict, in other words. So if a community is to come into existence, and persist, its potential members must find a way to bind the coorientational relationships to each other sufficiently to hold the delicate fabric of human relationships together.

This, I believe, is the role of authority. But I find no in-depth treatment of authority in activity theory that would furnish enlightenment on this challenge.

Division of Labor?

In the Engeström diagram illustrating his theory of activity, the axis of community is conceptualized as associated with rules and the division of labor. I want, to begin with, to focus on the latter, the division of labor. I will take up the question of rules later.

My initial formulation of coorientation theory posited a single agent and a single beneficiary. But that hardly adds up to a community. A community begins to form when there are many agents who relate to each other with respect to a certain cluster of objects and a shared class of beneficiaries. This then brings into focus the character of their internal relationships to each other as agents who typically occupy complementary roles in the performance of some task that is too complex for a single actor to undertake. Notice that word "complementary" again. There is still coorientation, except that now the object of exchange is a service, or the performance of a task. As Wittgenstein (1953) observed in his *Philosophical Investigations*, it is language that is the basic tool in this kind of interaction, and the object is no longer a consumable good, but a performance (Greimas, 1987). The A–B–X model still applies, except that the A–B axis of the relationship is mediated by the performance *of* B (X) acting as an agent *for* A. A is a beneficiary. Wittgenstein cites a trivial instance, where A is a builder, B an assistant, and the X is B handing stones to A. B's acting on an object (the stone) – his performance – is the object, in other words. It is A who asks B to pass the stone. That is his or her act. B is effectively a tool by means of which A acts on X.

For Hobbes (1996), B is an "actor," and that person, A, who "owneth" the words and actions of B, is the author: "In this case the actor acteth by authority" (p. 170). B is the *agent*, an actor-for; A is the source of the *authority* to act.

Austin (1962) baptized this function of language-as-acting-on-an-object by introducing a neologism, "illocutionary," and the outcome that is thereby brought about, in his jargon, as a "perlocutionary" effect. But he needn't have been so inventive, because using language as a tool to act on an object or subject in the quest for an outcome is a standard feature of language that linguists call *modality* (Bybee & Fleischman, 1995; Halliday, 1985; Palmer, 1986).

Notice that we have introduced a recursion – a transaction within a transaction: a performance (B's action on X) that is itself an object (B's acting on behalf of A or, in other words, A's action on B). Two outcomes are achieved in the performance of B: acting in a material world and, in doing so, constructing a social relationship, B with respect to A, and vice versa.

It is this recursiveness that is at the root of community formation, because in its absence the community has no permanence. It quickly dissolves once again into no more than a disparate collection of individual performances. Engeström's model treats this linking of performances as a "division of labor." But this has always prompted, for me, the troubling question of *who* is the "divider"? It must have been, should we presume (?), someone with the authority to make the division. But this is surely to beg the question, where did the divider's authority come from in the first place? For early management theorists such as F. W. Taylor and Henri Fayol there was no issue: The authority was lodged in the chief executive, by definition. But that is a view that is now outdated (other, of course, than in the minds of some executives and their mentors and disciples). I cannot believe that an analyst as subtle as Engeström actually subscribes to it.

How Authority Can Be Established from the Inside

The authority that reflects a stable social relationship has to be constituted in the transactional dynamic of interagent communication. That this occurs, spontaneously, seems to be empirically the case. A nice instance of this is furnished by Linde's (1988) research centered on "a cooperative work situation in which the authority status of the two participants is subject to a moment to moment negotiation" (p. 52). The context was a helicopter, in an airborne law enforcement agency, with a crew of two: a pilot (the aircraft commander) and a flight officer (the mission commander). The pilot was recruited from the Air Force, with supplementary training in police procedure; the flight officer from the police. Two parallel hierarchies were involved, in other words. Since each had authority over his own domain, their joint performance had to be negotiated: Neither could tell the other how to do his job. There were, in principle, two equals, each holding the rank of officer. Basing her analysis on hours of audio and video recordings of performance, Linde found, nevertheless, that there were clear signs that the pilot had the greater authority, perhaps because of a higher remuneration or because of a greater set of skills that had received official recognition. The emerging authority relationship could be discovered in the back-and-forth chitchat of the two. It emerged, for example, in off-work teasing and casual banter: Whereas the flight officer might be ribbed about poor job performance, the converse did not happen. But it entered into their work talk as well. The negotiation of authority, Linde found, was sensitive to the exigencies of the task, even though, overall, the distribution was skewed toward pilot primacy. The authority could shift, depending on the situation. But it was always present.

There are several reasons, I have concluded, for the stabilizing of authority in a community. In contemporary organizations, for example, the norm is exchange: labor for salary. The possession of finances and other key recourses by the executive thus constitutes a powerful instrument for the establishment of authority. Barnard (1938) points to another that has since found confirmation in the work of Barker (1993; Barker & Cheney, 1994): the discipline exerted on the individual within a work group by peers, who may not share the same resistance to authority as the individual plaintiff. The authority is now generated within the group, not imposed from without. And then there is a further factor that was emphasized by Arendt (1961). For her, modern society has witnessed a steady erosion of authority over the past century or more. As she wrote, "Authority has vanished from the modern world" (p. 91). I think that is to considerably overstate the case. But this is not to downplay the importance of tradition and the assumptions of hierarchy it projects onto the current experience of people in community. The "word" still matters, and so does the binding effect of origins.

Rules?

The Engeström model describes this set of background assumptions about the right and the wrong way to organize as "rules." I have the same question as before: Who wrote the rules? Whose rule is it? When I was teaching in Amsterdam, there was a sign outside the main building that read, "No bicycles allowed." Right in front of the sign were literally dozens of bikes, tied up. I asked my students about the rule. "Well, yes," they replied, "it's the rule but not really." Who wrote *their* rules? Where did *their* authority originate?

To me, the notion of rules does not capture the full significance of what people accept as the way to govern their life. Nor does the notion of rules, in the abstract, accurately reflect the authority a society accepts as "really" the rule. The pattern varies from country to country, and even between social configurations within a single society. Rules, explicitly enforced, are an instance of the overt exercise of authority and tend to be resented. As Sennett (1980) pointed out, the assertion of authority within the United States typically generates resistance. It seems plausible to hypothesize even greater intolerance to the imposition of authority in the Scandinavian countries, which are notorious for their egalitarianism (Heaton & Taylor, 2002). In other countries, however, the exercise of direct supervisory control may be more taken for granted. It depends.

There is another factor, this time structural. Let us return to Linde's case study. Presumably, her helicopter team had to report to a superior, who was in a position to sanction the team's performance as meeting the expected standard (the "rule") or failing to do so. In making their report, they would have had to be represented ("*re*-presented," for Cooren, 2006). Hobbes (1996) refers to this reconstitution of the team (minimum of two) in the voicing of its perspective as "personating" it: constituting the many (minimum two) of the team as a oneness, through its *im*-personation in a spokesperson. In doing so, it is making an account of its performance: justifying it. The representative assumes, literally, *authority*, since it is he or she who is responsible for authoring the account. And this process is itself a powerful instrumentality for the constitution of authority, because the members of the team may become intensely committed to their account (for good reason; it protects their collective face). And this tends to cement the authority relationship *within* the group, by establishing it as a *protagonist,* and the alien, outside judgmental authority as an *antagonist* (Greimas, 1987).

But the discipline need not stop there. Güney's (2006) research will serve to illustrate. She studied the steps leading to the development of a new product line in a globally known high-tech firm in the United States. Two centers were involved, which she whimsically dubbed "Hotville" and "Snowfield." One was famous for its high-end, technically sophisticated products, marketed mainly to very large clients, such as the military. The other specialized in user-friendly software and firmware aimed at a different market of midsize enterprises. Their cultures were totally different. Hotville was "cowboy": emphasis on individuality, low visible management intervention. Snowfield was conservative, and collaborative. Both had sunk investments in their establishment, and both counted on persuading the company to invest in their development priorities, because their status depended entirely on the continued financing. The company decided, however, that it needed a new line that would incorporate the best of the two centers, by combining their hardware and software excellence. But in its new fall plan, the objective was stated broadly, and much of the elaboration of the plan was left to the centers themselves to work out. The result was a form of open warfare, as Snowfield insisted that one of its new technically advanced innovations be incorporated into the new product line, whereas Hotville just as strongly rejected the proposal, on the grounds that the company's scheduled release time did not allow for its inclusion. For a couple of months, the schedule was frozen. Snowfield tried to bring in the higher-ups to buttress its argument, and Hotville found out about the move and blocked it. Finally, the company issued an ultimatum: They would have to sit in a room, for however long it took, and work out a solution. They did, because they had to. They eventually came up with a compromise, but not without strong residual feelings of resentment on both sides. Nevertheless, the project did finally go ahead.

Notice again, as in the instance of reporting to a superior, that the authority *within* the group was greatly enhanced by the conflict of perspectives *without.* No superior officer imposed a solution on Hotville and Snowfield. Instead, the company said, "Work it out yourselves" (the company did, however, establish the conditions). The result was an intensive concentration on developing a persuasive account that would satisfy both parties, but only more or less. Those days when the representatives of the two centers were locked in a room in Showfield were filled with PowerPoint presentations, highly detailed projections involving very sophisticated technical data, and arguments for and against. The result, finally, was an account that could be presented to management as the compromise. The whole process was one of engendering authority, from within.

Many of my colleagues in organizational communication studies favor dialogue over conflict, and I can understand, and sympathize with, the sentiment. But I think they are reluctant to grasp the nettle. I have a sense that to depend on dialogue, and the kind of "authentic" communication favored by someone like Habermas, is fundamentally misguided. Nobody likes authority when it is someone else who is exerting it. No one wants to be one-down in a one-up/one-down relationship (Watzlawick, Beavin, & Jackson, 1967). There is a great deal of empirical research showing that authority is accompanied by more or less covert resistance (e.g., Sennett, 1980). And yet it is my sense that in the absence of authority the community will dissolve, as Hobbes believed. In our own research, we have documented what can happen to a complex enterprise when the authority system fails (Taylor & Van Every, forthcoming). In two different environments we studied, broadcasting and police work, the result was catastrophic in its consequences and left permanent scars on the organization, with a very considerable weakening of its internal bonds of community and, externally, its capacity to carry out its mandate.

It is not a popular idea to celebrate, even in mitigated terms, authority. There is no doubt in my mind, moreover, that the constitution of authority is all too often characterized by its abuse. And yet, like Hobbes, it is hard for me to see the alternative, the absence of a system of authority, as an improvement. The existence of authority is an inconvenience we have to live with, as a condition of civilized society. At the very least, it seems to me, authority is a topic worthy of our close attention, as social scientists. In my own field, unfortunately, there is instead a resounding silence, and I am not aware that the literature on activity theory is much more informative.

CONCLUSION

I am a great admirer of Yrjö Engeström and the contribution he has made to the advancement of our field over his distinguished career. I continue to be astonished by his productivity: A whole shelf of my bookcase is stuffed with copies of the articles he has generated in an amazingly short time. What is even more impressive is the quality of the work. He is adept at taking empirical data and finding ways to illuminate its significance for the reader. This being said, I think there is a danger that his intense focus on the activity as such, a seductive positioning of his "camera," indeed, but not the only possible one, may have made him less sensitive to how the activity re-creates the larger system of activity. No system of activity is going to persist very long if it does not produce its own community in the very act of accomplishing the practical purposes of the people who make it up. I do not believe that activity theory has yet explained the genesis of community, in spite of its philosophical commitments. Partly, I think, this is because, while Engeström has from the beginning insisted on the empirical importance of communication, in practice activity theorists have paid little attention to its theoretical foundations. Yet as John Dewey (1944 [1916]) wrote, "communication" and "community" share a common Latin root.

The issue here is profound. The crux of the matter is the question of how a community reproduces itself. The self-reproductive loop has been described in more than one way. Maturana and Varela (1987), for example, have described it as *autopoietic* – self-reproducing. More recently, complexity theory, associated particularly with the work of the Santa Fe Institute in New Mexico, has borrowed the expression *auto-catalytic* to describe the indispensable mechanism that explains the origin of life in, and out of, the original chemical soup that was the world (Kauffman, 1995). The principle is the same. For any activity system, human or other, to reproduce itself and display continuity in its activities, beyond the immediate response to its environment, it must have the means to re-create the conditions of its own survival and perpetuation as a system. My sense is that this is the dimension of activity that has received less attention in the work of activity theorists than it merits.

How, then, can the omission be corrected? I think there is only one way: by an intensified concentration on the instrumental properties of human language – language as itself a tool. I do not mean by this a focus on ideology or discursive formations in the tradition of Foucault. I mean instead, as I have tried to outline in this chapter, how it is that in doing something together to deal with an object people are simultaneously doing something to themselves. There are always, where humans are concerned, *two* outcomes of activity, not one. One of those outcomes is an intervention in a practical world. The other is the formation of community, but here, I have tried to argue, there is a price to be paid. It is less appealing to be the done-to than the doer, to be the "object" of an exercise of authority than the subject, but if society is to perpetuate itself, there will have to be a good deal of "doing-to." Here I think Engeström has it just right. Every system of activity has within itself the seeds of its own contradiction. Complexity theorists have a term for this. They see organization as being possible only at what they call the "edge of chaos." The term may be a bit overdramatic, but I think the insight is authentic. Constant change is anathema to the formation of an organized community. Nothing ever settles down long enough to allow for coherent action. On the other hand, total order is equally the enemy of constructive activity. As Atlan (1979) described it, life is possible only between the crystal and the smoke.

Community is like that. It may seem stable as crystal, but that is only because the fire is, for the moment, damped down (Law & Mol, 1998). It can flame up into smoke at any time (and not infrequently does). But if community crystallizes *too* much, it dies. The "edge" is where learning and adaptation go on. This, I believe, is the challenge that still faces activity theory: to explain how community is constructed at the edge of chaos.

15

Research Leadership: Productive Research Communities and the Integration of Research Fellows

STEN LUDVIGSEN AND TURI ØWRE DIGERNES

In this chapter we focus on what can be described as especially productive research groups and communities. We take cultural-historical activity theory as the premise and focus on how we can understand research groups' work when using the concept of object as our main analytic concept (Engeström, 1987). Policy studies of research emphasize that the organization and funding of research are going through changes, from individual to collective models. The question then becomes, what does this mean for the researchers in their everyday activities? This trajectory, which has been seen for a long time within the research disciplines and communities of medicine, science, and technology, is starting to influence and play a significant role in the "text subjects" within social science, educational science, and the humanities. These areas are probably the fields of research where this trend in research development is currently at its weakest.

The shift in models can be illustrated by new arrangements like Centres of Excellence (CoE), Centres for Research-Based Innovation (CRIs), and Networks of Excellence in the European Union that aim to create better conditions for elite research, which will lead globalized knowledge production and in so doing expand research frontiers. As part of these efforts, the development of more focused and defined doctoral and postdoctoral research schools is taking place. These new research models are implemented across fields of sciences in Europe and in the United States.

We would like to thank all of the informants for sharing their time and experiences with us. This research is supported by the CMC, a strategic effort at the University of Oslo (http://www.intermedia.uio.no/), and the Norwegian Research Council–supported project Transform. Transform's focus is on understanding and characterizing productive learning communities. We thank Professor Olga Dysthe and Ph.D. student Cecilie F. Jahreie for very stimulating comments on different versions of this text. We also thank the anonymous reviewers and the editors for very helpful comments on the manuscript.

Research groups or communities can be seen as environments for work and learning, where collective demands, including intellectual agendas, are crucial for long-term success. This kind of work environment is often described as an intellectual community in which professors work closely with other professors, researchers, postdoctoral fellows, and Ph.D. students. Research leadership is very important when it comes to welding these kinds of work communities and creating productive learning conditions for research recruits.

Most studies of research communities are either historical (Kvale, 1997) or more structural analyses in which publishing patterns are identified (Kyvik & Sivertsen, 2005). However, in studies conducted by Latour and Woolgar (1986), we can see descriptions of "everyday life." Here, research work is described as a social activity, situated in practice, and strongly attached to theory, methods, and instruments, in other words, how scientific knowledge is produced (Latour, 1987; Pickering, 1995) or the machinery of knowledge construction, (Knorr Cetina, 1999). These studies are based on an epistemic perspective (Saari, 2003). Following in this tradition, we try to understand how the everyday life of research is unfolding and how the research community defines and follows its objects of research (Saari, 2003). In our study, we have chosen to look specifically at research leadership, aiming to understand how productive research communities are developed and maintained, and how Ph.D. students are integrated into these communities. Our study is based on the following questions:

1. How does one establish a joint object in a research community?
2. How are standards developed, and to what degree do these standards bring structure to the researchers' work and learning?
3. What kinds of implications will a joint object have for Ph.D. students' learning environment?

We have chosen two different research communities, and our analyses of the practices in these settings are based on interviews, observations, and document data. Both communities are recognized both nationally and internationally, and they have been awarded several large research grants. One of the communities is part of a larger research center. Both communities work within what we can describe as text-producing research, which means within a genre where the text itself and the arguments within the text are considered highly significant.

The aims of the chapter are twofold. First, we will give a set of empirical descriptions that can provide more insight into how productive research groups actually work and why they structure their research in specific ways. Second, we will demonstrate that cultural-historical activity theory gives us very sensitive analytic tools to understand how research groups construct their objects of research and why they do so.

CULTURAL-HISTORICAL ACTIVITY THEORY: A PERSPECTIVE AND SOME CONCEPTS

A theoretical perspective that gives us the opportunity to understand the constitution of a research community is cultural-historical activity theory (Engeström, 1987; Saari, 2003). On the basis of a cultural and historical understanding of human genesis through the concept of activity, a set of conceptual terms has been developed to understand how different communities and institutions develop through short-term actions and long cycles of activities. Concepts like tension, conflicts, breakdowns, and contradictions are emphasized, and the term *object* is especially significant (Engeström, 1987; Kaptelinin, 2005; Leont'ev, 1978) for understanding how change takes place and what direction it takes. In moment-by-moment interactions, tensions become visible at the empirical level, but in order to understand and explain how and why tensions occur, we must include institutional and historical analysis of long-term activities. Contradiction is seen as a feature that arises within these long cycles of activity.

An object is something potentially shared by several parties (Engeström, 1987). We make a distinction between two aspects of the object. The first applies to objects that work over a longer period of time and are part of institutional structures. These may be routines, standards, or procedures (Miettinen & Virkkunen, 2005). The other dimensions of the term *object* are the procedural aspects. When we enter into an activity, we must find objects that enable us to coordinate our actions. In research communities, these will often be texts, different kinds of methods, or methodological orientations that become the objects we use to coordinate our activities. More precisely, we must make decisions regarding the choice of theory or perspective, concepts, interpretation of data (either qualitative or quantitative), what to include in a summary of previous research, how far to stretch the analysis (in relation to reliability criteria as well as validity), and how to connect theory to data within the field of research.

The discipline of research, the epistemic area, and the research community will, of course, provide guidance with respect to several of the choices to be made, but within the actual research we still have to make many decisions on a "microlevel." These more general aspects will – in relation to the different phases a text goes through – not necessarily be the same, so in every single research project these aspects must be concretized and solutions must be developed.

The different aspects of the term *object* give us the opportunity to understand how structures and processes work over time within a research community. When using the expression *structures,* we mean standards, conventions, and genres within the field of research. One example is the manner in which one writes articles for certain scholarly journals. This can be seen as routine in other institutions; i.e., the routines are sturdy and seldom change. When using the expression *processes,* we mean the set of choices we have pointed to in this section, which form the core of the research work. Together, structures and processes create different kinds of communities of work and learning (Engeström, 2001; Leont'ev, 1978; Toiviainen, 2003). Given the discussion of objects as a concept, we would like to emphasize that this concept might help us understand how historical aspects are related to participants' meaning-making, which means that we can connect different timescales or what we can call multiple levels of human genesis (Engeström, 1987; Ludvigsen, Rasmussen, Krange, Moen, & Middleton, in press). In the next section, we will describe this on an empirical level.

METHODICAL ORIENTATION AND DATA COLLECTION

In this study, we chose to look at two communities, both consisting of professors, senior researchers, associate professors, postdoctoral researchers, and Ph.D. students. The size of these communities varies, but both can be described as having a collective organization of research. We chose one community within what we define as the humanities and one community within computer science. This difference offers possibilities for contrast, and at the same time, the communities exhibit some common traits with regard to how the research is organized. We used interviews as a primary database for our analysis for this chapter. We conducted 25 interviews, which were transcribed.

The interview guide consisted of the following main topics: biography, research community, research topics, research leadership (supervision situation), expectations (standards), aims, and engagement. Within each of these main topics, there were specifying questions. The interview data we collected gives us the opportunity to scrutinize and understand how the informants understand and potentially act in accordance with the topics they were asked about over longer stretches of time. These data will, to a limited degree, give answers about what exactly they do. For this, different kinds of data, for example, video recordings, are necessary. In this chapter, we have used data concerning a limited set of topics. The selected topics are aimed at the organization of the research community, research leadership, and the establishment of a joint focus. The significance this might have for research recruits is what we try to bring into focus.

EMPIRICAL ANALYSIS: SOME COMMON TRAITS AND DIFFERENCES

First, we will suggest some common traits and differences found in the two communities. All the research leaders emphasized the need for a joint focus and the need to establish it through work forms and publications. This may include concepts, methods, projects, or theoretical positions.

Both communities wished to make a substantial contribution to the research field, as well as take part in setting the agenda for forthcoming research priorities in their areas. In each community, the senior researchers spend a lot of time building the environment; that is, the research leadership engages in professional and economic decisions, as well as social organization. Research leadership is, for all interviewed leaders, a matter of moving within vertical axes from political and strategic decisions at the management level to actually being engaged in research, working with texts with other senior colleagues and Ph.D. students. The horizontal aspects of the activities are related to how the research is organized and enacted through participation in multiple activity systems (Engeström, 1987, 2004). By *multiple activity systems*, we mean that researchers and research students engage in research activities in a center or a department, but also in workshops, conferences, and other venues, which implies moving between the activity systems that constitute the larger field of knowledge.

Description of Research Community 1

This research community is based in media and communication research. It is situated at a university, and its roots go back to the establishment of this discipline at the university. Two research leaders (professors), two postdoctoral researchers, and four Ph.D. students are associated with this research community. In addition to this core of eight people, there are also a number of master's students.

Organization and Gradual Development

We will look at the organization and gradual development of the project from the perspective of the participants in this research community. This group is characterized by the fact that other researchers keep joining it.

Three aspects seem central to the research organization: First, each subproject may be dispersed. Second, these dispersed subprojects must contribute to the cumulative work within the research community. Third, integration appears to be a challenge, especially for research leader A:

> One has, in different ways, an idea, then one gets together, and then one has a small steering committee which first decides what to research … , and subsequently one will work together in different ways in the writing part. The idea is that the accumulative effect in the project, the gathering and finding of new, interesting issues, happens there, primarily. And the development of this paramount umbrella should also happen there, as much as possible.

Here, the research leader discusses how he tries to generate a common object for the research, the shared writing process being seen as essential. Nobody should own the text, and contributions from all participants are evaluated seriously and critically. A Ph.D. student (F) describes the research leaders' focus like this:

> The challenge is to find topics which everybody can work with. So we write lots of articles. This may not be very central for lots of people, but it's been immensely stimulating, because everybody has had enough interest in it to actually spend time on it. They have also managed to take advantage of each person's knowledge in a very good way, so that we've had good constellations – meaning we've shared the tasks between us in clever ways, which has made working together good.

The organization, in which one party uses the individual project as a base and then creates cross–writing groups, is seen by several of the participants as complicated and demanding. However, it provides an opportunity for in-depth study of some projects involving more than the owner, and at the same time the current projects' contribution to the mutual agenda can be articulated.

The timeline for this type of research is clearly strategic and long term. Every single contribution is valuable, and at the same time the cumulative effect over time is essential. Seen from the position of the postdoctoral researchers, these methods of work are both stimulating and challenging. Postdoctoral researcher C puts it this way:

> I can't throw myself into those joint experiments in the same way, even though I find them interesting. But the whole time I've been going around, considering: "What's in it for me?" because I'm just in a temporary position.

Here emphasis is placed on how topics may, under certain conditions, function as common objects for researchers who initially didn't have strong common interests. The dilemmas and tensions between personal research and the collective projects, from the point of view of a Ph.D. student, are evident from Ph.D. student A's comment:

> Sometimes I think we've noticed that the joint projects are given priority at the expense of individual projects, so we've had to raise that issue when we've all been together, because we get so excited, and then you come up with all these joint projects, but I can't be part of everything.

From the point of view of both postdoctoral researchers and fellow researchers, tensions related to the degree of joint focus are visible. The long-term agenda established by research leaders attempts to achieve a balance through the development of short-term projects headed by temporary employees. Even though there is a sharing of professional interests and the possibility of collaboration, this will not be sufficient if the tensions become too strong in relation to the objects steering the research. It is important to stress the fact that even though the researchers share their interests within one field of knowledge, the objects will be developed within the more limited and specified areas. This is what we refer to as the procedural part of the research work. This could cause trouble for the Ph.D. students if the research leaders and students don't share the same perspective on the concrete focus of the research.

The Research Leadership's Challenges

As indicated in the introduction, research leadership is offered as the solution to a series of problems identified at the policy level. In this section, we will take a closer look at the way our participants describe this. Research leader A expresses his ambitions for the community as follows:

> To achieve good research together, and explore how productive one can be as a team. ... we wanted to do something that was integrated pretty

tightly, both because of the professional development and the working processes. Simply the way we work together.

In this research community, the two research leaders have different roles and functions. The one who has been the longest in the field, and has guided numerous Ph.D. students on their way to their doctorates, contributes through professional inspiration and the maintenance of the social environment. The latter involves the promotion of an experimental and playful attitude toward the ways one can cooperate, which gives the research community a distinguished openness and a diversity of voices. The other research leader is described as having a more organizational function, and his role is to create boundaries and a strict focus. The two research leaders are described as complementing each other. They give the project direction, both internally, within their own unit, and in the external community in which the project is positioned. Postdoctoral researcher C puts it like this: "It seems like they [the research leaders] are incredibly coordinated."

During the interviews, different goals and ambitions related to the research community became apparent. The primary ambition seemed to be to develop research at a high international level of recognition through a strong and inclusive work environment. Another stated ambition is related to the social dimension of being a researcher. Emphasis is placed on areas like job satisfaction, well-being, and positive social interaction. Here, the different areas merge, and there is no strict division between the work context and social life outside the workplace. Ph.D. student A expresses it like this: "getting away from the loneliness and getting away from the feeling of being on your own." In other words, a picture is drawn of a work and learning environment in which the Ph.D. students face high expectations when it comes to production, but in return they receive a highly valued professional and social experience.

Summary

The first research community seems active and innovative. A researcher works directly with the development of conventions and genres of research within his or her own field. This field of knowledge is open to different methods of publishing so that the structures can't be taken for granted. Here we find that strong ambitions and different collective working methods are used to develop the research and the research genres. Three types of tension can be identified. The first is related to time. Different participants are operating with different timelines, depending on their institutional affiliations. Here norms about individuality and autonomy become important issues.

This influences the opportunities to participate in collective research and writing activities. For example, the Ph.D. students have to prioritize finishing their own projects before they are able to move on. A second tension exists between symmetry and asymmetry. On a social level, all can be seen as equal, but professionally the research community appears to have a distinct leadership. This is made clear, and is seen as obvious, by the participants. This is a tension between the rhetoric of equality and how the research is in fact framed and focused. The third tension is related to the degree of division of labor in the construction of the object of research. What is the single researcher's object of his or her own research, and what constitutes the joint research? The way we interpret this is that the project, as a collective activity, can be described as a negotiation zone, where all the participants are given the opportunity to give voice to their research agendas. But given that one has joined a research community, the negotiations aren't completely open. For the Ph.D. students and the postdoctoral fellows, this means that they must also enter into a set of joint activities, working with crosscutting problem areas within the projects, even if their own projects suffer as a result.

Description of Research Community 2

The computer science research community is part of a research center. The unit where we carried out the interviews is a department within this center. The community started as a small group in 1999, and since then has gradually grown to its current size. In the department there are research leaders, four senior researchers, three postdoctoral researchers, six Ph.D. students, and several master's students.

Organization and Gradual Development

The project has made its mark internationally and chooses new paths in relation to research organizing and types of projects. The department is divided into three areas.

The research leaders stress that a joint focus is central to the community's ability to produce good research results, and they support the department's division into three fields. According to research leader A:

> We've had a few strategy discussions where we say that we will focus on certain areas, three subareas ... , and then you have to stick with those areas. ... The philosophy is that if you want to become internationally

good, we all have to pull in the same direction, and you got to keep your focus.

The focus of this research community grew out of negotiations early in the process of the development, with a strong steer from the leadership. The object established by the leadership is not an object of research for general discussion. The aims and ambitions were articulated by research leader A through a consideration of three aspects:

> One has to work concentrated, several people in the same field over a period of time, if one wants to reach far out, internationally. So of course, focus is important in all parts of it, and then you have the thing about being stimulated, meaning getting people to perform, you've got to have fun, you've got to look at the things that unite hobbies and work, and of course resources, meaning that you shouldn't spend too much time on things interrupting the research, and things you can make other people do, other people should do.

The following seem to be important from the perspective of the research leader: focus, quality, support, and resources. These aspects point toward a strong degree of cohesion and continuity within the research work, and this is also mirrored in the subareas. Much emphasis is also placed on larger projects crosscutting smaller research groups. A reasonable interpretation is that this community places a strong emphasis on cohesion and continuity when it comes to the objects that drive its research. The negotiation of these objects takes place at the leadership level, with close reference to the development of the project itself.

The Challenges of the Research Leadership

As indicated in the introduction, this research group is described as hierarchical, with a clearly defined leadership and organizational structure. Taking a closer look at this structure, we will see how the participants describe the research leadership and their position in the group. One significant action is the arrangement of a three- to four-day internal seminar for the department twice a year. According to research leader B, "It's one hundred percent compulsory, and then we've got intense discussions and a tight schedule, nearly twenty-four hours a day for three to four days." These seminars are highly appreciated by the Ph.D. students and the postdoctoral researchers. Several of the informants mention the seminars as an important contribution to the social unity within the community.

High levels of pressure at work and clear organizational structures make the standards and the division of labor within the work environment clear. We can identify tensions between the different members of the group, in relation to the established standards and aims. One tension is between the Ph.D. students' need for cooperation and the research leaders' ambition to create tracks for the development of independence of the Ph.D. students and the postdoctoral researchers. This tension has made the Ph.D. students come together to form their own groups, in which they have provided each other with supervision based on their own experiences. When it comes to being included in different working arrangements and meetings, those who wish to participate need to take some sort of initiative. As one post-doctoral researcher said, "If you ask about it, he'll pass it on, but you've got to ask. If you're not being active yourself, you can easily end up just sitting there." It must be stressed that within the group, the different Ph.D. students have different perspectives – some value protection and quiet working environments, whereas others want more sparring with their seniors. Time is referred to and experienced as one of the most central tensions in this group. This is also related to the strong ambitions that exist.

In this group, much emphasis is placed on status, position, and ranking in the international research community. Activities are organized with regard to this, which means that one will experience tensions internally, within the group and the center (e.g., with regard to how much each individual contributes to strengthening the international position). For the Ph.D. students, this means that their contributions become part of this positioning. The support increases, but so does the pressure.

Summary

The second research community has a clear, institutional foundation in that it is part of a research center. This anchor provides clear directions for the work, and means that research is the main activity. Those working within this community have high ambitions, and the direction in which these ambitions are channeled is controlled primarily by the leadership. In this research community, different tensions are identified. First, the research community stands out as hierarchical, with a clear work division between researchers on different competence levels. There is little openness for researchers other than the senior researchers to negotiate the future agenda within the field of knowledge. From the Ph.D. students' perspective, this tension has implications for their integration into the community. This is strongly related to the fact that conventions and genres are established with regard to products such as scientific articles. The results produced by this center are collective and institutionally based, which means that the collective result is superior to the work each individual researcher contributes. This is expressed most clearly when it comes to the Ph.D. students. We could say that there are very few differences between the research leaders' projects and the Ph.D. students' projects.

This aspect is related to the second tension, the shared objects for research. As we have indicated, this means that the Ph.D. students' work is followed closely whenever that work is contributing to the research leadership's agenda. The Ph.D. students' work is closely integrated into the collective knowledge development of the research group. The tension here could also be described as that between individual contributions and development and the collective outcome for the research group.

The last tension is related to time and is concerned with the practice of prioritizing the research leaders' own research, strategic work, international participation and branding, co-writing with other senior researchers, as well as guiding Ph.D. students. We can describe this as a strong asymmetry between professors and Ph.D. students.

DISCUSSION AND CONCLUSION

In our analysis of the research group, we have pointed out learning potentials and affordances that are seen as crucial to the way Ph.D. students and research recruits get involved in their communities. Research organization and research leadership are crucial in this context. We have attempted to emphasize some of these main factors seen from the perspective of the research leaders and the Ph.D. students. In the empirical analyses, it becomes obvious that different kinds of negotiation zones are established. We can conceptualize this as emerging objects that direct and redirect the work and the meaning-making for the researchers (Engeström, 2004; Saari, 2003). Negotiation in this context is a process whereby one discusses and debates in order to achieve a common understanding. This involves structural aspects like standards, genres, and conventions and the micro-processes that constitute these activities.

In media and communication research, the most important thing seems to be the negotiations concerning the constitution of the object. The constitution of the object is not given and is gradually changed throughout a Ph.D. student's development. This is what Engeström (1987) and Saari (2003) describe as an emerging object, which means that the object gradually changes over time, redirecting the activities. The negotiation zone can be described as open, given that participants adhere to the set of thematic frameworks that this research group is based on, and the individual Ph.D. student will have many choices. Individuality and autonomy are strong norms in this group. These norms have a strong basis in many universities as knowledge institutions (Olsen & Maassen, 2007). If you choose to position yourself close to the joint focus, it means that the support from the research community increases. If you choose to position yourself at the periphery of the research group activities, there will necessarily be fewer overlapping interests, and direct support will be reduced. In the humanities field, constructing the object of research is part of the creative aspect of research activities. When the research group moves toward more collective models, contradictions can emerge.

In the computer science community, the Ph.D. students' learning activities are characterized by a relatively limited zone for negotiation. Here the objects also change, but the change process is not open to all the participants in the community. The main emphasis is placed on an overlapping of the research leaders' and Ph.D. students' focus. This means that the Ph.D. students increase their opportunities for support, and at the same time the pressure with regard to the production of a collective agenda increases. One possible contradiction here is between the creative aspects of research training and the collective outcomes. In this group, it is difficult for the Ph.D. students to be remote participants. The degree of overlap with the research leaders must be significant enough to create strong common areas of focus.

For the Ph.D. students, being included in different types of research groups necessarily gives rise to different experiences. This chapter gives us the opportunity to discuss how open versus closed the research focus can – or should – be. We have looked at concepts like conventions and genre to clarify what is given, and how and why negotiation is played out, and we have also examined the structural level of the research activities. In addition, we have described the process dimensions of the object, where one makes decisions on a microlevel within the research. This negotiation is aimed at making explicit which conventions and genres are valid. In the humanities communities, we see much more openness in both the structure and the process dimensions than in the computer science community. At the same time it is important to emphasize that on a general level the research leaders' work is similar; that is, their challenge is to offer direction, stimulate creative research contributions, and ensure that the Ph.D. students can manage the basic conventions and genres within their field of knowledge. They must also create conditions that can provide easy access to the forefront of research and determine how to develop contributions that are highly relevant to the accumulated knowledge within the respective field.

These findings seem important for a policy-related discussion when we use concepts like centers of excellence. When we describe the research leadership challenges on a more general level, they could be seen as the same, but at the microlevel the challenges are described differently. Here the traditions, rules, norms, organization of the research community, and their institutional context play a major role. It is at this level where the research activities are actually realized. Without detailed analysis of the everyday activities of the research work, we will have limited insight into how we can create more collective models in communities where individuality and autonomy stand as the most central norms.

We stated that object as an analytic concept is our key concept in this chapter. The reason for this choice is that in the field of learning theory and also in neighboring approaches to activity theory like actor network theory and microsociology (e.g., ethno-methodology), a strong concept that combines the material world and people's meaning-making is missing (Engeström, 1999b; Engeström & Middleton, 1996). We see this concept as a major contribution from activity theory and Engeström's work. In this chapter, we have used it at the empirical level to discern how different research groups and communities define and work with their object of research. Because the concept of object is often viewed as rather abstract when we come to empirical studies, we have used what we call *intermediate* concepts that come from the empirical data or from related studies. That is why we have found it productive to connect notions like standards, conventions, and genre to how the object was constituted and developed in the two research communities. The object as a concept becomes more securely anchored in the data that provide the empirical premise for the analysis. Notions like change and expansive learning are at the core of activity theory (Engeström, 1987, 2004). In this analysis, incremental change becomes transparent through the zones for negotiations. These processes do not capture expansive cycles, but provide us with an analysis of how boundaries get created and maintained over time. The duality of objects of research is central for the direction of the incremental processes that research leaders and their colleagues work with in their everyday activities.

Our purpose in this chapter has been to describe and in an analytical way point out resemblances and differences between two different research communities. If the focus becomes too open, the negotiations become time-consuming and unproductive compared with the collective agenda.

On the other hand, if the research focus is too closed, and the negotiations are not sufficiently transparent and substantiated, it reduces the Ph.D. students' opportunities to become participants and contributors to the collective agenda. Such tensions, dilemmas, and contradictions are part of most types of research communities and groups, but with new mechanisms like centers of excellence and collective research agendas, the contradictions will increase.

PART FIVE

INTERVENTIONS

16

Who Is Acting in an Activity System?

RITVA ENGESTRÖM

> How is it, are we the material or are we the producer of the outcomes
> or observations ... although I understand that it is difficult in a way,
> because it is as if emerging from discussions, but in what place can such
> observations be made that now the idea emerged and now we share the
> same opinion?
>
> (Excerpt from a Change Laboratory session, Spring 2006,
> in the project "Crossing Boundaries for
> Helping Families at Social Risk")

Having an educational background in Marxian sociology, I have been
inspired and affected by the research methodology proposed by Yrjö
Engeström for the dialectical study of links between the individual and
the society. Drawing on the cultural-historical school of psychology, he
has argued for a "radically new methodology" that incorporates historicity and developmental judgment into analyses that might "yet take fully
into account the diversity and multiplicity inherent in human activities"
(Engeström, 1999a, p. 28). This methodology became identified with
a collective learning activity from the very beginning. By introducing
the methodology of developmental work research with his colleagues,
Engeström broke new ground in the theory of his own disciplinary field
of adult education. The aim of developmental work research was to enable
workers to become conscious subjects of their own learning activity and to
combine independent learning activity with work.

The foundations of the methodology are presented in the book *Learning
by Expanding* (Engeström, 1987) in such a rich way that this text continues
to carry forward certain, partly unfulfilled ideas related to how to study
individual learning and societal change from the point of view of human
development. In this book, the author expands on Vygotsky's idea of the

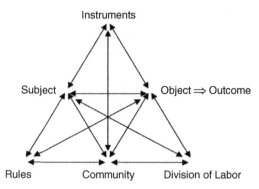

Figure 16.1. The structure of human activity (Engeström, 1987, p. 78).

zone of proximal development as the basic category of developmental work research. Behind the elaborated idea, there are two paths of theorizing. The first one is the model of an activity system. The second path uses the model in the analysis of the cultural evolution of learning. As should be obvious, the paths are intertwined and support each other in the theorizing process.

The model of the activity system developed by Engeström depicts the constituents of societal activity within a triangular structure of activity (Fig. 16.1). The model is suggested for grasping the systemic whole, not just separate connections, in order to analyze a multiplicity of relations (Engeström, 1987, p. 78). Furthermore, Engeström argues that the model is actually the smallest and simplest unit that still preserves the essential unity and integral quality of any human activity (p. 81). It therefore facilitates analysis of the dynamic relations and historical change of activity – for the understanding of developmental transformations.

In delineating the evolution of learning, Engeström utilizes Gregory Bateson's (1972) theory of a complex hierarchy of the processes of learning. In his reading of Bateson, "Learning I" indicates the object, which presents itself as mere immediate resistance, not consciously separated from the subject and instrument by the learner. In "Learning II," the object is conceived of as a problem, demanding specific efforts. The subject is no longer a nonconscious agent but an individual under self-assessment. In Learning III, the object is seen as a system containing the subject within it. Engeström (1987, p. 151) cites Bateson:

> Selfhood is a product or aggregate of Learning II. To the degree that a man achieves Learning III, and learns to perceive and act in terms of the

contexts of contexts, his "self" will take a sort of irrelevance. The concept of "self" will no longer function as a nodal argument in the punctuation of experience. (Bateson, 1972, p. 304)

The notion of Learning III made possible the questioning of existing learning theories and offered for Engeström the basis of expansive learning theory. In this theory, the individual self is replaced – or rather qualitatively altered – by a search for a collective subject, capable of mastering the complexity of "contexts of contexts," that is, of societal practices with a highly developed division of labor as well as multilevel technological and symbolic mediations (Engeström, 1987, p. 152). On the basis of the historical framing of learning activity, Engeström distinguishes among three types of development: the individual-explosive, the invisible-gradual, and the collective-expansive. He sees the third type as the one that requires conscious mastery – *the subjectification of the subject*. Although development can take place only as a "result" of learning, in Learning III development itself becomes the object of learning that is basically collective in nature (p. 158). Looking for the future of human activity, Engeström provides a view that activities are becoming increasingly societal. According to him, this is manifested in three different ways. First, different activity systems become gradually larger, more voluminous, and denser in their internal communication with a growing number of people. Second, different activity systems, and people within them, become increasingly interdependent, forming ever more complex networks and hierarchies of interaction. Third, this interdependence of activity systems is increasingly penetrated and saturated by the basic socioeconomic laws and by corresponding contradictions of the given society (p. 157).

From today's perspective, this theorizing of learning activity is coherent and convincing. However, there is an embedded dimension, continuously present, but left open or left to rely on the foundations of the school of cultural-historical psychology. This dimension concerns the question: Who is the collective subject, or "what kind of a subject is required and produced by learning activity?" (Engeström, 1987, p. 127). Engeström found the levels of human functioning introduced by A. N. Leont'ev (1978) relevant to his concept of a collective activity system. Operations bear certain typified features of actions in response to ongoing conditions of activity. Actions are artifactually mediated and carried out by individuals. They involve cultural interpretation. Activity is "an irreducible molar unit, an object-driven complex of goal-oriented actions" (Leont'ev, 1978, p. 61). On the basis of these levels, he views development "as the transitions between the levels of learning as movement from operations to actions to activity"

(Engeström, 1987, p. 163). He also applies the idea of the learning activity as a triadic process. According to him, "Each corner of the triangle would thus have three qualitatively different levels: that of the overall activity, that of actions, and that of operations." Instead of attempting "such a complex graphic presentation," he prefers to summarize the various characterizations of those three levels in a table entitled "The Proposed Hierarchical Structure of Activity" (pp. 153–154). In this table, the three levels of the subject are "non-conscious" (operation), "individual subject" (action), and "collective subject" (activity) (p. 154).

The aim of the present chapter is to examine subjectivity within the methodology of developmental work research. One reason for such an examination is the diversity of readings and interpretations of Engeström's unit of analysis. Another reason is that a future vision of activities seems to indicate movement toward increased subjectivity. I am also inspired by recent comments from followers of Holzkamp's (1995) "subject science of learning." For example, it has been asked whether or not the activity system itself has taken the place of the subject that realizes and reproduces itself by generating actions and operations. Or, put the other way around, it has been asked if the activity system is misattributed as "collective" regarding the expansive learning process (Langemeyer, 2006; Langemeyer & Roth, 2006).

On the basis of my own experiences from several developmental work research projects and on my long-term interest in processes of signification (R. Engeström, 1995, 1999), I consider theoretically promising the suggestion presented by Anna Stetsenko (2005). She points out that the dichotomy of individual and collective planes of activity is still insufficiently resolved in the research tradition of cultural-historical activity theory. She takes up for discussion the one-sided dependence of human subjectivity "on the processes of material production (especially in A. N. Leont'ev's works) and on associated societal forms of exchange between people (especially in Vygotsky's works)" (Stetsenko, 2005, p. 74). She calls for more attention to the subjective mechanisms allowing for individual participation in collective processes. For her, the three processes at the very foundation of human life and development are (1) the material production of tools, (2) the social exchanges among people, and (3) the individual mechanisms regulating this production and these exchanges.

All three processes need to be viewed as a unified system of interactions and truly dialectically connected, that is, as dependent on and – at the same time – conditioning and influencing each other. According to Stetsenko (2005, p. 85), human subjectivity can be conceptualized on this designated ontological foundation as an agentive and inherently necessary moment within unfolding activity processes. My argument is that the internal dialectics of the hierarchy of human functioning (proposed by Leont'ev) do not resolve the issue of subjectivity within the methodology of developmental work research and in the study of developmental transformations. I argue for the "immanent content" of the activity system as a unit of analysis, considering it conceptually as a collective activity "in itself" (Il'enkov, 1982, p. 102). This content is an object-driven complex that carries longitudinal-historical aspects of human functioning and has its own development (Leont'ev, 1978, p. 50). At the same time, actions performed by individuals can have analytical independence. People are usually positioned so as to inhabit multiple activities simultaneously, especially in the case of Learning III. Capturing the multilayered nature of different activities allows for creative configurations of individual actions. And most important, the unit of analysis should reflect conceptually and epistemologically the fact that subjectivity and society, in representing their emergent properties, differ in the specific mechanisms of their realization, in their degree of generality, in their power, and in their role in the genesis of practice (with the intersubjective level of practice being historically and ontogenetically prior to the intrasubjective level) – as pointed by Stetsenko (2005, p. 84).

I shall examine how subjectivity might be constructed when one is using the activity system as unit of analysis and keeping in mind the points made above. For this endeavor, I will discuss a set of intervention projects that used the methodology of developmental work research. The methodology (depicted also with the help of the cycle of expansive learning) basically redirects the attention to the knowledge we do not yet have and looks for ways in which to study the direction of societal change as not yet existing. The methodology implies a parallel conceptualization and constructive facilitation of social transformations of activity, utilizing principles originating from the method of double stimulation (on formative or developmental methodology; Cole, 1996; Engeström, 2007d; Lompscher, 1999; Vygotsky, 1978).

IN SEARCH OF SUBJECTIVITY

The analysis of developmental work research from the perspective of subjective mechanisms allowing for individual participation in collective processes requires special attention to participation. In order to interconnect the formation process with an open approach to the future, developmental work research compels people to face situations in which they are knowledge creators with opportunities to formulate a desirable culture. Thus, the approach, as Joachim Lompscher has put it, is used for societal transformations in directing research toward the formation of consciousness rather than simply describing what can be found in societal activities (Lompscher, 1999). For him, the potential of the methodology resides in solving the contradiction "that acquisition presupposes adequate activity, but that activity cannot emerge and develop outside of the respective acquisition process" (Lompscher, 1999, p. 141). Lompscher suggests three lines of logic in the "activity-and-formation strategy" of learning activity for dealing with the unity of the learning activity and learning object. I appropriate these logics and propose three intertwined activities that together constitute the context of the intervention methods of developmental work research: the central activity (logic of the "subject matter domain"), workplace learning activity (logic of the "acquisition process"), and experiencing and sense-making activity (logic of the "psychic development"). Object-relatedness makes each line of logic require a particular methodological attention based on the same ontology. The participants do not necessarily share the same meanings with regard to these activities, but they share *the process of engagement and construction of their subjectively unique understandings of their participation* based on the communicated messages across and within activities and participants' past experiences of certain practices (R. Engeström, 2005; Gutiérrez & Rogoff, 2003; Valsiner, 2001, pp. 95–96).

I will review three Finnish projects as examples of developmental work research methodology conducted together with Yrjö Engeström. Owing to the limits of space and the tentative nature of this examination, I will focus quite straightforwardly on the issue of subjectivity in these projects. I will concentrate on the function of the activity system model in these projects and on the ways in which the subject has been construed in these studies. The first project dealt with the development of cleaning work (1983–1984). The second one dealt with the functioning and development of a municipal health care center (1986–1989). The third example concerns applications of the Change Laboratory method in health care (1997–1998 and 2000–2002).

The Cleaning Work Project

The study was initiated by the professional trainers of cleaning work employed in a multi-business service company. Some of the trainers had taken a course in adult education (taught by Yrjö Engeström and his colleagues) that presented a new approach to workplace education. The trainers wanted to experiment with these ideas in the domain of cleaning, which they saw as neglected or underestimated, both in terms of education and in the daily practice of managers and clients. As this was the first developmental work research project, the researchers' motive was not only to study cleaners' thinking in a practical context, but also to use the possibilities to test some theoretical and methodological elements of the emerging research paradigm (Toikka, Engeström, & Norros, 1985). The empirical part of the research was carried out in collaboration with the training unit of the company. A researcher was employed by the company during the project and located in the trainers' unit. The study consisted of interviews, video recordings of a series of selected cleaning tasks performed by individual cleaners, and stimulated recall interviews based on the video recordings. The project also included so-called object-historical analysis, based on written narratives and reported studies on cleaning, and theory-historical analysis, based mainly on textbooks of cleaning (Engeström & Engeström, 1984). The cleaners' accounts of the meanings they attached to their cleaning actions (stimulated recall interviews) played a central role in switching the perspective from teaching to learning.

The findings produced two historical models of cleaning: the model of home cleaning and the model of rationalized cleaning work. Consequently, a zone of proximal development of cleaning work was suggested. In this, the strategic element was *a meta-thinking tool for planning local tasks of cleaning.* The object of cleaning had moved historically from the past object of "home" to the present object of rationalized cleaning work depicted as a measured "cleaning area." The present outcome was an agreed-upon (by the client and the cleaning service) "appropriate level of cleanliness" (based on functionality and health requirements of the cleaning area). The designed planning instrument contained a new vocabulary for understanding cleaning work and was meant to be used and further developed by the floor-level cleaners themselves. The trainers redesigned their instructions by taking into account the findings of the study, realizing that the company's principle of "acquiring cleaning experience at home" was misleading in the search for competency (Engeström & Engeström, 1986).

The subject of the activity system was a historically conceived subject changing from that of "housewife" (supposedly competent in cleaning) to that of the present "wage laborer with a minimal amount of specific training." The zone of proximal development implied a new subject in a restructured division of labor, with competencies and tasks expanding toward the functions of guidance, consultation, and joint planning, all of which gained in importance among the floor-level cleaners. The subject of the activity system was not the same as the subject of Learning III. This latter subject was formed through a collaboration between the members of the cleaning work training unit and the project researchers. The members of the training unit had a motive to look for new knowledge in order to make a qualitative change in training for cleaning work. Soon after the project was finished, the company in question acquired a new top manager, who brought in an alternative approach to training, based on distance learning. Four of the five trainers made the personal choice to give notice and terminate their employment. They chose to continue their developmental or consulting work in cleaning in or with other organizations. Their work later led to new development projects in this area and expanded into collaboration with the occupational health professionals.

The Health Center Project

This project was initiated by the health care management of a midsize city under nationwide pressure to find new ways to organize primary health care, which was increasingly criticized for functioning like a faceless assembly line. The reform focused on the principle of "a physician's population responsibility" (also called personal doctor practice) instead of the existing practice of arbitrarily allocating patients to physicians. The three-year project was conducted in the practitioners' workplace. The project was not, however, an implementation project in which a new model given by policymakers was supposed to take effect as an outcome of the project. The motive of the project was, rather, to produce a local interpretation and design based on the general principle. In the beginning, the focus was on physicians' work, but it was soon realized that general practitioners did not work with their patients alone, but were assisted by and worked in collaboration with public health nurses, health center assistants, radiologists, laboratory assistants, and physical therapists. These professional groups were included in the project.

The empirical data of the project comprised videotaped doctor–patient consultations and interviews with the participants. The data included stimulated recall interviews of all the videotaped consultations conducted by viewing the videotape with the patient and doctor separately in post-consultation interviews. On the basis of a historical analysis, three historically distinctive activity systems were drawn up as triangular representations: the district doctor system (1749–1882), the municipal doctor system (1882–1972), and the ongoing health center system (1972–). The use of systemic analyses conducted with the help of the triangular model made it possible for the participants to look at their own work from an outsider's point of view (see also Ahonen, Engeström, & Virkkunen, 2000). As noted by a participant interviewed after this health care project:

> The historical approach helped me to get rid of blaming myself and of need to explain my conduct. If I can understand that my own bad communication with the patient is embedded and relevant in time, it is easier for me to look at the present practice, to take it on the table and start to develop it.

After the first year's data-based analyses undertaken jointly by practitioners and researchers, the practitioners began to design a local model for reorganizing their activity system. The planning of the new model was carried out by five planning groups with the active participation of about 40 employees of the two health stations involved in the project. In this phase of the project, the researchers participated mainly by observing and making field notes. The key conceptual tool for planning, based on the analyses, was the idea of *a long-term care relationship* as the new object of work, meant to replace the existing object of an isolated patient visit. The design of the new model required a critical look both at the past municipal doctor system and at the present health center system (about the complex process of reconstructing organizational memory in this study, see R. Engeström, 1991). The final new model was based on the creation of small multiprofessional teams that were supposed to work on the continuous care of their patients. To realize this, not only were new practices necessary, but the physical structure of the stations had to be altered to support teamwork.

The activity system of primary health care was constructed from the perspective of the general practitioner. The medical consultation was considered a critical event in the patient's care. The subjects of the three historical systems were characterized by identifying their internal contradictions. The subject of Learning III was forged over a 3-year period of collaboration between and among the personnel of two health care stations and the research group. During the project, several individuals of the health care communities contributed by writing and publishing and by conducting additional small-scale studies based on the data collected by the project. Some 10 years after the completion of the project, practitioners of these two health care stations started a new project, to find ways to cope with excessive caseloads. In their publication, the authors reflect on their past developmental work research experiences as a springboard for their new study (Saarelma, 2003).

Change Laboratories in Health Care

The third project started with an invitation from the hospital management, which anticipated problems arising from the coming fusion of two hospitals (the City Hospital and the University Central Hospital) in children's medical care in Helsinki. The project's task was to support the formation of the new community with the Change Laboratory in order to produce collaborative solutions for reorganizing the work. The researchers were concerned not only with practical solutions. Indeed, another motivation was to study negotiations between different activity systems (two hospitals) and the potential of such negotiations for developing patient-centered care.

The Change Laboratory is a method for developing work practices in a temporally bounded process and physically recognizable place, in dialogue and debate among the practitioners themselves and with researchers, sometimes also including clients and representatives of the management of the activity in question (Engeström, Virkkunen, Helle, Pihlaja, & Poikela, 1996). Mirror data, gathered mostly by the researchers, on critical work situations and debates triggered by these data form a central part of the intervention. Initially, the method was designed to be used by a work team or local work unit, with an interventionist guiding the process. Subsequently expanded versions of the method have been developed for use with two or more interacting organizational units. The method continues the developmental work research tradition by making its interventions more compressed in time and systematically supported by representational artifacts.

The project was initially conducted as one Change Laboratory cycle with ten 2-hour laboratory sessions once a week and supported by the three-member research group. The focus group was the hospital outpatient clinic, but persons from hospital wards, the laboratory, and so on were also involved; in all about 80 persons participated in each session. This first round of the intervention dealt with the problems and prospects of physically merging two previously separate outpatient clinics.

To trace the object of medical work calls for the presence of the patient. It soon became evident that a second intervention round was needed in order to mend and integrate the often fragmented care of children with chronic illnesses. The responsibility for caring for these patients was divided between the hospital and local primary-care health centers; often other caregiver organizations were also involved. Data for this second laboratory round were collected by collaborating with and following patients.

The patients were followed through their visits to various caregivers, and the interactions and participants' interview statements were videotaped. Medical records were used to construct detailed descriptions of the care trajectories of these patients. The patient (in this case the parent of a child) was invited to attend the laboratory session in which her or his child's care was discussed and analyzed with the help of the mirror data. Also, responsible managers and practitioners from other clinics treating pediatric patients as well as from local primary-care health centers were invited to work together with practitioners from the Children's Hospital. This second intervention was called Boundary Crossing Laboratory.

During analysis of the captured trajectories of patients' care, the attention began to focus on issues of discontinuity of care and lack of a clear sense of who was responsible for the overall care of a patient. These newly revealed issues pointed toward a lack of horizontal and sociospatial relations beyond the singular clinic and challenged the participants to look at the object from the perspective of interactions between care providers located at different institutions, including the patient's family. In Excerpt 1, a specialist hospital physician reflects on the issue in the following interview (from Saaren-Seppälä, 2004, p. 113):

EXCERPT 1 (hospital specialist)

There has been a lot of talk that the general practitioner could have the care responsibility. I would see that he or she could be the central person and the hospitals would be consultants for the patient. ... But it is awfully difficult for me to see in these documents who actually is responsible for the care.

Concerning the same patient, the general practitioner gave her interpretation of responsible actors as follows (from Saaren-Seppälä, 2004, p. 113):

EXCERPT 2 (general practitioner)

I do think that the responsibility is elsewhere, not here at the primary care health center. I mean, I take responsibly for everything that happens here. But I think that at least in this phase, the care is located outside the health center. So in practice, since he [the patient] has contacts with the university hospital, it is surely the university hospital or the district hospital. But I don't really know the exact situation at the moment, in which one he receives more care, or by whom. And I don't know who the responsible physician is, and probably there isn't one.

The collaboration resulted in two other Change Laboratories (Implementation Laboratory and Piloting Laboratory) conducted jointly with the University Central Hospital and the primary-care health center in the City of Helsinki. Each laboratory consisted of ten 2-hour sessions (for a more comprehensive analysis of the project, see Kerosuo, 2006). These latter projects were based on the willingness of the participants to implement new ideas in the care of adult patients – ideas that were originally conceived in the Boundary Crossing Laboratory. The target of the projects was to re-tool the collaboration between the multiple, distributed actors of clinical work responsible for the care of patients with multiple illnesses.

Looking at the material produced in this set of Change Laboratories, the triangle model as a unit of analysis seems to be used in a varied way. Interesting uses can be found in the data from the Children's Hospital. The triangles were used to make visible contradictions between the present (old) state and the potential new state of the activity. This underlines change as an outcome of relations in which the two options are not mutually exclusive but dialectically produce a new perspective from which to look at the present actions. The modeling was forged in the course of the project (see Figures 16.2 to 16.4).

The project encountered a historical change of clinical practices: a shift from using hospitals for making diagnoses to an increasing number of specialized outpatient clinics working in collaboration with primary-care health centers. In the late 1980s and 1990s, hospitals began to design and implement critical paths for designated diseases or diagnostic groups. Critical paths were solutions created in response to particular historical sets of contradictions. The project identified critical paths as linear and temporal constructions of the object. Critical paths seemed to have great difficulties to represent and guide horizontal and sociospatial relations in order to produce comprehensive care.

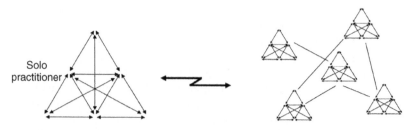

Figure 16.2. One activity system versus a network of activity systems.

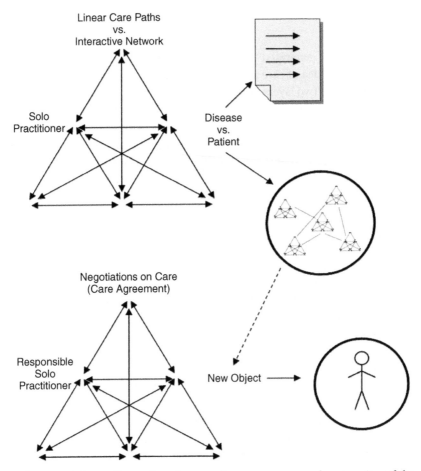

Figure 16.3. Linear disease-based care paths versus a comprehensive view of the patient's care.

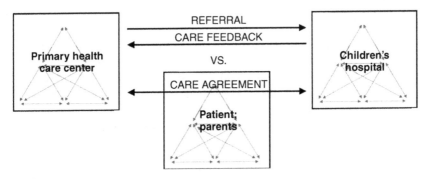

Figure 16.4. Unidirectional transactions (hierarchy) versus reciprocal transactions between equal collaborators.

The solution generated in the Boundary Crossing Laboratory was centered on the idea of care agreement. This projected new practice distinguished between two layers of responsibility: each practitioner's traditional responsibility for his or her patient's specific care and the shared responsibility for the formation, coordination, and monitoring of the patient's overall network and trajectory of care. The emergence of shared responsibility and "knotworking" make questionable the given forms of hierarchy and segmentation of professional and organizational authority (Engeström, Engeström, & Vähäaho, 1999).

The subjects of the depicted activity systems (Figs. 16.2, 16.3, and 16.4) are "solo practitioners" within a network. The subjects of Learning III in these applications of the Change Laboratory can be framed differently owing to the variation in the number of participants and their groupings. The obvious agentive actions of the individuals can be traced through three necessary policymaking events in the evolving problem-solving process: (1) The Boundary Crossing Laboratory was established in order to face the discovered challenges; (2) the new project was begun in order to apply ideas from children's health care to the care of adult patients; and (3) the health care practitioners of the Piloting Laboratory drafted together with the researchers the guidelines, which were signed by the CEOs of the two public health organizations as a joint executive order for implementing the care agreement and associated tools in the entire health care system in the region.

These events were achieved through multiple deliberations and debates. For example, the contradiction between disease-based care paths and the comprehensive view of the patient, summarized by the researchers (Fig. 16.3), evoked a multiplicity of meanings, including mixed emotions and conflicts. A senior doctor with a self-defined identity as a child-centered pediatrician started the discussion of the steering group meeting in which the decision to start Boundary Crossing Laboratory was made:

> I have to say, at least for my part, that never in my thoughts would I say that we have disease-based care paths. We always speak about the patients. ... But it doesn't mean that we would have eliminated these problems that we came across also in this Laboratory, that when a patient kind of has different problems, then her care, it disintegrates. ... And I want to note that at this point I see the problem, which is, a little contradiction, which is that we have to deal with these care paths by definition.

This excerpt indicates experience in the making – out of a blend of elements familiar from existing practices and new elements brought in by the intervention.

DISCUSSION

By way of discussion, I summarize the findings in Table 16.1. With the help of the table, we can return to the question posed at the beginning of this chapter, namely "Who is a collective subject?" The first apparent observation is that the approach requires that more than one subject be analytically taken into account in order to approach the processes of Learning III. The participants in the projects were producing a special kind of learning. In the projects presented in this chapter, the collective nature of the subject comes into being from the integration of science with its societal context. This integration calls for opportunities to collaborate outside a disciplinary structure and to work with a wider array of expertise, including innovative forms of social organization. In this regard, developmental work research projects act as settings consisting of co-construction processes between individual practitioners and researchers – each one contributing a different type of expertise. These situations go beyond the collaborative relations constructed by the actors, who are otherwise only loosely connected to each other.

The subjectification of the subject – making the collective subject of Learning III – requires consciously created conditions for co-construction and joint learning. Developmental work research is furnished with paradigmatic tools, such as the activity system model, the historical analysis of the inner contradictions, and systemic understanding of the expansive learning cycle. These tools were invented to facilitate "theoretical-genetic generalization" compared with the "abstract-empirical system of generalizing" (Davydov, 1990; Pihlaja, 2005). From a semiotic and sense-making vantage point, the tools, including the activity system model, can be seen to function as sign-creating anchors for contextualizing multiple practice-bound experiences of different practitioners, including the researchers.

These tools are also designed for carrying out the open-ended learning process, the unity of the learning activity and learning object, by using the zone of proximal development as a mechanism of subjectification. Anne Edwards and Carmen D'Arcy (2004) have begun to tease out the relational and affective aspects of the zone of proximal development. They see relational agency as being based on a fluid and open-ended notion of the zone of proximal development. Existing as more than merely a matter of collaboration on an object, it is "an ability to seek out and use others as resources for action and equally to be able to respond to the need for support from others" (Edwards & D'Arcy, 2004, p. 149).

Table 16.1. Summary of the Three Examples

Subject of activity system	Subject of Learning III	Actions of subjectification
Example 1: Cleaner	Five-member training unit, including the manager of the unit, in a middle-sized company Research group: 2 persons	Implementation of redesigned orientation course in cleaning; 4 of 5 of the trainers gave notice of employment termination and chose to continue their developmental work in other cleaning organizations
Example 2: General practitioner	Two health care stations; about 40 people (16 general practitioners) actively involved Research group: 4 persons; 2 persons added later A project group composed of a smaller number of practitioners, representatives of management, and the research group	Publications of practitioners (with and without the researchers); workshop of the "10th anniversary of the project" organized by the practitioners; a new developmental project conducted by the personnel and supported by an academic advisory group
Example 3: Solo practitioner in a network	1. Outpatient clinic, approx. 80 people in the Change Laboratory sessions from two merging hospitals Research group: 3 persons 2. Participants from different clinics, approx. 50 people in the Boundary Crossing Laboratory sessions Research group: 3 persons 3. Participants from different clinics, approx. 20 persons in the Piloting and Implementation Laboratory sessions Research group: 3 persons	Initiatives of political decisions on project management and implementation of new practices taken by individual professionals

In Table 16.1, actions of subjectification have analytic independence from the collective subject of Learning III in realizing transitions between different activities of intervention. The participants deal personally with issues of relevance and signification in participating in the agency, which "is forming itself while being formed at the same time" (Stacey, 2001, p. 62). The processes of individual and collective planes of activity are linked and coexist. Individual choices vary, as do the flows of participants within and between developmental transformations.

17

Past Experiences and Recent Challenges in Participatory Design Research

SUSANNE BØDKER

In 1987, I went to a conference on a rather remote farm in a rather remote corner of Finland. Here, most of the Scandinavian information systems and human–computer interaction community was gathered among Finnish lakes and smoke saunas.

I had recently finished my Ph.D. thesis, which would later be published internationally (Bødker, 1991). This thesis helped set the scene for what came to be known as second-generation human–computer interaction (HCI). I came to this topic with a background in early Scandinavian participatory design. My sources of theoretical inspiration were, among others, Leont'ev, whose works I had learned about from Danish colleagues in psychology – Henrik Poulsen, Jens Mammen, Klaus Bærentsen, Mariane Hedegaard, and others. Other sources included the recently published books of Winograd and Flores (1986), and Dreyfus and Dreyfus (1986), which served as vehicles for a joint study circle between psychology and computer science.

In two essays (Bannon & Bødker, 1991; Bertelsen & Bødker, 2002a), we summarized the state of our concerns at the time:

1. Many of the early advanced user interfaces assumed that the users were the designers themselves, and accordingly built on an assumption of a generic user, without concern for qualifications, work environment, division of work, and so on
2. In validating findings and designs, there was a heavy focus on novice users, whereas everyday use by experienced users and concerns for the development of expertise were hardly addressed.

I appreciate the discussions and comments of Olav Bertelsen and Joan Greenbaum on this chapter. Dorthe Haagen Nielsen provided many useful language comments.

3. Detailed task analysis was seen as the starting point for most user interface design, whereas much of the Scandinavian research had pointed out how limited explicit task descriptions were for capturing actual actions and conditions for these in use (Ehn & Kyng, 1984). The idealized models created through task analysis failed to capture the complexity and contingency of real-life action.

4. Classical systems focused on automation of routines, and this perspective on qualifications was carried over to HCI. As an alternative to this, the tool perspective was formulated (Ehn & Kyng, 1984) – to emphasize the anchoring of computer applications in classical tool use – the craftsman surrounded by his tools and materials with a historically created practice as his basis. However, this perspective was in dire need of a theoretical foundation that would make it relevant to the design and evaluation of computer applications, and available HCI theory was no answer to this.

5. From the point of view of complex work settings, it was striking how most HCI focused on one user–one computer in contrast to the ongoing cooperation and coordination of real work situations.

6. Users were seen mainly as objects of study. This was in striking contrast to the early Scandinavian experiences with active user participation, where users obviously were an active source of inspiration in design.

In particular, the role of the artifact as it stands between the user and the user's materials, objects, and outcomes was poorly understood, and this was exactly where the inspiration from Leont'ev and others came in. Accordingly, my contribution to second-generation HCI came to focus on analysis and design, with emphasis on artifacts in use, in particular the notion of the artifact as mediator of human activity, and the development of expertise and of use in general. With the inspiration from participatory design mentioned earlier, I was left with a need to conduct research on the multiplicity of use in terms of more users, more tools, and more complex use settings, and to find ways of addressing use as part of design.

In the cottage at Vaskievesi, I happened to be seated next to a young Ph.D. student from Oulu named Kari Kuutti. He had brought a copy of the book *Learning by Expanding*, by a Finnish researcher unknown to me: Yrjö Engeström. The book itself was not easy to get hold of, but I managed to find a copy. The man himself was even more difficult to meet, but this, too, I managed to do about a year later, when Ed Hutchins invited me to San Diego.

As I read the blue book, I realized that Engeström's work, in particular the methodological cycle and the focus on activity systems, matched my own recent work, which had been focused mainly on mediation and artifacts. And not only that; Engeström's work made it possible for me to see many relationships with my own background in the participatory design tradition.

Engeström's book provided the foundation of the Finnish approach to developmental work research (DWR). The methodology of DWR relies on interventions aimed at helping practitioners analyze and redesign their activity systems. As pointed out on the Center for Activity Theory and Developmental Work Research Web site, the idea of expansive learning, as coined in the blue book, is of central importance to the approach. Similarly, focusing on activity systems and the dynamics within them comes from Engeström's original work and has been used extensively.

Evidently, DWR, as well as participatory design, have taken many forms over the years, and many new insights and methods have been developed. In this chapter, I will trace the development of the participatory design research tradition and that of DWR. I will look at the perspectives they share, as well as the ones that pull them apart. I will look at the challenges they have been facing and the situation today. I will not discuss DWR in general, but mainly look at the influence that it has had on how I see and do participatory design. The chapter will end with a discussion of the current challenges facing participatory design and how DWR may join forces with it in embracing those challenges.

THE HISTORY OF PARTICIPATORY DESIGN RESEARCH

In Scandinavia, research projects on participatory design, or user participation in systems development, date back to the 1970s (Bødker, 1996). The main research school, the so-called collective resource approach, developed strategies and techniques for workers to influence the design and use of computer applications at the workplace: The Norwegian Iron and Metal Workers Union (NJMF) project took a first move from traditional research by working *with* people, directly changing the role of union clubs in the project (Ehn & Kyng, 1987).

The projects emphasized active cooperation between researchers and workers of the organization to help improve their work situation. While researchers got their results, the people they worked with were equally entitled to get something out of the project. The approach was building on people's own experiences, providing resources that would enable them to act in their current situation. The harmony view of organizations, according to which conflicts in an organization are regarded as pseudo-conflicts or "problems" dissolved by good analysis and increased communication, was rejected in favor of a view of organizations recognizing fundamental "un-dissolvable" conflicts in organizations (Bødker, Ehn, Knudsen, Kyng, & Madsen, 1988). In line with this, the tradition was largely a reaction to the sociotechnical tradition imported to Scandinavia from the United Kingdom. Although this tradition placed the human being as a focus point alongside the technology in the development of organizations and technology, it neither recognized the fundamental differences and discrepancies between management and workers, nor looked at changes beyond the fine-tuning of the sociotechnical system.

Participatory design research shared these roots and perspectives with DWR, socially and politically in terms of both philosophical stance and the development of the Nordic countries (see discussion in Spinuzzi, 2002). In particular, both traditions were rooted in Marx's ideas of concept formation (Israel, 1979) and his notion of conflicts as driving forces in societal change, which in participatory design led to the aforementioned focus on conflicts and contradictions as basic to understanding organizations and design processes within them, whereas in Engeström's work they are the roots of the primary contradictions in activity systems.

In the UTOPIA project (Bødker, Ehn, Kammersgaard, Kyng, & Sundblad, 1987; Ehn, 1988), the major achievements were experience-based design methods, developed through the focus on hands-on experiences, emphasizing the need for technical and organizational alternatives (Bødker et al., 1987). It can be argued that the techniques developed in the UTOPIA project were resistive to current technological developments rather than being innovative, because the aims were primarily to avoid the de-skilling, unemployment, and inferior product quality that came out of the deployment of page makeup technology in the United States. However, they were accompanied by techniques that more directly and exclusively addressed the issue of innovation (Bertelsen & Bødker, 2002b) in the unfolding of this discussion, and as such the projects did transcend the resistance of the traditional craft while debating which qualities were worth keeping. As discussed in Bødker (1996), the UPTOPIA project demonstrated the potentials as well as the problems of working with one group of workers (printers and typographers) in a world (of newspapers) where other groups, for example, journalists, as well as management also had significant interests, and this led to further projects, as discussed later in the chapter.

The parallel Florence project (Bjerknes & Bratteteig, 1987, 1988) started a long line of participatory design projects in the health sector. In particular, it worked with nurses and developed approaches for nurses to acquire a voice in the development of work and information technology (IT) in hospitals. The Florence project was important for putting gender on the agenda of participatory design research, with its starting point in a highly gendered work environment, and with its emphasis on how design for one group of (skilled, male) users might oppress other groups (unskilled, female), hence moving the focus on primary conflicts and oppression away from the traditional labor–management tension toward a wider set of contradictions similar to those of activity systems (Engeström, 1987).

As described, the first encounters between DWR and participatory design research were occasioned by the arrival of Engeström's (1987) dissertation. The theoretical framework was a great help in piecing together many of the theoretical fragments and practical experiences that participatory design research had worked with thus far. Several projects explicitly took the starting point in theoretical inspiration from Engeström's work (Bødker, Christiansen, Ehn, Markussen, Mogensen, & Trigg, 1991; Bødker, Grønbæk, & Kyng, 1993; Grønbæk, Kyng, & Mogensen, 1993, 1997). Also, the tool perspective, originating in the UTOPIA project, benefited from the confrontation with DWR (Engeström, 1990).

The AT project did participatory design research in a public organization with numerous branches (Bødker et al., 1991). The project focused on the tailoring and adaptability of standard technology and a long-term strategy for decentralized systems development. The project emphasized learning or resource acquisition for the participants, in a setting different from that of the earlier projects: first of all, because management as well as employees took part and, second, because the organization was to live with the technology after the project ended. Thus, the topics of resources, experiences, education, and so on were rethought, inspired by Pape and Thoresen (1987). The project proposed using learning strategies to improve the ability of the organization to cope with technological change in the long term, as well as in the immediate process.

Participatory design was initially brought to North America by people like Joan Greenbaum, Lucy Suchman, and Andrew Clement, and it got its current name in this transition (see also the critical discussion in Spinuzzi, 2002). Through this tour via North America, it was discussed and reframed into societal models other than the Scandinavian one (Grønbæk, Grudin, Bødker, & Bannon, 1993; Greenbaum & Kyng, 1991). The focus on quality of process and product that was introduced in the UTOPIA project was brought along, in preference to the political and organizational focus, which seemed less digestible to a U.S. audience. To a large extent, this perspective filled a hole in the cognitivistic U.S. HCI research: Bannon (1991) aptly frames this needed transition as "from human factors to human actors." Unfortunately, the influence of cognitive science also led to a largely individualistic focus, such as in the work of Norman (1991), rather than a focus on praxis, as mentioned earlier.

Grudin (1993) has pointed out that much participatory design was in practical terms directed mostly at in-house development and was less concerned with the development of technology beyond the immediate users. To pick up this challenge, the relationship between specific user participation and general technology development came further into focus, for example, in EuroCoop/EuroCODE (Grønbæk et al., 1993, 1997). The situation within EuroCODE was that IT design was distributed, geographically as well as with respect to the organization of work. The group of designers was too big and widely dispersed for all to be involved in the investigation of, and cooperation with, the actual users. The users worked in two organizations with heavy multimedia documentation and communication needs: a large bridge construction site and distributed hospital setting. The challenge for participatory design research was to make participatory design happen, so as to support the transfer of knowledge within the project, systematize and theoretically ground the empirical experiences, and focus the development while provoking thoughts and ideas and providing alternatives (Bødker & Christiansen, 1997).

The project developed the use of scenarios as the backbone of the design (Bødker & Christiansen, 1997; Kyng, 1995). Scenarios were used to set the stage for, and point at, problems and solutions to be dealt with in cooperative prototyping (Bødker & Grønbæk, 1991). As an essential element of building the bridge between the general development of technology and participatory design, the project carried out a long-term systematic exploration of a running computer application in the bridge construction organization (Bouvin, Nielsen, & Sejersen, 1991). The overall participatory design strategy developed by the project Cooperative Experimental Systems Development (CESD; Grønbæk et al., 1997) combined iterative cycles of general development of technology and specific participatory design cycles in the two empirical settings. CESD shared with the AT project the concern for multiple use situations and multiple groups of users in different organizational positions. In contrast to many participatory design approaches (Kensing, Simonsen, & Bødker, 1998;

see also Muller, Haslwanter, & Dayton, 1997), it reached beyond early analysis of the work setting and embraced participatory design in the entire development process.

In recent years, it has been a major challenge for participatory design to embrace the fact that much technology development no longer happens as the design of isolated systems in well-defined communities of work (Beck, 2002). At the dawn of the 21st century, we use technology at work, at home, in school, and while on the move. We use a variety of technologies with overlapping capacities, and we transfer experiences between them. We use technology for playing, contemplating, and so on, as well as for working, and in that sense participatory design and participatory design research have had to deal with use situations that are not as directly motivated as the rather work-specific use situations that were the focus in the past (Bødker & Christiansen, 2004, 2006).

It is evident that, throughout Scandinavia, there are many groups and projects that apply participatory design research methods on a regular basis and hence are part of the development and appropriation of the methods, as well as of disseminating the methods to industrial practice, among the more prominent, the Center for User-Oriented IT-Design (CID) at the Royal Institute of Technology. With his background in the UTOPIA project, Yngve Sundblad has, with a number of collaborators, developed a platform for a number of projects in which industrial partners, as well as partners from the labor movement and nongovernmental organizations, participated. This way, the labor movement has been brought back into the loop of participatory design, and the community has been enriched by the participation of active stakeholders in other arenas of human life.

This strategy reflects the observations made by many colleagues that the Nordic countries are among the least hierarchical and authoritarian in the world.[1] This has been acknowledged as a fact since the 1970s, and it still is today, which may continue to provide rather unique opportunities for participatory design research. After a further analysis of the current situation, I will return to what kind of possibilities this situation might yield.

---

[1] "HCI Knowledge – Fit for Transfer, Share or Co-Construction?" panel discussion with Olav W. Bertelsen, Susanne Bødker, Tom McEwan, Dag Svanæs, and Rob Procter. British HCI conference, Edinburgh, 2005. See also the Edinburg daily newspaper *Information*, April 28, 2007.

LIVING AND WORKING WITH TECHNOLOGY TODAY

The current situation is such that users do not work at just one workstation at a time. People apply multiple devices, with overlapping functionality, some moveable, some more permanently located in a meeting room or, for example, at home. Most of these technologies are not designed from scratch – rather, they are based on standards and to some extent are open to adjustment and tailoring, and to being used together with other devices. Although this may not seem so surprising from the perspective of activity theory, many projects developing these technologies nevertheless seem to make assumptions about designing for isolated use. However, the changing configurations of technology and the understandable design of tailorable and reconfigurable technology are the main focus of the EU project Palcom. Whereas many proponents of ubiquitous or pervasive technology consider it to be the ideal that such technologies basically disappear from the attention of users, Palcom acknowledges that technologies will also always be the focus of users at certain points, and hence that in design, invisibility must be coupled with visibility, control, and understandability (see also Bødker, 2006).

Active user participation is taken for granted in many design settings. This taken-for-grantedness of participatory methods (Bødker & Iversen, 2002) leads to a lack of reflection among designers on their own ways of working. For that reason alone, we should be ready to take on new methodological challenges. In addition, as discussed elsewhere (Bødker, 2006), we are facing a world where we do not design one technology in isolation, but must deal with multiple, reconfigurable artifacts that are used across contexts, including the boundary crossing between work life and home life and so on. To do participatory design research in such settings, we need to work with users who are not only workers in a particular practice. These users need to participate in design as persons who bring their entire life to the design.

Currently, use contexts and application types are broadened and intermixed. Computers are increasingly being used in the private and public spheres. Technology is spreading from the workplace to our homes and everyday lives and culture. New elements of human life, such as culture, emotion, and experience, need to be considered in design. Although new design methodologies are being developed toward this end, they are focusing mainly on a number of perceived negations of work – leisure, fun, emotion, and so on.

THE CHALLENGES OF PEOPLE'S CURRENT
EVERYDAY SITUATIONS

Multiplicity

Many challenges still pertain to work. Work across different and changing locations, in particular cross-organizational project work, reflects many of these: ongoing streams of new collaborators, changing configurations of technological infrastructure, new locations and work environments (physical and virtual), and new project goals. DWR recognizes the need to work with multiple streams of activity in terms of knotworking, temporary and changing configurations of collaborators, and so on, and that in this respect, there has been a need to replace such concepts as activity systems and communities of practice with something more dynamic. In my own work, I have happily embraced these ideas and worked with them (Bødker & Christiansen, 2004, 2006). However, when I look, for example, at Virkkunen's dilemmas for DWR (Virkkunen, 2006a), it seems that there is a contrast here between DWR and the reality of participatory design. While visions and ideas may be all-encompassing, we rarely get a chance to disentangle design entirely from what is already there.

While participatory design has been thoroughly inspired by the cycle of expansive learning (Bødker & Christiansen's, 1997, talk about springboards and microcosm, and Mogensen's, 1992, notions of prototyping and provotyping), it has never been easy to point to *one* solution, or to one better world. This is why alternatives are important. In this respect, participatory design research, perhaps even more than DWR, must constantly embrace the dilemma between the understood motive of the development and acute problem solving, the dilemma between applying old concepts and finding new ones, and ultimately, the dilemma between expansion and regression that Virkkunen (2006a) talks about.

Beyond Communities of Work

In the current situation where IT stretches beyond a particular work praxis and into people's everyday lives, what is gained and what is lost when introducing some kind of change may cross these boundaries as well. For example, while 24/7 access to e-mail may support flexible working conditions, it also has an impact on family life; and although the always-on condition may in some ways seem expansive, it may cause regression in terms of leisure and family time. To participatory design, this emphasizes the need to consider human users not only as workers within a particular community of practice, but in their entire life context (Bødker, 2006). Although we may learn from newer methods (Dunne & Raby, 2001) emphasizing what work is not, we need to look for methods that transcend this proposed dichotomy between work and nonwork. I think that DWR, as well as participatory design research, needs to focus on people's lived lives (McCarthy & Wright, 2004), across communities of practice, whether these are at work or in other human capacities.

Furthermore, this type of focus emphasizes the need to look at design as a process that stretches beyond the implementation of the technology (Floyd, 1987) and into the realm where the technology is used and further developed in everyday activity. I believe that participatory design research and DWR both have roles in providing reconfigurable alternatives, participatory design through technology in a wide sense, and DWR with its main focus on the organizational side. In both instances we talk about instruments that do not just solve immediate problems – they provide seeds for further development. I believe that this way we can make more out of the cooperation and learning possibilities within and across communities.

The Vision, the New, and Alternatives

Just like DWR, participatory design puts a lot of work into formulating the vision, and sorting between small and large problems. An example of how this has often been done is through future workshops, which help participants air critiques and move beyond them (Kensing & Madsen, 1991). The future workshop (Jungk & Müllert, 1987) is a modest example of what Engeström (1987) refers to as a springboard. Participatory design research has very explicitly expressed the need to do experimental prototyping and working with alternatives. The way in which mock-ups and prototypes were developed in the UTOPIA project (Bødker et al., 1987) served exactly to address the skills and experiences of the typographers, while providing hands-on experience with a future technology that was not there yet. The idea of games and simulations has been developed into ways of helping people formulate visions together (Halskov & Dalsgård, 2006; Hornecker & Buur, 2006). It is not obvious that DWR would see the visionary model of many a participatory design project as visionary enough. However, in my understanding of alternatives in participatory design, these are often not so much about providing running computer technology to specific users as they are about pointing toward alternatives on many societal and social levels, and about setting up processes through which people can make better-informed choices.

Ehn (1988) places design between tradition and transcendence. Although we may discuss how visionary the vision is and might be, one of the challenges that participatory design and DWR are both facing is exploration beyond the known. Engeström's early work builds heavily on Vygotsky's zone of proximal development and the notion of the more capable peer, and he has extended this perspective significantly. Nonetheless, Bødker and Christiansen (2006) discuss how the situation is much more open when it comes to exploring, for example, awareness in open, flexible work settings, simply because there are no well-understood more advanced use situations and more capable peers. Discussing support for awareness in organizations, Bødker and Christiansen (2004) point out that designers know little about participatory processes focusing on emergent social encounters and that such design needs to be even more exploratory than exploratory prototyping. The paper proposes using technological prototypes to help explore which questions to ask. In these situations, we do not yet know what the new might be, and accordingly, there are neither zones of proximal development nor more capable peers. Engeström formulated his perspective on this challenge as *from breakthrough to breaking away*. In my view, both approaches need to work further on methods and instruments for exploring the unknown.

Consumerism

Elsewhere (Bødker, 2006), I have expressed my concern that much technology designed and introduced today in our homes and everyday lives is developed in a manner that differs from, or even contrasts with, the underlying co-determination framework of Scandinavian societies. As I discussed (Bødker, 2006), it seems ironic that currently the citizens of Nordic societies have more democratic influence on the technology they apply at work than they do on the technology developed for the rest of their lives, be this for leisure, for school use, or for health purposes. I believe that there are alternatives to this: I imagine making use of people's experiences of cooperating and learning, and hence supporting them in making informed choices that would radically shape their lived lives with technology. I imagine that researchers provide reconfigurable alternatives, through design prototyping. As I point out (Bødker, 2006), Scandinavian research may have a chance of doing such projects because of the profoundly non-hierarchical societies and the tradition of participating in the development of work and technology in the workplace. However, neither the settings nor the methods for such development are clear: Participatory design has little to offer when it comes to specific methods for bringing together life and work experiences, and for empowering life beyond work. Although DWR has focused on other elements of human life, like health and the role of patients in various kinds of activities, Change Laboratories, for instance, are still very much rooted in work and the work setting.

CONCLUSION

I hope that DWR is ready to join forces with participatory design in finding new ways of dealing with our changing everyday lived lives, beyond the take-it-or-leave-it voting with the feet that underpins the above-described consumerism and beyond the equally individualistic expansion of cognitivism (Norman, 2002) that seems to inspire many technology development projects. After all, with its roots in sociocultural psychology, DWR is well suited to this. To a large extent, this invitation is offered to the young researchers of our communities. At the same time, researchers of my generation should not give up doing interesting research just yet. With a bit of luck, we could well be ready to harvest the fruits of the endeavor as active participants in technology-enhanced everyday life experiences among the elderly.

18

Clinic of Activity: The Dialogue as Instrument

YVES CLOT

This chapter highlights three important dimensions of Yrjö Engeström's work. It then examines some objections that have been recently addressed to him. Finally, the chapter presents an original French approach that is not sufficiently well known internationally, although some publications in languages other than French have recently appeared (Béguin & Clot, 2004; Clot, Fernandez, & Carles, 2002; Clot & Scheller, 2006). Engeström has, in his own way, allowed the "French-speaking school" of analysis of activity to come into contact and enter into discussions with the Anglo-Saxon world. In France this discussion was recently relaunched with the symposium "Situated Action and Activity Theory" (ARTCO) in Lyon, where researchers from different countries met to debate their conceptions of "action," "activity," and "collective" (Clot, 2005a; Engeström, 2006b).

TRANSFORMING FOR UNDERSTANDING

The position given by Engeström to transformative action in the workplace brings him very close to the French-speaking school of analysis of work and activity. Whereas international ergonomics focused on the engineering of task and artifacts, French-speaking ergonomics was organized around activity and health with the intention of preserving and developing the operators' power to act in the workplace. Vygotsky's work is indeed inseparable from this perspective on action. When Vygotsky

---

This chapter is a translation from the French by Annalisa Sannino. The quotes of Vygotsky and Leont'ev were originally taken by the author from the available French translations of the works by these Russian psychologists. In the present chapter, these quotes have been replaced by the translations available in English.

analyzed the crisis of psychology, he pointed to practice as a means to overcome the crisis. He even presented practice as a real alternative to the blind empiricism that can paralyze psychology (Vygotsky, 1997a), as is still the case today. That is why the perspective opened by Vygotsky is not only the perspective of a new psychological theory. It is primarily a new way to do psychology, as we will see later in this chapter. That is why it is so difficult to reduce it to a *theory* of activity, even if we connect it with the later work by Leont'ev.

For Engeström, positivism is not the only possible horizon for scientific activity. I share with him a determined opposition to what Comte (2004) himself called the positivist catechism. This positivist catechism adheres to the principle *From science comes foresight, from foresight comes action.* In other words, this principle emphasizes knowing in order to foresee before acting. Within this perspective, real human work becomes in the best case the projection or application of concepts. In the worst case, real human work becomes a simple residue for science and an obstacle to be surmounted for the sake of management. Yet there is indeed an alternative to positivism that leads not to a weakening of scientific activity but rather to a bigger demand for it. Its principle could be the following: acting, without being able to foresee everything, in order to know. In this perspective, aimed at action, the production of knowledge not only remains on the scene but turns out to be strongly developed. Therefore, the question is to understand the mechanisms of action, to understand not only how singular things are in general but rather how, *in general*, singular things are generated. What is at stake is not to explain the eternal but to analyze how the new is produced. It is not a question of examining the general *without* the singular, but of discovering the general *in* the singular that is produced.

In a word, it is a question of provoking through action a movement in ordinary activity in order to reveal the development of the subjects' action. Not only is this radically antiempiricist epistemological concern not bothered by action, but by being basically practical it finds its own object in action. This concern has to be brought together with the indirect methods proposed by Vygotsky. It is necessary to transform in order to understand, because activity does not allow its enigmas to be resolved until it is put into movement. This is also the principle of the laboratory methods used by Engeström (2007d) within the framework of his theory of expansive learning and developmental work research. In this perspective, development is at the same time the object and the method of psychology. The transformation of actions for developing the subjects' power to act is the object itself of a basic and field-based science of psychology. This is the only way to break away from the false dilemma between applied science and action research, about which Vygotsky could have written that they are less enemies than twins.

MODELS, SCIENTIFIC CONCEPTS,
AND EVERYDAY CONCEPTS

The second contribution of Engeström pertains to the theory of intervention. On this question he has repeatedly shown that the nature of a general model of activity is such that it can become an instrument of action for professionals themselves and not only for researchers: "The essential instruments of learning activity are models. With the help of models the subject fixes and objectifies the essential relations of the object. However, the construction of theoretical models is accomplished with the help of a more general instrument – a methodology. Learning activity may be conceived of as expansive movement from models to the methodology of making models – and back" (Engeström, 1987, p. 116). As Virkkunen (2005) points out, learning activity "is a transitory, intermediate kind of activity which lies between science and work activities" (p. 52). In other words, it is a question of engaging in an action of remediation aimed at constructing "new solutions, new model for the practice" (Virkkunen, 2005, p. 54).

In this perspective, it is important to point out that the interventionist's action is not the establishment of a model of transformation that brings solutions or even gives advice. Interventionists aim at providing professionals with tools within the development of their own activity. Research therefore has to be defined as devising instruments of actions for the practitioners themselves. Virkkunen has recently insisted once more on this by mentioning the dilemmas encountered in actions of this type (Virkkunen, 2006a). The project is, however, very clear and has been the object of convincing realizations: "The framework is general and does not prescribe any solutions. It is valuable as a tool for analysis and planning only when people involved start to analyze their work practices by using it, relate the abstract model to concrete facts about their everyday activity, give meanings to the elements and their relations, and change their work themselves" (Virkkunen & Kuutti, 2000, p. 316).

It is striking to realize how in terms of this issue developmental work research comes close to the concerns brought to maturity throughout the history of French analyses of work. We can also connect developmental work research to the approach implemented by Oddone (1981) in Italy at the end of the 1960s. In both cases it is not so much a question of proposing a new academic discipline, for instance, a new work psychology; it is a question of experimenting with a new way of producing knowledge. This new way consists in testing a different system of knowledge production in action, by changing the principal characters of this production. Professionals become themselves agents of reconceptualization of their activity, by transforming researchers into instruments – in a Vygotskian sense – for developing their professional activity.

Within this developmental perspective, we can observe two properties. The first property is that generalization is not an abstraction; it happens by developing the local and the concrete itself. Generalization is realized downward rather than upward. The second property is that professionals are invited to step outside their present situation in order to turn it into a means for living something different. As a consequence, the difference between developmental work research and the approaches to situated action is important. Developmental work research consists less in localizing the routines of action or identifying the communities of practices than in encouraging their reconfiguration by proposing "a collective mirror in front of the practitioners" (Engeström, 2000c, p. 153). Developmental work research engages in encounters that renew each community – the community of researchers and the community of professionals – by getting involved in practices that are different from habitual routines. It is a question of transforming the social division of labor by means of producing new instruments of action.

Here I would like to provide a psychological remark drawing on Vygotsky (1987). In *Thinking and Speech* he writes, "It [was] also important for us to show that scientific concepts are as inadequate in some contexts as everyday concepts are in scientific contexts, and that this pattern corresponds with the fact that the strengths and weaknesses of native and foreign languages are manifested in different contexts" (p. 222). On this basis one can understand that the development of instruments of professionals' action could not be only one-way, by appropriating the conceptual instruments of researchers. According to Vygotsky, the development of scientific concepts and of everyday concepts takes shape in a discordant way. The two develop in opposite directions.

For Vygotsky scientific concepts and everyday or spontaneous concepts are two sources of intelligibility that can meet but can never become identical. Everyday concepts are saturated with empirical contents, filled up with the sense of the singular experience. Scientific concepts do not take things directly as starting points, and their relation to the object is itself mediated by the system of concepts. They are indeed really two ways of thinking that do not coincide. And we can without doubt affirm that this is the case for both the professionals concerned with the intervention and the interventionists themselves. Consequently, development cannot consist in eliminating the difference between these two ways of thinking. Vygotsky (1987) justifiably criticized Piaget, for whom "development is comparable to a process in which one liquid – forced into a vessel from the outside – replaces another that had previously filled the vessel" (p. 175). Understanding everyday concepts would then be useful only "in the same sense that we must understand an enemy" (p. 176). Yet it was difficult for Vygotsky to admit that we could acquire scientific concepts "without reworking them, that they simply drop into his mouth like hot cakes" (p. 179).

For Vygotsky the formation of scientific concepts and spontaneous concepts starts when we acquire a new meaning. The two forms of conceptualization develop, therefore, simultaneously without eliminating each other, and this creative mismatch must be the focus of research efforts. Each one of the modalities of thinking must become an instrument of development for the other so that the opposition between practical and theoretical models of action develops the power of the subject to act. It is precisely this tension that is the source of effective thinking. Theoretical thinking does not generate action. It does not explain real activity. It is rather this real activity and its unpredictability that *explicates itself* – in the two senses of the term – with theoretical knowledge. Theoretical knowledge is a decisive resource but certainly not the source of thinking with regard to reality. When Vygotsky (1987) anticipated the future of the two modes of thinking, he clearly mentioned a double development: "The links between the two processes and the tremendous influence they have on one another is possible because their development takes such different paths" (p. 220).

The fact that these two modes of grasping reality intellectually are not "encapsulated or isolated in the child's consciousness" (Vygotsky, 1987, p. 177) has as a consequence a double generalization. Speaking of generalization, one often thinks about a formal and categorical approach. This line of thinking is very important. Vygotsky, however, insists on the other line: the discovery of the connections and the relations between a given object and other objects of the real world, the diversification that does not move away from materiality but, on the contrary, multiplies the connections between the objects of practical activity in order to reorganize the activity. This second generalization belongs to the development of spontaneous concepts, and although it can be served by the first type of generalization and therefore by scientific models, it is realized in the field of practice itself. This is what is simply called the development of experience.

One may think that interventions in the workplace have, first of all, the objective of development of experience and that the scientific models utilized must serve the interlocutors for this purpose. However, the changes they make of their own experience are for us researchers inversely instruments of development of our scientific models.

NO ACTIVITY WITHOUT THE COLLECTIVE

Another important contribution of Engeström concerns the promotion of the collective dimensions of human activity. He has seen better than others that the cultural-historical approach was in opposition, without possible reconciliation, with the cognitivist paradigm that looks for the source of action in the subject (Engeström & Blackler, 2005). Engeström's work stands against mentalism, according to which the subject learns by finding in him- or herself resources of a constructive activity for acting on a physical world of material objects. Engeström has highlighted the rupture that Vygotsky introduced when he affirmed that the subject's constructive activity does not belong primarily to the subject. It originates in the relations that the subject has to build with others in order to live. The subject of Vygotsky does not live in a context. He needs to build a context in order to live. This is possible only if the subject succeeds in appropriating constructs that others put more or less at the subject's disposal. The subject's constructive activity is nothing but a reconstruction of the world of others. It originates primarily in collective work.

Vygotsky's (1987) critique of Piaget is original because it is made by utilizing data from Piaget's work from which Piaget himself did not draw full conclusions. In *Thinking and Speech*, Vygotsky writes that for Piaget it was necessary to explicate the genesis of the child's reflection starting from controversy: "Piaget demonstrated that reflective thinking appears in the child only after argument appears in the child's social collective, that reflective thinking develops only when – in argument and discussion – the child encounters the functional characteristics which provide its beginnings" (Vygotsky, 1987, pp. 74–75).

Consequently, for Vygotsky social activity appears twice in the individual activity, considered here to be the only way in which subjects connect to objects and the people with whom they live. Being first the source of individual activity, social activity becomes a resource for this individual activity. It changes status in the history of development. It changes place through the life of the subject. In this movement of sources and resources, collective life obeys what might be called functional migrations (Vygotsky, 1987, pp. 334, 337). First, individual activity develops *in* social activity. The subject does what he or she has first experimented with and built with others by being with them "above his or her head," in a zone of proximal development.

This activity redeems itself from social forms of conduct in a precise way: not by denying them, but through their development. Subjects, by engaging their own activity in the history of somebody else, can bring in their personal contribution and, paradoxically, become unique in their genre. For Vygotsky, and in contrast to Piaget, psychological development does not go from the subject to the social, but inversely, from the social to the subject. Individuals become psychological subjects when they start using for themselves and in their own ways forms of conduct that others have used first with respect to them. Subjects appropriate the social and reshape it for their own activity. That way social activity develops by means of the activity of each subject. This is why for Vygotsky it is simplistic to understand the social only as an external collective. The social is not a collection of individuals. It is there even when the individual is alone. In other words, if the human subject originates in collective work and is always engaged in it, the collective never remains outside the subject. It is in the subjects and reappears in the subjects as a resource of their individual activity. This is what leads Vygotsky (1971) to write that the object of social psychology is "the psyche of the single individual" (p. 17).

Although Engeström has mainly insisted on the collective as cooperation between subjects, on social and collaborative activity, I believe that my own emphasis as a psychologist on the psychological function of the social in individual activity does not contrast with his main concern, which I deeply share: rehabilitating the collective dimensions of human activity. The system of collective activities around the objects of the world exists in two forms: between the subjects and within each of them. This is why it can develop between them and in each of them, but it can also die between them and in each of them. A. N. Leont'ev (1978) writes: "Actions and operations have various origins, various dynamics, and various fates. Their genesis lies in the relationships of exchange of activities; every operation, however, is the result of a transformation of action that takes place as a result of its inclusion in another action and its subsequent 'technization'" (p. 66). The force of this proposition is in the definition that the architecture of human activity applies to both the practical external activity and to the internal thinking activity of the subjects.

For Leont'ev (1978), the most interesting issue is the movement of one into the other: "These transitions are possible because external and internal activity have a similar general structure. The disclosure of the common features of their structure seems to me to be one of the more important discoveries of contemporary psychological science" (p. 61). Of course, the similarity of structure between individual and collective activity does not at all imply their correspondence. Given that individual activity is derived from collective activity, on the contrary, it is their conflict that is a source of development when these mismatches are creatively used. They can also be destructive and a source of obstacles. Engeström (2000a) and Virkkunen (2005) have already pointed out this problem: "Resistance is often interpreted as an obstacle to development and learning. However, resistance is not only an obstacle but also a dynamic force that may be triggered to generate learning. The 'foreign' or 'unknown' must be one's own. This requires attacking, testing and questioning the new" (Engeström, 2006a, p. 22).

With regard to both the individual and the social, as Vygotsky (1997a) has shown, activity is a "continual struggle or collision" (p. 70), and "man is every minute full of unrealized possibilities" (p. 70). Let us imagine, he says, "the narrow doors of some big building through which a crowd of many thousands of people wishes to enter in panic. Only a few people can enter through the doors. Those who enter successfully are but a few of the thousands who were shoved aside and who perished. This better conveys the catastrophic character of that struggle, that dynamic and dialectic process between the world and man and within man which is called behavior" (p. 70). This idea is also applicable to the action and its object, coming out of the conflicts of activity. Observable action realized at both the social and the individual levels is most often the possibility that remains after what was ideally wished had to be dismissed. This does not take anything away from the action. On the contrary, it allows the collectives and the subjects to delineate a transformable object, never completely definitive. It also allows action, by means of the operations that carry it out, to make visible what might be realizable and what one had not even suspected. The object of the action has its own life. It is, however, a double life. The action, by realizing itself, reduces the activity, but simultaneously opens it up to other possibilities.

Let us take an example:[1]

In June 2005, Sally Ramsey, a 63-year-old chemist, was about to make an experiment. Her company, Ecology Coating, specialized in very

---

[1] From *Le Monde*, December 18, 2005.

fine coats of substitute paint based on nanoparticles. She recollects: "I wanted to show to a potential client that one of our products for coating plastics dried rapidly under ultraviolet." The experiment, however, did not go as she expected. "I stained my clothes, and some product fell on the floor, which I protected with paper sheets." To repair the damage caused by her clumsiness, Mrs. Ramsey collected the paper sheets and dried them under ultraviolet "in order to safely throw them away."

As a scientist she was tempted to see "whether the sheets show interesting properties." She found out that "The appearance, the color, and the softness of the paper have not changed; I am even able to write on it with ink or paint. I rinse the sheets under running water and I realize that they are completely impermeable!" The result is visibly permanent. "I still have some paper sheets soaking since June on which I have written. Nothing has disappeared." Mrs. Ramsey has even removed them from water, written again on them, and then reimmersed them. The ink and the paper remain intact.

Impermeable paper is not a new product, but it is expensive – about 30 U.S. dollars for 50 sheets – because its manufacture requires mixing vinyl and polypropylene. Mrs. Ramsey's discovery should make it possible to reduce the manufacturing expenses by 10 times. She explains: "One has to be able to use ordinary paper. This will be easier to make and less harmful for the environment." Mrs. Ramsey's company, too small to produce the impermeable paper by itself, is at the moment negotiating with manufacturing companies.

Ecology Coating now sharpens its commercial arguments. The company affirms that this paper could first serve logistics groups such as DHL or FedEx, by protecting tags on packages and eliminating the need for the current plastic wrapping. Important official documents could also be printed on impermeable paper. The company also mentions the creation of impermeable surfaces – sleeping bags or sports equipment – on which all kinds of text could be written.

In this particular example, we can precisely locate how the new emerges and the conflicts in which development originates. The objects of the action in progress are transformed under the impact of the real world in which the discovery happens. The surprising occurrence of the initial action, first in the service of a commercial activity with a client, transforms the commercial activity of Mrs. Ramsey into a scientific activity, which is then realized in a new action of experimentation. In this collision between two objects we can see disconnection and reconnection of the action in progress. This action re-indexes itself. It changes its sense, to use Leont'ev's (1978) terminology.

Facing the result of this action, the commercial activity regains the upper hand to search for new manufacturing services and new clients. We observe that the emergence of new aims of action implies an exchange between scientific and commercial activities within Mrs. Ramsey's activity itself. And it is this mismatch in the internal activity – source of new actions and of concrete operational achievements – that transforms, by means of a backward shock, the external recipients of her activity: from the initial client, to the new manufacturing company, to finding potential clients. Here the "psychological division of labor" in the subject's own activity, between scientific and commercial activity, and the internal exchanges of activities that follow the surprising initial action, authorize fine movements between individual and social activity.

Mrs. Ramsey's social cooperation finds itself transformed by new collective connections. But this can only happen because there are many potential activities that lie dormant within her] – in other words, because there is indeed "the collective" in the individual. The concrete movement of activity "goes" from external activities to internal activities. It happens in immediate actions that are accomplished in effective operations and that "wake up" other possible but "sleeping" activities in the life of the subject. These other activities, first dismissed without being abolished in her life, are then revitalized in the course of the action.

There are, therefore, different types of collectives. Besides the collaboration that brings people into a relationship with one another within action on an object, there exists another type of "collaboration": Each subject tries to "resist" the internal "collectivity" of activities that push each other and that the subject tries to contain. This effort of containment is challenged in the action. The movement from these internal activities to external activities and inversely is one of the most difficult problems to solve for a psychological theory of activity. This direction of the research, however, is without doubt very promising for a developmental approach to subjectivity in the workplace.

To sum up, work activity is defined by two conflicts that cannot be suppressed. First, activity is always addressed (always has a recipient). It is simultaneously directed toward its object and toward the activity of others on this object. As a consequence, this object is always an object of collision in transformation, even when an agreement on it is reached. Second, all activities are never realized in the action. The activity realized in the action inhibits other possible realizations, which do not disappear and explain further development.

OBJECTIONS AND DISCUSSION: AN EXAMPLE

Some objections to Engeström's work have been voiced. In the field of ergonomics, Bedny and Karwowski (2004a) criticize the West European use of activity theory. In order to restore the function of the task in defining activity, they take up the following example:

> We can consider Engeström's (2000a) study of children's medical care. He described different actions performed by a junior physician. However, what he describes as actions are really tasks in the framework of activity theory. For example, examination and diagnosis of patients is not an action as was stated by Engeström, but rather a diagnostic task. This task includes distinct actions, and not only subject–object interaction, but also subject–subject interrelationships as well. Engeström, in this example, formulates a physician as the subject and the patient and his father as the object. However, in the rubrics of activity theory the patient and his father are subjects; the object of the physician's activity is the health condition of his patients. Moreover social interaction is also critically important. Therefore, in the physician's diagnostic tasks the subject–object relationship is transformed into subject–subject relationship, and vice-versa. When a physician evaluates a patient's health, we refer to subject–object aspects of a task; when a physician speaks with a patient and his father we refer to that as subject–subject aspects of a task. (p. 135)

We can discuss the assimilation of the patient and his father into the object of the action while we accept the idea that the patient's health is this object. This allows us to understand the emergence of a conflict in which the doctor's activity is simultaneously oriented toward its object and toward the patient's activity on the same object. The activity of the patient and of his father are better understood that way in the activity of the doctor. I do not believe, however, that the task directly determines the activity, as Bedny and Karwowski maintain. What we can do is discuss collectively ways to work within this tradition in our concrete research. This is the only way to keep this tradition alive, by our willingness to put it at risk in different contexts.

Moreover, it is difficult to accept what Bedny and Karwowski (2004a) affirm in the following: "The concept of task is fundamental in activity theory and it is the major object of study from the activity point of view" (p. 135). One may agree with Bedny (see also Bedny & Meister, 1997; Bedny, Seglin, & Meister, 2000), but the argument cannot be defended on the basis of Vygotsky's or Leont'ev's texts. Also, in France, for instance, the tradition of analysis of work has for a long time made a distinction between task and activity. Activity is always a re-creation of the task. And even if we retain Leont'ev's (1978) definition of the task, we realize that it concerns the action or, more precisely, the relation between aims and means: "The action being carried out is adequate to the task; the task then is a goal assigned in specific circumstances" (p. 65). According to Leont'ev, activity gives its sense to the task or makes the task lose sense. Drawing on the relation between sense and meaning (Leont'ev, 1978), we can say that it is the activity that is concretized in the task, rather than the task being manifested in the activity. Activity is in no way potentially contained in the task. Activity is generated by practical contact with concrete objects that solicit, resist, deviate from, modify, or enrich it.

The subject's practical activity is never only an effect of external conditions, and psychological activity is not the internal reproduction of these conditions. The activity – practical and psychological – is always a site of vital investments: It transforms the objects of the world into means for living. The subject's activity is not mechanically determined by its context; it makes the context undergo a metamorphosis. It frees the subject – by always taking the risk of failing – from dependency on the concrete situation and subordinates to itself the given context. The object of activity is this very subordination, or rather this taming, so specific to the human species, which turns everything, in one way or another, simultaneously into a social object and a psychological object. Even in the most constrained work situations, we know now that this is the case and, when this is not the case, psychopathology of work is never far away. In other words, activity does not exist in a context but rather produces the context in order to exist.

This is why, for the subject *in the course of an activity*, external dimensions are internal and internal dimensions are external. We can therefore speak about activity as an appropriation, always original, reciprocal, and practical, of the world and of the subject. As Vasilyuk and Zinchenko point out in the epilogue of the French edition of Leont'ev's book (Vassiliouk & Zinchenko, 1984), "The object is then not simply a thing, it is a thing integrated into the human being and becomes a necessary organ of this being, subjectivized by the vital process itself before any specific cognitive assimilation" (p. 345). In this movement of appropriation, the immediate object of action is thus never only an object functional to the activity of the subject. For the subject, the object is a means to live. If it loses this status, the object of the action is devitalized, it becomes disused in the activity of the subject, and loses its value for the subject. In these dynamics of valuation and devaluation in the formation of objects of the action, the sense is located as the central regulator of activity. A task may have or not have a sense in the activity of the subjects. This is where its psychological energy is developed or lost. This is where new aims of action are invented and formed. That is why the activity of the subjects has never had its last word, which is not the case for an action. We can always define action by its expected or obtained results. The activity or the interaction between activities can therefore produce or fix tasks to be accomplished, but the task does not produce the activity, contrarily to what Bedny and Karwowski (2004a, p. 136) so much want us to believe.

We may recall Leont'ev's (1978) commentary on the work of Galperin, in which he at the same time praised its fecundity and highlighted its limits. Galperin studied the directed and "non-spontaneous" formation of mental processes, while subjects accomplished tasks given from the outside: "The analysis concentrated on carrying out assigned actions; as far as their origins were concerned, that is the process of goal formation and motivation of activity that they realized (in the given case, training), that remained beyond the limits of direct investigation" (Leont'ev, 1978, p. 87). Psychological inquiries start when one is interested in this latter aspect of the life of the subjects, added Leont'ev. The task realizes or solicits the subjects' activity. If this is not the case, the task loses its sense for the subjects. If we do not pose the problem in those terms, we risk diverting the analysis from human subjectivity.

This is, by the way, what Bedny and Karwowski seem to recognize in another very interesting article: "The difference in the interpretation of the same task by different subjects, or an analysis of how the subject interprets the task as different task components are either excluded or included, makes the discovery of the unconscious elements of activity possible" (2004b, p. 138).[2] In the example of the medical doctor discussed by Engeström (2000a), one can demonstrate the impact of this "subjective" approach, which is necessary to analyze the activity. In the example it was actually a question of a "junior" practitioner. His activity is certainly not the same as that of a "senior" practitioner, yet the diagnostic task is identical.

The junior practitioner, for instance, has to demonstrate something to his peers, to the patient, to the patient's father, and to himself. His actions directed toward the object and toward his interlocutors are affected by these aspects in a different way than in the case of a senior practitioner who no longer has anything to prove. If, in addition, the junior practitioner has,

---

[2] It would be useful to discuss the conceptualization of the unconscious in this article by Bedny and Karwowski (2004b), in which it is defined only as "nonverbal."

for instance, to account for his work to a supervising senior practitioner, his action is going to be affected differently once more, and he will give it yet another sense. In this case not only will he need to engage in the action, but in the action he will have to prepare himself to explicate later how he performed with the patient. We could continue imagining possible variations of activities that are realized in the action. I prefer, instead, to focus on the Clinic of Activity, which allows provoking these variations in order to develop thinking and action at work.

CLINIC OF ACTIVITY: A DIALOGICAL INTERVENTION

The method I present in this section can be defined as a historical and developmental method (Clot, 2005b; Clot, Prot, & Werthe, 2001; Yvon & Clot, 2003). One may describe it in terms of its phases, each of which includes multiple steps.

The first phase includes the following steps.

1. The construction of a collective of professionals who volunteer to design with researchers what we can call the social perimeter of the zone of proximal development of a trade.
2. The systematic observation of situations in which the work is "difficult to do" and is likely to be the object of a critical reevaluation by "experts."
3. The selection of a shared sequence of activity to be video-recorded. This is by definition a sequence in which the activity of each professional is at same time unique and replaceable.

In this first phase the activity is observed in great detail in its real conditions, as in the French ergonomic tradition. The analyses are elaborated at the level of the collective with the aim of "denaturalizing" the activity. We rediscover each time that the subjects at work carry history and experience that an observer from the outside easily confuses with automatisms and routines. These are in fact supported by choices, subjective engagement, and social determinations. The first phase aims at instructing individually and collectively this rediscovery of experience, of its richness but also of its limits and dilemmas. In this phase, subjects search for a connection-to-the-object, which is "difficult to explain."

The second phase involves three steps.

1. Video recordings of a few minutes of a sequence of activity. This way we establish traces of the activity that will become the object of repeated analyses.

2. Confrontation of the professional with the video recording of his or her activity in the presence of the researcher. This step is called "simple autoconfrontation."

3. Confrontation of the same professional with the same video recording in the presence of the researcher and of a colleague who has already been confronted with his or her own sequences of activity. This step is called "crossed autoconfrontation."

The second phase is devoted to collecting two types of video data: data of the activity and data of the confrontation. The researcher does not aim at understanding "why" what is done is done. This "truth" is not directly accessible. The researcher rather aims at making the practitioners question themselves on what they see themselves doing in the video. In other words, the researcher invites them to describe as precisely as possible the gestures and the operations observable in the video, until the point at which the limits of this description appear. This is the point at which *conventional truths* fail in the face of unexpected developments of the dialogic exchange.

The organized "professional dispute" opens up ways of dissecting professional gestures. The reevaluated activity acquires another status: it turns from object of thinking into means of thinking of other possibilities. Instead of isolating the elements of the activity, which the researcher then logically recomposes, the subjects make over and over again the connections between what they see themselves doing, what needs to be done, what they would like to do, what they could have done, or what should be done over again. In other words, the result of the analysis does not lead to knowledge about the activity. It rather leads to astonished reactions about real events that are difficult to interpret within the rules of established discourses. Crossed commentaries orient the dialogue to confrontation between different "ways of doing" in order to pursue the same objectives or in order to determine other objectives. The diffusion of professional experience opens up a cycle between what practitioners do, what they say they do, and, finally, what they do of what they say.

The third phase allows us to move the confrontation "upward" or "downward" to other levels of engaged cooperation:

1. The initial collective of professionals
2. The steering committee of the action, where the organizers and those who conceive the work can rethink their own trade.
3. The extended professional collective, that is, the overall group of pairs facing the same professional challenges

This is the moment when the analyses are returned to the collective with the help of the videos of the work. The confrontation between the different contexts that research and researchers cross is accentuated by the limits of participants' interpretations of the concrete activity, which leave the subjects without defense. This movement of dialogic confrontation on the work activity has a priori no limits. It is not possible to have the last word in these circumstances, even if decisions can be made and must be made. Experience shows, however, that this interpretative movement of reevaluation and action meets numerous obstacles, in particular in finding its place in the history of the organization and of the professional collective, sometimes against generic expectations mobilized at different levels of the organization.

A DIALOGIC ARTIFACT

The exercise of a Clinic of Activity implies that researchers and practitioners are deliberately equipped with a specific developmental device, namely simple and crossed autoconfrontation. These consist in organizing a new directed activity that overlays the ordinary activity. The latter is the activity that researchers and practitioners aim at transforming and analyzing. The commentary on the video by the practitioner who is autoconfronted is first addressed to a researcher, then to a colleague from the same workplace. The change of recipient of the analysis changes the analysis itself.

The words of the subjects are oriented not only toward their object (the visible situation), but also toward the activity of the one who solicits this activity. It is a directed activity (Clot, 1999) in which language, far from being for the subject just a means of explaining what he or she does or sees, becomes a means of action, of bringing somebody else to think, to feel, and to act also according to his or her own perspective (Kostulski, 2005). A psychologist of work and a colleague in the sessions of autoconfrontation do not have the same doubts; they do not convey, even by their silences, the same impatience, the same astonishment.

The subject looks for ways of acting on the psychologist and the colleague. He or she does not look first at him- or herself, but at the other one. The subject struggles against an incomplete comprehension of his or her activity by the interlocutors. The subject aims at appropriating their respective thoughts concerning his or her work, in order to modify them, and consequently the subject sees his or her own activity "with the eyes" of another activity. The subject experiences, deciphers, and sometimes develops his or her emotions through the emotions of the other. That is how the subject finds, without necessarily searching for it, something new in him- or herself. However, the differences between the two recipients become crucial. The subject looks at his or her own activity "with the eyes" of the other two activities, in themselves discordant. Our methodological inquiries are attempts to fully utilize the resources of this social dissonance within a historical and developmental perspective. For us, the conflicts between accounts addressed to different recipients mobilize the activity, serve to develop thinking, and renew the objects of action. The double address of the autoconfrontation provokes the development of everyday concepts, and this development is an object of scientific inquiry.

CONCLUSION

In this chapter I have explored Engeström's contribution to the development of intervention studies in workplaces. Three results have been obtained. The first result stresses that action for transforming work is the condition of the production of scientific knowledge. This is an alternative to the dominant positivism. The second result attests to the importance of the collective in the development of activity. I wanted to show that this is true up to personal activity. This is important in order to promote an alternative to dominant conceptions of subjectivity. The third result concerns the question of models in the intervention. The development of the scientific concepts of the interventionist and the spontaneous concepts in the action of the professionals is accomplished along lines that cross but do not become identical.

I also discussed objections to Engeström's work, choosing those coming from ergonomics literature published in the Anglo-Saxon language sphere. The example I presented results in an open discussion that testifies to the vitality of studies on activity up to the problem of subjectivity. Finally, in order to open discussion, I presented the perspective of the Clinic of Activity, focusing in particular on the methodological device of dialogic intervention that defines it.

The outcome is stimulating. Engeström has demonstrated that our theoretical tradition can stay alive, on the condition that we use it for acting on the world and for transforming it. In the action, this approach is confronted with original problems and unpredicted events that impose on us the challenge of innovation. Engeström dared to take this challenge. His example must be followed.

19

The Future of Activity Theory: A Rough Draft

YRJÖ ENGESTRÖM

In a previous attempt to outline the challenges facing cultural-historical activity theory, I observed two opposite tendencies in our field:

> One force pulls researchers toward individual applications and separate variations of certain general, often vague ideas. The other force pulls researchers toward learning from each other, questioning and contesting each other's ideas and applications, making explicit claims about the theoretical core of the activity approach. (Engeström, 1999a, p. 20)

This volume is a welcome example of the second tendency. I see it as a formative intervention, a virtual Change Laboratory (Engeström, 2007e), attended by a diverse group of scholars interested in pushing forward the development of activity theory. Looking at this effort through Vygotsky's (1997b) idea of double stimulation, the first stimulus or "problem space" for the contributors was the body of research and theorizing I have produced over the years. The second stimulus consisted of the critical reviews written by other authors and colleagues.

However, the resulting chapters are not merely commentaries on my work. Double stimulation is an expansive method. It pushes the subject to go beyond the problem initially given, to open up and expand on an object behind the problem. In this case, the object is activity theory, embedded in its relations to other theories and to the societal reality it tries to grasp and change.

It is my privilege to take the next step in this chapter. By using the chapters of this volume as raw material, I will try to construct a new first stimulus, namely a rough draft agenda for the future of activity theory. Perhaps this will serve a new round of virtual Change Laboratories.

RUNAWAY OBJECTS

Activity theory is a theory of object-driven activity. Objects are concerns; they are generators and foci of attention, motivation, effort, and meaning. Through their activities, people constantly change and create new objects. The new objects are often not intentional products of a single activity but unintended consequences of multiple activities.

The societal relevance and impact of activity theory depend on our ability to grasp the changing character of objects. In the present era, we need to understand and deal with what I have called "runaway objects" (Engeström, 2008b). Runaway objects have the potential to escalate and expand to a global scale of influence. They are objects that are rarely under anybody's control and have far-reaching, unexpected effects. Such objects are often monsters: They seem to have a life of their own that threatens our security and safety in many ways. Klein (2007) argues that in present-day capitalism, disasters and shocks are becoming a dominant object, exploited by the economic and political elites to reorganize societal conditions in line with the neoliberal doctrine.

Runaway objects are contested objects that generate opposition and controversy. They can also be powerfully emancipatory objects that open up radically new possibilities of development and well-being. The Linux operating system is a well-known example. There are other, less known but potentially very significant new objects being created:

> In Brazil, the phenomenon is best seen in the million and a half farmers of the Landless People's Movement (MST) who have formed hundreds of cooperatives to reclaim unused land. In Argentina, it is clearest in the movement of "recovered companies," two hundred bankrupt businesses that have been resuscitated by their workers, who have turned them into democratically run cooperatives. For the cooperatives, there is no fear of facing an economic shock of investors leaving, because the investors have already left.(Klein, 2007, p. 455)

Contrary to mega-projects (Altshuler & Luberoff, 2003; Flyvbjerg, Bruzelius, & Rothengatter, 2003), most runaway objects do not start out big and risky. More commonly, they begin as small problems or marginal innovations, which makes their runaway potential difficult to predict and utilize. They often remain dormant, invisible, or unseen for lengthy periods of time, until they burst out into the open in the form of acute crises or breakthroughs.

Leont'ev's (1978) well-known dictum was that there is no activity without an object. With runaway objects, we may ask: Are there objects without an activity? Whose object is global warming, for example? Of course, runaway objects do not emerge and exist without human activities. To begin with, they must be identified and named by humans. The very concept of global warming would not exist if experts, researchers, politicians, and journalists had not articulated the phenomenon. But which activities take responsibility for such a huge object as global warming?

I have often used the representation depicted in Figure 19.1 to capture the challenge of constructing a shared object between two or more activity systems.

However, with large runaway objects, the challenge would look more like Figure 19.2. There are typically numerous activity systems focused on or affiliated with the object. But the object is pervasive and its boundaries are hard to draw. Thus, the positions of the activity systems are ambiguous, and they often seem to be subsumed by the object rather than in control of it.

Big runaway objects tend to be either what used to be regarded as "natural forces" (diseases, environmental threats) or technological innovations. Such runaway objects are typically seen as objects for relatively exclusive professional expert activities. Patients, victims, and users become marginal, or "rubbish" (Engeström & Blackler, 2005).

The task of activity theory is to recycle rubbish and to turn it into diamonds. This calls attention to being ill, suffering and recovering, rebuilding, using, and tinkering as *productive* activities. We need intermediate runaway objects that are less spectacular and more inviting.

Various social movements try to meet this need. Organic farming, Wikipedia, open models of scientific research and publishing are examples. Most such attempts fail or remain marginal. A crucial question is: What gives some objects inherent drawing power?

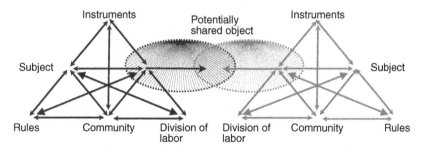

Figure 19.1. Two activity systems and a potentially shared object.

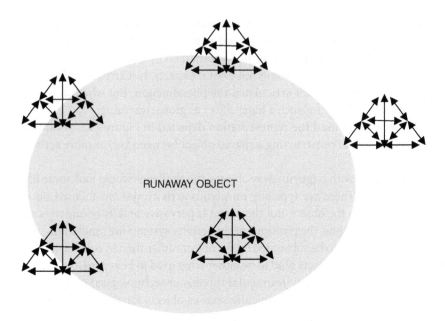

RUNAWAY OBJECT

Figure 19.2. Large runaway object and activity systems.

In a very tentative way, I would suggest some prerequisites. First of all, a benign runaway object must have intrinsic properties that transcend the limits of utilitarian profit motive. In this sense, a benign runaway object is at the boundary between legitimate and illegitimate, sensible and crazy, work and leisure, technology and art. These properties are experienced in acting on and with the object over a long haul, with persistence and patience, oscillating between intensity and withdrawal. The object must yield useful intermediate products, yet remain an incomplete project. The object must be visible, accessible, and cumulable – allowing participants to return time and again. There must be effective feedback from and exchange among the participants acting on the object. In the following sections, I will discuss the five themes of this book in the light of the challenges posed by the emergence of runaway objects.

UNITS OF ANALYSIS: THIRD-GENERATION ACTIVITY THEORY AND BEYOND

I have suggested that the evolution of activity theory may be seen in terms of three generations, each building on its own version of the unit of analysis

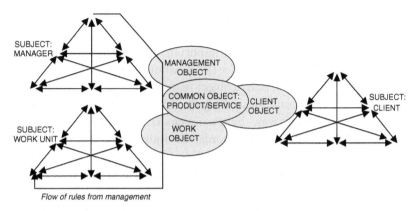

Figure 19.3. A possible unit of analysis for examining power relations at work.

(Engeström, 1996b). The first generation built on Vygotsky's notion of mediated action. The second generation built on Leont'ev's notion of activity system. The third generation, emerging in the past 15 years or so, built on the idea of multiple interacting activity systems focused on a partially shared object.

In this volume, Frank Blackler (Chapter 2) takes up the issue of power in activity systems. It is indeed not easy to depict and analyze hierarchical power relations within a single activity system. Third-generation activity theory may open up new possibilities. In an organization, managing is usually best seen as an activity system of its own, relatively independent of the activity systems of primary productive work. A useful minimal unit of analysis might in some cases look like the diagram in Figure 19.3. In the diagram, the relationship between the activities of management and work, specifically the flow of rules from management to work units, is opened up for scrutiny. Yet these two activity systems and their takes on the potentially shared object are looked at in relation to the activity system of the client. Examination of the horizontal relations with the client should prevent the vertical power relationship from being turned into a closed iron cage.

Wolff-Michael Roth (Chapter 4, this volume) calls for the inclusion of sensuous aspects of work into the unit of analysis. He names emotions, identity, and ethico-moral dimensions of action as salient sensuous aspects. Roth suggests that the sensuous aspects may be approached by focusing on actions together with their effects. This is basically the same insight that drives Sannino's (2008) analysis of conflictual discourse.

Analyzing actions together with their social and material consequences is indeed a promising way to approach emotions and other sensuous aspects of activity empirically. But it is also important to ask: Why emotions? What is their role in activity? For Leont'ev (1978), emotions were, above all, signals of the subjective construction of object-related motives that are difficult to access and explicate consciously. To gain access to motives, one must proceed in a "round-about way," by tracing emotionally marked experiences (Leont'ev, 1978, p. 125). In other words, the study of action-level emotional experiences is an avenue to understanding activity-level motives. Mäkitalo (2005) took this route in his study of employees' work-related emotions in nursing homes. The analysis of emotional experiences led to the identification of motives and different emotionally significant objects, which led to the identification of historically different but coexisting layers of the work activity.

Third-generation activity theory expands the analysis both up and down, outward and inward. Moving up and outward, it tackles multiple interconnected activity systems with their partially shared and often fragmented objects. Moving down and inward, it tackles issues of subjectivity, experiencing, personal sense, emotion, embodiment, identity, and moral commitment. The two directions may seem incompatible. Indeed, there is a risk that activity theory is split into the study of activity systems, organizations, and history, on the one hand, and subjects, actions, and situations, on the other. This is exactly the kind of split the founders of activity theory set out to overcome. To bridge and integrate the two directions, serious theoretical and empirical efforts are needed.

Coming from the study of written communication, David Russell (Chapter 3, this volume) suggests "genre as social action" as a unit of analysis complementary to the unit of activity system. For Russell, genres are classifications of artifacts-plus-intentions. They are links between subjects, tools, and objects. Genres provide relatively stable ways of seeing what acts are available and appropriate in a given situation.

I see genre and activity, indeed, as complementary concepts, much as Bakhtin's (1982) concepts of social language and voice may be seen as complementary to the concept of activity. The concept of genre is very flexible and open-ended. This is both a strength and a weakness. Perhaps the most serious limitation has to do with the strong anchoring of genre to writing and written text. Activities are mediated by multiple modalities, from bodily movements and gestures to pictures, sounds, tools, and all kinds of signs. Written text is but one of the mediational modalities. It is not clear to what extent the concept of genre can be useful for analyses of activities in which multiple modalities work in concert and interpenetrate one another.

What is particularly interesting about genres as systems of typified written communication is their mobility and ability to cross organizational boundaries. As Russell points out, printed forms, records, genres of e-mail, and other forms of documentation travel across activity systems and make trails that change the landscape. This is directly relevant to our attempts to understand current historical transformations in the organization of human activities.

The recent rise of new forms of Internet-based social production, or "commons-based peer production" (Benkler, 2006, p. 60; see also Shirky, 2008), prompts us to rethink the shape of activity systems. Third-generation activity theory still treats activity systems as reasonably well-bounded, although interlocking and networked, structured units. What goes on between activity systems is processes, such as the flow of rules from management to workers depicted in Figure 19.3. Processes are commonly assumed to be relatively straightforward, stepwise movements from point A to point B.

In social production or peer production, the boundaries and structures of activity systems seem to fade away. Processes become simultaneous, multidirectional, and often reciprocal. The density and crisscrossing of processes make the distinction between process and structure somewhat obsolete. The movements of information create textures that are constantly changing but not arbitrary or momentary. The textures are made up of traces or trails that are both cognitive, "in the mind," and material, "in the world" (Cussins, 1992). Wikipedia is a good example in that every alteration of an entry is automatically stored and retrievable by anyone as a cumulative record of previous versions and alterations. So the constantly moving texture is also multilayered and historically durable.

I have characterized these new forms of activity as "wildfire activities" and "mycorrhizae activities," in which interaction takes the shape of knotworking without a single stable center (Engeström, 2006b, 2007b, 2008b). Although greatly enhanced and accelerated by the Web, I don't think they are necessarily dependent on the Internet. Perhaps the new grassroots cooperatives spreading in Latin America, described by Klein (as mentioned earlier), are to some extent also examples of this kind of organizing.

If largely invisible, weakly bounded textures of crisscrossing trails become the foundation of an activity, will the model of an activity system become obsolete as a unit of analysis? It seems clear that social production or peer production does not eliminate more bounded and vertically structured organizational units. Mycorrhizae are symbiotic forms that require trees and plants to survive and spread. Similarly, social production requires and generates bounded hubs of concentrated coordination efforts. Thus, Wikipedia has the Wikimedia Foundation, which collects funds, oversees the operation, and occasionally institutes new rules and controls. The Wikimedia Foundation has a small paid staff working out of a main office in San Francisco. The Web page of the foundation even displays a classic vertical organization chart. Activity system models are very appropriate for the analysis of such hubs. The challenge is to integrate such analytical tools with new concepts appropriate for the analysis of trails and mycorrhizae. Perhaps this implies a need for a fourth generation of activity theory.

MEDIATION AND DISCOURSE

Georg Rückriem (Chapter 6, this volume) argues that activity theory as it presently exists is a captive of the historically passing medium of print and writing. For Rückriem, the whole idea of mediation of specific activities by specific tools and signs misses the point of the ongoing societal and cultural transformation engendered by digital media, especially by Web 2.0. Mediation is an issue of the historically leading or dominant media. The entire scope and character of human activities is determined by the dominant media.

Rückriem is right that in much of activity-theoretical literature, probably including much of my own work, print and writing are taken for granted as the dominant cultural media. Such tacit assumptions may indeed blind us to the consequences and potentials of digital media.

If Rückriem is right, it is media that determine the nature and possibilities of human activity. This means that the object of activity is of secondary importance. Here I disagree with Rückriem. I see his insistence on the decisive role of media as a particular form of technological determinism. His argument ignores what media are used for – what ends and objects they serve. Consequently, it also ignores the internal contradictions of objects in capitalism. To me the most interesting issues of Web 2.0 have to do with the aggravation of contradictions between exchange value and use value, between private ownership and public good, between proprietary and freely accessible or open forms of knowledge and production. While this aggravation is greatly facilitated by Web 2.0, it is not simply a consequence of digital media. Forms of similar aggravation are seen in struggles over the production and distribution of generic drugs, or indeed in the struggles over the uses of land and other natural resources in Latin America as reported by Klein.

Sweeping technological determinism leaves little room for human agency in concrete activities. Focusing on contradictory objects in specific activities calls for new forms of agency. When we take a closer look at the uses of digital media, much of the mythical omnipotence disappears. Thus, Shirky (2008, p. 136) characterizes Wikis (as well as other elements of Web 2.0) as "a hybrid of tool and community." This characterization fits well in the classic analytical vocabulary of activity theory.

We do also need new concepts to make sense of Web 2.0. For example, the notions of "open" and "closed" have great potential, although they remain theoretically underdeveloped for the time being. Perhaps more important, digital media make very problematic the Vygotskian distinction between tool and sign.

Vladislav Lektorsky (Chapter 5, this volume) puts agency into the notion of mediation. He argues that the creation of new activity is a process of reflective re-mediation. A mediating concept or device can open up an entirely new question and lead to the formation of a new object and a new activity. This kind of re-mediation is radically different from goal-rational theories of change. The limitation of goal-rational models of creation and change is that they require that the investigator or interventionist define the desired outcome of the change effort at the beginning. This leads to a paradox: How can you create something new if you know ahead of time what it is? Lektorsky shows that re-mediation involves a shift from the predefined or "given new" goal to an unexpected or "created new" object (Engeström, 1987).

Åsa Mäkitalo and Roger Säljö (Chapter 7, this volume) discuss the mediational role of categories in institutional practices. When categories are imposed on people, they often become iron cages that reduce and rule out possibilities. Such closed "stabilization knowledge" (Engeström, 2007c) is commonly the result of exclusively empirical generalizations taught in schools as authorized "correct knowledge" (Davydov, 1990). On the other hand, existing social categories can also be turned into discursive tools that generate new, emancipatory meanings when blended with new contents and new categories. The president of Bolivia, Evo Morales, never made a secret either of being indigenous or of being a former coca farmer. These ordinarily very constraining categories, when blended with the category of president, were turned into a strength, in fact into symbols of entirely new possibilities and potentials. Such transitions from "stabilization knowledge" to "possibility knowledge" are at the core of zones of proximal development. The zone is never an empty space to be simply filled with the new. It is inhabited by previous categories that need to be opened up, challenged, and transformed.

In radical transformations aimed at the creation of new activity concepts, opening up and blending existing categories are not enough. What is needed is re-mediation by new theoretical concepts that serve as "germ cells" for expanded horizons of possibilities. Davydov's (1990) idea of theoretical generalization has nothing to do with scientism, which regards "scientific concepts" as superior to everyday concepts. Davydov carefully showed that science as taught in schools is in fact dominated by empirical generalizations. The roots of theoretical generalization are in our primordial attempts to change our conditions and to experiment with new solutions.

EXPANSIVE LEARNING AND DEVELOPMENT

Development is a burdened, yet necessary concept. As Rist (2006, p. 10) put it, "The principal defect of most pseudo-definitions of 'development' is that they are based upon the way in which one person (or set of persons) pictures the ideal conditions of human existence." He proposes an alternative notion of development, based not on an ideal end state but on a realistic observation of what is being done in the name of development:

> "Development" consists of a set of practices, sometimes appearing to conflict one another, which require – for the reproduction of society – the general transformation and destruction of the natural environment and of social relations. Its aim is to increase the production of commodities (goods and services) geared, by way of exchange, to effective demand. (Rist, 2006, p. 13)

Although Rist's realism is a useful antidote to the taken-for-granted teleologies often present in theories of human development, it does not give us much in terms of understanding the destructive and constructive mechanisms of development. I will suggest a set of potential mechanisms that may stimulate further work in activity-theoretical studies of development. These mechanisms are (1) living movement, (2) breaking away, (3) double stimulation, (4) stabilization, and (5) boundary crossing.

(1) In the tradition of activity theory, a key metaphor for development is that of a zone. Often the zone of proximal development is interpreted as a vertical step that leads to a higher stage or level. I find it more useful to think of the zone as a terrain of activity to be dwelled in and explored, not

just a stage to be achieved or even a space to be crossed. The zone is explored by movement within it. The movement may take various directions and patterns. In craft activity, the dominant pattern was from the periphery toward the center. In mass production, the dominant pattern is linear. At present, we see the emergence of patterns of pulsation, swarming, and multidirectional crisscrossing.

(2) The dwellers create trails and the intersecting trails gradually lead to an increased capability to move in the zone effectively, independently of the particular location or destination of the subjects. However, the zone is never an empty space to begin with. It has preexisting dominant trails and boundaries made by others, often with heavy histories and power invested in them. More than that, the existing trails, landmarks, and boundaries are inherently contradictory, possessing both exchange value and use value, being both controlled by proprietary interests and opening up possibilities of common good. When new dwellers enter the zone, they both adapt to the dominant trails and struggle to break away from them. The latter leads to critical conflicts and double binds. The troublesome trail of a student through a mass university is an example, aptly characterized as "an obstacle course" by Sannino (2005, p. 188).

(3) Breaking away from a preexisting trail or terrain requires expansive agency. This can be achieved by employing external cultural artifacts that are invested with meaning and thus become powerful mediating signs that enable the human being to control his or her behavior from the outside. This is the mechanism of double stimulation. It is often interpreted merely as a way to enhance performance in specific tasks of learning and problem solving. Such a technical interpretation neglects the developmental significance of double stimulation as essentially a mechanism of building agency and will.

(4) New trails and intersections are marked, stabilized, and made durable mainly in three ways, namely by means of critical conflicts, by means of authority, and by means of reification into artifacts and conceptualizations. Critical conflicts are often seen as merely situational problems. However, as therapy researchers such as Vasilyuk (1988) have shown, conflicts can become durable emotional blocks or sources of recurrent irritation that restrict and channel the actions of human beings for years. The formation and execution of authority is an obvious source of stability, yet it is an issue barely touched by activity theorists thus far (I return to it later in this chapter). Reification into artifacts and concepts, the "ratchet effect" as Tomasello (1999) calls it, is the most visible and palpable form of stabilization.

(5) Boundary crossing occurs because human beings are involved in multiple activities and have to move between them. A student must move

from home to school to peer culture and back home. Boundary crossing also happens between collective activity systems and organizations, in partnerships and mergers, but also in espionage and hostile takeovers. Boundary crossing provides material for double stimulation. It requires negotiation and re-orchestration. It is the most obvious aspect of the horizontal or sideways dimension of development.

These five mechanisms partly overlap the conceptual framework of expansive learning (Engeström, 1987, 2001). Obviously, breaking away is closely connected to facing and resolving contradictions in the different steps of a cycle of expansive learning. And stabilization is closely connected to the construction of a new model and new tools for the activity. But expansive learning as a stepwise process of ascending from the abstract to the concrete by means of specific learning actions is not reducible to the five mechanisms. I see it as the sixth and most important mechanism of development.

Michael Cole and Natalia Gajdamashko (Chapter 8, this volume) show that much research and theorizing in developmental psychology is compatible with the idea of development as "breaking away and opening up." Perhaps what is missing is sustained research programs that would integrate the psychological, institutional, and societal aspects of development, not only observationally and retrospectively but also proactively and by means of interventions. To make it more concrete, the emergence of new forms of work that Reijo Miettinen (Chapter 10, this volume) discusses and the alternative forms of organizational knowledge creation examined by Jaakko Virkkunen (Chapter 9, in this volume) are still domains that seem to have nothing to do with core issues of developmental psychology. Yet the cultural teleology of development is largely forged in the spheres of work, technology, and organizational strategy. Shuta Kagawa and Yuji Moro (Chapter 11, this volume) add a crucial ingredient to this challenge by taking up the politico-affective nature of activity. Development happens – and should be studied – in the forging of the future in politically and affectively loaded everyday discursive actions, decisions, and change efforts.

AGENCY AND COMMUNITY

James Taylor (Chapter 14, this volume) makes the powerful argument that authority is foundational for the sustained existence of a community – yet there is no in-depth treatment of authority in activity theory. I think Taylor is right, and much of his theorizing on the recursive character of language as source of authority is highly relevant. However, I would approach authority from a historical point of view. In my recent book, *From Teams to Knots* (Engeström, 2008b), I try to capture something of the historical evolution of authority by means of a condensed table (Table 19.1).

Coordination is not exactly the same as authority. However, the achievement of coordination is a central manifestation of authority. Thus, it may be useful to think of organizational authority in terms of the dominant mode of coordination, including its tools.

The fourth column of Table 19.1 lists the typical coordinating mechanisms in very broadly conceived historical types of production. In craft-based organizations, when each individual practitioner is focused on his or her own object or fragment of the object, practitioners are commonly held together by externally imposed or tradition-based identification and subordination. In industrial organizations, teams emerged as units for cooperative solving of problems. Their efforts are typically coordinated by various forms of explicit process management. However, teams run into troubles and find their limits when faced with objects that require constant questioning and reconfiguration of the division of labor, rules, and boundaries of the team and the wider organization – in short, negotiation across horizontal and vertical boundaries of the given process.

Negotiation is a central coordinating mechanism of the distributed agency required in knotworking within social production. Negotiation is required when the very object of the activity is unstable, resists attempts at control and standardization, and requires rapid integration of expertise from various locations and traditions. Negotiation is more than an instrumental search for a singular, isolated compromise decision. It is basically a construction of a *negotiated order* (Strauss, 1978) in which the participants can pursue their intersecting activities. As Firth (1995) put it, "In quite implicit ways, negotiation activity implicates the discourse process itself, revolving around such things as acceptability of categories used to describe objects or concepts, and the veridicality of facts, reasons or assessments" (p. 7). Putnam (1994) goes a step further and points out that successful negotiations tend to transform the dispute, not just reach an instrumental end:

> By transforming a dispute, I refer to the extent that a conflict has experienced fundamental changes as a result of the negotiation. Fundamental changes might entail transforming the way individuals conceive of the other person, their relationship, the conflict dilemma, or the social-political situation. ... In the transformative approach, conflicts are no longer problems to be resolved; rather, they are opportunities to create a new social reality, a new negotiated order, a different definition of a relationship, or a transformed situation. (pp. 339–340)

Table 19.1. A Historical Sketch for Conceptualizing Authority, Agency, and Community

	Nature of object	Locus of agency	Dominant mode of interaction	Coordinating mechanism	Learning movement
Craft	Personal object	Individual actor	Coordination	Identification and subordination	Peripheral participation, gradual transition toward the center
Mass production	Problematic object	Team	Cooperation	Process management	Focal involvement, linear and vertical improvement
Social production	Runaway object	Knots in mycorrhizae	Reflective communication	Negotiation and peer review	Expansive swarming engagment, multidirectional pulsation

Social production, such as the open source software movement or Wikipedia, is dependent on constant, publicly accessible critical commentary and peer review. When peer review becomes reciprocal, open, and continuous, it actually coincides with Putnam's notion of transformative negotiation.

Authority and agency are closely related. In agentic actions, we gain authority and become authors of our lives. This happens within historically changing patterns of activity and mediation. In Table 19.1, historical change in the locus of agency is described as shifts from the individual to the team and further to pulsating "knots in mycorrhizae." This does not mean that the agency of an individual subject disappears. It means that the individual faces new challenges in his or her attempts to attain the position of an agentive subject. These challenges can be characterized by means of the notion of relational agency, put forward by Anne Edwards (Chapter 12, this volume). It seems clear that individuals engaged in multi-agency collaboration aimed at the creation of a new activity need to nourish and manifest relational agency in order to achieve, as a collective, the expansive agency described by Katsuhiro Yamazumi (Chapter 13, this volume). Relational agency and expansive agency are complementary lenses, one focused on the individual, the other focused on the distributed collective.

The analysis of agency is still in its infancy. We need to link Il'enkov's (1977a) concept of contradiction with Leont'ev's (1978) concepts of need, object, and motive, and these further with concrete manifestations of will and agentive action. In between, there is space for intermediate concepts such as conflict, envisioning, identification, responsibility, experiencing, and commitment.

One gains authority and agency by being recognized by a community and by receiving support from a community. Sten Ludvigsen and Turi Øwre Digernes (Chapter 15, this volume) point out that the character of a community is to a significant extent determined by how open or closed is the shared object of the community. Table 19.1 implies that we are moving toward increasingly open, amoeba-like communities characterized by multidirectional swarming, weak boundaries, and no single stable center. If this is the case, authority and agency may also grow in unexpected ways, as multiple simultaneous and interacting "minority influences" (Moscovici, Mugny, & van Avermaet, 2008) from the peripheries rather than as a single dominant majority influence from the center.

INTERVENTIONS

In the past few years, U.S. educational authorities have aggressively launched legislation and national guidelines that define the "gold standard" of educational research. The "gold standard" emphasizes the use of randomized controlled trials, the selection of valid control groups, and "scalability" implying large statistical samples and multiple research sites.

The "gold standard" correctly sees educational research as interventionist research. The randomized control trials are meant to assess the effectives of educational interventions. The model of intervention research is taken from fields such as medicine and agriculture. As one observer put it:

> For instance, if I want to test the effectiveness of weed control measures, I randomly assign different plots of crops to the experimental or control conditions. Then, they all get treated the same otherwise as far as weather, fertilizer, hours of day light and other pests. The crops are monitored and observations are made throughout the growing season and a person might be able to see the result visually if the results are remarkable enough. But the telling evidence is in the yield, when the crops are harvested. If there is a significant difference in yield in all the experimental plots as opposed to the control plots, then we might attribute it towards the independent variable, which in this case is weed control. (http://specialed.wordpress.com/2006/02/10/educational-researchthe-gold-standard/)

The "gold standard" thinking in educational research starts from the assumption that researchers know what they want to implement, how they want to change the educational practice. In other words, the intervention and its desired outcomes are well defined in advance. The task of research is to check whether or not the desired outcomes are actually achieved.

This predetermined and linear view of interventions is actually shared by much of the literature on design experiments. For example, in the account of Collins, Joseph, and Bielaczyc (2004, p. 33), the methodology of design research is basically a linear progression of six steps, starting from "implementing a design" and ending with "reporting on design research." As the process begins with implementation, the making of the design in the first place is not even included in the methodology. Thus, there is no need to problematize the issue of who makes the design and guided by what theory or principles. In a similar vein, Cobb, Confrey, DiSessa, Lehrer, and Schauble (2003) seem to take it for granted that it is the researchers who determine the "end points" for the design experiment:

> In addition to clarifying the theoretical intent of the experiment, the research team must also specify the significant disciplinary ideas and forms of reasoning that constitute the prospective goals or endpoints for student learning. (p. 11)

The main difference between "gold standard" interventions and design experiments seems to be that the former expect the design of the intervention to be complete at the outset while the latter, recognizing the complexity of educational settings, expect the design to proceed through multiple iterations of "refinement." But even design experiments aim at closure and control:

> Design experiments were developed as a way to carry out formative research to test and refine educational designs based on theoretical principles derived from prior research. This approach of progressive refinement in design involves putting a first version of a design into the world to see how it works. Then, the design is constantly revised based on experience, until *all the bugs* are worked out. (Collins et al., 2004, p. 18; emphasis added)

Collins et al. (2004, pp. 18–19) compare educational design research to the design of cars and other consumer products, using *Consumer Reports* as their explicit model for evaluation. They don't seem to notice any significant difference between finished mass products and such open-ended, continuously co-configured products as educational innovations (for co-configuration, see Engeström, 2008b; Victor & Boynton, 1998). A strange obsession with "completeness" runs like a red thread through their argument:

> Thus, in the jigsaw, all pieces of the puzzle come together to form *a complete understanding.* (Collins et al., 2004, p. 23; emphasis added)

What this overlooks is that "one can never get it right, and that innovation may best be seen as a continuous process, with particular product embodiments simply being arbitrary points along the way" (von Hippel & Tyre, 1995, p. 12).

Sociological intervention studies differ from educational ones in that there are usually no safe institutional walls to protect the intervention from the vagaries of the outside world. Perhaps this is why the linear view common to both "gold standard" interventions and design experiments is much less easily adopted in sociology. A good case in point is the work of Norman Long:

> Intervention is an on-going transformational process that is constantly re-shaped by its own internal organisational and political dynamic and by the specific conditions it encounters or itself creates, including the responses and strategies of local and regional groups who may struggle to define and defend their own social spaces, cultural boundaries and positions within the wider power field. (2001, p. 27)

Long uses words like "struggle," "strategy," "power," and "position" – words that are conspicuously absent in recent literature on both "gold standard" interventions and design experiments:

> Crucial to understanding processes of intervention is the need to identify and come to grips with the strategies that local actors devise for dealing with their new intervenors so that they might appropriate, manipulate, subvert or dismember particular interventions. (Long, 2001, p. 233)

In other words, resistance and subversion are not accidental disturbances that need to be eliminated. They are essential core ingredients of interventions, and they need to have a prominent place in a viable intervention methodology. Melucci (1996) extends this point into a threefold methodological guideline for intervention research:

> What we must recognize is that actors themselves can make sense out of what they are doing, autonomously of any evangelical or manipulative interventions of the researcher. ... Secondly, we need to recognize that the researcher–actor relation is itself an object of observation, that it is itself part of the field of action, and thus subject to explicit negotiation and to a contract stipulated between the parties. ... Lastly, we must recognize that every research practice which involves intervention in the field of action creates an artificial situation which must be explicitly acknowledged. ... a capability of metacommunication on the relationship between the observer and the observed must therefore be incorporated into the research framework. (pp. 388–389)

Interventions in human beings' activities are met with actors with identities and agency, not with anonymous mechanical responses. If agency is not a central concern in the methodology, there is something seriously wrong with it.

In educational research, one of the few scholars who have taken this seriously is David Olson:

> Research in the human sciences, it may be argued, is less designed to dictate what one does than to provide information that agents, both teachers and students, can use in making informed decisions about what to do in the multiple and varied contexts in which they work. (2004, p. 25)

Vytgotsky's methodological principle of double stimulation leads to a concept of formative interventions that are radically different from the linear interventions advocated both by the "gold standard" and by the literature on design experiments. The crucial differences are as follows:

1. In linear interventions, the contents and goals of the intervention are known ahead of time by the researchers. In formative interventions, the subjects (whether children or adult practitioners) construct a novel solution or novel concept the contents of which are not known ahead of time to the researchers.
2. In linear interventions, the subjects are expected to receive the intervention without argument; difficulties of reception are interpreted as weaknesses in the design that are to be corrected. In formative interventions, the contents and course of the intervention are subject to negotiation and the shape of the intervention is eventually up to the subjects.
3. In linear interventions, the aim is to control all the variables and to achieve a standardized intervention module that will reliably generate the same desired outcomes when transferred and implemented in new settings. In formative interventions, the aim is to generate intermediate concepts and solutions that can be used in other settings as tools in the design on locally appropriate new solutions.

Vygotsky himself described the method of double stimulation as follows:

> The task facing the child in the experimental context is, as a rule, beyond his present capabilities and cannot be solved by existing skills. In such cases a neutral object is placed near the child, and frequently we are able to observe how the neutral stimulus is drawn into the situation and takes on the function of a sign. Thus, *the child actively incorporates these neutral objects into the task of problem solving.* We might say that when difficulties arise, neutral stimuli take on the function of a sign and from that point on the operation's structure assumes an essentially different character. (1978, p. 74; emphasis added)
>
> By using this approach, we do not limit ourselves to the usual method of offering the subject simple stimuli to which we expect a direct response. Rather, we simultaneously offer a *second series of stimuli* that have a special function. In this way, we are able to study the *process of accomplishing a task by the aid of specific auxiliary means;* thus we are also able to discover the inner structure and development of higher psychological processes. The method of double stimulation elicits manifestations of the crucial processes in the behavior of people of all ages. Tying a knot as a reminder, in both children and adults, is but one example of a pervasive regulatory principle of human behavior, that of

signification, wherein people create temporary links and give significance to previously neutral stimuli in the context of their problem-solving efforts. We regard our method as important because it helps to *objectify* inner psychological processes. (1978, pp. 74–75)

It is important to note that the second stimuli, the mediating means, were not necessarily given to the subjects in any ready-made form:

> In experimental studies, we do not necessarily have to present to the subject a prepared external means with which we might solve the proposed problem. The main design of our experiment will not suffer in any way if instead of giving the child prepared external means, we will wait while he spontaneously applies the auxiliary device and involves some auxiliary system of symbols in the operation. … In not giving the child a ready symbol, we could trace the way all the essential mechanisms of the complex symbolic activity of the child develop during the spontaneous expanding of the devices he used. (Vygotsky, 1999, p. 60)

Van der Veer and Valsiner (1991) point out the fundamental challenge this methodology poses to the experimenter who wants to control the experimental situation:

> The notion of "experimental method" is set up by Vygotsky in a methodological framework where the traditional norm of the experimenter's maximum control over what happens in the experiment is retained as a special case, rather than the modal one. The human subject always "imports" into an experimental setting a set of "stimulus-means" (psychological instruments) in the form of signs that the experimenter cannot control externally in any rigid way. Hence the experimental setting becomes a context of investigation where the experimenter can manipulate its structure in order to trigger (but not "produce") the subject's *construction* of new psychological phenomena. (p. 399)

In other words, the subject's agency steps into the picture. To fully appreciate the radical potential of the methodology of double stimulation, we need to reconstruct Vygotsky's more general conception of intentionality and agency. Vygotsky described this artifact-mediated nature of intentional action as follows:

> The person, using the power of things or stimuli, controls his own behavior through them, grouping them, putting them together, sorting them. In other words, the great uniqueness of the will consists of man having no power over his own behavior other than the power that things have over his behavior. But man subjects to himself the power of things over behavior, makes them serve his own purposes and controls that power

as he wants. He changes the environment with the external activity and in this way affects his own behavior, subjecting it to his own authority. (1997b, p. 212)

Vygotsky (1997b, p. 213) pointed out that voluntary action has two phases or "two apparatus." The first one is the design phase in which the mediating artifact or "the closure part of the voluntary process" is, often painstakingly, constructed. The second one is the execution phase or "actuating apparatus," which typically looks quite easy and almost automatic, much like a conditioned reflex.

Classic examples of culturally mediated intentionality include devices we construct and use to wake up early in the morning. Vygotsky's examples of voluntary action are mostly focused on individual actors. This must not be interpreted as neglect of collective intentionality. According to Vygotsky's famous principle, higher psychological functions appear twice, first interpsychologically, in collaborative action, and later intrapsychologically, internalized by the individual:

> V. K. Arsen'ev, a well-known researcher of the Ussuriysk region, tells how in an Udeg village in which he stopped during the journey, the local inhabitants asked him, on his return to Vladivostok, to tell the Russian authorities that the merchant Li Tanku was oppressing them. The next day, the inhabitants came out to accompany the traveler to the outskirts. A gray-haired old man came from the crowd, says Arsen'ev, and gave him the claw of a lynx and told him to put it in his pocket so that he would not forget their petition about Li Tanku. The man himself introduced an artificial stimulus into the situation, actively affecting the processes of remembering. Affecting the memory of another person, we note in passing, is essentially the same as affecting one's own memory." (1997b, pp. 50–51)

Vygotsky's colleague A. N. Leont'ev (1932) focused on the social origins of intentional action. He pointed out that signals given by foremen, the rhythmic sounds of a drum, and working songs gave collective work the necessary direction and continuance. The interpsychological origins of voluntary action – and collective intentionality – would thus be found in rudimentary uses of shared external signals, prompts, as well as in reminders, plans, maps, and so on.

We see the radical potential of double stimulation and mediated intentionality every day in educational practice. Cheating in school is an enlightening example. What does a student do when he or she constructs a cheating slip while preparing for an exam?

The exam questions and the texts one must master are the "first stimuli," or the object, for the student. The cheating device, for example, a slip of paper, is the "second stimulus," or the mediating tool. The cheating slip is typically a small piece of paper that can be hidden from the teacher's eyes and on which one writes what one considers the most essential information about a topic one expects to be included in the exam questions. Since the slip is small, there cannot be too much text. To create a good cheating slip, the student must carefully select the most relevant and useful aspects of the topic and represent them in an economic and accessible way on the slip. Thus, the construction of a cheating slip is truly what Vygotsky described as creating an external auxiliary means for mastering an object. The construction, contents, and use of the cheating slip bring into light and objectify the inner psychological process of preparing for the test. If we get access to the construction, contents, and use of cheating slips we learn much more about students' learning than merely by reading and grading their exam answers. That is why I occasionally ask my students to prepare cheating slips and to cheat in my exam; then at the end of the exam I collect their slips and the actual answers.

Cheating is an important form of student agency. By creating and using a cheating slip, students control their own behavior with the help of a tool they have made. The hard part is the construction of a good cheating slip – the design phase or the "closure part" of the agentic action. When asked, students often report that the execution part is surprisingly easy. If the slip has been well prepared, it is often enough that the student merely glances at it – the details seem to follow from memory as if a floodgate had been opened. This is the phenomenon of instantaneous recollection or reconstruction of a complex meaningful pattern with the help of a good "advance organizer" (Ausubel, 2000), "orientation basis" (Haenen, 1995; Talyzina, 1981), or "germ cell model" (Davydov, 1990). In other words, learning to cheat well is extremely valuable.

At the same time, cheating is contestation of the given activity of school going. By constructing and using a cheating slip, the student takes a risk but also creates a new mediating tool for the mastery of the entire testing situation, which is really the core of traditional schooling. This goes far beyond merely quantitatively enlarging or "amplifying" one's memory. Good cheating is a way to beat the system, to be more clever than the given activity. Long ago John Holt (1964) gave a vivid picture of the beginnings of this type of agency when he described how elementary school kids learn to calculate the risk: When the teacher asks a question to which you don't know the answer, it is reasonably safe to raise your hand if most of the other kids also raise their hand. You look good and the probability of getting caught is low. Agency is by definition testing and going beyond the limits of what is required and allowed. Students are themselves making double-stimulation experiments in these situations.

Intervention may be defined simply as "purposeful action by a human agent to create change" (Midgley, 2000, p. 113). This definition makes it clear that the researcher does not have a monopoly on interventions. Institutional activity systems such as schools and workplaces are bombarded by interventions from all kinds of outside agents (e.g., consultants, administrators, customers, competitors, partners, and politicians). And inside the activity system, practitioners and managers incessantly make their own interventions. Thus, taking the notion of intervention as a starting point is a way to remind us that we as researchers should not expect nicely linear results from our efforts.

Activity theory takes the subjects, the participants, and the local practitioners very seriously. But it does not assume that the researcher has a magic formula with which he or she can objectively decipher how the participants understand and judge the unfolding events. Instead, the practitioners themselves are asked to look at, comment on, and make sense of the researcher's initial data and provisional analysis. Ever since our initial workplace studies in the early 1980s (e.g., Engeström & Engeström, 1986), we have routinely shown work sequences we have videotaped to the workers themselves and asked them to interpret the events. The ensuing dialogue itself becomes a new layer of data that gives voice to the practitioners' interpretations (Engeström, 1999c). This methodological principle is independently and imaginatively developed in the French methodology of the Clinic of Activity presented by Yves Clot (Chapter 18, this volume).

In our Change Laboratory interventions (Engeström, 2007e), such a dialogic and longitudinal relationship forms the foundation for practical, material generalization of novel solutions and developmental breakthroughs. These solutions are articulated with the help of new concepts and models. For the researcher, such new concepts and models become findings that can acquire significant theoretical import. For the practitioners, those concepts and models are tools that either die out or stabilize and spread. In the latter case, they are typically borrowed and hybridized with other concepts and conditions in other activity systems. This complex process of generalization through practice-bound hybridization represents an alternative way to look at generalizability.

Vygotsky was keenly aware of the need for genuine theoretical generalizations. He pointed out that Marx analyzed the "cell" of capitalist society in the form of the commodity value: "He discerns the structure of the whole social order and all economical formations in this cell" (Vygotsky, 1997a, p. 320). Vygotsky continued citing Engels (1925/1978, p. 497), for whom such a cell "represents the process in a pure, independent and undistorted form." In the first chapter of *Thinking and Speech*, Vygotsky (1987) presented the famous contrast between analysis into elements and analysis into units:

> In contrast to the term "element," the term "unit" designates a product of analysis that possesses *all the basic characteristics of the whole*. The unit is a vital and irreducible part of the whole. (1987, p. 46)

A genuine theoretical generalization is thus based on a "cell" that represents a complex system in a simple, "pure" form. Such a cell retains all the basic characteristics and relationships of the whole system. It is also an ever-present, common part of the whole.

Davydov (1990) subsequently developed these insights into a fully elaborated theory of generalization. His view of the process of theoretical generalization can be summarized with the help of Figure 19.4. In Davydov's analysis, theoretical generalization is a multi-step process in which an abstract germ cell is first constructed by means of transforming

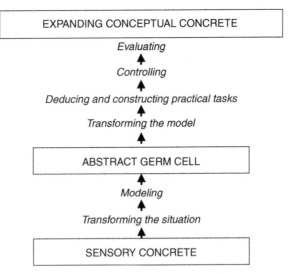

Figure 19.4. Summary of Davydov's view of theoretical generalization (Davydov, 1982, p. 42).

the initial situation experimentally and analytically, and then modeling the emerging idea. The cell is studied by testing and transforming the model. Subsequently, the cell is used to construct increasingly complex extensions and applications, as well as to reflect on and control the very process of generalization. The process leads to a rich, continuously expanding living system, the conceptually mastered concrete.

As I have pointed out before, Davydov's theory is oriented toward learning processes within the confines of a classroom where the curricular contents are determined ahead of time. This probably explains why it does not explicitly question existing dominant practices and concepts. Similarly, the last actions of Davydov's model do not clearly imply the construction of culturally novel material practices. In my theory of expansive learning, the beginning and the end of the process of ascending from the abstract to the concrete are conceptualized differently (Engeström, 1999e).

Significant change is not made by singular actors in singular situations but in the interlinking of multiple situations and actors accomplished by virtue of the durability and longevity of objects (Engeström, Puonti, & Seppänen, 2003). This calls for a conscious expansion of attention beyond the subjects, to include and center on the objects of work and discourse.

Expansive learning is above all stepwise expansion of the object. The potential for such expansion is best discovered by means of interventions that open up the zone of proximal development of the activity system. The study of expansive learning in complex settings requires a longitudinal intervention approach that can be crystallized in the form of three methodological rules (Engeström, Engeström, & Kerosuo, 2003): (1) *follow the objects* of activity in their temporal and sociospatial trajectories; (2) *give the objects a voice* by involving the clients or users in dialogues where the object is made visible, articulated, and negotiated; (3) *expand the objects* by organizing intervention sessions and assignments where the producers and clients construct new shared models, concepts, and tools to master their objects.

The Change Laboratory sessions are a *purposeful blend* of elements familiar from existing practices and new elements brought in by the researchers. They are designed to serve as *microcosms* in which potentials of co-configuration and knotworking can be experienced and experimented with:

> A microcosm is a social testbench and a spearhead of the coming culturally more advanced form of the activity system. . . . the microcosm is supposed to reach within itself and propagate outwards reflective communication while at the same time expanding and therefore eventually

dissolving into the whole community of the activity. (Engeström, 1987, pp. 277–278)

In practice, the aforementioned methodological rules mean that selected objects of activity in the research settings are first followed ethnographically. Critical incidents and examples from the ethnographic material are brought into a series of Change Laboratory sessions to stimulate analysis and negotiation between the participants. As Ritva Engeström (Chapter 16, this volume) points out, these formative interventions also allow us to observe the formation of the subjectivity of participants, not only as subjects of their central activity (e.g., work), but also as subjects of learning and design, and finally as subjects of self-change or experiencing. The Change Laboratory sessions themselves are videotaped for analysis and used as stimuli for reflection. The participants in the sessions engage in constructing shared models and tools to enhance their collaborative mastery of the object. The objects are again followed as the new tools and models are being implemented. The procedure allows for the collection of rich longitudinal data on the microinteractions and cognitive processes involved in expansive learning as the participants make their work visible, moving between actions and activity, between the past, the present, and the envisioned future.

Susanne Bødker (Chapter 17, this volume) invites developmental work research and Change Laboratory interventions to work with multiple alternatives and artifacts, and with people's lives beyond work. She uses the key phrase "informed choice." If I read her correctly, she suggests that radical overall transformations of activity may often be beyond the reach of research-based interventions – thus, we might use our energies in smaller and more accessible change efforts. This argument seems to run counter to my emphasis on global runaway objects. However, my tentative conclusion was: "We need intermediate runaway objects which are less spectacular and more inviting." This is indeed a task for activity theory: bringing together the big and the small, the impossible and the possible, the future-oriented activity-level vision and the here-and-now consequential action.

BIBLIOGRAPHY

Ackroyd, S., Batt, R., Thompson, P., & Tolbert, P. (Eds.) (2005). *The Oxford handbook of work and organization*. Oxford: Oxford University Press.

Adler, P.S., & Hecksher, C. (2006). Towards collaborative community. In C. Hecksher & P.S. Adler (Eds.), *The firm as collaborative community* (pp. 11–100). Oxford: Oxford University Press.

Ahonen, H., Engeström, Y., & Virkkunen, J. (2000). Knowledge management – second generation: Creating competencies within and between work communities in the Competence Laboratory. In Y. Malhotra (Ed.), *Knowledge management and virtual organizations* (pp. 282–305). London: Idea Group.

Altshuler, A., & Luberoff, D. (2003). *Mega-projects: The changing politics of urban public investment*. Washington, DC: Brookings Institution.

Alvesson, M., & Willmott, H. (Eds.) (1992). *Critical management studies*. London: Sage.

Arendt, H. (1961). *Between past and future*. New York: Viking Press.

Argyris, C., Putnam, R., & Smith, D. (1985). *Action science: Concepts, methods and skills for research and intervention*. San Francisco: Jossey-Bass.

Armstrong, D. (2005). *Organization in the mind: Psychodynamics, group relations and organizational consultancy*. London: Karnac Books.

Atlan, H. (1979). *Entre la crystal et la fumée* [Between the crystal and the smoke]. Paris: Éditions du Seuil.

Austin, J. L. (1962). *How to do things with words*. Oxford: Oxford University Press.

Ausubel, D. P. (2000). *The acquisition and retention of knowledge: A cognitive view*. Dordrect: Kluwer.

Avis, J. (2007). Engeström's version of activity theory: A conservative praxis? *Journal of Education and Work*, *20*(3), 161–177.

Bakhtin, M.M. (1982). *The dialogic imagination: Four essays by M. M. Bakhtin*. Austin: University of Texas Press.

Bakhtin, M.M. (1987). *Speech genres and other late essays*. Austin: University of Texas Press.

Bakhtin, M.M. (1993). *Toward a philosophy of the act*. Austin: University of Texas Press.

Bakhtin, M. M., Holquist, M., & Emerson, C. (1986). *Speech genres and other late essays*. Austin: University of Texas Press.

Bakhurst, D. (1990). *Consciousness and revolution in Soviet philosophy: From the Bolsheviks to Evald Ilyenkov.* Cambridge: Cambridge University Press.

Balibar, E. (1994). Spinoza, the anti-Orwell: The fear of the masses. In E. Balibar, *Masses, classes, ideas: Studies on politics and philosophy before and after Marx* (pp. 9–38). New York: Routledge.

Bannon, L. (1991). From human factors to human actors: The role of psychology and human–computer interaction studies in system design. In J. Greenbaum & M. Kyng (Eds.), *Design at work: Cooperative design of computer systems* (pp. 25–44). Hillsdale, NJ: Erlbaum.

Bannon, L., & Bødker, S. (1991). Beyond the interface: Encountering artifacts in use. In J. M. Carroll (Ed.), *Designing interaction: Psychology at the human-computer interface* (pp. 227–253). Cambridge: Cambridge University Press.

Barash, D. P. (1986). *The hare and the tortoise: Culture, behavior, and human nature.* New York: Viking.

Barker, J. (1993). Tightening the iron cage: Concertive control in self-managing teams. *Administrative Science Quarterly, 38,* 408–437.

Barker, J., & Cheney, G. (1994). The concept and the practice of discipline in contemporary organizational life. *Communication Monographs, 21,* 19–43.

Barker, R. G., & Wright H. F. (1954). *Midwest and its children: The psychological ecology of an American town.* Evanston, IL: Row, Peterson.

Barley, S., & Kunda, G. (2001). Bringing work back in. *Organization Science, 12*(1), 76–95.

Barnard, C. (1938). *The functions of the executive.* Cambridge, MA: Harvard University Press.

Bateson, G. (1972). *Steps to an ecology of mind: A revolutionary approach to man's understanding of himself.* New York: Chandler.

Bazerman, C. (1988). *Shaping written knowledge: The genre and activity of the experimental article in science.* Madison: University of Wisconsin Press.

Bazerman, C. (1994). Systems of genres and the enactment of social intentions. In A. Freedman & P. Medway (Eds.), *Genre and the new rhetoric* (pp. 79–101). London: Taylor & Francis.

Bazerman, C. (1997). Discursively structures activities. *Mind, Culture, and Activity, 4*(4), 296–308.

Bazerman, C. (1999). *The languages of Edison's light.* Cambridge, MA: MIT Press.

Bazerman, C. (2000). Singular utterances: Realizing local activities through typified forms in typified circumstances. In A. Trosberg (Ed.), *Analysing the discourses of professional genres* (pp. 25–40). Amsterdam: Benjamins.

Bazerman, C. (2004). Speech acts, genres, and activity systems: How texts organize activity and people. In C. Bazerman & P. Prior (Eds.), *What writing does and how it does it: An introduction to analyzing texts and textual practices* (pp. 309–339). Mahwah, NJ: Erlbaum.

Bazerman, C. (2006). The writing of social organization and the literate situating of cognition: Extending Goody's social implications of writing. In D. Olson & M. Cole (Eds.), *Technology, literacy and the evolution of society: Implications of the work of Jack Goody* (pp. 215–240). Mahwah, NJ: Erlbaum.

Bazerman, C., Little, J., & Chavkin, T. (2003). The production of information for genred activity spaces. *Written Communication, 20*(4), 455–477.

Bazerman, C., & Russell, D. R. (Eds.). (2003). *Writing selves/writing societies: Research from activity perspectives.* Fort Collins, CO: WAC Clearinghouse.

Beach, K. (2003). Consequential transitions: A developmental view of knowledge propagation through social organizations. In T. Tuomi-Gröhn & Y. Engeström (Eds.), *Between school and work: New perspectives on transfer and boundary-crossing* (pp. 39–62). New York: Earli.

Beck, E. E. (2002). P for political: Participation is not enough. *Scandinavian Journal of Information Systems, 14*(2), pp. 77–92.

Beck, U. (1992). *The risk society.* London: Sage.

Bedny, G. Z., & Karwowski, W. (2004a). Activity theory as a basis for the study of work. *Ergonomics, 47*(2), 134–153.

Bedny, G. Z., & Karwowski, W. (2004b). Meaning and sense in activity theory and their role in the study of human performance. *Ergonomia IJE&HF, 26*(2), 121–140.

Bedny, G. Z., & Meister, D. (1997). *The Russian theory of activity: Current applications to design and learning.* Hillsdale, NJ: Erlbaum.

Bedny, G. Z., Seglin, M., & Meister, D. (2000). Activity theory: History, research and application. *Theoretical Issues in Ergonomics Science, 1*(2), 168–206.

Béguin, P., & Clot, Y. (2004). Situated action in the development of activity. *@ctivité, 1*(2), http://www.activites.org.

Benkler, Y. (2006). *The wealth of networks: How social production transforms markets and freedom.* New Haven, CT: Yale University Press.

Berkenkotter, C., & Huckin, T. (1995). *Genre knowledge in disciplinary communication: Cognition/culture/power.* Hillsdale, NJ: Erlbaum.

Bertelsen, O. W., & Bødker, S. (2002a). Activity theory. In J. Carroll (Ed.), *HCI models, theories and frameworks* (pp. 291–324). San Francisco: Morgan Kaufmann.

Bertelsen, O. W., & Bødker, S. (2002b). Discontinuities. In C. Floyd, Y. Dittrich, & R. Klischewski (Eds.), *Social thinking: Software practice* (pp. 409–424). Cambridge, MA: MIT Press.

Best, J. (1987). Rhetoric in claims-making: Constructing the missing children problem. *Social Problems, 34*(2), 101–121.

Bhaskar R. (1977). *A realist theory of science.* London: Verso.

Billett, S. (2006). Relational interdependence between social and individual agency in work and working life. *Mind, Culture, and Activity, 13*(1), 53–69.

Billig, M. (1996). *Arguing and thinking: A rhetorical view of social psychology.* Cambridge: Cambridge University Press.

Bion, W. (1961). *Experiences in groups and other papers.* New York: Basic Books.

Bjerknes, G., & Bratteteig, T. (1987). Florence in wonderland: Systems development with nurses. In G. Bjerknes, P. Ehn, & M. Kyng (Eds.), *Computers and democracy: A Scandinavian challenge* (pp. 279–296). Aldershot: Avebury.

Bjerknes, G., & Bratteteig, T. (1988). The memoirs of two survivors – or evaluation of a computer system for cooperative work. In D. Tatar (Ed.), *Proceedings of the 2nd conference on computer supported cooperative work* (pp. 167–177). New York: Association for Computing Machinery Press.

Blackler, F., Crump, N., & MacDonald, S. (1999). Managing experts and competing through innovation: An activity theoretical analysis. *Organization, 6*(1), 5–31.

Blackler, F., & McDonald, S. (2000). Power, mastery and organisational learning. *Journal of Management Studies, 37*(6), 833–851.

Blackler, F., & Regan, S. (2006). Institutional reform and the reorganisation of family support services. *Organization Studies, 27*(12), 1843–1862.

Blau, P. (1955). *The dynamics of bureaucracy.* Chicago: Chicago University Press.

Bødker, S. (1991). *Through the interface.* Hillsdale, NJ: Erlbaum.

Bødker, S. (1996). Creating conditions for participation: Conflicts and resources in systems design. *Human–Computer Interaction, 11*, 215–236.

Bødker, S. (2006). When second wave HCI meets third wave challenges, NordiCHI keynote. In A. Mørch, K. Morgan, T. Bratteteig, G. Ghosh, & D. Svanæs (Eds.), *NordiCHI 2006: Proceedings of the 4th Nordic conference on human-computer interaction* (pp. 1–8). Oslo: Association for Computing Machinery Press.

Bødker, S., & Christiansen, E. (1997). Scenarios as springboards in design. In G. Bowker, L. Gasser, S. L. Star, & W. Turner (Eds.), *Social science research, technical systems and cooperative work* (pp. 217–234). Hillsdale, NJ: Erlbaum.

Bødker, S., & Christiansen, E. (2004). Designing for ephemerality and proto-typicality. In D. Benyon, P. Moody, D. Gruen, & I. McAra-McWilliam (Eds.), *Proceedings of the 5th conference on designing interactive systems: Processes, practices, methods, and techniques* (pp. 255–260). New York: Association for Computing Machinery Press.

Bødker, S., & Christiansen, E. (2006). Computer support for social awareness in flexible work. *Journal of CSCW, 15*(1), 1–28.

Bødker, S., Christiansen, E., Ehn, P., Markussen, R., Mogensen, P., & Trigg, R. (1991). *Computers in context: Report from the AT-project.* Arbejdets Udvikling: NES/SAM.

Bødker, S., Ehn, P., Kammersgaard, J., Kyng, M., & Sundblad, Y. (1987). A utopian experience. In G. Bjerknes, P. Ehn, & M. Kyng (Eds.), *Computers and democracy: A Scandinavian challenge* (pp. 251–278). Aldershot: Avebury.

Bødker, S., Ehn, P., Knudsen, J. L., Kyng, M., & Madsen, K. H. (1988). Computer support for cooperative design. In I. Grief (Ed.), *Proceedings of the 2nd conference on computer-supported cooperative work* (pp. 377–394). New York: Association for Computing Machinery Press.

Bødker, S., & Grønbæk, K. (1991). Design in action: From prototyping by demonstration to cooperative prototyping. In J. Greenbaum & M. Kyng (Eds.), *Design at work: Cooperative design of computer systems* (pp. 197–218). Hillsdale, NJ: Erlbaum.

Bødker, S., Grønbæk, K., & Kyng, M. (1993). Cooperative design: Techniques and experiences from the Scandinavian scene. In D. Schuler & A. Namioka (Eds.), *Participatory design: Principles and practices* (pp. 157–76). Hillsdale, NJ: Erlbaum.

Bødker, S., & Iversen, O. (2002). Staging a professional participatory design practice: Moving PD beyond the initial fascination of user involvement. In O. Bertelsen, S. Bødker, & K. Kuutti (Eds.), *NordiCHI 2002: Proceedings of the 2nd Nordic conference on human–computer interaction* (pp. 11–18). Aarhus: Association for Computing Machinery Press.

Böhme, G. (1998). The structures and prospects of knowledge society. *Social Science Information, 37*(1), 447–468.

Bolz, N. (1993). *Am Ende der Gutenberg-Galaxis: Die neuen Kommunika-tionsverhältnisse* [At the end of the Gutenberg galaxy: The new conditions of communication]. Padeborn: Wilhelm Fink.

Bouvin, N. O., Nielsen, A. C., & Sejersen, C. M. (1991). *Spirits in a material world: An activity theory based evaluation of Ariel, a demonstrator in the EuroCODE CSCW project, aimed at supporting inspection work at the Great Belt bridge.* DAIMI/Eurocode. Unpublished master thesis. University of Aarhus.

Boyle, J. (2003). The second enclosure movement and the construction of the public domain. *Law and Contemporary Problems, 66,* 33–74.

Bujarski, M, Hildebrand-Nilshon, M., & Kordt, J. (1999). Psychomotor and socioe-motional processes in literacy acquisition: Results of an ongoing case study involving a nonvocal cerebral palsic young man. In Y. Engeström, R. Miettinen, & R.-L. Punamäki (Eds.), *Perspectives on activity theory* (pp. 206–227). New York: Cambridge University Press.

Bülow, P. (2004). Sharing experiences of contested illness by storytelling. *Discourse & Society, 15*(1), 33–53.

Burrell, G., & Morgan, G. (1979). *Sociological paradigms and organizational analysis.* London: Heinemann.

Bybee, J., & Fleischman, S. (1995). *Modality in grammar and discourse.* Amsterdam: John Benjamins.

Caplow, T. (1968). *Two against one.* Englewood Cliffs, NJ: Prentice-Hall.

Carter, M. (2004). Teaching genre to English first-language adults: A study of the laboratory report. *Research in the Teaching of English, 38,* 395–413.

Castells, M. (1996). *The rise of the network society.* Oxford: Blackwell.

Castells, M. (2000). Materials for an explanatory theory of the network society. *British Journal of Sociology, 51*(1), 5–24.

Chaiklin, S. (1993). Understanding the social scientific practice of *Understanding Practice.* In S. Chaiklin & J. Lave (Eds.), *Understanding practice: Perspectives on activity and context* (pp. 379–402). Cambridge: Cambridge University Press.

Cherns, A. (1979). *Using the social sciences.* London: Routledge & Kegan Paul.

Child, J., & Smith, C. (1987). The context and process of organizational transforma-tion: Cadbury Ltd. in its sector. *Journal of Management Studies, 24,* 656–594.

Christensen, M., & Kirby, S. (2003). *Language evolution.* Oxford: Oxford University Press.

Clark A. (1998). Embodiment and the philosophy of mind. In A. O'Hear (Ed.), *Contemporary issues in the philosophy of mind* (pp. 35–51). Cambridge: Cambridge University Press.

Clark, A., & Chalmers, D. J. (1998). The extended mind. *Analysis, 58,* 10–23.

Clot, Y. (1999). *La fonction psychologique du travail [The psychological function of work].* Paris: Presses universitaires de France.

Clot, Y. (2005a, July). *Pourquoi et comment s'occuper du développement en clinique de l'activité ?* [Why and how to focus on development in the Clinic of Activity]. Paper presented at the international symposium *Artefacts and collectives: Situated action and activity theory* (ARTCO), Lyon, http://sites.univ-lyon2.fr/artco/home.html.

Clot, Y. (2005b). L'auto-confrontation croisée en analyse du travail: L'apport de la théorie bakhtinienne du dialogue [Crossed self-confrontation in the analysis of work: The contribution of Bakhtin's theory of dialogue]. In L. Filliettaz & J. P. Bronckart (Eds.), *L'analyse des actionss et des discourse en situation de travail: Concepts, méthodes et applications* (pp. 37–55). Louvaine-La-Neuve: Peters.

Clot, Y., Fernandez, G., & Carles, L. (2002). Crossed self-confrontation in the "Clinic of Activity." In S. Bagnara, S. Pozzi, A. Rizzo, & P. Wright (Eds.), *Proceedings of the 11th European conference on cognitive ergonomics, ECCE 11* (pp. 13–18). Rome, Italy: Istituto di Scienze e Tecnologie della Cognizione.

Clot, Y., Prot, B., & Werthe, C. (2001). Clinique de l'activité et pouvoir d'agir [Clinic of Activity and power to act]. *Éducation Permanente, 146,* 12–37.

Clot, Y., & Scheller, L. (2006). La "clinica dell'attività." Analizzare il lavoro per trasformarlo [The Clinic of Activity: Analyzing work for transforming it]. In C. Zucchermaglio & F. Alby (Eds.), *Psicologia culturale delle organizzazioni.* Rome: Carocci editore.

Cobb, P., Confrey, J., diSessa, A., Lehrer, R., & Schauble, L. (2003). Design experiments in educational research. *Educational Researcher, 32,* 9–13.

Cohen, J. E. (2006). Copyright, commodification, and culture: Locating the public domain. In L. Guibault & P. B. Hugenholz (Eds.), *The future of public domain* (pp. 121–166). Dordrecht: Kluwer.

Cole, M. (1985). The zone of proximal development: Where culture and cognition create each other. In J. V. Wertsch (Ed.), *Culture, communication, and cognition: Vygotskian perspectives* (pp. 146–161). Cambridge: Cambridge University Press.

Cole, M. (1996). *Cultural psychology: A once and future discipline.* Cambridge, MA: Harvard University Press.

Collins, A., Joseph, D., & Bielaczyc, K. (2004). Design research: Theoretical and methodological issues. *Journal of the Learning Sciences, 13,* 15–42.

Comte, A. (2004). *The catechism of positive religion.* Whitefish, MT: Kessinger.

Cooren, F. (2006). The organizational world as a plenum of agencies. In F. Cooren, J. R. Taylor, & E. J. Van Every (Eds.), *Communication as organizing: Empirical explorations into the dynamic of text and conversation* (pp. 81–100). Mahwah, NJ: Erlbaum.

Cussins, A. (1992). Content, embodiment and objectivity: The theory of cognitive trails. *Mind, 101,* 651–688.

Czarniawska, B. (2003). The styles and stylists of organization theory. In H. Tsoukas & C. Knudsen (Eds.), *The Oxford handbook of organizational theory* (pp. 237–261). Oxford: Oxford University Press.

Dalton, M. (1950). *Men who manage.* New York: Wiley.

Damasio, A. R. (2000). *Descartes' error: Emotion, reason, and the human brain.* New York: HarperCollins.

D'Andrade, R. (1996). Culture. In A. Kuper & J. Kuper (Eds.), *Social science encyclopedia* (pp. 161–163). London: Routledge.

Daniels, H. (2001). *Vygotsky and pedagogy.* London: Routledge Falmer.

Daniels, H., Brown, S., Edwards, A., Leadbetter, J., Martin, D., Middleton, D., Parsons, S., Popova, A., & Warmington, P. (2005). Studying professional learning for inclusion. In K. Yamazumi, Y. Engeström, & H. Daniels (Eds.), *New learning challenges: Going beyond the industrial age system of school and work* (pp. 79–101). Osaka: Kansai University Press.

Daniels, H., Cole, M., & Wertsch, J. V (2007). *The Cambridge companion to Vygotsky.* Cambridge: Cambridge University Press.

Daniels, H., Leadbetter, J., Warmington, P., Edwards, A., Martin, D., Popova, A., Apostolov, A., Middleton, D., & Brown, S. (2007). Learning in and for multi-agency working. *Oxford Review of Education, 33*(4), 521–538.

Dartington, T. (1998). From altruism to action: Primary task and the not-for-profit organization. *Human Relations, 51,* 1495–1508.

Darwin, C. (1859). *The origin of species.* New York: Penguin.

Davydov, V. V. (1982). The psychological structure and contents of the learning activity in school children. In R. Glaser & J. Lompscher (Eds.), *Cognitive and motivational aspects of instruction* (pp. 37–44). Berlin: Deutscher Verlag der Wissenschaften.

Davydov, V. V. (1988). Problems of developmental teaching. *Soviet Education, 30*(9), 3–83.

Davydov, V. V. (1990). *Types of generalization in instruction: Logical and psychological problems in the structuring of school curricula.* Reston, VA: National Council of Teachers of Mathematics.

Davydov V. V. (1996). *The theory of developmental teaching.* Moscow: In-Tor Publishers (in Russian).

Davydov, V. V. (1999a). A new approach to the interpretation of activity structure and content. In S. Chaiklin, M. Hedegaard, & U. J. Jensen (Eds.), *Activity theory and social practice* (pp. 39–50). Aarhus: Aarhus University Press.

Davydov, V. V. (1999b). The content and unsolved problems of activity theory. In Y. Engeström, R. Miettinen, & R.-L. Punamäki (Eds.), *Perspectives on activity theory* (pp. 39–52). Cambridge: Cambridge University Press.

Davydov, V. V., & Radikhovskii, L. A. (1985). Vygotsky's theory and activity-oriented approach in psychology. In J. Wertsch (Ed.), *Culture, communication, and cognition* (pp. 35–65). Cambridge: Cambridge University Press.

Dawydow, W. W. (1977). *Arten des Verallgemeinerung im unterricht* [Types of generalizations in instruction]. Berlin: Volk und Wissen.

Deibel, E. (2006). Open source in biotechnology and return of common property. *Tailoring Biotechnologies, 2*(2), 49–84.

Deleuze, G., & Guattari, F. (1987). *A thousand plateaus: Capitalism and schizophrenia.* Minneapolis: University of Minnesota Press.

Derry, J. (2004). The unity of intellect and will: Vygotsky and Spinoza. *Educational Review, 56*(2), 113–120.

De Vries, M. W. (1987). Cry babies, culture, and catastrophe: Infant temperament in the Masai. In N. Scheper-Hughes (Ed.), *Child survival: Anthropological approaches to the treatment and maltreatment of children* (pp. 165–186). Boston: Reidel.

Dewey, J. (1944). *Democracy and education.* New York: Free Press.

Dias, P., Freedman, A., Medway, P., & Paré, A. (1999). *Worlds apart: Acting and writing in academic and workplace contexts.* Mahwah, NJ: Erlbaum.

Donaldson, M. (1978). *Children's minds.* London: Fontana.

Dreyfus, H. L., & Dreyfus, S. D. (1986). *Mind over machine: The power of human intuition and expertise in the era of the computer.* Glasgow: Basil Blackwell.

Dunne, A., & Raby, F. (2001). *Design noir: The secret life of electronic objects.* Basel: Birkhäuser.

Dyer-Witheford, N. (1999). *Cyber-Marx: Cycles and circuits of struggle in high-technology capitalism.* Urbana: University of Illinois Press.

Edwards, A. (2004). The new multi-agency working: Collaborating to prevent the social exclusion of children and families. *Journal of Integrated Care, 12*(5), 3–9.

Edwards, A. (2005). Relational agency: Learning to be a resourceful practitioner. *International Journal of Educational Research, 43*, 168–182.

Edwards, A. (in press). Learning how to know who: Professional learning for expansive practice between organisations. In S. Ludvigsen, A. Lund, I. Rasmussen, & R. Säljö (Eds.), *Learning across sites: New tools, infrastructures and practices.* London: Pergamon.

Edwards, A., Barnes, M., Plewis, I., & Morris, K. (2006). Working to prevent the social exclusion of children and young people: Final lessons from the National Evaluation of the Children's Fund. Research Report 734. London: DfES.

Edwards, A., & D'Arcy, C. (2004). Relational agency and disposition in sociocultural accounts of learning to teach. *Educational Review, 56*(2), 147–155.

Ehn, P. (1988). *Work-oriented design of computer artifacts.* Hillsdale, NJ: Erlbaum.

Ehn, P., & Kyng, M. (1984). A tool perspective on design of interactive computer support for skilled workers. In M. Sääksjärvi (Ed.), *Proceedings from the 7th Scandinavian research seminar on systemeering* (pp. 211–242). Helsinki: Helsinki Business School.

Ehn, P., & Kyng, M. (1987). The collective resource approach to systems design. In G. Bjerknes, P. Ehn, & M. Kyng (Eds.), *Computers and democracy: A Scandinavian challenge* (pp. 17–58). Aldershot: Avebury.

Engels, F. (1925/1978). *Dialektik der Natur* [Dialectics of nature]. Berlin: Dietz.

Engeström, R. (1991). Reconstructing organizational memory in a health center. *Multidisciplinary Newsletter for Activity Theory, 9/10*, 20–26.

Engeström, R. (1995). Voice as communicative action. *Mind, Culture, and Activity, 2*, 192–215.

Engeström, R. (1999). Imagine the world you want to live in: A study on developmental change in doctor–patient interaction. *Outlines: Critical Social Theory, 1*(1), 33–50.

Engeström, R. (2005). Polyphony of activity. In Y. Engeström, J. Lompscher, & G. Rückriem (Eds.), *Putting activity theory to work* (pp. 49–74). Berlin: ICHS.

Engeström, Y. (1970). *Koulutus luokkayhteiskunnassa: Johdatus kapitalistisen yhteiskunnan koulutusongelmiin* [Education in class society: Introduction to the educational problems of capitalism]. Jyväskylä: Gummerus.

Engeström, Y. (1979). *Koululaisten mielikuvitus ja käyttäytyminen rauhankasvatuksen kannalta tarkasteltuna* [The imagination and behavior of school students analyzed from the viewpoint of education for peace]. Tampere: Institute of Peace and Conflict Research.

Engeström, Y. (1982). Teoreettisen yleistämisen kehittäminen opetuksessa: Esimerkki historianopetuksesta [Developing theoretical generalization in instruction: An example from history teaching]. In P. Hakkarainen (Ed.), *Opetuksen ja sen evaluoinnin tutkiminen* (pp. 43–64). Jyväskylä: Kasvatustieteiden tutkimuslaitos.

Engeström, Y. (1983). *Oppimistoiminta ja opetustyö* [Learning activity and instructional work]. Helsinki: Tutkijaliitto.

Engeström, Y. (1987). *Learning by expanding: An activity-theoretical approach to developmental research.* Helsinki: Orienta-Konsultit.

Engeström, Y. (1990). *Learning, working and imagining: Twelve studies in activity theory.* Helsinki: Orienta-Konsultit.

Engeström, Y. (1991a). Developmental work research: Reconstructing expertise through expansive learning. In M. I. Nurminen & G. R. S. Weir (Eds.), *Human jobs and computer interfaces* (pp. 265–290). Amsterdam: Elsevier.

Engeström Y. (1991b). Non scolae sed vitae discimus: Toward overcoming the encapsulation of school learning. *Learning and Instruction: An International Journal, 1,* 243–259.

Engeström, Y. (1996a). Development as breaking away and opening up: A challenge to Vygotsky and Piaget. *Swiss Journal of Psychology, 55*(2/3), 126–132.

Engeström, Y. (1996b). Developmental work research as educational research: Looking ten years back and into the zone of proximal development. *Nordisk Pedagogik: Journal of Nordic Educational Research, 16,* 131–143.

Engeström, Y. (1999a). Activity theory and individual and social transformation. In Y. Engeström, R. Miettinen, & R.-L. Punamäki (Eds.), *Perspectives on activity theory* (pp. 19–38). Cambridge: Cambridge University Press.

Engeström, Y. (1999b). Communication, discourse and activity. *Communication Review, 3,* 165–185.

Engeström, Y. (1999c). Expansive visibilization of work: An activity-theoretical perspective. *Computer Supported Cooperative Work, 8,* 63–93.

Engeström, Y. (1999d). From iron cages to webs on the wind: Three theses on teams and learning at work. *Lifelong Learning in Europe, 4*(2), 101–110.

Engeström, Y. (1999e). Innovative learning in work teams: Analyzing cycles of knowledge creation in practice. In Y. Engeström, R. Miettinen, & R.-L. Punamäki (Eds.), *Perspectives on activity theory* (pp. 377–404). Cambridge: Cambridge University Press.

Engeström, Y. (1999f). Learning by expanding: Ten years after. Foreword to the Japanese edition of *Learning by Expanding.* Tokyo: Shin-yo-sha (in Japanese).

Engeström, Y. (2000a). Activity theory as a framework for analyzing and redesigning work. *Ergonomics, 43*(7), 960–974.

Engeström, Y. (2000b). Comment on Blackler et al., activity theory and the social construction of knowledge: A story of four umpires. *Organization, 7*(2), 301–310.

Engeström, Y. (2000c). From individual action to collective activity and back: Developmental work research as an interventionist methodology. In P. Luff, J. Hindmarsh, & C. Heath (Eds.), *Workplace studies* (pp. 150–166). Cambridge: Cambridge University Press.

Engeström, Y. (2001). Expansive learning at work: Toward an activity theoretical reconceptualization. *Journal of Education and Work, 14*(1), 133–156.

Engeström, Y. (2004). New forms of learning in co-configuration work. *Journal of Workplace Learning 16*(1/2), 11–21.

Engeström Y. (2005a). *Developmental work research: Expanding activity theory in practice.* Berlin: Lehmanns Media.

Engeström, Y. (2005b). Introduction. In Y. Engeström, J. Lompscher, & G. Rückriem (Eds.), *Putting activity theory to work: Contributions from developmental work research* (pp. 11–17). Berlin: Lehmanns Media.

Engeström, Y. (2005c). Knotworking to create collaborative intentionality capital in fluid organizational fields. In M. M. Beyerlein, S. T. Beyerlein, & F. A. Kennedy (Eds.), *Collaborative capital: Creating intangible value* (pp. 307–336). Amsterdam: Elsevier.

Engeström, Y. (2006a). Activity theory and expansive design. In S. Bagnara & G. Crampton Smith (Eds.), *Theories and practice of interaction design* (pp. 3–23). Mahwah, NJ: Erlbaum.

Engeström, Y. (2006b). Development, movement and agency: Breaking away into mycorrhizae activities. In K. Yamazumi (Ed.), *Building activity theory in practice: Toward the next generation* (Vol. 1, pp. 1–43). Osaka: Center for Human Activity Theory (CHAT), Kansai University.

Engeström, Y. (2006c). From well-bounded ethnographies to intervening in mycorrhizae activities. *Organization Studies, 27*(2), 1783–1793.

Engeström, Y, (2006d). *Triangles, strands, objects, and contradictions: A commentary on Bakhurst.* Unpublished manuscript.

Engeström, Y. (2007a). Enriching the theory of expansive learning: Lessons from journeys toward co-configuration. *Mind, Culture, and Activity, 14*(1–2), 23–39.

Engeström, Y. (2007b). From communities of practice to mycorrhizae. In J. Hughes, N. Jewson, & L. Unwin (Eds.), *Communities of practice: Critical perspectives* (pp. 41–54). London: Routledge.

Engeström, Y. (2007c). From stabilization knowledge to possibility knowledge in organizational learning. *Management Learning, 38*, 271–275.

Engeström, Y. (2007d). Putting activity theory to work: The Change Laboratory as an application of double stimulation. In H. Daniels, M. Cole, & J. V. Wertsch (Eds.), *The Cambridge companion to Vygotsky* (pp. 363–382). Cambridge: Cambridge University Press.

Engeström, Y. (2007e). Putting Vygotsky to work: The Change Laboratory as an application of double stimulation. In H. Daniels, M. Cole. & J. V. Wertsch (Eds.), *The Cambridge companion to Vygotsky* (pp. 363–382). Cambridge: Cambridge University Press.

Engeström, Y. (2008a). Enriching activity theory without shortcuts. *Interacting with Computers, 20*, 256–259.

Engeström, Y. (2008b). *From teams to knots: Activity-theoretical studies of collaboration and learning at work.* Cambridge: Cambridge University Press.

Engeström, Y., & Blackler, F. (2005). On the life of the object. *Organization, 12*(3), 307–330.

Engeström, Y., & Engeström, R. (1984). *Siivoustyön hallinta ja työntekijöiden laadullinen koulutustarve* [The mastery of janitorial cleaning work and the workers' qualitative need for training]. Helsinki: ServiSystems.

Engeström, Y., & Engeström, R. (1986). Developmental work research: The approach and the application of cleaning work. *Nordisk Pedagogik, 6*, 2–15.

Engeström, Y., Engeström, R., Helenius, J., & Koistinen, K. (1989). *Tereyskeskuslääkärien työn kehittämistutkimus* [Developmental study of the work of health center physicians: Third interim report]. Espoo: Espoon kaupungin terveyskeskus.

Engeström, Y., Engeström, R., & Kärkkäinen, M. (1995). Polycontextuality and boundary crossing in expert cognition: Learning and problem solving in complex work activities. *Learning and Instruction: An International Journal, 5,* 319–336.

Engeström, Y., Engeström, R., & Kerosuo, H. (2003). The discursive construction of collaborative care. *Applied Linguistics, 24*(4), 286–315.

Engeström, Y., Engeström, R., & Vähäaho, T. (1999). When the centre does not hold: The importance of knotworking. In S. Chaiklin, M. Hedegaard, & U. J. Jensen (Eds.), *Activity theory and social practice* (pp. 345–374). Aarhus: Aarhus University Press.

Engeström, Y., Hakkarainen, P., & Hedegaard, M. (1984). On the methodological basis of research in teaching and learning. In M. Hedegaard, P. Hakkarainen, & Y. Engeström (Eds.), *Learning and teaching on a scientific basis: Methodological and epistemological aspects of the activity theory of learning and teaching* (pp. 119–189). Aarhus: University of Aarhus.

Engeström, Y., Kerosuo, H., & Kajamaa, A. (2007). Beyond discontinuity: Expansive organizational learning remembered. *Management Learning, 38*(3), 319–336.

Engeström, Y., & Middleton, D. (Eds.) (1996). *Cognition and communication at work.* Cambridge: Cambridge University Press.

Engeström, Y., Miettinen, R., & Punamäki, R.-L. (Eds.) (1999). *Perspectives on activity theory.* Cambridge: Cambridge University Press.

Engeström, Y., Pasanen, A., Toiviainen, H., & Haavisto, V. (2005). Expansive learning as concept formation at work. In K. Yamazumi, Y. Engeström, & H. Daniels (Eds.), *New learning challenges: Going beyond the industrial age system of school and work* (pp. 47–77). Osaka: Kansai University Press.

Engeström, Y., Puonti, A., & Seppänen, L. (2003). Spatial and temporal expansion of the object as a challenge for reorganizing work. In D. Nicolini, S. Gherardi, & D. Yanow (Eds.), *Knowing in organizations: A practice-based approach* (pp. 151–186). Armonk, NY: Sharpe.

Engeström, Y., & Toiviainen, H. (in press). Co-configurational design of learning instrumentalities: An activity-theoretical perspective. In S. Ludvigsen, A. Lund, I. Rasmussen, & R. Säljö (Eds.), *Learning across sites: New tools, infrastructures and practices.* London: Pergamon.

Engeström, Y., Virkkunen, J., Helle, M., Pihlaja, J., & Poikela, R. (1996). Change Laboratory as a tool for transforming work. *Lifelong Learning in Europe, 1*(2), 10–17.

Etzkowitz, H., & Webster, A. (1995). Science as intellectual property. In S. Jasanoff. G. Mankle, S. Peterson,. & T. Pinch (Eds.), *Handbook of science and technology studies* (pp. 480–505). London: Sage.

Featherstone, M., & Lash, S. (Eds.) (1999). *Spaces of culture.* London: Sage.

Field, J. (2002). *Social capital.* London: Routledge.

Firth, A. (1995). Introduction and overview. In A. Firth (Ed.), *The discourse of negotiation: Studies of language in the workplace* (pp. 3–39). Oxford: Pergamon.

Floyd, C. (1987). Outline of a paradigm change in software engineering. In G. Bjerknes, P. Ehn, & M. Kyng (Eds.), *Computers and democracy: A Scandinavian challenge* (pp. 191–212). Aldershot: Avebury.

Flusser, V. (1998). *Kommunikologie* [Communicology]. Frankfurt: Fischer.

Flyvbjerg, B. (2001). *Making social science matter: Why social enquiry fails and how it can succeed again.* Cambridge: Cambridge University Press.

Flyvbjerg, B., Bruzelius, N., & Rothengatter, W. (2003). *Megaprojects and risk: An anatomy of ambition.* Cambridge: Cambridge University Press.

Fournier, V., & Grey, C. (2000). At the critical moment: Conditions and prospects for critical management studies. *Human Relations, 53*(1), 7–32.

Freeman, C., & Louçã, F. (2000). *As time goes by: From the Industrial Revolutions to the Information Revolution.* Oxford: Oxford University Press.

Friebe, H., & Lobo, S. (2006). *Wir nennen es Arbeit. Die digitale Bohème oder intelligentes Leben jenseits der Festanstellung* [We call it work: The digital bohemian or life beyond permanent jobs]. Munich: Heyne.

Friedland, R., & Boden, D. (Eds.) (1994). *NowHere: Space, time and modernity.* Berkeley: University of California Press.

Fuyuno, I. (2007). Brain craze. *Nature, 447*(3), 18–20.

Geertz, C. (1973). *The interpretation of cultures.* New York: Basic Books.

Gergen, K. (1999). *An invitation to social construction.* London: Sage.

Giddens, A. (1991). *The consequences of modernity.* Cambridge, MA: Polity Press.

Giddens, A. (2000). *Runaway world: How globalization is reshaping our lives.* London: Routledge.

Giesecke, M. (1998). *Sinnenwandel, Sprachwandel, Kulturwandel: Studien zur Vorgeschichte der Informationsgesellschaft* [Transformation of sense, language and culture: Studies on the prehistory of the information society]. Frankfurt: Suhrkamp.

Giesecke, M. (2002). *Von den Mythen der Buchkultur zu den Visionen der Informationsgesellschaft* [From myths of the book culture to visions of information society]. Frankfurt: Suhrkamp.

Giesecke, M. (2006). *Die Eentdeckung der kommunikativen Welt* [The discovery of the communicative world]. Frankfurt: Suhrkamp.

Goldin-Meadow, S. (2002). Constructing communication by hand. *Cognitive Development, 17*(3–4), 1385–1405.

Goodwin, R. (2005). Why I study relationships and culture. *Psychologist, 18*(10), 614–615.

Gould, S. J. (2007). A tale of two work sites. In S. J. Gould, S. Rose, & P. McGarr (Eds.), *The richness of life: The essential Stephen J. Gould* (pp. 546–563). London: Jonathan Cape.

Gouldner, A. (1954). *Industrial bureaucracy.* New York: Free Press.

Greenbaum, J., & Kyng, M. (Eds.) (1991). *Design at work: Cooperative design of computer systems.* Hillsdale, NJ: Erlbaum.

Greenfield, P. M. (1999). Historical change and cognitive change: A two-decade follow-up study in Zinacantan, a Mayan community in Chiapas, Mexico. *Mind, Culture, and Activity, 6*(2), 92–108.

Greenfield, P. M. (2004). *Weaving generations together: Evolving creativity in the Maya of Chiapis.* Santa Fe, NM: School of American Research.

Greeno, J. G. (1997). On claims that answer the wrong question. *Educational Researcher, 26*(1), 5–17.

Greeno, J. G. (2006). Authoritative, accountable positioning and connected general knowing: Progressive themes in understanding transfer. *Journal of the Learning Sciences, 15*(4), 537–547.

Greimas, A. J. (1987). *On meaning: Selected writings in semiotic theory.* Minneapolis: University of Minnesota Press.

Griffin, P., & Cole, M. (1984). Current activity for the future. In B. Rogoff & J. Wertsch (Eds.), *Children's learning in the "zone of proximal development": New directions for child development* (pp. 45–64). San Francisco: Jossey-Bass.

Groleau, C. (2006). One phenomenon, two lenses: Understanding collective action from the perspectives of coorientation and activity theories. In F. Cooren, J. R. Taylor, & E. J. Van Every (Eds.), *Communication as organizing: Empirical and theoretical explorations in the dynamic of text and conversation* (pp. 157–180). Mahwah, NJ: Erlbaum.

Grønbæk, K., Grudin, J., Bødker, S., & Bannon, L. (1993). Achieving cooperative system design: Shifting from product to process focus. In D. Schuler & A. Namioka (Eds.), *Participatory design: Perspectives of systems design* (pp. 79–98). Hillsdale, NJ: Erlbaum.

Grønbæk, K., Kyng, M., & Mogensen, P. (1993). CSCW challenges: Cooperative design in engineering projects. *CACM, 36*(4), 67–77.

Grønbæk, K., Kyng, M., & Mogensen, P. (1997). Toward a cooperative experimental system development approach. In M. Kyng & L. Mathiassen (Eds.), *Computers and design in context* (pp. 201–238). Cambridge, MA: MIT press.

Grudin, J. (1993). Obstacles to participatory design in large product development organizations. In D. Schuler & A. Namioka (Eds.), *Participatory design: Principles and practices* (pp. 99–119). Hillsdale, NJ: Erlbaum.

Guile, D. (2007). Moebius strip enterprises and expertise in the creative industries: New challenges for lifelong learning? *International Journal of Lifelong Learning, 23*(3), 241–261.

Güney, S. (2006). Making sense of a conflict as the (missing) link between collaborating actors. In F. Cooren, J. R. Taylor, & E. J. Van Every (Eds.), *Communication as organizing: Empirical and theoretical explorations in the dynamic of text and conversations* (pp. 19–36). Mahwah, NJ: Erlbaum.

Gutiérrez, K. D., & Rogoff, B. (2003). Cultural ways of learning: Individual traits or repertoires of practice. *Educational Researcher, 32*(5), 19–25.

Hacking, I. (1995). *Rewriting the soul: Multiple personality and the science of memory.* London: Sage.

Haenen, J. (1995). *Pjotr Gal'perin: Psychologist in Vygotsky's footsteps.* Hauppauge: Nova Science Publishers.

Hakkarainen, K., Palonen, T., Paavola, S., & Lehtinen, E. (2004). *Communities of networked expertise: Professional and educational perspectives.* Amsterdam: Elsevier.

Hall, C., Slembrouck, S., & Sarangi, S. (2006). *Language practices in social work: Categorisation and accountability in child welfare.* London: Routledge.

Halliday, M. A. K. (1985). *An introduction to functional grammar.* London: Edward Arnold.

Halpern, D. (2005). *Social capital.* Cambridge, MA: Polity Press.

Halskov, K., & Dalsgård, P. (2006). Inspiration card workshops. In J. M. Carroll, S. Bødker, & J. Coughlin (Eds.), *Proceedings of the conference on designing interactive systems* (pp. 2–11). New York: Association for Computing Machinery Press.

Harré, R. (1984). *Personal being: A theory for individual psychology.* Cambridge, MA: Harvard University Press.

Harré, R. (1986). *Varieties of realism: A rationale for the natural sciences.* Oxford: Blackwell.

Haug, W. F. (2003). *High-tech-capitalismus.* Hamburg: Argument Verlag.

Heaton, L., & Taylor, J. R. (2002). Knowledge management and professional work: A communication perspective on the knowledge-based organization. *Management Communication Quarterly, 16*(2), 210–236.

Hegel, G. W. F. (1977). *Phenomenology of spirit.* Oxford: Oxford University Press.

Heller, M. A., & Eisenberg, R. S. (1998). Can patents deter innovation? The anti-commons in biomedical research. *Science, 280,* 698–701.

Helmuth, L. (2001). From the mouths (and hands) of babes. *Science, 293,* 1758–1759.

Hicks, D. (2000). Self and other in Bakhtin's early philosophical essays: Prelude to prose consciousness. *Mind, Culture, and Activity, 7*(3), 227–242.

Hinings, C., & Greenwood, R. (1988). *The dynamics of strategic change.* Oxford: Basil Blackwell.

Hirschhorn, L. (1999). The primary risk. *Human Relations, 52*(1), 5–23.

Hobbes, T. (Ed.). (1996). *Leviathan.* Oxford: Oxford University Press.

Hobsbawm, E. (1995). *Age of extremes: The short twentieth century 1914–1991.* London: Abacus.

Holland, D., & Lave, J. (Eds.) (2001). *History in person.* Oxford: James Currey.

Holland, D., Skinner, D., Lachicotte, W., & Cain, C. (1998). *Identity and agency in cultural worlds.* Cambridge, MA: Harvard University Press.

Holt, J. (1964). *How children fail.* New York: Dell.

Holzkamp, K. (1983). *Grundlegung der psychologie* [Foundations of psychology]. Frankfurt: Campus.

Holzkamp, K. (1995). *Lernen: Subjektwissenschaftliche Grundlegung* [Learning: Subject-scientific foundation]. Frankfurt am Main: Campus.

Holzman, L. (2006). What kind of theory is activity theory? *Theory & Psychology, 16,* 1, 5–11.

Hopwood, A., & Miller, P. (Eds.) (1994). *Accounting as social and institutional practice.* Cambridge: Cambridge University Press.

Hornecker, E., & Buur, J. (2006). Getting a grip on tangible interaction: A framework on physical space and social interaction. In R. Grinter, T. Rodden, P. Aoki, E. Cutrell, R. Jeffries, & G. Olson (Eds.), *Proceedings of the SIGCHI conference on human factors in computing systems* (pp. 437–446). New York: Association for Computing Machinery Press.

Iljenkow, E. W. (1975). Die dialektik von abstraktem und konkretem [The dialectics of the abstract and the concrete]. In M. M. Rosental (Ed.), *Geschichte der marxistichen dialektik* (pp. 211–233). Berlin: Dietz Verlag.

Il'enkov, E. (1977a). *Dialectical logic: Essays on its history and theory.* Moscow: Progress.

Il'enkov, E. V. (1977b). The problem of the ideal. In *Philosophy in the USSR: Problems of dialectical materialism.* Moscow: Progress.

Il'enkov, E. V. (1982). *The dialectics of the abstract and the concrete in Marx's "Capital."* Moscow: Progress.

Ingold, T. (2000). *The perception of the environment: Essays on livelihood, dwelling and skill.* London: Routledge.

Israel, J. (1979). *The language of dialectics and the dialectics of language.* London: Harvester Press.

Jaffe, A.B., & Lerner, J. (2004). *Innovations and its discontents: How our broken patent system is endangering innovation and progress, and what to do about it.* Princeton, NJ: Princeton University Press.

Jensen, K. (2007). The desire to learn: An analysis of knowledge-seeking practices among professionals. *Oxford Review of Education, 33*(4), 489–502.

Johnson, S. C., Dweck, C. S., & Chen, F.S. (2007). Evidence for infants' internal working models of attachment. *Psychological Science, 18*(6), 501–502.

Johnstone, T., & Scherer, K.R. (2000). Vocal communication of emotion. In M. Lewis & J. Haviland (Eds.), *Handbook of emotion* (pp. 220–235). New York: Guilford Press.

Judin, E.G. (1984). Das Problem der Tätigkeit in Philosophie und Wissenschaft [The problem of activity in philosophy of science]. In D. Viehweger (Ed.), *Grundfragen einer Theorie der sprachlichen Tätigkeit* (pp. 216–270). Berlin: Akademie-Verlag.

Jungk, R., & Müllert, N. (1987). *Future workshops: How to create desirable futures.* London: Institute for Social Inventions.

Kagawa, S., & Moro, Y. (2006). Student nurses' experiencing and construction of "heterochrony": Learning process in the classroom–practicum transition. *Japanese Journal of Educational Psychology, 54*(2), 346–360 (in Japanese).

Kain, D., & Wardle, E. (2005). Building context: Using activity theory to teach about genre in multi-major professional communication courses. *Technical Communication Quarterly, 14*(2), 113–139.

Kaptelinin, V. (2005). The object of activity: Making sense of the sense-maker. *Mind, Culture, and Activity, 12*(1), 4–18.

Kasavin, I.T. (1990). Activity and rationality. In V.A. Lektorsky (Ed.), *Activity: Theories, methodology, and problems* (pp. 93–98). Orlando, FL: Paul M. Deutsch.

Kauffman, S. (1995). *At home in the universe: The search for the laws of self-organization and complexity.* New York: Oxford University Press.

Keating, P., & Cambrosio, A. (2003). *Biomedical platforms. Realigning the normal and the pathological in late-twentieth-century medicine.* Cambridge, MA: MIT Press.

Keiler, P. (2002). *Lev Vygotskij: Ein leben für die psychologie* [Lev Vygotsky: A life for psychology]. Weinheim: Beltz.

Kelly, K. (2005). We are the web. *Wired, 13*, 8.

Kensing, F., & Madsen, K.H. (1991). Generating visions: Future workshops and metaphorical design. In J. Greenbaum & M. Kyng (Eds.), *Design at work: Cooperative design of computer systems* (pp. 155–168). Hillsdale, NJ: Erlbaum.

Kensing, F., Simonsen, J., & Bødker, S. (1998). MUST: A method for participatory design. *Human–computer interaction, 13*(2), 167–198.

Kerosuo, H. (2006). *Boundaries in action: An activity-theoretical study of development, learning and change in health care for patients with multiple and chronic illnesses.* Helsinki: Helsinki University Press.

Klein, N. (2007). *The shock doctrine: The rise of disaster capitalism.* New York: Penguin.

Knorr Cetina, K. (1999). *Epistemic cultures: How sciences make knowledge.* Cambridge MA: Harvard University Press.

Knorr Cetina, K., & Bruggar, U. (2002). Traders' engagement with markets. *Theory Culture and Society, 19*(5–6), 161–185.

Konkola, R., Tuomi-Gröhn, T., Lambert, P., & Ludvigsen, S. (2007). Promoting learning and transfer between school and workplace. *Journal of Education and Work, 3*(20), 211–228.

Kostulski, K. (2005). Activité conversationnelle et activité d'analyse. L'interlocution en situation de co-analyse du travail [Conversational activity and activity of analysis: Interlocution in the context of co-analysis of work]. In L. Filliettaz & J. P. Bronckart (Eds.), *L'analyse des actions et des discours en situation de travail. Concepts, méthodes et applications* (pp. 57–75). Louvain-La-Neuve: Peeters.

Kozulin, A. (1986). The concept of activity in soviet psychology: Vygotsky, his disciples and critics. *American Psychologist, 41*(3), 264–275.

Kvale, S. (1997). Research apprenticeship. *Nordisk Pedagogik, 17*(3), 186–194.

Kyng M. (1995). Creating contexts for design. In J. M. Carroll (Ed.), *Scenario-based design: Envisioning work and technology in system development* (pp. 85–108). New York: Wiley.

Kyvik, S., & Sivertsen, G. (2005). Vitenskapelig publisering [Scientific publication]. In M. Gulbrandsen & J. C. Smeby (Eds.), *Forskning ved Universitetene. Rammebetingelser, relevans og resultater* (pp. 149–163). Oslo: Cappelen Academic Press.

Langemeyer, I. (2006). Contradictions in expansive learning: Towards a critical analysis of self-dependent forms of learning in relation to contemporary socio-technological change. *Forum: Qualitative Social Research, 7*(1). http://www.qualitative-research.net/fqs-texte/1–06/06–1-12-e.htm.

Langemeyer, I., & Roth, W.-M. (2006). Is cultural-historical activity theory threatened to fall short of its own principles and possibilities as a dialectical social science? *Outlines, 2*, 20–42.

Latour, B. (1987). *Science in action.* Cambridge, MA: Harvard University Press.

Latour, B. (2005). *Reassembling the social: An introduction to actor-network-theory.* Oxford: Oxford University Press.

Latour, B., & Woolgar, S. (1986). *Laboratory life: The construction of scientific facts.* Princeton, NJ: Princeton University Press.

Latour, B., & Woolgar, S. (1979). *Laboratory life.* London: Sage.

Lave, J. (1988). *Cognition in practice: Mind, mathematics and culture in everyday life.* New York: Cambridge University Press.

Lave, J., & Wenger, E. (1991). *Situated learning: Legitimate peripheral participation.* Cambridge: Cambridge University Press.

Law, J., & Mol, A. (1998). Metrics and fluids: Notes on otherness. In R. Chia (Ed.), *Organised worlds: Explorations in technology, organisation and modernity* (pp. 20–38). London: Routledge.

Lawrence, W., & Robinson, P. (1975). *An innovation and its implementation: Issues of evaluation.* London: Tavistock Institute of Human Relations.

Learmonth, M., & Harding, N. (2006). Evidence-based management: The very idea. *Public Administration, 84*(2), 245–266.

Lee, C.D., & Smagorinsky, P. (Eds.) (2000). *Vygotskian perspectives on literacy research.* Cambridge: Cambridge University Press.

Lee, G. K., & Cole, R. C. (2003). From a firm-based to a community-based model of knowledge creation: The case of Linux kernel development. *Organization Science, 14*(6), 633–649.

Lektorsky, V. A. (1999). Historical changes of the notion of activity: Philosophical presuppositions. In S. Chaiklin, M. Hedegaard, & U. J. Jensen (Eds.), *Activity theory and social practice* (pp. 100–113). Aarhus: Aarhus University Press.

Lemke, J. (1990). *Talking science: Language, learning and values.* Norwood, NJ: Ablex.

Leont'ev, A. A. (2005). The life and creative path of A. N. Leontiev. *Journal of Russian and East European Psychology, 43*(3), 8–69.

Leont'ev, A. N. (1932). The development of voluntary attention in the child. *Journal of Genetic Psychology, 40*, 52–81.

Leont'ev, A.N. (1964). Problemy inzhenernoy psikhologii [Problems of engineering psychology]. In A.N. Leont'ev, V.P. Zinchenko, & D.J. Panov (Eds.), *Inchenernaya psikhologiya* (pp. 5–23). Moscow: Izd-vo Mosk.

Leont'ev, A. N. (1966). Automatization and control. In A. N. Leont'ev, I. Yeremenko, V. P. Zinchenko, B. F. Lomov, & V. Rubakhin (Eds.), *Technique and equipment* (pp. 36–43). Publisher unknown (in Russian).

Leont'ev, A.N. (1968). On the issue of tension/extension, caused by the supplementary stress of operators in follow up systems. In *Problems of engineering psychology* (pp. 36–322). Moscow: Unknown publisher (in Russian).

Leont'ev, A. N. (1970). Automation and the human being. In *Psychological studies* (Vol. 2, pp. 3–12). Moscow: Izd-vo Mosk (in Russian).

Leont'ev, A. N. (1977). Automation and the human being. In *Scientific-technical revolution and the human being* (pp. 172–181). Moscow: Nauka (in Russian).

Leont'ev, A.N. (1978). *Activity, consciousness, and personality.* Englewood Cliffs, NJ: Prentice-Hall.

Leont'ev, A.N. (1980). *Activity, consciousness, and personality.* Tokyo: Meijitosyo (in Japanese).

Leont'ev, A. N. (1981). *Problems of the development of the mind.* Moscow: Progress.

Leont'ev, A. N. (2001). *Lectures on general psychology.* Moscow: Smysl (in Russian).

Leont'ev, A.N. (2005). *Frühe Schriften* [Early works], Vol. 2. Berlin: Lehmann's Media.

Leont'ev, A.N., & Lomov, B. F. (1963). The human being and technology. *Voprosy psikhologii, 5*, 29–37 (in Russian).

Leont'ev, A.N., & Panov, D.J. (1963). The psychology of the human being in the technological process. In *Filosofskie voprosy fiziologii vysshey nervnoy deyatelnosti i psykhologii* (pp. 393–424). Moscow: Izd-vo AN CCCR (in Russian).

Leont'ev, A.N., & Zaporozhets, A. V. (1960). *Rehabilitation of hand function.* New York: Pergamon.

Leont'ev, A.N. (1990). Notes on consciousness. Part 2. Translation of an unknown manuscript from 1933. *Multidisciplinary Newsletter for Activity Theory, 5/6*, 1–8.

Leontjew, A. N. (1973). *Probleme des entwicklung des psychschen* [Problems of the development of the mind]. Berlin: Volk und Wissen.

Levi-Strauss, C. (1962). *The savage mind: Nature of human society.* Chicago: University of Chicago Press.

Levitin, K. (1982). *One is not born a personality: Profiles of Soviet education psychologists.* Moscow: Progress.

Linde, C. (1988). Who's in charge here? Cooperative work and authority negotiation in police helicopter missions. In I. Grief (Ed.), *Proceedings of the 2nd conference on computer-supported cooperative work* (pp. 52–64). New York: Association for Computing Machinery Press.

Linell, P. (1998). *Approaching dialogue: Talk, interaction and contexts in dialogical perspectives.* Amsterdam: John Benjamins.

Lompscher, J. (1999). Learning activity and its formation: Ascending from the abstract to the concrete. In M. Hedegaard & J. Lompscher (Eds.), *Learning activity and development* (pp. 139–166). Aarhus: Aarhus University Press.

Lompscher, J. (2004). *Lernkultur und Kompetenzentwicklung aus kulturhistorischer Sicht* [Learning culture and competence development in cultural-historical perspective]. Berlin: Lehmanns Media.

Long, N. (2001). *Development sociology: Actor perspectives.* London: Routledge.

Lotman, Y. M. (1988). The semiotics of culture and the concept of a text. *Soviet Psychology, 26*(3), 52–58.

Ludvigsen, S., Rasmussen, I., Krange, I., Moen, A., & Middleton, D. (in press). Intersecting trajectories of participation: Temporality and learning. In S. Ludvigsen, A. Lund, I. Rasmussen, & R. Säljö (Eds.), *Learning across sites: New tools, infrastructures and practices.* London: Pergamon.

Lumsden, C. J., & Wilson, E. O. (1983). *Promethean fire.* Cambridge, MA: Harvard University Press.

Lundvall, B.-A. (1996). *The social dimension of the learning economy.* DRUID Working Paper 96-1. Aalborg: Aalborg University.

Luria, A. R. (1979). *The making of mind: A personal account of Soviet psychology.* Cambridge, MA: Harvard University Press.

Luria, A. R. (2005). The making of mind: A personal account of Soviet psychology. In M. Cole, K. Levitin, & A. R. Luria (Eds.), *The autobiography of Alexander Luria: A dialogue with "The Making of Mind."* Mahwah, NJ: Erlbaum.

Mäkitalo, J. (2005). An analysis of the employees' work-related emotions in two homes for the elderly. In Y. Engeström, J. Lompscher, & G. Rückriem (Eds.), *Putting activity theory to work: Contributions from developmental work research* (pp. 495–600). Berlin: Lehmanns Media.

Mäkitalo, Å., & Säljö, R. (2002a). Invisible people: Institutional reasoning and reflexivity in the production of services and "social facts" in public employment agencies. *Mind, Culture, and Activity, 9*(3), 160–178.

Mäkitalo, Å., & Säljö, R. (2002b). Talk in institutional context and institutional context in talk: Categories as situated practices. *TEXT, 22*(1), 57–82.

Marx, K. (1973). *Grundrisse: Introduction to the "Critique of Political Economy."* Harmondsworth: Penguin Books.

Marx, K. (1976). Theses on Feuerbach. In K. Marx & F. Engels, *Collected works,* Vol. 5. London: Lawrence & Wishart.

Marx, K. (1977). *Capital*, Vol.1. New York: Vintage.

Maturana, H. R., & Varela, F. J. (1987). *The tree of knowledge: The biological roots of human understanding.* New York: Random House.

McCarthy, J., & Wright, P. (2004). *Technology as experience.* Cambridge, MA: MIT Press.

McLuhan, H. M. (1962). *The Gutenberg galaxy: The making of typographic man.* Toronto: University of Toronto Press.

Mehan, H. (2007). Inter-organizational collaboration: A strategy to improve diversity and college access for underrepresented minority students. *Actio: An International Journal of Human Activity Theory, 1*, 63–91.

Melucci, A. (1996). *Challenging codes: Collective action in the information age.* Cambridge: Cambridge University Press.

Merton, R. K. (1968). *Social theory and social structure.* New York: Free Press

Meshcheryakov, A. (1979). *Awakening to life.* Moscow: Progress.

Midgley, G. (2000). *Systemic intervention: Philosophy, methodology, and practice.* New York: Kluwer.

Miettinen, R. (2005). Object of activity and individual motivation. *Mind, Culture, and Activity 12*(1), 52–69.

Miettinen, R., & Virkkunen, J. (2005). Epistemic objects, artefacts and organizational change. *Organization, 12*, 437–456.

Miller, C. R. (1984). Genre as social action. *Quarterly Journal of Speech, 70*, 151–167.

Miller, C. R. (1994). Rhetorical community: The cultural basis of genre. In A. Freedman & P. Medway (Eds.), *Genre and the new rhetoric* (pp. 67–78). London: Taylor & Francis.

Miller, E. (1993). *From dependency to autonomy: Studies in organization and change.* London: Free Association Books.

Miller, E., & Gwynne, G. (1974). *A life apart: A pilot study of residential institutions for the physically handicapped and young chronically sick.* London: Tavistock.

Miller, E., & Rice, A. (1967). *Systems of organization: Task and sentient systems and the boundary control.* London: Tavistock.

Minnis, M., & John-Steiner, V. P. (2001). Are we ready for a single, integrated theory? *Human Development, 44*(5), 296–310.

Mogensen, P. (1992). Towards a provotyping approach in systems development. *Scandinavian Journal of Information Systems, 4*, 31–53.

Moon, J. Y., & Sproul, L. (2002). Essence of distributed work: The case of the Linux kernel. In P. Hinds & S. Kiesler (Eds.), *Distributed work* (pp. 381–404). Cambridge, MA: MIT Press.

Morson, G. S., & Emerson, C. (1990). *Mikhail Bakhtin: Creation of a prosaics.* Stanford, CA: Stanford University Press.

Moscovici, S., Mugny, G., & van Avermaet, E. (Eds.) (2008). *Perspectives on minority influence.* Cambridge: Cambridge University Press.

Muller, M. J., Haslwanter, H., & Dayton, J. (1997). Participatory practices in the software lifecycle. In M. Helander, T. Landauer, & P. Prabhu (Eds.). *Handbook of human–computer interaction* (pp. 255–298). Amsterdam: North Holland.

Nardi, B. A. (2005). Objects of desire: Power and passion in collaborative activity. *Mind, Culture, and Activity, 12*(1), 37–51.

Nardi, B. A., Whittaker, S., & Schwarz, H. (2002). NetWORKers and their activity in intensional networks. *Computer Supported Cooperative Work, 11*(1–2), 205–242.

Nelson, R. R. (2001). Observations on the post-Bayh-Dole rise of patenting at American universities. *Journal of Technology Transfer, 26,* 13–19.

Nerlove, S., Munroe, R. H., & Munroe, R. (1971). Effect of environmental experience on spatial ability: A replication. *Journal of Social Psychology, 84*(1), 3–10.

New, T. L., Foo, S. W., & De Silva, L. C. (2003). Emotion recognition using hidden Markov models. *Speech Communication, 41,* 603–623.

Newcomb, T. (1953). An approach to the study of communicative acts. *Psychological Review, 60,* 393–404.

Nonaka, I., & Takeuchi, N. (1995). *The knowledge creating company.* New York: Oxford University Press.

Norman, D. A. (1991). Cognitive artifacts. In J. M. Carroll (Ed.), *Designing interaction* (pp. 17–38). Cambridge: Cambridge University Press.

Norman, D. A. (2002). Emotion and design: Attractive things work better. *Interactions Magazine, 9*(4), 36–42.

Obholzer, A. (2001). The leader, the unconscious, and the management of the organization. In L. Gould, L. Stapley, & M. Stein (Eds.), *The systems psychodynamics of organizations: Integrating the group relations approach, psychoanalytic, and open systems.* London: Karnac.

Oddone, I. (1981). *Redécouvrir l'expérience ouvrière* [Rediscovering workers' experience]. Paris: Éditions sociales.

Olsen, J. P., & Maassen, P. (2007). European debates on the knowledge institution: The modernization of the university at the European level. In P. Maassen & J. P. Olsen (Eds.), *University dynamics and European integration* (pp. 3–24). Dordrecht: Springer.

Olson, D. R. (2004). The triumph of hope over experience in the search for "what works": A response to Slavin. *Educational Researcher, 33,* 24–26.

Padden, C., & Humphries, T. (2005). *Inside deaf culture.* Cambridge, MA: Harvard University Press.

Palmer, F. R. (1986). *Mood and modality.* Cambridge: Cambridge University Press.

Pape, T. C., & Thoresen, K. (1987). Development of common systems by prototyping. In G. Bjerknes, P. Ehn, & M. Kyng (Eds.), *Computers and democracy: A Scandinavian challenge* (pp. 297–314). Aldershot: Avebury.

Park, D., & Moro, Y. (2006). Dynamics of situation definition. *Mind, Culture, and Activity, 13*(2), 100–128.

Pettigrew, A. (1985). *The awakening giant.* Oxford: Blackwell.

Pfeffer, J. (1993). Barriers to the advance of organization science: Paradigm development as a dependent variable. *Academy of Management Review, 18*(4), 599–620.

Pfeffer, J. (1995). Mortality, reproducibility, and the persistence of styles of theory. *Organization Science, 6*(6), 681–686.

Pfeffer, J. (2007). *Testimony submitted to the US House of Representatives Committee on Oversight and Government Reforms, March 8.* Available from www.evidence-basedmanagement.com (accessed June 2007).

Pickering, A. (1993). The mangle of practice: Agency and emergence in the sociology of science. *American Journal of Sociology, 99*(3), 559–589.

Pickering, A. (1995). *The mangle of practice: Time, agency and science.* Chicago: University of Chicago Press.

Pihlaja, J. (2005). *Learning in and for production: An activity-theoretical study of the historical development of distributed systems of generalizing.* Helsinki: Helsinki University Press.

Polanyi, M. (1958). *Personal knowledge.* London: Routledge & Kegan Paul.

Popper K. (1975). *Objective knowledge: An evolutionary approach.* Oxford: Oxford University Press.

Postman, N. (1988). *Wir amüsieren uns zu tode* [Amusing ourselves to death: Public discourse in the age of show business]. Frankfurt: Suhrkamp.

Potter, J. (1996). *Representing reality. Discourse, rhetoric and social construction.* London: Sage.

Powell, W. W. (1990). Neither market nor hierarchy: Network forms of organization. *Research in Organizational Behavior, 12,* 295–336.

Powell, W. W., & Snellman, K. (2004). The knowledge economy. *Annual Review of Sociology, 30,* 199–220.

Prahalad, C. K., & Hamel, G. (1990). The core competence of the corporation. *Harvard Business Review, 68*(3), 79–91.

Putnam, L. (1994). Challenging the assumptions of traditional approaches to negotiation. *Negotiation Journal, 10,* 337–346.

Rafael, V. L. (2003). The cell phone and the crowd: Messianic politics in the contemporary Philippines. *Public Culture, 15,* 399–425.

Ravier-Gaxiola, M., Silva-Pereyra, J., & Kuhl, P. K. (2005). Brain potentials to native and non-native speech contrasts in 7- and 11-month-old American infants. *Developmental Science, 8*(2), 162–172.

Raymond, E. (1999). *The cathedral & the bazaar.* Beijing: O'Really.

Reed, J. (1935). *Ten days that shook the world.* New York: Modern Library.

Rheingold, H. (2002). *Smart mobs: The next social revolution.* Cambridge, MA: Perseus Books.

Rice, A. (1958). *Productivity and social organization: The Ahmedabad experiment.* London: Tavistock.

Rice, A. (1965). *Learning for leadership.* London: Tavistock.

Rist, G. (2006). *The history of development: From Western origins to global faith.* London: Zed Books.

Robbins, D. (2001). *Vygotsky's psychology-philosophy: A metaphor for language theory and learning.* New York: Kluwer Academic / Plenum Publishers.

Robichaud, D. (2006). Steps toward a relational view of agency. In F. Cooren, J. R. Taylor, & E. J. Van Every (Eds.), *Communication as organizing: Empirical explorations into the dynamic of text and conversation* (pp. 101–114). Mahwah, NJ: Erlbaum.

Rogoff, B. (2003). *The cultural nature of human development.* New York: Oxford University Press.

Rogoff, B., Correa-Chávez, M., & Cotuc, M. N. (2005). A cultural/historical view of schooling in human development. In D. B. Pillemer & S. H. White (Eds.), *Developmental psychology and social change: Research, history and policy* (pp. 225–263). Cambridge: Cambridge University Press.

Roth, W.-M. (2007a). Emotion at work: A contribution to third-generation cultural historical activity theory. *Mind, Culture and Activity, 14*, 40–63.

Roth, W.-M. (2007b). Identity in scientific literacy: Emotional-volitional and ethico-moral dimensions. In W.-M. Roth & K. Tobin (Eds.), *Science, learning, and identity: Sociocultural and cultural historical perspectives* (pp. 153–184). Rotterdam: Sense Publishers.

Roth, W.-M., & Lee, Y. J. (2007). "Vygotsky's neglected legacy": Cultural-historical activity theory. *Review of Educational Research, 76*, 186–232.

Rotkirch, A. (1996). The playing 80s: Russian activity games. In D. Saunders, F. Percival, & M. Vartiainen (Eds.), *The simulation and gaming yearbook: Games and simulations to enhance quality learning* (Vol. 4, pp. 34–40). London: Routledge.

Rozov, M. A. (1981). The ways of scientific discoveries. *Voprosi Filosofii, 8*, 143–154 (in Russian).

Rubtsov, V. V. (1991). *Learning in children: Organization and development of cooperative actions.* Happauge, NY: Nova Science.

Russell, D. R. (1995). Activity theory and its implications for writing instruction. In J. Petraglia (Ed.), *Reconceiving writing, rethinking writing instruction* (pp. 51–77). Mahwah, NJ: Erlbaum.

Russell, D. R. (1997a). Rethinking genre in school and society: An activity theory analysis. *Written Communication, 14*(4), 504–554.

Russell, D. R. (1997b). Writing and genre in higher education and workplaces: A review of studies that use cultural-historical activity theory. *Mind, Culture, and Activity, 4*(4), 224–237.

Russell, D. R. (2002). *Writing in the academic disciplines: A curricular history.* Carbondale: Southern Illinois University Press.

Russell, D. R. (2007). Rethinking the articulation between business and technical communication and writing in the disciplines: Useful avenues for teaching and research. *Journal of Business and Technical Communication, 21*(3), 248–278.

Russell, D. R., & Bazerman, C. (Eds.) (1997). The activity of writing: The writing of activity. *Mind, Culture, Activity, special issue, 4*(4), 223–308.

Russell, D. R., & Yañez, A. (2003). "Big picture people rarely become historians": Genre systems and the contradictions of general education. In C. Bazerman & D. R. Russell (Eds.), *Writing selves/writing societies: Research from activity perspectives* (pp. 331–362). Fort Collins, CO: WAC Clearinghouse and *Mind, Culture, and Activity.*

Saarelma, O. (Ed.) (2003). *Työtulvan hallinta terveysasemalla.* [To manage work flood in health care clinic]. Espoo: STAKES/Publications 271.

Saaren-Seppälä, T. (2004). *Yhteisen potilaan hoito.* [The care of a shared patient]. Tampere: Tampere University Press.

Saari, E. (2003). *The pulse of change in research work.* Helsinki: University of Helsinki.

Sahlins, M. (1976). *Culture and practical reason.* Chicago: University of Chicago Press.

Sannino, A. (2005). Cultural-historical and discursive tools for analyzing critical conflicts in students' development. In K. Yamazumi Y. Engeström, & H. Daniels

(Eds.), *New learning challenges: Going beyond the industrial age system of school and work* (pp. 165–196). Osaka: Kansai University Press.

Sannino, A. (2008). From talk to action: Experiencing interlocution in developmental interventions. *Mind, Culture, and Activity, 15*, 3, 234–257.

Säljö, R. (2003). Epilogue: From transfer to boundary-crossing. In T. Tuomi-Gröhn & Y. Engeström (Eds.), *Between school and work: New perspectives on transfer and boundary-crossing* (pp. 311–321). New York: Pergamon.

Sartre, J.-P. (2000). *Being and nothingness: An essay on phenomenological ontology.* Moscow: Republic (in Russian).

Schatzki, T. R., Knorr Cetina, K., & von Savigny, E. (2000). *The practice turn in contemporary theory.* London: Routledge.

Schaufeli, W., & Enzmann, D. (1998). *The burnout companion to study and practice: A critical analysis.* London: Taylor & Francis.

Schryer, C. F. (1993). Records as genre. *Written Communication, 10*(2), 200–234.

Schryer, C. F., Lingard, L., & Spatford, M. M. (2003). Structure and agency in medical case presentations. In C. Bazerman & D. R. Russell (Eds.), *Writing selves/writing societies: Research from activity perspectives* (pp. 62–96). Fort Collins, CO: WAC Clearinghouse and *Mind, Culture, and Activity.*

Schutz, A., & Luckmann, T. (1973). *The structures of the life-world.* Evanston, IL: Northwestern University Press.

Scott, W. (2001). *Institutions and organizations.* London: Sage.

Scribner, S. (1997). Three developmental paradigms. In E. Tobach, R. Joffe Falmagne, M. Brown Parlee, L. M. W. Martin, & A. Scribner Kapelman (Eds.), *Mind and social practice: Selected writings of Sylvia Scribner* (pp. 281–288). Cambridge: Cambridge University Press.

Scribner, S., & Cole, M. (1981). *The psychology of literacy.* Cambridge, MA: Harvard University Press.

Searle, J. (1969). *Speech acts.* Cambridge: Cambridge University Press.

Searle, J. (1990). Collective intentions and actions. In P. R. Cohen, J. Morgan, & M. E. Pollack (Eds.). *Intentions in communication* (pp. 401–416). Cambridge, MA: Harvard University Press.

Senghas, R. J., Senghas, A., & Pyers J. E. (2005). The emergence of Nicaraguan Sign Language: Questions of development, acquisition, and evolution. In J. Langer, S. T. Parker, & C. Milbrath (Eds.), *Biology and knowledge revisited: From neurogenesis to psychogenesis* (pp. 287–306). Mahwah, NJ: Erlbaum

Sennett, R. (1980). *Authority.* New York: Knopf.

Sennett, R. (1998). *The corrosion of character.* New York: Norton.

Sennett, R. (1999a). Growth and failure: The new political economy and culture. In M. Featherstone & S. Lash (Eds.), *Spaces of culture* (pp. 14–26). London: Sage.

Sennett, R. (1999b). *The corrosion of character: The personal consequences of work in the new capitalism.* New York: Norton.

Sennett, R. (2003). *Respect: The formation of character in an age of inequality.* London: Allen Lane.

Shchedrovitsky, G. P. (1995). *Selected works.* Moscow: School of Cultural Politics Publishers (in Russian).

Sherrod, L., Flanagan, C., Kassimir, R., & Syvertsen, A. (2006). *Youth activism: An international encyclopedia.* Westport, CT: Greenwood.

Shirky, C. (2008). *Here comes everybody: The power of organizing without organizations.* New York: Penguin Press.

Shotter, J. (1993). *The cultural politics of everyday life.* Buckingham: Open University Press.

Silverman, D. (1968). Review of Miller and Rice: Systems of Organization. *British Journal of Industrial Relations, 6,* 393–397.

Silverman, D. (1970). *The theory of organizations: A sociological framework.* London: Heinemann.

Smart, G. (2006). *Writing the economy: Activity, genre, and technology in the world of banking.* London: Equinox.

Smedslund, J. (1953). The problem of what is learned? *Psychological Review, 60*(3), 157–158.

Smith, D. E. (2005). *Institutional ethnography: A sociology for people.* Oxford: Alta Mira Press.

Snyder, B. R. (1971). *The hidden curriculum.* New York: Knopf.

Spinoza, B. de (1955). *On the improvement of the understanding: The ethics correspondence.* New York: Dover.

Spinoza, B. de (1994). *Ethics.* London: Penguin Books.

Spinoza, B. de (2004). A political treatise. In *A theologico-political treatise and a political treatise* (pp. 278–198). New York: Dover.

Spinuzzi, C. (2002). A Scandinavian challenge, a US response: Methodological assumptions in Scandinavian and US prototyping approaches. In K. Haramundanis & M. Priestley (Eds.), *Proceedings of the 20th annual international conference on computer documentation* (pp. 208–215). New York: Association for Computing Machinery Press.

Spinuzzi, C. (2003). *Tracing genres through organizations: A sociocultural approach to information design.* Cambridge, MA: MIT Press.

Stacey, R. D. (2001). *Complex responsive processes in organisators: Learning and knowledge creation.* London: Routledge.

Stalk, G. P., Evans, P., & Shulman, L. E. (1992). Competing on capabilities: The new rules of corporate strategy. *Harvard Business Review, 70*(2), 57–69.

Stallman, R. (2002). *Free software, free society: Selected essays of Richard M. Stallman.* Boston: GNU Press.

Starbuck, W. (2003). The origins of organizational theory. In H. Tsoukas & C. Knudsen (Eds.), *The Oxford handbook of organizational theory.* Oxford: Oxford University Press.

Stetsenko, A. (2005). Activity as object-related: Resolving the dichotomy of individual and collective planes of activity. *Mind, Culture, and Activity, 12*(1), 70–88.

Strauss, A. L. (1978). *Negotiations: Varieties, contexts, processes, and social order.* San Francisco: Jossey-Bass.

Swan, J., Robertson, M., & Bresnen, M. (2003). Knowledge management and the colonization of knowledge. *Electronic Journal of Radical Organisation Theory, 7*(2), http://www.mngt.waikato.ac.nz/ejrot/EJROT(newdesign)Vol7_2_front.asp.

Talyzina, N. F. (1981). *The psychology of learning: Theories of learning and programmed instruction.* Moscow: Progress.

Taylor, C. (1977). What is human agency? In T. Mischel (Ed.), *The self: Psychological and philosophical issues* (pp. 103–135). Oxford: Oxford University Press.

Taylor, C. (1991). *The ethics of authenticity.* Cambridge MA: Harvard University Press.

Taylor, J. R. (1983). Conceptual impediments to productivity. *Optimum: A Forum for Management, 14*(1/2), 19–42.

Taylor, J. R. (1993). *Rethinking the theory of organizational communication: How to read an organization.* Norwood, NJ: Ablex.

Taylor, J. R. (2006). Coorientation: A conceptual framework. In F. Cooren, J. R. Taylor, & E. J. Van Every (Eds.), *Communication as organizing: Empirical and theoretical explorations in the dynamic of text and conversation* (pp. 141–156). Mahwah, NJ: Erlbaum.

Taylor, J. R., & Cooren, F. (2006). Making worldview sense: And paying homage, retrospectively, to Algirdas Greimas. In F. Cooren, J. R. Taylor, & E. J. Van Every (Eds.), *Communication as organizing: Empirical explorations into the dynamic of text and conversation* (pp. 115–138). Mahwah, NJ: Erlbaum.

Taylor, J. R., Gurd, G., & Bardini, T. (1997). The worldviews of cooperative work. In G. Bowker, L. Gasser, S. L. Star, & W. Turner (Eds.), *Social science research, technical systems and cooperative work* (pp. 379–413). Mahwah, NJ: Erlbaum.

Taylor, J. R., & Robichaud, D. (2004). Finding the organization in the communication: Discourse as action and sensemaking. *Organization, 11*(3), 395–413.

Taylor, J. R., & Van Every, E. J. (2000). *The emergent organization: Communication as its site and surface.* Mahwah, NJ: Erlbaum.

Taylor, J. R., & Van Every, E. J. (forthcoming). *Dilemmas of authority: A communicative analysis.*

Thompson, M. (2004). Some proposals for strengthening organizational activity theory. *Organization, 11*(5), 579–602.

Toikka, K. (1984). *Kehittävä kvalifikaatiotutkimus* [Developmental qualification research]. Helsinki: Valtion Painatuskeskus.

Toikka, K., Engeström, Y., & Norros, L. (1985). Entwickelnde Arbeitsforschung. Theoretische und methodologische Elemente [Developmental work research: Theoretical and methodological elements]. *Forum Kritische Psychologie, 15,* 5–41.

Toiviainen, H. (2003). *Learning across levels: Challenges of collaboration in a small-firm network.* Helsinki: University of Helsinki.

Tolman, C. W. (2001). The origin of activity as a category in the philosophies of Kant, Fichte, Hegel and Marx. In S. Chaiklin (Ed.), *The theory and practice of cultural-historical psychology* (pp. 84–92). Aarhus: Aarhus University Press.

Tomasello, M. (1999). *The cultural origins of human cognition.* Cambridge, MA: Harvard University Press.

Tsoukas, H. (2003). New times, fresh challenges: Reflections on the past and future of organizational theory. In H. Tsoukas & C. Knudsen (Eds.), *The Oxford handbook of organizational theory* (pp. 607–622). Oxford: Oxford University Press.

Tsoukas, H., & Knudsen, C. (Eds.) (2003). *The Oxford handbook of organizational theory.* Oxford: Oxford University Press.

Tudge, J. R. H., Winterhoff, P. A., & Hogan, D. M. (1996). The cognitive consequence of collaborative problem solving with and without feedback. *Child Development, 67,* 2892–2909.

Tuomi-Gröhn, T. (2003). Developmental transfer as a goal of internship in practical nursing. In T. Tuomi-Gröhn & Y. Engeström (Eds.), *Between school and work: New perspectives on transfer and boundary-crossing* (pp. 199–231). New York: Pergamon.

Tuomi-Gröhn, T., & Engeström, Y. (Eds.) (2003a). *Between school and work: New perspectives on transfer and boundary-crossing.* New York: Pergamon.

Tuomi-Gröhn, T., & Engeström, Y. (2003b). From transfer to boundary-crossing between school and work as a tool for developing vocational education: An introduction. In T. Tuomi-Gröhn & Y. Engeström (Eds.), *Between school and work: New perspectives on transfer and boundary-crossing* (pp. 19–38). New York: Pergamon.

Turner, J.H. (2002). *Face to face: Toward a sociological theory of interpersonal behavior.* Stanford, CA: Stanford University Press.

Ueno, O. (2006). *Spinoza: An atheist can affirm religions?* Tokyo: NHK Press (in Japanese).

Valsiner, J. (2001). Process structure of semiotic mediation in human development. *Human Development, 44*(2/3), 84–97.

Van der Veer, R. (1984). Early periods in the work of L. S. Vygotsky: The influence of Spinoza. In M. Hedegaard, P. Hakkarainen, & Y. Engeström (Eds.), *Learning and teaching on a scientific basis: Methodological and epistemological aspects of activity theory on learning and teaching* (pp. 87–98). Aarhus: Aarhus University, Institute of Psychology.

Van der Veer, R. (1996). The concept of culture in Vygotsky's thinking. *Culture and Psychology, 2,* 247–263.

Van der Veer, R., & Valsiner, J. (1991). *Understanding Vygotsky: A quest for synthesis.* Oxford: Basil Blackwell.

Van Oers, V. (1998). The fallacy of decontextualization. *Mind, Culture and Activity, 5*(2), 135–142.

Vasilyuk, F. (1988). *The psychology of experiencing.* Moscow: Progress.

Vassiliouk, F., & Zinchenko, V. P. (1984). Epilogue. In A.N. Léontiev, *Activité, conscience, personnalité* (pp. 339–349). Moscow: Progress.

Victor, B., & Boynton, A. C. (1998). *Invented here: Maximizing your organization's internal growth and profitability.* Boston: Harvard Business School Press.

Virkkunen, J. (2005). Developmental intervention in work activities: An activity-theoretical interpretation. In T. Kontinen (Ed.), *Development intervention: Actor and activity perspectives* (pp. 37–66). Helsinki: University of Helsinki, Center for Activity Theory and Developmental Work Research and Institute for Development Studies.

Virkkunen, J. (2006a). Dilemmas in building shared transformative agency. *@ctivités, 3*(1), http://www.activites.org.

Virkkunen, J. (2006b). Hybrid agency in co-configuration work. *Outlines, 8*(1), 61–75.

Virkkunen, J., & Ahonen, H. (2004). Transforming learning and knowledge creation on the shop floor. *International Journal of Human Resources Development and Management, 4*(1), 57–72.

Virkkunen, J., & Kuutti, K. (2000). Understanding organizational learning by focusing on "activity system." *Accounting Management and Information Technology, 10,* 291–319.

von Hippel, E. (2005). *Democratizing innovation.* Cambridge, MA: MIT Press.

von Hippel, E., & Tyre, M. J. (1995). How learning by doing is done: Problem identification in novel process equipment. *Research Policy, 24*, 1–12.

Vygotsky, L. S. (1971). *The psychology of art*. Cambridge, MA: MIT Press.

Vygotsky L. S. (1978). *Mind in society: The development of higher psychological processes*. Cambridge, MA: Harvard University Press.

Vygotsky, L. S. (1986). *Thought and Language*. Cambridge MA: MIT Press.

Vygotsky, L. S. (1987). *The collected works of L. S. Vygotsky*. Vol. 1: Problems of General Psychology. New York: Plenum Press.

Vygotsky, L. S. (1994). The socialist alteration of man. In R. van der Veer & J. Valsiner (Eds.), *Vygotsky reader* (pp. 175–184). Oxford: Blackwell.

Vygotsky, L. S. (1997a). *The collected works of L. S. Vygotsky*. Vol. 3: Problems of the theory and history of psychology. New York: Plenum.

Vygotsky, L. S. (1997b). *The collected works of L. S. Vygotsky*. Vol. 4: The history of the development of higher mental functions. New York: Plenum.

Vygotsky, L. S. (1998). *The collected works of L. S. Vygotsky*. Vol. 5: Child Psychology. New York: Plenum.

Vygotsky, L. S. (1999). *The collected works of L. S. Vygotsky*. Vol. 6: Scientific legacy. New York: Plenum.

Waddington, C. H. (1947). *Organizers and genes*. Cambridge: Cambridge University Press.

Walker, C., & Guest, W. (1952). *The man of the assembly line*. Cambridge, MA: Harvard University Press.

Watzlawick, P., Beavin, J., & Jackson, D. (1967). *The pragmatics of communication*. New York: Norton.

Weber, S. (2004). *The success of open source*. Cambridge, MA: Harvard University Press.

Weiser, M. (1991). The computer for the 21st century. *Scientific American, 265*(3), 94–104.

Wenger, E. (1990). *Toward a theory of cultural transparency: Elements of a social discourse of visible and the invisible*. Unpublished doctoral dissertation, University of California, Irvine.

Wertsch, J. V. (1985). *Vygotsky and the social formation of mind*. Cambridge, MA: Harvard University Press.

Wertsch, J. V. (1991). *Voices of the mind: A sociocultural approach to mediated action*. Cambridge, MA: Harvard University Press.

Wertsch, J. V. (1994). *Voices of the mind: A sociocultural approach to mediated action*. London: Harvester Wheatsheaf.

Whiting, B. (1980). Culture and social behavior. *Ethos, 8*, 95–116.

Wilde, L. (1989). *Marx and contradiction*. Aldershot: Avebury.

Willke, H. (1998). *Systemisches Wissensmanagement* [Systemic management of knowledge]. Stuttgart: Lucius und Lucius.

Willke, H. (2001). *Atopia: Studien zur atopischen Gesellschaft* [Atopia: Studies on atopian society]. Frankfurt: Suhrkamp.

Winograd, T., & Flores, F. (1986). *Understanding computers and cognition: A new foundation for design*. Norwood, NJ: Ablex.

Winsor, D. A. (2003). *Writing power: An ethnographic study of writing in an engineering center*. Albany, NY: SUNY Press.

Wittgenstein, L. (1953). *Philosophical investigations*. Oxford: Oxford University Press.

Yamazumi, K. (2001). Orchestrating voices and crossing boundaries in educational practice: Dialogic research on learning about the Kobe earthquake. In M. Hedegaard (Ed.), *Learning in classrooms: A cultural-historical approach* (pp. 97–120). Aarhus: Aarhus University Press.

Yamazumi, K. (2005). School as collaborative change agent. In K. Yamazumi, Y. Engeström, & H. Daniels (Eds.), *New learning challenges: Going beyond the industrial age system of school and work* (pp. 11–45). Osaka: Kansai University Press.

Yamazumi, K. (2006a). Activity theory and the transformation of pedagogic practice. *Educational Studies in Japan: International Yearbook of Japanese Educational Research Association, 1,* 77–90.

Yamazumi, K. (2006b). Learning for critical and creative agency: An activity-theoretical study of advanced networks of learning in New School project. In K Yamazumi, K. (Ed.). *Building activity theory in practice: Toward the next generation* (pp. 73–107). Technical Report No. 1. Osaka: Center for Human Activity Theory, Kansai University.

Yamazumi, K. (2007). Human agency and educational research: A new problem in activity theory. *Actio: An International Journal of Human Activity Theory, 1,* 19–39.

Yamazumi, K. (2008). Creating a hybrid activity system for school innovation. *Journal of Educational Change, 9*(4), 365–373.

Yañez, A., & Russell, D. R. (in press). The world is too messy: The challenge of historical literacy in a general-education course. In J. Castner (Ed.), *Teaching writing in the liberal arts*. Kreskill, NJ: Hampton Press.

Yaroshevsky, M. (1989). *Lev Vygotsky*. Moscow: Progress.

Yates, J. (1989). *Control through communication: The rise of system in American management*. Baltimore: Johns Hopkins University Press.

Yourgrau, P. (2005). *A world without time: The forgotten legacy of Gödel and Einstein*. New York: Basic Books.

Yovel, Y. (1989) *Spinoza and other heretics: The adventures of immanence*. Princeton, NJ: Princeton University Press.

Yudin, E. G. (1978). *The system approach and the principle of activity*. Moscow: Izdatelstvo Nauka (in Russian).

Yvon, F., &Clot, Y. (2003). Apprentissage et développement dans l'analyse du travail enseignant [Learning and development in the analysis of teachers' work]. *Pratiques psychologiques, 76,* 25–32.

Zagier Roberts, V. (1994). The organization of work: Contributions from open systems theory. In A. Obholzer & V. Zagier Roberts (Eds.), *The unconscious at work: Individual and organizational stress in the human services* (pp. 28–38). London: Routledge.

Zinchenko, V. P. (2002). From classical to organic psychology: In commemoration of Lev Vygotsky's birth. In D. Robbins & A. Stetsenko (Eds.), *Voices within Vygotsky's non-classical psychology: Past, present, and future* (pp. 3–26). New York: Nova Science Publishers.

Zinchenko V. P. (2006a). The nature of the creative act. *Voprosi Filosofii, 8*, 27–35 (in Russian).

Zinchenko, V. P. (2006b). Thought and word: The approaches of L. S. Vygotsky and G. G. Shpet. In H. Daniels, M. Cole, & J. V. Wertsch (Eds.), *The Cambridge Companion to Vygotsky* (pp. 212–245). Cambridge: Cambridge University Press.

Zuboff, S. (1988). *In the age of the smart machine: The future of work and power.* New York: Basic Books.

Zysman, J., & Newman, A. (2004). *How revolutionary is the revolution: Will there be a "political economy" of the digital era?* Working Paper, 161. Berkeley Round Table on the International Economy, Berkeley, CA. Available at http://brie.berkeley.edu/publications/working_papers.html (accessed January 2008).

AUTHOR INDEX

SUBJECT INDEX

Lightning Source UK Ltd.
Milton Keynes UK
UKOW05f1822101216
289637UK00010B/368/P